Introduction to Policing

Introduction to Policing

PERCEPTIONS VERSUS REALITY

REVISED FIRST EDITION

Chernoh Wurie
Virginia Commonwealth University

cognella®
SAN DIEGO

Bassim Hamadeh, CEO and Publisher
Carrie Baarns, Manager, Revisions and Author Care
Kaela Martin, Project Editor
Christian Berk, Production Editor
Jess Estrella, Senior Graphic Designer
Alexa Lucido, Licensing Manager
Natalie Piccotti, Director of Marketing
Kassie Graves, Vice President of Editorial
Jamie Giganti, Director of Academic Publishing

Printed in the United States of America.

cognella® ACADEMIC PUBLISHING
3970 Sorrento Valley Blvd., Ste. 500, San Diego, CA 92121

Taking into consideration the various life-altering unfortunate events that have transpired between police and the community members they serve, as an advocate of social justice and change, I am dedicating this book to a twofold foundation. First, I am dedicating this book to those brave individuals that are currently serving as law enforcement officers in all levels and especially those that have lost their lives in the line of performing their sworn duties.

Secondly, this book is dedicated to those citizens who have lost their lives due to the innumerable negative situations between law enforcement and community members. Regardless of the justification to use lethal force, each incident affected not only the individuals killed. Their families were affected, their entire livelihoods were affected, and in addition the officers involved were also affected. I proudly dedicate this book to all those involved in these situations that have transformed the face of law enforcement for generations to come.

BRIEF CONTENTS

DETAILED CONTENTS

CHAPTER 3

The Career of a Police Officer 47

CHAPTER 4

Law Enforcement Administration 83

CHAPTER 5

Police and Homeland Security 109

ACKNOWLEDGMENTS

Writing the acknowledgement page is always one of the most difficult portions of a publication, because it is necessary to make sure everyone is acknowledged. I would like to start from a holistic perspective and then moved inward to the folks that were with me throughout. First, I would like to acknowledge the Prince William County Police. I was employed by this prestigious agency for over 15 years, since my volunteer and intern days. This agency has brought me so much joy and laughter, some sadness, and most importantly shaped me to be the disciplined individual I am today. I would also like to thank former Chief Charlie Deane for taking that chance in hiring me—that foreign kid that he could barely understand because of my thick African accent. Chief Barry Barnard also took a chance on me and continued to play the mentor role for me when Chief Deane retired. These two men played an astronomical part in my policing and personal life. I am grateful for these two faithful men. In addition, I am grateful to my good friends that contributed to this book, Lt. Dave Smith and Sgt. Leandro Pena. Dave always made time for my requests, lecturing in my classes and contributing to this book. Your knowledge and dedication to this profession is admirable. Leo, my boy, our friendship is unique. We have been through a lot and have saved each other's lives, and you have always been there for me and has responded every time I called about issues with any and everything. I appreciate your continuous support and his believing in me and my ability to complete this project. Lastly, I acknowledge Officer Chris Yung, may your soul rest in perfect peace—my dear friend who lost his life in the line of duty—we will never forget you.

My next gratitude goes to the brave members of the Henrico Police Department. This department has been very receptive and helpful throughout this project and in the short time since my transition to VCU. Sgt. Jermaine Alley has been truly instrumental in making all this possible. This brother has so much energy and is always there to help when called upon. A great deal of appreciation should be directed to Chief Cardunel, Lt. Col. Linda Toney, and Lt. Col. Mike Palkovics. These individuals were always willing to help when I requested pictures and initiated other partnering ventures for this text and beyond. Their dedication and commitment to their services are commendable. Lt. Rachel Heinig, I appreciate our spirited conversations in reference to motivating our students to pursue this illustrious career. Lt. Col. A.J. Scott was and is always willing to guest lecture in my classes. Your dedication to this service is also commendable. I want to truly thank Officer Jerome Goodine Jr. for his services. Your representation in recruiting qualified personnel for your department is one of a kind, please continue the hard work. I truly appreciate the continuous support in partnering with our students at VCU. Lastly, I would like to express my gratitude to Retired Lt. Col. Clearance Hunter of the Henrico PD. I truly appreciate your friendship and knowledge in fair and impartial policing. Your passion for this work demonstrates the dying need for this venture for current and future policing initiatives. Thank you for all you do; I charge you to continue your passion in this venture.

My next gratitude goes to the Chesterfield Police Department. I want to personally thank Lt. Col. Dan Kelly and Captain A. J. Starke for their continuous support in partnering with our students at VCU. Thank you for always responding to my requests, coming to VCU, and presenting a wealth of information to our students. A personal thank you also to you Dan Kelly for always being there and always providing the support and advice needed on various topics. Thank you for everything.

To my very own VCUPD, Captain Butters was instrumental in always being there, providing support, and addressing any questions asked by my students. Thank you for having a calm demeanor and for always reaching out to say hello when you can. To Officer Anthony Wojno, my very own former student and now a VCU police officer, I am grateful for you, you helped me craft the title for this textbook. I truly appreciate your hard work and dedication in my classes and beyond the classroom. All the best on your future endeavors, sir. Not to forget Chief John Venuti, thank you for your leadership and inspiration to the VCUPD. To some of my esteemed students, Amy Mills, Haley Smith, Monica Bains, Jordan Devers, and many more, thank you for all your support and assistance in helping me develop this project. I truly am appreciative for your support and hard work throughout this process. Amy Mills, you were there with me throughout this process and assisted me in various ways and means to complete this project. Thank you for your dedication and for always being willing to help. To my colleagues at VCU, Professors Jay Albanese, Christina Mancini, Ashlee Barnes and all, thank you for your continuous support and mentorship through this process. I truly appreciate the conversations we have had throughout this process.

To my friends Gregory Lawson, Quentin Bolton, and Stephanas Lynch, I want to take a special moment to thank these special brothers. They all played a significant role on this venture: Greg contributed to a section in one of my chapters and also engaged me in several rich conversations about policing and the communities they serve. Q's in-depth conversations and curious questions about policing, not to mention his experiences with police officers, helped shaped my stance in many of the things I wrote in this book. Lastly, Stephanas, even though he did not contribute to this book, spent many mornings during breakfast with me talking about it. I listened and took back several of the things he mentioned in our conversations. I am grateful for friends like these!!

To my publishing team, MJ Peluso, Lisa Kramer, Lynn Tramonte, Alisa Munoz, Alaina Munoz, Alia Bales, Kassie Graves, and Jamie Giganti. These individuals have all played an integral part in this publication. I am very pleased with their work and our interactions. Alisa, you have been there from the start, and I cannot thank you enough for all your hard work and dedication to this project. You are an amazing person and very knowledgeable in your work. My dear editor Lisa's calm demeanor and character took me through some difficult times with this book. Thank you for the confidence you have in me. To my production editor Celeste Paed, thank you for your hard work and dedication to completing this project. You are very professional and easy to work with.

I would also like to thank Dr. LaNina N. Cooke at Farmingdale State College, and Dr. Christopher Martinez at City University of New York for their early and encouraging reviews of my manuscript. I am very appreciative of their time and effort in contributing their expert suggestions to this textbook.

Lastly, to my family: Krista Shires's passion for helping and knowledge shows how much she was willing to help in my book project. Thank you for your contribution. Continue the thirst for knowledge. To my parents Alimamy Rassin Wurie and Aminata Wurie, thank you for always supporting me to pursue my dreams. Even though they did not approve of my career as a police officer, they supported me throughout. Their strict rules and regulations made me the man I am today. Thank you!! My brothers Manny, Abdul, and Alhaji, thank you for always supporting me to pursue my ambitions. I truly appreciate all the positive comments and encouragements. I am thankful for my in-laws Deborah aka "Moms" and Neal Burroughs aka "Big Guy" (no, he is not actually big, it is just a nick name). They inquired about the book process throughout the duration of this publication, and they encouraged me and pushed me to complete it. The simple check-ins meant a lot to me and primarily added to my motivation to complete it. Lastly, to my unwavering family structure (Jamessin, Eliza, and Jennifer): They have been there with me from the beginning to the end. I have always carved out time for family and made certain that my work and writing did not conflict with our family time. Thank you for always being there for me. For the times that I put my work first, I am very sorry and look forward to building a stronger family structure. Jennifer, my rock, my best friend, my wife, and my partner, ever since I met you, you have always supported, encouraged, and believed in me. Your steady motivation and confidence in me keep me pushing forward.

CHAPTER ONE

Policing History

Welcome to the history and evolution of policing. In this chapter, you will explore the historical perspective and evolution of policing—where the concept of policing came from and how it migrated to the United States and North America. Documented in this chapter are the various types of historical policing methods and the use of various police tools for law enforcement. This chapter incorporates active learning to help you gain a better understanding of what life was like for police, including such aspects as ancient policing tools, uniforms, badges, patrols, and modes of transportation—from horses to motor vehicles.

A REAL-LIFE POLICE SCENARIO FOR DISCUSSION

from Chernoh Wurie's personal accounts

Early on a Saturday, around 2:30 a.m., as a Prince William County, Virginia, police officer, I was conducting a routine patrol when I noticed a gray Honda Civic with one headlight traveling on the opposite side of the road. I made a legal U-turn and followed the car based on suspicion. I called in the vehicle registration number, activated my emergency lights, and mentioned the location for the stop. Everything was going as planned until the driver decided to flee. I followed the vehicle for a short distance until the driver crashed and ran from the scene. As a rookie officer less than a year out of the academy, my own **reasonable suspicion** (an innate suspicion of seemingly regular activities helpful for detecting wrongdoings that might seem regular/normal to the regular citizen) alerted me that something was not right. The driver fled from the vehicle for a reason; it was my duty and responsibility to determine that reason. As a young officer, I made the split decision to chase the driver without any back-up assistance.

Using my flashlight to shine the way in hot pursuit through the morning darkness, I climbed four 4-foot fences in two different backyards before catching up with the driver. Standing approximately 8 to 10 feet from the driver, I drew my gun, pointed it at the driver, and told him to "get on the ground" and show his hands.

The driver, a young Hispanic male dressed in black, fully complied with my commands. I carefully placed him on an investigative detention and radioed his location. Several other officers arrived on the scene to provide investigative assistance. They discovered that someone reported the Honda Civic as stolen from a nearby location. The driver confessed to stealing the car and joyriding. We informed the driver that he was under arrest and transported to him to a local station for processing. Since he was a juvenile, he was placed in a secure room away from the other arrestees, advised of his rights, and sent to the on-call juvenile intake officer who reviewed the case and issued a detention order for a charge of grand larceny auto.

Learning Objectives

- Discuss the meaning and origination of the concept of "policing"
- Identify key players for the evolution of policing
- Recognize the difference between English and American policing
- Identify the various influential American policing eras

Chapter Outline

1. A Real-Life Police Scenario for Discussion
2. Exploring the Concept of "Policing" and Its Perceptions
3. Background and Evolution of American Policing
4. Perception versus Reality
5. Key Players in the Evolution of American Policing
6. Summary of American Policing Eras and Evolution
7. Chapter Summary
8. Discussion Questions

This scenario involves several key events that will help us understand the historical concepts of policing. Some points to consider include the following: What was the reason and justification for the stop? Why did the officer give chase without waiting for back-up officers? What tools did the officer possess? Why did the officer draw his weapon and point it at the driver? And, why did the officer place the juvenile in handcuffs while he was questioning him?

Exploring the Concept of "Policing" and Its Perceptions

The real-life scenario described in the previous section can help us understand the concept of "policing." To answer the questions at the end of the section, it's important to understand several variables involved in the chase. These factors include reasonable suspicion, probable cause, officer safety, police pursuit, officer orders, juvenile intake processing and procedures, and interviewing/interrogations. In addition, before exploring the word "police," the perception-versus-reality standpoint should be addressed. Witnesses only see an officer pointing his or her loaded gun at the driver. They may perceive the situation as excessive force because the driver was unarmed. They would likely ask, "Why was the officer pointing a loaded weapon at someone who was unarmed?" Secondly, witnesses may believe the officer stopped the individual because of his or her race and sex.

In reality, the officer relied on his or her professional training in issuing verbal commands to a fleeing subject. Whether the individual has a weapon or not, officers are trained to draw their weapon and issue clear verbal commands during/after a pursuit. In addition, just because the officer drew his or her weapon doesn't mean he or she is going to use it. It's a tactic officers use to warn the subject and keep the subject's physical movements visible. Another important point to consider is that the stop itself was justifiable. The officer saw a vehicle with one headlight driving during the early morning hours, which raised reasonable suspicion. It's also important to note that there have been cases where an officer could stop someone based on his or her own reasons and biases. This concept will be discussed in later chapters.

The term "police" engenders both positive and negative feelings depending on the era or social climate. For instance, during the summers of 2015 and 2016, several police shootings involving unarmed African American males received a great deal of media attention. These incidents led many people to perceive the police as a negative enforcing factor—a stark change in attitudes from the early 2000s. Shortly after the 9/11 attacks, public perceptions of police were largely positive. Law enforcement's response to the tragedies were viewed as heroic, helping to build a unified relationship between the police and its citizens.

Today, the term "police" elicits some unique interpretations. An online search revealed several possible acronyms for the term "police," including People Often Lie In Confidence Everywhere, Protection of Life In Civil Establishments, and Polite Obedient Loyal Intelligent Courageous And Encouraging (Abbreviations.com, n.d.). In further researching the true meaning of the word "police," Merriam-Webster dictionary noted that it was originally derived from the Greek word "polis" meaning community or city. In addition, it is interesting to note how perceptions of policing and the community have changed over time wherein originally the word "police" meant community. Debo P. Adegbile (2017) noted in an article titled "Policing Through an American Prism" that policing practices are under constant inquiry due to the various police and community incidents recently, including Eric Garner in New York, Walter Scott in South Carolina, Philando Castile in Minnesota, and Yvette Smith in Texas. But the author also notes that officers, too, are the victims of shootings, including recent incidents that led to the deaths of Officer Ashley Guindon in Virginia and New York City Police Department Officers Rafael Ramos and WenJian

Liu. The author pointed out that these incidents created further divisions between the police and the community. To help bridge the divide, the majority of police departments as well as federal, local, state, and community leaders are opening dialogue with the public to develop police and community reforms. Police and community reforms include various partnership endeavors by police and the community to include Santa Cops, Faith Coalitions, Business Watches, Neighborhood Watches, and Shop with a Cop. The conversations should focus on reaching common ground on public safety, liberty, and equality (Adegbile, 2017).

In addition to use-of-force scenarios, another concept that is often misperceived are various police procedures, such as stop and frisks and interactions with suspects. Many individuals would describe police responses to various incidents as too aggressive and intimidating, often citing their use of militaristic weapons and surplus equipment in response to these situations. For instance, during the Ferguson, Missouri, demonstrations, state and local agencies responded with armored tanks and other militaristic gear to control potentially violent protesters (Radil, Dezzani, & McAden, 2017). The federal 1033 program provides a path for police to acquire surplus military gear, weapons, and other movable equipment to fight the war on drugs. There are varied arguments and perceptions on this endeavor. Some researchers have suggested that military equipment is necessary because crimes are becoming increasingly violent. From the law enforcement and public safety perspective, police access to high-powered equipment is essential to protect the public, especially given recent events involving mass shootings and other violent incidents.

Other people have argued that the use of surplus military equipment demonstrates the police are too powerful and have become more militaristic in nature. Therefore, the original community policing model has been changed due to this new development in policing. The original community policing model was geared toward establishing a relationship between the police and the community they serve. As noted, recent police encounters with community members—primarily young, African American males—have created a barrier between the community and policing initiatives. In the wake of modern challenges and scrutiny in policing, several organizations have dedicated and enhanced their missions and goals to improve police and community relations. These organizations include the International Association of Chiefs of Police (IACP), Police Executive Research Forum (PERF), community advocates groups, the Department of Justice (DOJ), and the Final Report of the President's Task Force on 21st Century Policing. Each entity has identified various strategies and collaborative endeavors to increase public safety and improve relationships between police officers and the communities they serve. This book will explore these issues and help readers understand the differences between perceptions and realities.

Background and Evolution of American Policing

The history of policing can be very confusing for beginning criminal justice students. This textbook will present such concepts in a straightforward and concise manner for students to understand. The history of policing in the United States closely mirrors the history of law enforcement in England, and it dates back to the early U.S. settlers who were migrants from Great Britain. Most of these settlers longed for protection and order of maintenance (addressing minor improper behaviors that threaten the well-being and normalcy of a society). They sought protection from neighbors, friends, volunteers, and random individuals who would charge high prices for the guarantee of freedom and safety on their new properties.

Policing in the early colonies took two distinct forms: **communal form** and **informal form** (Spitzer, 1979). In explaining these forms further, communal forms of policing in the colonial era were mainly shared by everyone in the community. Anyone could be a police officer or a protector. There were no distinctions, directives, general orders, duties, or responsibilities. Regarding informal form of policing, it also had no defined structure and hierarchy; it was merely a form of policing comprising a group of volunteers who were willing to serve as protectors. The "watch" system also emerged from these early forms of policing.

There were two forms of the watch system, **night watch** and **day watch** (Potter, 2013). The night watch was not very effective because it consisted of volunteers who had no prior training or experiences. These volunteers were notorious for engaging in inappropriate activities while on duty, including drinking, gambling, and sleeping. The day watch had its share of issues as well. The volunteers were basically individuals who were volunteering as a form of punishment. According to police historians, individuals who were continually breaking minor rules were ordered by the local magistrates to serve as volunteers in the day watch system. Not surprisingly, they didn't perform as expected. However, the colonies desperately needed protection and order of maintenance, so they were forced to use these forms of policing as their only means of protection from criminals. With regards to important dates in early policing, Gaines, Kappeler, and Vaughn (1999) noted that Boston in 1636, New York City in 1658, and Philadelphia in 1700 were the primary cities that implemented the night watch system. In addition to enforcing criminal laws, the night watch was charged with lighting street lamps at night, patrolling on foot from dusk to dawn, cleaning the garbage from the streets, and extinguishing fires. Regarding the day watch, Philadelphia was the first to adopt this form of policing in 1833, followed by New York in 1844 (Gaines, Kappeler, & Vaughn 1999).

While the North was creating and fine tuning the watch system, the South was relying on "slave patrols" as their primary enforcers. The North and South were still two distinct regions as they believed in two separate ideologies about human rights and freedoms. The South at the time still favored and practiced slavery. The famous researcher on law and history in early America, Sally E. Hadden, noted the slave patrol system formed the basis for earlier policing in the United States. These were individuals who were authorized to track runaway slaves and protect the White population from slave revolutions. Hadden (2003) explains in her book *Slave Patrols: Law and Violence in Virginia and the Carolinas* that these patrollers were usually White men or women, some poor Whites, all equipped with ships, whistles, firearms, and other forms of weaponry. These individuals had the authority from their southern localities to enter any dwelling without a warrant to enforce slave codes.

Readers might wonder how this ties into modern-day policing. During the days of early policing, there were designated slave codes developed by designated states (McFadden, 2017). Because slaves were viewed as property, they were bound by these codes. Examples of slave codes included

- interacting with a White person without authorization,
- having relations with a White person,
- stealing from a White person,
- impregnating a White person, and
- running away.

The codes were created to provide and maintain social order for Whites. To gain a better understanding of the slave codes, Robert Paquette (2016) noted that the 1857 *Dred Scott v. Sandford* Supreme Court decision declared that slaves were treated as property. The chief justice Roger Taney, who wrote the majority of the decision, stated that Dred Scott—even though he had moved with his family to a free state—because he was considered "property," had no right to sue in a federal court. These conflicts between the North and South continued for decades, and these perceptions of policing varied until the implementation of the "**constable**" system (Potter, 2013).

Prior to the constable system, communal families were expected to police themselves through the tithing systems. These tithing systems were made up of 10 families. These families were expected to police within themselves and protect the families from outside wrongdoings. The next level was made up of 10 tithings, which was a collected group of 100 families. These tithings were under the supervision of the constable. Eventually, a constable (who was assigned by the king) was the higher authority and was authorized to oversee these families (Dobrin, 2017). Adam Dobrin further noted that these individuals were originally not paid; however, in later years they were paid with collected public taxes. The constable system was a bit more stable than the tithing systems. The constables were somewhat organized and had minimal training and experiences. Some were former servicemen with prior military experiences. Some of the constable system responsibilities included catching thieves, arresting criminals, transporting and serving warrants and other government papers, and supervising the watchmen entirely. The constable system can be attributed as the first formalized police force in early America. The role and title of the constable further evolved into the county or area **shire reeve**, later called the sheriff.

The sheriff was the law enforcement officer for the county, a specific region, or sometimes an entire province depending on the locality. In further examining the evolution of policing in the United States, students frequently ask, "What was the first state to develop a formalized police force?" The states that initiated the first police department and dates they started vary in some scholarly texts. Some researchers identified the first city that implemented a formal police force as Boston in 1838. Others contended that New York City was the first city to implement a formal police agency in 1844. Harlan Hahn and Judson Jefferies (2003) illustrated the reasons for implementing early American policing in large cities such as Boston, New York, and Philadelphia clearly in their book, *Urban America and its Police: From Postcolonial Era Through the Turbulent 1960s*. The authors confirmed that Boston was one of the first cities in early America to create a formal police force in 1838. Police scholars and other police researchers also noted that Boston was the first because of its political and socioeconomic climate. Several city riots took place during the 1830s and 1840s. Some of these riots were culturally driven, wherein German or Irish immigrants would face off with native-born English Protestants (Walker & Katz, 2018). These scholars further noted that other reasons for these riots were related to closing houses used for prostitution, opposition to medical research participants, and the issue of slavery. Many still favored slavery and would protest in the city regarding their rights to own and purchase slaves.

The second city known to have established a formal police department was New York City in 1844. Following Boston and New York were Chicago and New Orleans in 1851 and 1852, respectively. Subsequently, Philadelphia established its department in 1854, followed by Baltimore in 1857, and Washington, DC in 1861 (Hahn & Jefferies, 2003).

The majority of the early forces had formal uniforms and were equipped with a stick and whistle. Carrying a firearm was always a controversial topic as the level of use of deadly force was very high during these times. As a result, early police officers without training or experience were not equipped with firearms. They would also have a star-shaped badge that was made from copper. This became the famous nickname for police officers as either "copper" or "cops." These early officers had no formalized training or experience. They were mainly locals who wanted to serve or were forced to serve as a punishment for various wrongdoings.

During this time, **state and federal law enforcement agencies** were being formed as well, at the same time or even earlier (Corcoran, 1924). Some of the earliest state police agencies included the Massachusetts District Police, the Connecticut State Police Department, the Texas Rangers, South Dakota State Constabulary, and the Idaho Department of Law Enforcement. The author noted that these agencies were created as early as 1865 to 1870. It was further noted that the Texas Rangers (1823) and the Pennsylvania State Police (1905) agencies were among the first two state police agencies established. The Texas Rangers were initiated due to several Indian attacks and other Mexican-American social and political conflicts. The Pennsylvania State Police agency was founded after the **Coal Strike of 1902** (Cornell, 1957). According to Jeffery Bumgarner (2006), one of the first federal law enforcement agencies was the U.S. Marshals Service in 1789. President George Washington initially appointed the first 13 U.S. Marshals as established by the Judiciary Act. Another federal law enforcement agency that was created after the U.S. Marshals was the United States Secret Service in 1865. Another early federal law enforcement agency was the United States Postal Inspectors. This agency was primarily created to enforce crimes related to the U.S. mail services.

The Marshals' original duties and responsibilities were focused on pursuing and apprehending counterfeiters. Later on, their duties focused on targeting fugitive slaves and eventually other criminals or civil fugitives. Following was the Bureau of Investigations, currently known as the Federal Bureau of Investigations (FBI), which was created in 1908 (Bumgarner, 2006). This agency originally investigated antitrust land fraud and other civil matters. In the late 1920s, this agency gained wide popularity when new director J. Edgar Hoover took over. He was a controversial director—very ambitious and aggressive. He pursued several high-profile cases, including various mobsters and the kidnapping of the Charles Lindbergh baby. Because of the FBI's high visibility, its duties and responsibilities shifted toward federal criminal and civil investigations against and within the federal government. The levels of policing are more thoroughly covered in chapter 4.

Box 1.1 Perception Versus Reality

Why are police officers called "**cops**"? Reality: As mentioned under the history section, there are various reasons. First, the majority of the early police agencies equipped their officers with copper badges. They were widely known as "cops" because they were sworn to their badges. Other historians have noted that the word "cops" meant citizens on patrol, which was essentially true as well because the majority of the early police officers were volunteers. Some negative perceptions of the word "cops" have been influenced by the current social and economic climate that has wrecked the relationship between police and the community. Therefore, the majority relates to "COPS" as a negative force that violates individual rights, uses excessive force, and makes unnecessary arrests. This book will shed light on these various perceptions and causes of such perceptions. It will also examine the various initiatives several police departments are using to rebuild these relationships.

Key Players in the Evolution of American Policing

Several key players can be credited to the evolution of policing in the United States. It is important to note that earlier police systems in the United States mirror the police systems in England due to the migration and early colonial settlers from England. As a result, the majority of these key players were from England. This section will list and explore each player's role and influence in today's policing strategies. The individuals who seem to be most common among most policing mediums are Henry Fielding and his brother John Fielding, Patrick Colquhoun, Sir Robert Peel, August Vollmer, O.W. Wilson, Alice Stebbins Wells, and Lola Baldwin.

Henry Fielding

Figure 1.1 Henry Fielding

Between the early and mid-1700s, corruption, theft, disorderliness, and other civil unrest plagued London (Lemmings, 2017). Young Henry Fielding (see figure 1.1), who was a playwright and a novelist, accepted a deputy magistrate position of Bow Street Court in 1748. As a renowned writer, his primary mission was to spread information about crimes and other disorderliness throughout the city through his connections with local medium channels to effect a change. In his new role as the magistrate of Bow Street, he sought to organize a small team of non-uniformed individuals who later became known as the "Bow Street Runners." These individuals were tasked with preventing crimes, arresting and charging criminals, investigating crimes, and pursuing social justice. It is important to note that prior to being a magistrate, Henry Fielding completed several publications on authority and justice (Lemmings, 2017). These publications detailed criminal facts and current social-order enforcers addressed them. Later, in his role as a magistrate—a paid government employee—his main goal was to counteract the writings of the newspapers to comfort the citizens of London. He was effectively enforcing crimes, thus reducing crime rates. As an author, Fielding could not resist displaying in his writings humor and admiration for various encounters with criminals via the Bow Street Runners, but as a government official, his intentions were serious. His Bow Street Runners were indeed somewhat successful in carrying out their duties and responsibilities.

Sir John Fielding

Figure 1.2 John Fielding

Following Henry Fielding, another noteworthy police evolutionist was his younger half-brother Sir John Fielding (see figure 1.2). According to John McMullan (1996), Sir John Fielding was the assistant to his brother in his business at Henry Fielding's residence in Bow Street. This is the origin of the nickname "Bow Street Runners." It was also noted that Sir John Fielding was a cofounder of this initial group. Police historians also noted that Sir John Fielding became blind at an early age due to an accident. However, this impairment did not stop his drive and motivation in fighting crime with his older brother. He became a police magistrate and was notorious as the "Blind Beak," as he recognized thousands of criminals through their voices (McMullan, 1996). Sir John Fielding was appointed the magistrate when his older brother died in 1754. According to a review by M. D. George (1936), Fielding strived to continue his brother's legacy in fighting crime, crime prevention, and maintaining law and order in the city of London.

Historical manuals pointed out the irony that in current police hiring standards, where vision is a much-needed requirement, one of the very first police officers happened to be blind. It should also be noted that even though he was blind, he used his skills predominantly in interviewing, exploring, and interrogating criminals and offenders. The streets of London were filled with young, abandoned children who eventually became unemployed and, as a result, fought to survive, whether as male criminals or female prostitutes (Lemmings, 2017). Sir John Fielding dedicated his service to cleaning up the streets. He helped save these children by taking them in and advocating for teaching programs such as math, reading, and writing. His philosophy was simple: to eliminate future crimes and catch them early. He would pour his resources into young children to mold them into positive young individuals and role models so that they would not choose the path of crime.

Patrick Colquhoun

Another prominent name in the evolution of American policing is **Patrick Colquhoun** (see figure 1.3). As the others noted in this chapter, Colquhoun was also motivated to bring about social justice and order to the city of London. To explore his contribution toward the evolution of policing, it's important to examine an informative article entitled "Patrick Colquhoun, the Scottish Enlightenment and Police Reform in Glasgow in the Late Eighteenth Century" (Barrie, 2008). According to author, David Barrie, this police reformer was born in Dumbarton, Scotland, and was the son of an earlier sheriff of Dumbarton. At 16, he was sent to Virginia in the United States to learn the tobacco trade. Upon returning to London at the age of 22, he became concerned about the crime rates, social disorder, and, most importantly, the corrupt trade systems. This includes the channel on the River Thames in London. He was also a writer and published several controversial books on the current trade systems, poverty, and security. He wanted to make something of himself, so he teamed up with another very prominent utilitarian thinker, Jeremy Bentham, to initiate a private police force, which would later be called the Thames River Police force.

Figure 1.3 Patrick Colquhoun

Colquhoun was very much interested in reducing the increasing crime rates that were plaguing the Thames River to include merchant ships and other cargo marine transportations entities (Filtness, 2014). To protect the transportation route on the Thames River, Colquhoun initiated this endeavor with about 50 men. Financial difficulties continued to affect their new police force initiation. However, Colquhoun reached out to wealthy merchants for support in return for protection of their precious cargoes. He promised them a 1-year trial period for sponsorship on his enforcing initiatives. After a year, he would provide his supporters with a progress report, noting the positives and beneficial factors of his endeavor. He promised protection and prevention of crime efforts for the wealthy merchants and their cargoes. He and his men faced some critics from the riverfront workers who did not want to lose their wages. But Colquhoun was able to convince his supporters that his force was successful. Several other prominent merchants and wealthy politicians saw the positive outcome of his initiatives. As a result, in July of 1800, the British government passed the Marine Police Bill, which transformed the private police force to a public police force (Barrie, 2008). Patrick Colquhoun often is left out of police history literature. However, it is important to note that as a statistician, magistrate, and merchant his primary focus was on protecting and preserving commerce, private properties, and trade (Filtness, 2014).

Sir Robert Peel

Another prominent police reformer is **Sir Robert Peel** (see figure 1.4). Unlike other reformers, Sir Robert Peel was not a police officer or a magistrate, but he was heavily involved in politics. He served two terms as a prime minister for the United Kingdom and twice as home secretary (Williams, 2003). He made it his life's passion to motivate the British government to pass the famous police act called the **Metropolitan Police Act of 1829**. This act established the first formalized police force of London. It replaced the disorganized police force of the Watchmen, Constable, and other private police forces. These individuals were uniformed and were paid by the British government. They were equipped with blue tail-coat uniforms and a top hat (Lyman, 1964). Their uniforms were carefully selected to be blue so they would blend in with the general population to strictly differentiate them from the military uniforms and practices. Peel wanted to have his officers relate to the public and present a simplistic look as civilians on patrol. He wanted his officers to be regular citizens, but he also wanted them to be easily identified as officers.

Figure 1.4 Sir Robert Peel

These officers also were equipped with a wooden rattle—which later became the whistle used for signaling when trouble occurs—a truncheon, and a pair of handcuffs. Officers on the force needed to be fit and could not have any history of wrongdoings (Williams, 2003). Peel also geared these new police concepts to be more community oriented. He feared that citizens would perceive the police as the military, so he instituted the quasi-military structure in policing with a defined hierarchy, general orders, rules, and regulations (see Box 1.1). While there are significant similarities between the military system and the quasi-military, Peel wanted his police force to be distinct. Sir Robert Peel's first formalized police force was known as the "Bobbies" or the "Peelers." There are various localities currently in London that still refer to the London Metropolitan Police Force as the "Bobbies."

These principles—although implemented over 100 years ago—are still relevant to today's law enforcement agencies. Although not all of these principles are applicable, several are being used by various large police agencies such as the LAPD, the NYPD, and others.

Before introducing the other prominent police reformers, it is imperative to note that the reformers mentioned previously were originals of specified European nations. One would ask, why are they considered important in the evolution of policing in America? The main answer to this is that these reformers were the initiators, the implementers, the great thinkers for solving the rampant rising crime rates at that time. Their methods and strategies carried over into the early American society as the majority of the early settlers migrated from Great Britain to include London. Their thoughts and methods of crime fighting, crime prevention, and criminal investigations carried over into the early American nation. It is also important to give credit to these English reformers as the majority of the American values and norms were derived from the English system. As mentioned previously, various police departments, such as the Boston Police Department and the New York Police Department, were already formed. However, they were facing several corruption and unethical standard challenges from American citizens. Policing reforming was inevitable. Individuals like August Vollmer and O.W. Wilson were brought into the spotlight due to the much-needed police reforms the country was seeking.

Box 1.2 Peel's Nine Principles

1. The basic mission for which the police exist is to prevent crime and disorder.
2. The ability of the police to perform their duties is dependent on public approval of police actions.
3. Police must secure the willing cooperation of the public in voluntary observance of the law to be able to secure and maintain the respect of the public.
4. The degree of cooperation of the public that can be secured diminishes proportionally to the necessity of the use of physical force.
5. Police seek and preserve public favour not by catering to public opinion, but by constantly demonstrating absolute impartial service to the law.
6. Police use physical force to the extent necessary to secure observance of the law or to restore order only when the exercise of persuasion, advice and warning is found to be insufficient.
7. Police, at all times, should maintain a relationship with the public that gives reality to the historic tradition that the police are the public and the public are the police; the police being only members of the public who are paid to give full-time attention to duties which are incumbent on every citizen in the interests of community welfare and existence.
8. Police should always direct their action strictly toward their functions and never appear to usurp the powers of the judiciary.
9. The test of police efficiency is the absence of crime and disorder, not the visible evidence of police action in dealing with it (Williams, 2003).

Discussion question: Examine each principle and determine which ones are still in use. Give concrete examples as to which agency is using which principle.

August Vollmer

While Sir Robert Peel was known as the founder of modern policing, **August Vollmer** (see figure 1.5) was known as the founder of modern American professional policing. Wilson (1953), one of Vollmer's many protégés and former students, published a detailed account on Vollmer life's accomplishments and noted him as being one of the most influential police reformers in American history. Vollmer was the son of German immigrants who migrated to the United States in the late 1800s to pursue the evolving American dream. He was born in New Orleans, and his father died at an early age. In response, his mother moved his entire family to San Francisco, and they eventually settled in the small town of Berkeley. During the Spanish-American war, he enlisted and performed exceptionally and also volunteered for dangerous frontline missions. Upon returning home as a hero, he worked for local businesses, and, based on his heroic nature and demeanor, his friends convinced him to run for the town marshal (Wilson, 1953). His family was completely against this initiative because they viewed the local police as corrupt and felt that being an officer was a disgraced career.

Figure 1.5 August Vollmer

Vollmer listened to advice from his close friends and ran for town marshal. He won the election and assumed the post. The previous marshals were notorious for being corrupt and taking bribes or illegal payments for their services. Vollmer stayed true to his values and ethics. He was not known as a corrupt public official. Furthermore, when the town of Berkeley obtained its city charter, Vollmer was appointed the first police chief for the Berkley Police Department. He served from 1905 to 1932.

In addition, according to Wilson's account, Vollmer accomplished a number of police reformation initiatives, such as equipping his entire police department with bicycles, motorcycles, and patrol cars. He was also known to be the first police chief to implement police radios in police vehicles to ease communications between officers and their bases or units. On top of these accomplishments, Vollmer was also credited for creating the first centralized police systems, wherein the information collected and documented can be safely stored and accessed by other agencies for criminal and investigative purposes. Another controversial endeavor he undertook was making sure his department valued diversity. For example, he was the **first chief to hire African American and female police officers**. He faced much criticism for this initiative, but he once again stood his ground and remained true to his values.

With regards to Vollmer's educational achievements and police professionalization, Willard Oliver (2016) noted that Vollmer developed a keen interest in police administration and studies. He would approach and befriend the professors at the University of California (UC) at Berkeley to educate himself on criminal psychology. Because of his interests and contributions, he published several articles along with books in police sciences and administration. Oliver (2016) further noted that he was asked to teach police sciences at the University of Chicago and at UC Berkeley. He performed excellently on his teaching services and as a result was appointed to full professor at UC Berkeley. Upon being exposed to all these classes, Vollmer developed a profound understanding of the importance of higher education in policing. As a result, he required all his officers to have a college degree. Later, he made arrangements with the university to provide a common police training model and university credit system that recognized officers for their enrollment and successful completion of these classes and degrees.

Lastly, Vollmer was known as a humanitarian. Other police historians noted that he treated his arrestees with respect. He would offer them meals and eat with them upon being released. Many related that they returned to his agency just to thank him for being respectful to them while they were in his custody. August Vollmer is truly the police reformer. Without his contributions, modern American policing would be without several new initiatives and technologies. His initiatives are still in practice, and they have been implemented and significantly improved for the modern era.

O.W. Wilson

O.W. Wilson, one of August Vollmer's students, prides himself on carrying out his mentor's legacy. According to Oliver (2016), while a student, O.W. Wilson was also a patrol officer working under Vollmer at the Berkeley Police Department. Later, in his police career, he worked his way up the ranks within his department and also outside of his department. He was an author, a police chief, and a criminology professor. Wilson followed the path of his mentor regarding his educational endeavors and contributions. Wilson also was passionate about police work. He wanted to carry on the legacy of professionalizing police forces across the United States. He studied constantly and befriended several university professors across the country. He later became a professor of criminology at UC Berkeley (Bopp, 1988).

Wilson has been credited as the founder of the law enforcement code of ethics, and he initiated psychological testing requirements for police officers. In addition, he became the dean of the Criminology Department at UC Berkeley. Wilson's connections and accomplishments led Chicago Mayor Richard Daley to contact him about restoring Chicago's police department, which was plagued with corruption and scandal (Oliver 2016). The mayor asked Wilson to chair a search committee to hire a new commissioner for the department. The search committee couldn't find a well-suited, qualified, and disciplined commissioner. The mayor later turned to Wilson and asked him to take the position. He accepted the position for a short period of time and reorganized the entire police department. He successfully restored confidence in the police department. Later in his career, Wilson authored one of the most famous policing textbooks in the nation, titled *Police Administration*. Several police agencies and higher educational institutions used his book to teach his professional standards of policing.

Alice Stebbins Wells and Lola Baldwin

Lastly, in the spirit of diversity, it is of key importance to note the first female police officers in the United States. Among the many candidates who were called the first police women, two stood out: **Alice Stebbins Wells** (see figure 1.6), with the Los Angeles Police Department, and **Lola Baldwin** (see figure 1.7) with the Portland Police Bureau in Oregon (Schultz, 1993). Baldwin was mainly a social worker who, along with her female force, saved and rescued young girls and women from unimaginable living conditions. They were granted police powers by the City of Portland. Their affairs were mainly focused on social work (Shultz, 1993).

Figure 1.6 Alice Stebbins Wells

Figure 1.7 Lola Greene Baldwin

Wells was recognized as the first female officer appointed by the LAPD commissioner in 1910 (Ramsland, 2011). She spent more than 30 years with the department before retiring. Not only was she a reformer, she was also a leader, speaker, and writer who motivated other women to join the ranks. Previously, the officer designation was a symbolic gesture for women, typically granted to women as a consolation when they lost a loved one. Wells received a badge, which she proudly carried in her purse and would display when necessary. She was assigned to patrol special areas, including marketplaces and movie theaters, among others. One of her greatest accomplishments was during her term as an officer. She established the International Policewomen's Association. This organization was later called the International Association of Women Police. It is pertinent to note that these two prominent women diversified police work. They paved the way for many other women in law enforcement. Their dedication and commitment to bringing about change in this male-dominated career was remarkable.

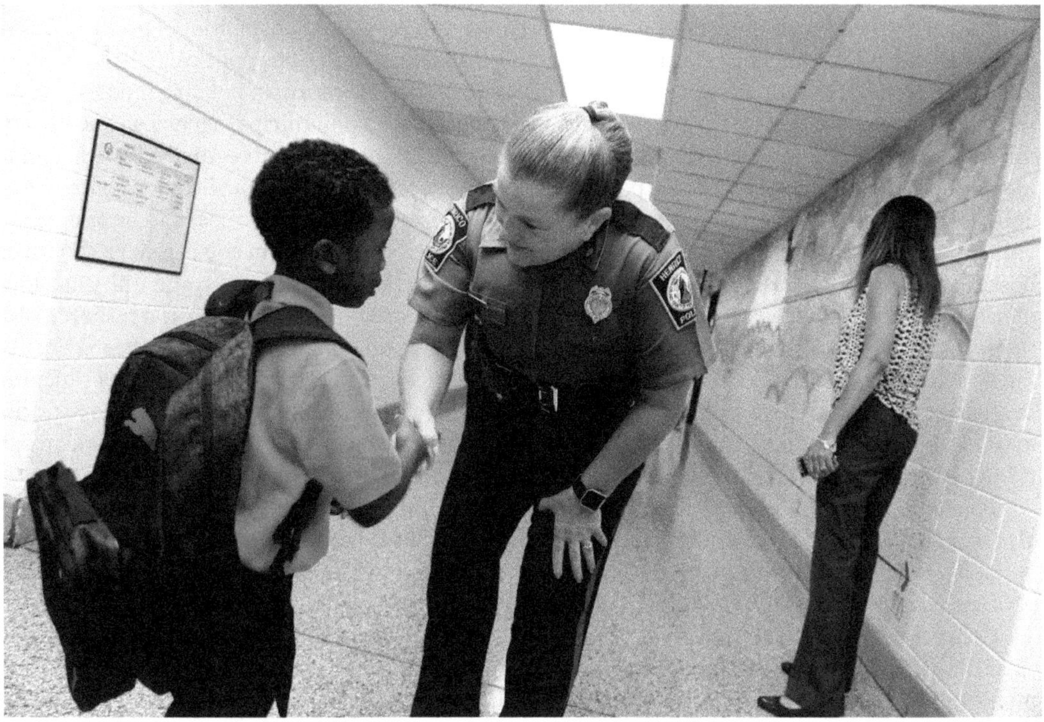

Figure 1.8 Linda Toney Greeting Child

Summary of American Policing Eras and Evolution

It is strange to evaluate the various changes and reformation that American policing has undergone over the past century. Several factors influenced the need for a change and professionalization of policing from the early 1800s to the late 1900s. Evidently, the reformers mentioned in this chapter made significant contributions in professionalizing American policing. However, before their involvement, the policing in the United States experienced turbulent times, including the political era, the reform era, and the community era. More specifically, these eras included sub-eras, noted as the riot, the immigration, the corruption, the post-9/11, and excessive-use-of-force eras. It is also important to note that the sub-eras morphed within the three major eras.

In elaborating on the learning objectives for this chapter, the presentation of these eras will be illustrated very simply with a focus on **the political era**, **the reform era**, and **the community era**. According to Oliver (2006), the political era was from 1840 to 1930. The reform era covered periods from 1930 to 1980, and the community era covered periods from 1980 to present. The author further mentioned the groundbreaking work by Kelling and Moore, *"To Serve and Protect": Learning from Police History*. Of these three eras, the political era was indeed the most turbulent.

The Political Era

As American policing was at its implementation stages, officers were very corrupt and so was their leadership. This sort of behavior characterized **the political era**. The political era (1840–early 1900s) was known as the period where politicians dictated the duties and responsibilities of police officers. Their responsibilities and job securities were highly influenced by various political figures. Most of the police agencies during this era were mainly **decentralized**—the form of policing model wherein the majority of police services are spread within various local and municipal agencies. Since policing was in its early stages, the authority was dispersed into several subunits—this included several locations and jurisdictions that could perform police services in their own localities. Accountability and disciplinary measures for officers' misconduct were minimal. Excessive use of force and police corruption were rampant. The era was heavily characterized by clientelism and catered to political bosses and their agendas. Departments were less guided by performance and community engagement and more through local politicians from whom they acquired authorization and resources for their subsistence. Politics played a heavy influence on the hiring process of police officers. Securing a position as an officer in New York City required a $300 payout, while those in San Francisco neared $400. Just the same, policemen could be expected to pay anywhere from $1,600 to $15,000 in order to be considered for promotional positions (Walker, 1999). All revenue accumulated from these payouts would support the activities of the dominant political party.

Police officers would strictly enforce the rules and regulations (Oliver, 2006). Most notable also was that during this era politicians heavily dictated the dealings of police hiring and terminations. Therefore, there was a simple level of understanding between the police agencies and the political figures.

Conversely, even though the police agencies in the political era were very strict in carrying out their duties and responsibilities, their primary focus was building a relationship with their communities and its citizens. The author further noted, however, that the police force focused mostly on protecting the powerful politicians and other dominant and rich citizens.

In addressing the federal government's dealings with the widespread corruption and excessive use of force complaints by police departments, the current president at the time, President Herbert Hoover, initiated the **Wickersham Commission**. This entity was established in 1929 to examine current police practices and all criminal justice practices at the time (Silver, 1968). The commission focused on some of the many issues, including but not limited to enforcement of prohibition laws, criminal statistics, prosecution, criminal procedure, lawlessness in law enforcement, cost of crime, police, and causes of crime. The commission found a widespread occurrence of unethical and unprofessional behaviors from various police agencies. As a result, a reformation in police practices was documented thoroughly in the commission's reports, to which August Vollmer contributed heavily. This led to the second important era known as the reform era.

The Reform Era

The reform era (1930–1980) is also known as the professional era due to the works and contributions of August Vollmer and O.W. Wilson. They were the frontrunners in reforming the early police systems and organizations. Based on the results and outcomes recommendations from the Wickersham reports, these two police pioneers were dedicated to carrying out major police reformation throughout the entire country. Police agencies during this era became highly **centralized** with the contributions of Vollmer and Wilson (Joanes, 2000). The centralized model of policing is wherein fewer agencies such as state agencies have the authority to undertake criminal investigations and patrol state highways. In this case, state police agencies perform centralized duties and maintain central database systems for criminal records and other biographical information.

These noted reformers sought education and solicited advice from various higher educational institutional scholars to implement professionalism in policing. Carrying out this professionalization of policing was no easy task, as they were attempting to uproot the political influence in policing (Oliver, 2016). Some of the first steps in professionalizing policing included the following:

- Incorporating college degree requirements for police officers
- Improving the basic standards for police recruiting
- Recruiting more college graduates
- Implementing automobiles in police patrolling
- Incorporating the telephone and the police radio systems for easier communications

Vollmer and Wilson are highly credited for implementing these police technology initiatives.

It is also important to note that during this era, the use of the television became widespread, thus police activities were broadcast on a grand scale. Communities and citizens now have an easier way to view police actions and criticize or praise their efforts. Although this era experienced many improvements for policing, it also introduced this profession to an entirely transparent spectrum.

The Community Era

In keeping up with this new transparency—being visible to an entire new world of the booming media through television—the policing era entered **the community era**. This era spans from 1980 to the present. For a more in-depth understanding of this era, it is advisable to examine Gayle Fisher-Stewart's prominent project with the U.S. Department of Justice's Office of **C**ommunity **O**riented **P**olicing **S**ervices (COPS). This project, led by Fisher-Stewart, is titled "Community Policing Explained: A Guide for Local Governments." This project, published in 2007, is still in effect and its practices have been adopted by agencies around the country.

Fisher-Stewart (2007), lead author, noted that the rise of this era was a result of several instances of police use of excessive force in the late 50s and 60s, causing nationwide civil unrest and leading to multi-city riots. Crime rates and gang participation and related offenses were on the rise as well. The author further noted that police administrators realized they had to revisit the original foundation as to why police agencies were initiated—community outreach, keeping the peace, and maintaining order (see figure 1.9).

Figure 1.9 School Supplies Giveaway

As a result, the community policing era was born. In further examining this era, it is important to acknowledge that the majority of the police agencies have initiated community-based programs to include the major dynamics of a community—businesses, faith-based institutions, schools, and neighborhoods. Furthermore, the author noted that in addressing this community era reformation, agencies should address the three main ingredients: **problem solving**, **community partnerships**, and **organizational transformation** (Fisher-Stewart, 2007).

PROBLEM SOLVING

Problem solving deals with police administrators meeting with community members to hear and listen to problems the communities are facing. These administrators then solicit professional consultants externally and internally to come up with strategic solutions for mending the concerns raised by the community members.

COMMUNITY PARTNERSHIP

After listening to the problems and concerns from community leaders, police administrators will then create initiatives such as community partnerships. These partnerships could be with faith-based organizations and other businesses to encourage a clearer understanding of, and open communications on, policies and procedures of their departments.

ORGANIZATIONAL TRANSFORMATION

Lastly, organizational transformation deals with the internal organizational changes within the agencies. Some administrators have sought to change the entire structure of their organizations wherein they are more transparent, incorporating technologies such as the use of body-worn cameras and creating more community-related officer positions.

Chapter Summary

This chapter covered a variety of historical aspects of policing. In examining the perception of policing, various perceptions were mentioned and documented. Police perceptions drive our nation to include the media and other distributing entities of social events. Police officers are under serious scrutiny in every aspect of their duties and responsibilities. With the implementation of the body worn cameras, this endeavor has been noted to bring more transparency to police officers.

Reflecting on the history of policing, several contributors were noted, including Henry Fielding and John Fielding, Sir Robert Peel, August Vollmer, O.W. Wilson, Alice Stebbins Wells, and Lola Baldwin. These contributors were the frontrunners of policing. Their contributions to the evolution of policing in America will always be acknowledged by police scholars and historians. Lastly, examining the police eras was also very important as this demonstrates how social and environmental climates tend to direct policing strategies and methodologies.

Discussion Questions

1. Upon reading the three ingredients listed by author Gayle Fisher-Stewart—problem solving, community partnerships, and organizational transformation—explain each ingredient briefly and give a specific example of each ingredient being practiced by an agency.

2. Examine Box 1.2 on Peel's nine principles. Which ones are still in use today? Give an example of a program and a department that is currently practicing the selected principle.

3. Upon reading the police scenario mentioned at the beginning of the chapter, what historical aspects can you apply to this scenario?

4. During the policing reform era, many positive initiatives were implemented to include several police technologies (police cruisers, forensic scientists, radios, fingerprinting, etc.) However, can you note a major disadvantage this era contributed to the relationship between the police and its citizens?

5. August Vollmer and O.W. Wilson were very prominent police reformers. What fueled their motivation to succeed in their reformation initiatives?

6. After reading the Supreme Court case on the *Dred Scott* decision, what impact does this case have on modern policing?

7. Which police reformer was known as the "Blind Beak"? Discuss the current police hiring and recruiting requirements, specifically addressing this question: How can police departments use individuals who are blind or accommodate such impairments in today's law enforcement strategies?

References

Abbreviations.com. (n.d.). *Police.* Retrieved from http://www.abbreviations.com/POLICE

Adegbile, D. P. (2017). Policing through an American prism. *Yale Law Journal, 126*(7), 2222–2259.

Barrie, D. (2008). Colquhoun, the Scottish Enlightenment and police reform in Glasgow in the late eighteenth century. 12(2), 59–79.

Bopp, W. J. (1988). O.W. Wilson: Portrait of an American police administrator. *Police Journal, 61*(3), 219–225.

Bumgarner, J. B. (2006). *Growth of federal law enforcement in America.* Connecticut, Westport: Praeger.

Corcoran, M. (1923). State police in the united states. *Journal of the American Institute of Criminal Law and Criminology, 14*(4), 544–555.

Cornell, R. T. (1957). *The anthracite coal strike of* 1902. Washington, D.C. : Catholic University of America Press.

Dobrin, A. (2017). Volunteer police: History, benefits, costs and current descriptions. *Security Journal, 30*(3), 717–733. doi:10.1057/sj.2015.18

Filtness, D. (2014). Poverty's policeman. *History Today, 64*(2), 32–39.

Fisher-Stewart, G. (2007). Community policing explained: A guide for local governments. *Community Policing Explained: A Guide for Local Governments,* https://cops.usdoj.gov/pdf/vets-to-cops/cp_explained.pdf

Gaines, L. K, Kappeler, V. E, & Vaughn, J. B. (1999). *Policing in America.* (3rd. ed.). Cincinnati, Ohio: Anderson Publication.

George, M. D. (1936). *History, 21*(81), 72–74. Retrieved from http://www.jstor.org/stable/24401289

Hadden, S. E. (2003). *Slave patrols: Law and violence in Virginia and the Carolinas.* Cambridge, MA: Harvard University Press.

Hahn, H., & Jeffries, J. L. (2003). *Urban America and its police: From the postcolonial era through the turbulent 1960.* Colorado, Boulder: University Press of Colorado.

Lemmings, D. (2017). Henry Fielding and English crime and justice reportage, 1748–52: Narratives of panic, authority, and emotion. *Huntington Library Quarterly, 80*(1), 71–97.

Lyman, J. L. (1964). The Metropolitan Police Act of 1829: An analysis of certain events influencing the passage and character of the Metropolitan Police Act in England. Journal of Criminal Law, Criminology & Police Science, 55(1), 141-145. doi:10.2307/1140471

McFadden, S. (2017). Slavery in America: History, culture, and law. *Reference & User Services Quarterly, 56*(3), 207–208.

McMullan, J. L. (1996). The new improved moneyed police: Reform, crime control, and the commodification of policing in. *British Journal of Criminology, 36*(1), 85.

Merriam-Webster. (n.d.). *Police.* Retrieved from https://www.merriam-webster.com/dictionary/police

Moore, M. H., & Kelling, G. L. (1983). To serve and protect: Learning from police history. *The Public Interest, 70,* 49–65.

Oliver, W. (2006). The fourth era of policing: Homeland security. *International Review of Law, Computers & Technology, 20*(1), 49–62. doi:10.1080/13600860600579696

Oliver, W. M. (2016). Celebrating 100 years of criminal justice education, 1916–2016. *Journal of Criminal Justice Education, 27*(4), 455–472. doi:10.1080/10511253.2016.1186992

Paquette, R. (2016). The mind of Roger Taney: New light on the Dred Scott decision. *Academic Questions, 29*(1), 34–48. doi:10.1007/s12129-016-9549-9

Potter, G. (2013). The history of policing in the United States. *Eastern Kentucky University.* Retrieved from http://plsonline.eku.edu/insidelook/history-policing-united-states-part-1

Radil, S. M., Dezzani, R. J., & McAden, L. D. (2017). Geographies of U.S. police militarization and the role of the 1033 program. *Professional Geographer, 69*(2), 203–213. doi:10.1080/00330124.2016.1212666

Ramsland, K. (2011). The thin blue thread: 100th anniversary. *Forensic Examiner, 20*(1), 138–142.

Silver, I. (1968). The president's commission revisited. *New York University Law Review, 43*(5), 916–967.

Spitzer, S. (1979). The misplaced emphasis on urbanization in police development. *Contemporary Crisis and Society, 3*(1). 1–12.

Walker, S. (1999). *The Police in America* (3rd ed.) Boston, MA: McGraw-Hill.

Walker, S. & Katz, C. (2018). *The police in America* (9th ed.). New York, NY: McGraw-Hill Education.

Williams, K. L. (2003). Peel's principles and their acceptance by American police: Ending 175 years of reinvention. *Police Journal, 76*(2), 97–120.

Wilson, O.W. (1953). Police science. *Journal of Criminal Law, Criminology & Police Science, 44*(1), 91–103.

Figure Credits

Fig. 1.1: Source: https://commons.wikimedia.org/wiki/File:Henry_Fielding.png.
Fig. 1.2: Source: https://commons.wikimedia.org/wiki/File:John_fielding.jpg.
Fig. 1.3: Source: https://commons.wikimedia.org/wiki/File:Patrick_Colquhoun_L.L.D._engraving_by_Freeman.png.
Fig. 1.4: Source: https://commons.wikimedia.org/wiki/File:Robert_Peel.jpg.
Fig. 1.5: Source: https://commons.wikimedia.org/wiki/File:August_Vollmer_cph.3b17374.jpg.
Fig. 1.6: Source: https://en.wikipedia.org/wiki/File:Alice_stebbins_wells.jpg.
Fig. 1.7: Source: https://commons.wikimedia.org/wiki/File:Lola_Greene_Baldwin.jpg.
Fig. 1.8: Copyright © by Henrico County Police Division. Reprinted with permission.
Fig. 1.9: Copyright © by Henrico County Police Division. Reprinted with permission.

CHAPTER TWO

Perceptions of Policing (Then and Now)

In this chapter, you will learn about the perceptions of policing from multiple dimensions (including race, gender, and age). In addition, you will have the chance to examine several incidents that lead to these perceptions; these events are briefly listed. It is pertinent to present these perceptions, as they have changed over time. As mentioned in chapter 1, the original reason for and implementation of policing was to protect and maintain order for the community. However, situations and encounters have shifted this focus from positive police perceptions to negative police perceptions. This chapter explores these perceptions from various mediums and also documents the initiatives police departments are taking to rebuild these negative perceptions.

Learning Objectives

- Demonstrate an understanding of both early and current police practices and perceptions
- Identify current trends in police perceptions to include race, age, gender, media, and college students' perceptions on policing
- Understand the meaning and reasoning behind militarization of policing, also known as police paramilitary units (PPU)
- Explore the community policing aspect, the broken trust, and rebuilding the trust between police and community

Chapter Outline

A REAL-LIFE POLICE SCENARIO FOR DISCUSSION

from Chernoh Wurie's personal accounts

I was patrolling my assigned beat area as usual—the busiest sector of the eastern district of the county. I was on the dayshift squad from 7:00 a.m.–5:00 p.m. Multitasking like always, I was listening to the police radio, typing on my computer, and visually observing my surroundings. At about 10:30 a.m., dispatch called to report a domestic dispute in progress at a nearby street. The dispatcher stated that a neighbor had phoned the police explaining that they heard a physical and verbal altercation between a couple who lived next door to the caller. The caller also stated that he or she did not see or witness the disagreement; he or she simply heard the commotion and what appeared to be a physical quarrel in progress. I read the call thoroughly and started toward the location of the dispute.

Upon arrival, I radioed in to determine the estimated arrival time of my back-up officer. I listened carefully but heard no noise and approached the residence with caution. The house was a small, older-style townhome comprised of red and brown brick. It had no awning or front porch. I chose to approach the front door, knock, and wait for a response. After about 10 seconds, a young, African American female between 20 and 30 years of age appeared at the front door. Her appearance was somewhat surprising, as her clothes and hair were ruffled. She seemed very nervous when opening the door and revealed to me that her name was "Fatima." Relying on my training and experience, I determined that Fatima had been involved in a physical altercation. She asked what I was doing at the residence and who called. She further stated that she did not call the police and did not need our services. I instructed her that an anonymous person called stating that there appeared to be a verbal and physical altercation at her residence and that she fit the description of the person involved in the incident. Through questioning, I determined that she was the victim of a domestic assault and battery by her husband.

As she was talking with me, I noticed a young child between the ages of 2 and 4 years emerging from behind the woman. The little girl seemed nervous and was not making any eye contact with me. She managed to say, "Mommy, why is the police officer here?" and then returned to hide behind her mother's leg again. As I continued to talk with the young lady, the young child emerged again; this time she was physically scared and trembling, saying "Mommy, why is the police officer here? Is he here to shoot me? I am afraid of the police officer." My heart melted and I decided to let down my guard and my officer safety techniques and got down on my knees and spoke directly to the little girl saying, "I am sorry you feel that way about the police, I am not here to hurt you; I am here to keep the peace and make sure everyone is okay."

At that point, my back-up arrived and made contact with the other party—the husband of the young lady who opened the door. Upon further investigation, it was determined that the primary aggressor was the husband. He was arrested for domestic assault and battery and was transported to the substation for processing by the backup officer.

I stayed on the scene to reassure the mother and her little girl that this would not happen again and that the situation was being handled by the police department. I also explained the domestic protective order measures and what would be allowable in order for the husband to not violate the order.

I realized that I let down my guard and jeopardized my officer safety training and techniques by getting down to the level of the child to address her. My back was exposed and, fortunately, the husband did not make his presence known until the other officer showed up. I felt very disturbed that a young child would have such a perception of the police. Where did she get that perception? How did she come to view police officers in this way?

Early Police Practices and Perceptions

This scenario is just one of many stories experienced at various levels and encounters between police and citizens. For this chapter, community members and citizens will be used interchangeably as they relate to the same construct. In addition, police agencies and law enforcement agencies will also be used interchangeably, as they are the same entities. Most policing textbooks do not address police perceptions. However, the author, editors, and contributors of this text made it a point to address and present this concept in its own chapter to show its importance.

The situation presented is appalling; the reaction of the young girl is a result of what is being portrayed around her on a regular basis. Why does she perceive the police as she does? Why does she have such a negative perception of the police? What negative stimuli has she encountered? To explore the early perceptions of policing, it is vital to examine the works of Oliver (2006), which include descriptions of the various policing eras—the political era, the reform era, and the community era. As mentioned in chapter 1, each era represented the policing spectra and its perceptions from the community. As the famous police historian Gary Potter (2013) noted, these eras formed the foundation of policing in the United States.

For this section, we'll review the eras again briefly, presenting the influences each contributed in the early perceptions of policing. The political era (from 1840 to 1930) is most applicable as it features accurately thc early perceptions of policing (Oliver, 2006). During the middle-to-late 1800s and early 1900s, the only forms of mass media communication that existed were the portable radio and the common telegram. The community members and citizens relied on radio communications and other slower means of communications to be in tune with current times. During this era, the relationship between the police and politicians was reciprocal in nature—they both looked out for each other. For instance, the politicians directly influenced the hiring and retaining of police officers, and in return police officers encouraged citizens to vote for politicians in order for them to stay in office. Sometimes, changes in political figures brought about changes within entire police organizations.

Based on this mutual understanding and relationship between the police and the politicians, the citizens started feeling that police departments were corrupt; therefore, the police perceptions during these times were negative.

In examining the reform era (1930–1980) (Oliver, 2006), also known as the professional era, it helped shape the perception of policing somewhat in a positive way. Police reformers such as August Vollmer and O.W. Wilson both influenced this era. Both pioneers sought the help of academic professionals and other scholars in the criminal justice system to address the police corruption that the previous era had created. These individuals implemented the police communications systems, police bicycles, and police cars and established stringent police professional standards for the hiring of police officers. The political era had become so influenced by politics that the hiring requirements of policing were practically nonexistent. Vollmer and Wilson brought about the professionalism in policing. Because of their rigorous reformation in police practices, the perception of policing was somewhat accepting and positive. Citizens and community members started seeing police officers as experts in their field, educated, and professionally trained.

Last, the community era—1980 to the present (Oliver, 2006)—is the most controversial era and has the greatest influence on police perception, whether positive or negative. Debo Adegbile (2017) noted that current police perceptions are being seen through the eyes of citizens who are constantly being exposed to the evolving social media and other technological means of communications. It is satirical knowing that this era primarily deals with community policing and reinforces the relationship between the police and the community. However, due to the recent turbulent times, these relationships have been negatively impacted by several unfortunate encounters between officers and citizens.

In summary, early perceptions varied from being negative due to corruption and favoritism between politicians and officers to somewhat respectful perceptions during the reform era, and then, during the community era, police perceptions became distorted. The next section discusses in detail the current police perceptions.

Current Police Perceptions

In exploring the current police perceptions, it is imperative to examine this construct from a myriad of entities including race and police perceptions, age and gender and police perceptions, college students and police perceptions, the media and police perceptions, and militarization of policing (see figure 2.1).

Figure 2.1 Police in tactical gear

Race and Police Perceptions

When discussing race in the United States it is imperious to note how diverse the country is; it is essentially known as the "**melting pot**." Race plays a significant role in the perceptions of policing in America. In further examining this construct, in 2016, the National Institute of Justice (NIJ) published a paper titled, "Race, Trust and Police Legitimacy." The paper further noted that people of color rather often view police officers with distrust and suspicion unlike the way White individuals might often view the police. Furthermore, people of color feel that they are disproportionately being stopped, searched, and detained in comparison to Whites. Therefore, the support and respect for police officers are in peril. The publication further noted that **legitimacy** and **lawfulness** are the key ingredients in a successful police and community partnership. However, some research shows that people of color's perceptions of the police lack lawfulness and legitimacy. In a thriving democratic nation such as the United States it is important for these two ingredients to be present; without them, the police cannot function effectively (NIJ, 2016). Additionally, most current police agencies are pursuing transparent endeavors in order to improve this legitimacy and lawfulness by allowing outside entities and community members to come in and closely examine their policies and procedures, for instance, citizen police academies, police cadet programs, police volunteer programs, and other collaborative programs to incorporate community partnership. Some of these endeavors have proven to be positive in improving these agencies' legitimacy and lawfulness.

Still, is it also noteworthy to mention that even though Whites hold high regard for policing and have positive perceptions, recent studies have shown that race is not the sole factor in how citizens form their opinions on police officers (NIJ, 2016). The researchers from NIJ also concluded that affected variables such as age, income, and educational level were more of an influential factor than race when it comes to police perceptions. In further examining the construct of race and police perceptions, another prominent work from Devon Johnson, David Wilson, Edward Maguire, and Belen

Figure 2.2 San Francisco, California, United States

Lowrey-Kinberg (2017) should be highlighted: "Race and Perceptions of Police: Experimental Results on the Impact of Procedural (In) Justice." The authors brilliantly conducted a social experiment with 546 participants who were randomly assigned to watch one of three simulated traffic stop videos. The videos depicted perceptions of procedural justices from a positive, negative, and a neutral perception. The results showed non-African American respondents assessing police strategies more favorably than African American respondents who assessed police less favorably (Johnson et al., 2017). The authors also referenced the famous **stop-and-frisk** data from the New York Police Department, wherein African American and Hispanic pedestrians were more likely to get stopped than White pedestrians (see figure 2.2). This concept of stop and frisk has always been a controversial issue between police and its citizens.

The concept of **driving while Black** (DWB) also emerged in the early 1990s due to the higher number of police and citizens contact between African American drivers and police officers. In presenting another scholar's perception on this construct, a study was conducted in the Marietta, Georgia Police Department by Sutham Cheurprakobkit (2006) titled "The Impact of Race, Police Experience, and Feeling of Safety on Attitude Toward the Police." This study surveyed 393 citizen respondents, mostly crime victims and complainants. All respondents were asked questions relating to police demeanor and performances during various types of interactions. The study revealed that the respondents felt safe in their communities and were confident in the officers working their cases. Secondly, regarding race, the same number of African Americans reported negative perceptions of policing as Whites (Cheurprakobkit, 2006). Lastly, the study revealed that although race was the primary perception tested, the study highlighted the citizen satisfaction to include attitudes of police officers toward their community members. This is impactful as citizen satisfaction is paramount wherein police daily interaction with the communities they serve influences whether they trust the police or not. It is also important to note that this study revealed that four demographic variables were identified: gender, income, educational level, and length of stay in the neighborhood. All these subsets affected the outcome of this study.

Although the excerpts discussed here illustrate a significant influential factor when it comes to race and policing, acknowledging that other factors do affect the general realm of police perception is key. Other factors include socioeconomic circumstances, generational differences, income and class levels, and age differences. Various studies have suggested that there is no direct influence to race and perceptions of policing while others negate this construct, insisting that race is the primary influential factor when it comes to police perceptions. The key takeaway here is that various other factors are at play, as mentioned; researchers should focus on all these other factors to get an accurate depiction of this factor whether it affects police perceptions. For instance, a low-income person of color might have a different perception of policing compared to that of a middle- or high-income person of color. The next section will explore age and gender and police perceptions.

Age and Gender Views on Policing

To take into account an international approach to examining the age and gender construct perception on policing, a study by Katy Sindall, McCarthy, & Brunton-Smith (2017) titled, "Young People and the Formation of Attitudes Towards the Police" will be explored. This was a study conducted in England and Wales wherein 1,500 young individuals between 10–15 years of age were interviewed about their perceptions toward the police, along with their parents' perceptions of police. The researcher noted a strong similarity in responses between the young participants and their parents, who shared that they are aware of the police presence and have experienced police victimization at a young age.

Sindall further noted that young individuals' attitudes toward police continue to be negative in the United Kingdom. Various factors might be attributed to this notion, including crime rates, police encounters, localities, and other public places. Even though the English police system shaped the

United States police system, both systems have morphed into two distinct and dissimilar types of systems. It is intriguing to see the same type of perception of policing in the United States, wherein young individuals view the police more negatively than middle-aged or older individuals (Lee, Steinberg, Piquero, & Knight, 2011). From the correctional point of view (Lee et al., 2011), researchers examined several young individuals—primarily young, African American male juvenile offenders, ages 14–18, who were adjudicated for serious misdemeanor or felony charges. In addition, the majority of the participants stated that they have had negative experiences during their encounters with the police.

Gender expectedly plays an important role when measuring submissive behavior of citizens toward the police. Results from the Cato Institute's (Ekins, 2016) national criminal justice survey compared opinions and perceptions toward police officers across multiple demographics. Among the 4,000 participants approached to take this survey, it was found that women and men have strikingly similar views toward the police where 64% of women, and 65% of men, expressed favorability toward local police officers (Ekins, 2016). While the majority of the American population opposed warrantless searches, such tolerance for unconstitutional searches and phone monitoring were shared alongside high school graduates, but not college graduates. In contrast to men (26%), the survey revealed that a strong majority of women (41%) believe law enforcement officials should obtain search warrants before conducting searches of suspected criminals. It is also important to emphasize that women across all races and ethnic groups are more likely than men to report a crime (74% vs. 70%) (Ekins, 2016). Examining the influence that police interactions have on different gender roles allows law enforcement officials to evaluate the public-to-police relationship so the perceptions of police can be measured in today's contemporary society for betterment.

Additionally, Paul Blackhurst's (2013) thesis, "Examining the Role of Race, Gender, and Class in African-American Police Perceptions in Rural Kentucky" posited that age and gender have also been an influential factor to police perception. To illustrate a somewhat different type of research on this subject, it is important to examine Joshua Cochran and Patricia Warren's (2012) work on "Racial, Ethnic, and Gender Differences in Perceptions of the Police: The Salience of Officer Race Within Context of Racial Profiling." This study used data from the Bureau of Justice Statistics' (BJS) Police-Public Contact Survey to reiterate their point on negative perceptions of policing regarding underrepresented individuals. The study also examined whether the perception might vary based on the race of the officer. The authors concluded their study with findings of positive interactions between officers of color and citizens from the same community, thus providing a slow restoration toward police citizen contact (Cochran & Warren, 2012). It is also important to note that in the findings of this study, the authors reiterated various other factors that tend to influence the perceptions of policing, whether positive and negative. These factors include but are not limited to vicarious experiences, the community context, neighborhood context, neighborhood crime rates, and the media.

The next section will delve more deeply into the media and perceptions of policing. Various scholars, governmental entities, and community groups have collectively closely researched the causes for the lower trust and confidence levels between citizens from underrepresented communities and the police. Based on all the research presented in this section, the fact can be argued that a sincere effort is being undertaken by all parts of the spectrum—community, policing, and the government. Young scholars are encouraged to take on this endeavor, as bridging the trust and confidence is an ongoing effort. In addition, students—who will be the change-makers carrying us forward—can, with focus and hard work in their future criminal justice careers, bring about positive change to our justice system.

College Students' Perceptions on Policing

The basic college student's perception on policing can vary significantly depending on various factors. Most colleges have their own campus police or safety officers. Dr. Andrea Allen, an assistant professor at Clayton State University and expert in campus policing studies, has published several works on campus policing and interactions with college students. She wrote an article in 2016 titled "Stop and Question Campus Policing," which involved 73 participants from a metropolitan university in Atlanta, Georgia. The premise of the study was based on a concept called the **stop and question policing** (SQP). This initiative is the same as the Terry stop derived from the ***Terry v. Ohio*** United States Supreme Court decision that an officer can stop any citizen based on **reasonable suspicion**.

The study concluded that most participants perceived this concept as positive. They believe SQP reduces crime rates on campus and is part of officers' duties and responsibilities. Furthermore, many people believe that widespread alcohol use on college campuses leads to various crimes, such as underage drinking and driving under the influence, so campus police officers must make these enforcement strategies their priority (Dowdall, 2013). Students involved in alcohol-related offenses are more likely to engage in violent property and other disorderliness (Allen & Jacques, 2013). Taking into consideration these crimes, campus police officers are under enormous pressure to enforce the law and control these incidents. However, how far can they go to enforce these crimes?

Additionally, Allen (2016) noted that if these enforcement strategies are overly enforced, this might dissuade prospective students from attending these colleges and universities. The author also commented that both parents and college administrators tend to put the officers in a sort of catch-22 situation, which can be problematic. For example, based on studies and some practical experiences, these officers might feel pressured by their administration to enforce alcohol-related violations in order to get rid of the party-town reputation and mentality of these campuses, yet on the other hand and simultaneously, the university administration is pressuring them not to enforce

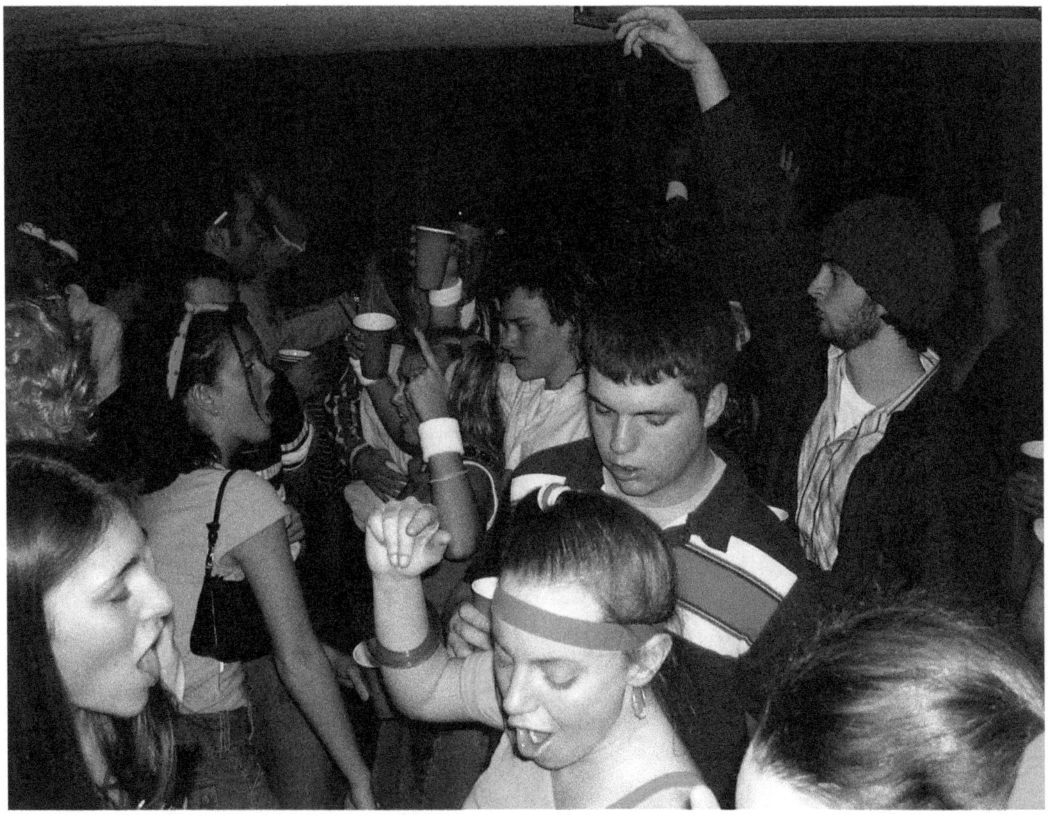

Figure 2.3 Party People

too much as they still want to attract positive enrollment. After all, too much enforcement could turn students and their parents away from enrolling at these campuses.

So, the questions become, "How much policing is necessary in a campus setting? How much policing can officers conduct without losing the confidence or appreciation of students and their parents?" In continuing to explain college students' perceptions on policing, most students say they feel as though officers are empowered to protect and serve these campuses initiatives. These students tend to be more cooperative with officers. Students who believe officers should be less empowered tend to be more disobedient to these officers (Allen, 2016).

Traditionally, college students have viewed their campus police as security officers whose primary responsibilities include enforcing alcohol-related violations, such as dispersing loud parties and other student gatherings. Some students refer to campus officers as "rental cops," which is a demeaning term that suggests the officers have no police powers. However, after several tragic campus shootings, most colleges are equipping their law enforcement officers with similar gear that municipal and local police officers receive. Most campus police agencies are requiring their officers to complete full police academy training to be employed as a campus police officer. In addition, most campus police officers are either recent graduates from the university where they're employed or from other colleges, or they're older officers who want to work in a slower-paced environment. The younger officers are primarily recent graduates and can relate to the typical college demographic. They also tend to know the hot spots for illegal parties, drinking, and other alcohol-related disorderliness. It's important to illustrate that even though alcohol-related enforcement can lead to negative student perceptions of police, research indicates that the majority of students perceive campus officers positively. They feel they're conducting their duties and responsibilities in an appropriate manner.

It is imperative to note that all the listed contributing factors should be taken into consideration when looking into police perceptions. Also, researchers have highly regarded the media as one of the major influential factors when it comes to police perceptions. The media presents on daily news and situations; are they presenting the events accurately, or are they putting their spin on things in order to make it more believable? The next section addresses this concept thoroughly.

The Media and Police Perceptions

When exploring the **media's** influence on police perception, it's important to understand how the media has evolved. The original meaning of the word "media" has changed dramatically with the Internet expanding the availability of 24-hour news, notes Dr. Nelson Granados (2016), an associate professor of information systems and the director of the Institute for Media, Entertainment, and Culture at Pepperdine Graziadio School of Business.

Figure 2.4 Mesa Police Department Responds to two publicized use of force situation

According to the Oxford English Dictionary, the media can be defined as the body or means that divulges information through various means to include broadcasting, publishing, and the internet. Granados (2016) further noted when people refer to the media they can be describing the message, the medium, or the messenger. The message is the content itself (e.g., information on a website, comments on a Facebook feed, or a YouTube video); the medium is advertising media or promotional content delivered through various channels (e.g., movies, TV, or radio); and the messengers include the actual news outlets. Now that a simple understanding and definition of the media has been presented, let's examine how it influences police perceptions.

As mentioned in chapter 1, police perceptions started changing during the reform era, especially with the invention of the television. TV broadcasts included news related to excessive use of force and other negative police-citizen encounters. The coverage raised public awareness of mostly negative police practices. August Vollmer and O.W. Wilson transformed policing through their professional initiatives and endeavors to include educational standards, training, and newer police technologies. Moving to current times, the use of cellphone cameras and other technologies have led to more scrutiny of police practices. Following are two recent incidents that serve as relevant examples of this scrutiny. See Boxes 2.1.

Box 2.1 Scrutiny of Police Practices

EXAMPLE INSTANCE #1

Our first example of police practice scrutiny was an incident that took place in Prince William County, Virginia, involving a 15-year-old boy who police shot and killed (NBC Washington, 2017). According to reports, police were responding to someone holding his family hostage. An officer responded and encountered the boy. A news report stated the subject approached the officer in a threatening manner with a crowbar. The officer responded by shooting and killing the suspect. The news reporter questioned why the officer didn't use a Taser or other methods to stabilize the situation instead of his gun.

From a criminal justice scholar's point of view, discuss the use of force continuum and apply it to this scenario.

Describe the role of the media in this scenario.

Describe the role of the police department in this scenario.

EXAMPLE INSTANCE #2

Another recent incident that serves as an example of police practice scrutiny involved a robbery suspect who was shot by Upper Merion police in King of Prussia, Pennsylvania, on October 29, 2017 (WPVI-TV, Philadelphia) (Ileto, 2017) . The news station that reported the incident said the subject was attempting to flee the scene, rammed two police cars, and was attempting to run over officers on foot. At that point, officers decided to shoot the suspect.

Apply the use-of-force continuum to the particular situation.

Discuss the role of the media and the police in the particular situation.

The news reports of the incidents outlined can influence the way the public views police interactions with citizens. The public perceives the media as independent reporting agents with no criminal justice background or biases. They are bound to report on what they see and their understanding of the specific situations they're covering.

For instance, when examining the Prince William County shooting (Box 2.1), most people would agree that nobody should face such a tragic death. But the situation involved several undetermined factors. From a criminal justice standpoint, officers are trained to confront threats with the use-of-force continuum strategy, which involves an officer quickly assessing the situation and utilizing one higher level of force than that of the perceived threat. In this situation, the officer faced a suspect with a crowbar. He believes his use of force is justified because he needs to stop the suspect from causing harm. In the eyes of the family and the community, this is uncalled for and unimaginable. Most police departments are implementing programs wherein community members and media reporters are invited to the police academy to view simulations of shoot-don't-shoot scenarios. It is understandable why the family and community react so strongly toward police departments' actions. But various factors determine why an officer chooses to use his or her weapon. These factors, as stated, are based on the officer's training and experiences regarding the use of force. The community events help bring transparency to the department's use-of-force policies and help the public understand situations that may lead to such events. We'll explore this topic more in depth in the following chapters.

In the King of Prussia situation (see figure 2.5 and box 2.1), the media reported on the reason for the shooting, but some intricate details were left out. These are details that could help the public understand use-of-force policies and why the officers chose a lethal option. As mentioned in the first scenario (Box 2.1), officers are trained to determine the level of force necessary for any serious situation. It's important to show both perspectives when it comes to reporting news stories involving use of deadly force. It's also important that criminal justice students understand the intricate details of all these cases. Future law enforcement officers, defense attorneys, and other local, state, or federal positions of authority must be aware of both sides of reasoning because they will have a major impact on new decisions and policies regarding use of force.

Pew Research Center's John Gramlich and Kim Parker (2017) conducted a profound study examining how the media impacts perceptions of police. The study was conducted by the National Police Research Platform for the Pew Research Center, covering a wide range of large and small police departments. It illustrated that eight in 10 officers totaling 81% agree that the media treat police dishonestly. The study also revealed that about 18% of officers disagree that the media does not treat them unfairly. Lastly, about 42% strongly agree that the media treats the police unfairly (Gramlich & Parker, 2017). In further analyzing these results, various other factors influenced these outcomes,

Figure 2.5 King of Prussia Mall Garage Shooting

including the race, gender, and rank of the officers. African American officers seemed less concerned and stated lower unfairness levels by the media, whereas the majority of the White officers felt that they were primarily being treated unfairly by the media. The rank of the officer also plays a key role. Line officers expressed more unfair treatment by the media than higher-ranking supervisors. In addition, officers who stated they "strongly agree" that they were treated unfairly by the media also said they feel somewhat disengaged from the communities they serve. Why are these officers feeling this way?

In exploring the negative aspect of police and media relations, John Dempsey and Linda Frost (2016) illustrated in their textbook, *An Introduction to Policing*, that the media primarily focuses on reporting on negative impacts on police encounters. For instance, in a use-of-physical-force incident involving an officer and a subject, the media typically reports on the situation from the subject's perspective. In this situation, the subject typically has the opportunity to tell his or her side of the story repeatedly. Meanwhile, officers cannot comment because departmental policies and state regulations prohibit them from discussing ongoing investigations, which may take several months (Dempsey & Frost, 2016). As such, the media's portrayal of the police department's actions is overly negative. The authors also noted, though, that the media has a positive partnership with police, which is normally not understood by the public. The police often rely on the media to solve cases through Crime Stoppers programs, persons-of-interest investigations, and lookouts, and by conducting mass media campaigns for the police department (Dempsey & Frost, 2016). For example, in a person(s)-of-interest situation, a police department that has a positive partnership with a media outlet may ask the station to broadcast the pertinent details of a subject to help identify and apprehend the suspect. In a mass media campaign, a news organization will broadcast suspect or other crime-related information. TV shows such as *America's Most Wanted* have also helped police locate wanted suspects. In a nutshell, while the media and police can have a volatile relationship, their collective efforts often result in positive outcomes.

The media continues to evolve as technology advances. This includes the use of body-worn cameras, cellphones, and video cameras that allow anyone to be the source of incident-related news. How can we ensure the media is reporting all perspectives equally? One solution is to inform the public by inviting community members, reporters, and students to various police academy training sessions that include use-of-force scenarios. This will broaden the public's understanding of why police officers take various actions, thus improving the perception of policing through the eyes of the citizens.

Militarization of Policing? Reasoning? Is This Necessary?

Several law-enforcement critics say the militarization of policing is unwarranted. They claim it violates the **Posse Comitatus Act**. Enacted in 1878, this law prohibits federal military and the National Guard from conducting or participating in local law enforcement endeavors (Schmalleger & Worrall, 2010). In exploring this concept and determining how it affects police perceptions it's important to note the law's origin, reasoning, and necessity. Police militarization can also be classified as **police paramilitary unit (PPU)**, which means local and state police agencies are training with specific branches of the military and are using military gear, techniques, and concepts in fighting crime (Schmalleger & Worrall, 2010). PPU also stems from the **1033 program**, which Peter Kraska and Victor Kappeler (1997) describe as the transfer of surplus and excess military equipment to local and state agencies to fight

Figure 2.6 Heckler & Koch MP5-1

Figure 2.7 Special Forces Soldier

crime and the war on drugs. These programs also led to the creation of special weapons and tactics teams (SWAT), which are common in most police departments.

As noted by Kraska and Kappeler (1997), some of the key tools and tactics used by PPUs include:

- Military-style equipment and technology
- The Heckler & Koch MP5 submachine gun
- Deployment of sophisticated weaponry, including tactical semiautomatic shotguns, M16 automatic rifles, sniper rifles, and automatic shotguns known as street sweepers
- Deployment of less-than-lethal technology, such as percussion grenades
- Use of tools for "dynamic entries," such as the service of high-risk warrants
- Use of battering rams, hydraulic door spreaders, and even C-4 explosives
- Deployment of armored or military personnel carriers and specifically equipped "tactical cruisers"
- Organizational structures that parallel those of military special operations groups
- Deployment of officers dressed in black or urban camouflage and wearing Kevlar helmets, body armor, etc.
- A tactical focus on "high-risk" work, including serving warrants, managing civil riots, responding to terrorism, and dealing with hostage situations and barricaded suspects.

(Kraska & Kappeler, 1997).

To understand the concept of PPUs fully, we need to explore how they're perceived by both the public and police. Citizens want to know why local and state police, who were established for community policing, need surplus military equipment and technologies to fight crime. They also want to know why police need to wear military-style uniforms that can inflict fear in the minds of innocent citizens. The local and state police systems should be completely distinct from the military. Citizens are becoming increasingly fearful of these paramilitary responses because they feel like the actual military is responding to crimes in their neighborhoods. The preliminary reasoning behind justifying the use of paramilitary responses stems from incidents such as the Ruby Ridge incident in 1992, the Branch Davidian siege in 1993, and the North Hollywood Bank robbery in 1997. In addition, some street protests have become deadly and destructive, so various law enforcement agencies have improved how they respond to similar incidents. In analyzing the police militarization concept, both police and citizens have valid arguments. Citizens have the right to express their opinions on PPUs, and it has been noted in some research reports that paramilitary responses to peaceful gatherings does inflict fear in the minds of innocent citizens. These concepts can be controversial when local and state agencies use military technologies and equipment during protests and other peaceful gatherings. The police are being cautious and prepared because of past incidents that have turned violent. Sam Bieler (2016) noted in his paper, "Police Militarization in the USA: The State of the Field," that there are advantages and disadvantages related to police militarization.

The researcher presented both spectrums of this concept using various studies. He continued to note that some researchers have concurred that police militarization brings hostility and chaos in neighborhoods but also gives police additional peace of mind knowing that they can use these types of forces, if necessary. Other researchers have illustrated that police militarization is a positive initiative because it encourages accountability and professionalism (Bieler, 2016). Police departments that utilize this surplus equipment are held to higher standards by the federal government mostly in providing justification for use of such equipment. They are also required to provide feedback in support for the program. Many view these collaborations as professional endeavors as they demonstrate that both the military and police can form a positive and mutually valued collaboration.

It is important to note that both parties—police and citizens—have listed very important points and reasoning on their perspectives on this initiative. The future and continuation of police militarization is highly political. Depending on the political administration, it will continue or it will be cut back. Police departments will also continue to deploy improved technologies to either keep pace with criminals or surpass them.

Box 2.2 Lieutenant David M. Smith: Prince William County Police Department

Over the last decade the debate about the militarization of the nation's local law enforcement has grown and is often a heated discussion on both sides of the issue. There are arguments that the use of "military equipment," such as weapons, body armor, uniforms, and vehicles, only help to alienate officers from the community they serve and create the appearance of a police state. There is also a counter-argument that the police need to be equipped to respond to the increasingly complex and frequent incidents of terrorism across the nation.

Figure 2.8 David Smith

The use of the word *militarization* is commonly used to describe outfitting law enforcement agencies with military equipment, but it is, in reality, not what the term means. Militarization is in principle the process of becoming ready for war or conflict. This term, when applied to law enforcement, is often confused with the advancement of equipment, weapons, and tactics based on a changing world. No one is advocating for local law enforcement to become the military, and as long as constitutional checks and balances exist and the criminal justice system maintains an independent review by magistrates and judges, we can maintain a balance to avoid a militarized society.

That being said, citizens have an expectation, and local law enforcement has an obligation, to respond to and prevent the increasingly frequent incidents of domestic terrorism. To understand why police must maintain the capability to protect the community in these types of incidents, one must look at the specific incidents themselves and how they were carried out. In the 2017 Las Vegas shooting, the gunman had access to 23 firearms, thousands of rounds of ammunition, high-capacity magazines, surveillance cameras, as well as ammonium nitrate and Tannerite for use in improvised explosive devices. In under 10 minutes he was able to inflict massive carnage on a crowd of concert-goers from an elevated position, killing 58 people and wounding 546.

The Las Vegas Metropolitan Police Department responded to the incident with hundreds of officers, many equipped with patrol rifles, ballistic shields, and tactical medical kits to render aid. A SWAT team also breached the hotel room to engage and neutralize the shooter. This is only one of many instances where the access to "military equipment" made the difference between the local police having the ability to respond to an incident effectively and the absence of such equipment, which would have left the police unable to stop the threat and protect the public from further harm.

Box 2.3 Perception Versus Reality

In this chapter of perceptions of policing, it's important to explore a perception that has plagued the criminal justice system for decades—the idea that the police are becoming more militarized due to their cooperative training with the military, use of military surplus equipment, and use of military tactics and technologies. In reality, there are specific policies and laws in place in the United States that sets the levels of government. The United States Constitution specifically categorizes the federal government into the three major branches: the legislative (makes laws—Congress), the judicial (evaluates the laws such as the supreme courts and other lower courts), and the executive branch (carries out and enforces the laws such as those passed by the president, vice president, cabinet, and the various enforcement agencies). This is specifically established by the U.S. Constitution in order to prevent one branch from becoming too powerful. This creates a system of checks and balances, providing higher accountability for every agency and governmental enforcing arm. Policies, such as the Posse Comitatus Act, prevent such a takeover and intrusion from the military.

Community and Policing

While chapter 6 covers community policing extensively, this section will discuss the relationship between communities and the police. The community has always played an important role in police formation and enforcement. Various police departments have partnered with communities to collectively sponsor programs such as Citizens on Patrol (COP), Neighborhood Watch programs, Shop With a Cop, Santa Cops, Dunk a Cop, and other initiatives involving faith-based and business coalitions. The community's perception of the police is sometimes based only on the current era, media representation, and crime rates. For instance, a community will be happy with their local police department if crime rates are down and there are significant higher case closures. This demonstrates to a community that the police department is effective.

On the other hand, if the police department is engaged in a questionable use-of-force scenario or the media portrays the police department as being unfair and immoral during an arrest, then the community's perception will become negative based on a single incident or officer's action.

In examining various studies, Jack Green and Scott Decker (1989) published an intriguing study titled "Police and Community Perceptions of Community Role in Policing: The Philadelphia Experience." In this study, they conducted a perception study from both groups—the police officers and community participants. They interviewed more than 50 Philadelphia police officers and 24 community residents. Most of the questions covered police and citizen interactions. The findings of the study revealed a somewhat peculiar result, noting that these perceptions are being affected mostly by the officers' attitudes themselves and the department's acceptance of public criticism (Green & Decker, 1989). In explaining this further, it's important to note that police officers are resistant to change. Police officers also are very critical of each other and their agencies. As a result, some officers may respond negatively toward these stimuli, which can affect their daily interactions toward the citizens they serve.

Rachel Stein and Candace Griffith (2017) also illustrated in their study "Resident and Police Perceptions of the Neighborhood: Implications for Community Policing," that the structure and context of the neighborhood plays an important part in shaping police and community perceptions. In this particular study, the authors conducted a police and neighborhood perceptions survey in three high-crime neighborhoods in a Midwestern U.S. city. The preliminary findings show responses from the residents in all three neighborhoods were similar to the perceptions of the police and their interactions with residents. The officers' perceptions of residents were based on various factors, including employment, unemployment, class structure, income level, and demographics. Positive police interactions were primarily found in White neighborhoods, while predominantly neighborhoods composed of underrepresented individuals expressed less-positive perceptions. The authors also point out the benefits of implementing a successful crime-prevention program in a neighborhood, which should include cultural diversity training for officers to help them understand and connect with the residents they're serving (Stein & Griffith, 2017). Current research also shows that agencies that have invested in mandatory cultural diversity training for their officers have received positive police perceptions and encounters from citizens and community members. Most local and state agencies are implementing these programs and requiring their officers to attend them on an annual basis.

Officer/Community Leader Experiences

The following excerpt includes insights from a community member who was asked to provide input into his perception on policing:

> As a career educator, I have always viewed law enforcement as an integral partner of the public school system. School systems rely on local law enforcement agencies to assist

in providing a safe, welcoming learning environment for students. I have witnessed how our police partners foster a positive relationship with the school community by educating stakeholders on local laws and crime prevention strategies.

– Gregory Lawson, Henrico Public School, Virginia

As mentioned previously, community and policing make up the fabric of society; without an understandable working relationship between the two, the mutual understanding that has existed between these two groups will always be strained. Endeavors on both ends are being addressed on all aspects. Police agencies are becoming more transparent and are involving their communities in decision making, policy revisions, and sometimes disciplinary measures of officers. Some community leaders are taking it upon themselves to help build positive relationships with their local and state police departments by attending open police forums and also by inviting their local and state agencies to community events.

The Broken Trust: How Did This Happen?

As mentioned under the community and policing section, various strategies are being explored in creating a positive relationship between the two entities. As important as this relationship is, it is imperative to examine how this trust has become broken, and what has contributed to this deterioration. Box 2.4 contains a personal note from this book's author on broken trust.

Box 2.4 A Personal Note From the Author, Chernoh Wurie, Ph.D.

In conducting the research for this section, I experienced a lot of mixed emotions, as I can relate to all sides of the spectrum. I am all of these: an African American immigrant, a former police officer, and currently a university professor. Given these life experiences, it is sometimes very difficult to stay neutral on this topic. As an African immigrant, I have experienced stereotypical treatment from various forms of law enforcement agencies from all levels—local, state, and federal. When I was a police officer, I also experienced a double marginality wherein I was somewhat accepted as a police officer by the community I served and somewhat accepted by my African family who mostly reported poor treatment from police in general. I felt as if I had no place—not fully accepted by my family because of my career choice, and not fully accepted by the community as they viewed me as just another police officer with too much power and authority. In addition, another issue that I struggled with as a former police officer was that it was very challenging to relate to the incidents involving the shooting of unarmed African American males by police during 2014–2016. As a former police officer who has been involved in all levels of use of force, it was very difficult to cast blame or judge any of the involved officers. On the other hand, as African American male, I can relate to each of the individuals involved in these shootings, their families, and friends. I resorted to listing all aspects of these voices in order to stay neutral to this audience and to reflect progressing movement toward healing this community distrust.

The majority of this section of the broken trust will cover the trust between members of underrepresented communities—predominantly African American communities—and the police. It was evident that the trust between the police and the communities they protect and serve has been broken after a series of incidents surrounding high-profile, police-involved deaths of African Americans. The trust that existed between police and the community before these high-profile incidents was somewhat manageable. An article published by Boston's NPR News Station, WBUR, "After 9 High-Profile Police-Involved Deaths Of African-Americans, What Happened To The Officers?", accurately listed the series of events that changed the entire face of policing across the United States. The dates of these incidents range from 2014 to 2016 and include the following:

- Eric Garner, NY, July 17, 2014
- Michael Brown, MO, August 9, 2014
- Laquan McDonald, IL, October 20, 2014
- Tamir Rice, OH, November 23, 2014
- Walter Scott, SC, April 4, 2015
- Freddie Gray, MD, April 12, 2015
- Sandra Bland, TX, July 10, 2016
- Alton Sterling, LA, July 5, 2016

From a researcher's perspective, these represent a cluster of unfortunate incidents. However, why did these events occur within a certain timeframe, from 2014–2016? Were police officers receiving similar training on the use of deadly force? Were police officers being taught to be hypervigilant when encountering persons of color, particularly African American males? From the community's perspective, these incidents occurred in a cluster form because the police were becoming too powerful, and because the police seemed to have no regard for the lives of persons of color—especially African American males. Thus began the **Black lives matter movement** (BLM) (BLM, 2013).

The Black lives matter movement was originally founded by three African American organizers—Alicia Garza, Patrisse Cullors, and Opal Tometi—who created the movement soon after the Trevon Martin acquittal of George Zimmerman. The BLM's main focus is to bring to light to the world that the lives of African Americans are not being valued; that instead, African Americans are being treated poorly by individuals of authoritative stature (including those involved at all levels of the enforcement and correctional arms globally, not just in the United States; see figure 2.9). The BLM currently has over 40 chapters worldwide. From the law enforcement perspective, these series of events happened due to heightened alert and cognitive responses toward officer safety initiatives. Current research suggests that because of the number of officers who were killed in the line of duty, the BLM has grown immensely, and as a result, most police departments initiated and continue to take various steps to train officers how to more effectively and successfully respond to various scenarios.

In analyzing each of the tragedies listed, it is challenging to determine the cause of each incident. One thing for certain is that an administrative investigation was initiated for all the officers who were involved and charges were brought against those who were deemed to have used excessive and unnecessary force. Both the police departments and the community members have a contributing hand in the reasoning for these tragedies. Some may disagree with this notion; however, various factors should be taken into account when examining these incidents, including but not limited to the following:

- Cultural diversity between officers and subjects
- Use-of-force trainings
- Less lethal options
- Neighborhood contexts
- Community and social stimuli due to constant media portrayal
- Officers' and subjects' demeanors during these encounters

Consider a specific BLM incident and think about how it could have been prevented. Examine both spectrums: What could the police departments have done differently to prevent such atrocities? What could the community have done differently to have possibly prevented such occurrences?

Figure 2.9 Black Lives Matter Protest

After the tragic incidents listed, much of the perception between police and members of underrepresented communities became negative, therefore breaking the fragile trust these communities once had for the police. Some White communities sympathized with underrepresented communities and joined them in peaceful protesting across the nation. Their voices were heard around the world calling for various police reforms. The majority of police departments developed various plans to rebuild this broken trust, as it is much needed for the productive operation of a police department and the communities it serves. The next section delves in details about rebuilding initiatives between law enforcement and the community.

Rebuilding the Trust Between the Community and the Police

In order to properly document the various initiatives being explored to rebuild this trust, it is imperative to cover the political aspect of this concept as it is the driving force behind the change in police departments. Under the Obama administration, the president formed a task force to reexamine police practices and solicit community leaders, police leaders, and criminal justice scholars in order to come up with ways to rebuild this trust.

In summation of President Obama's plans to rebuild this trust, three key points were noted by former associate director of content for the Office of Digital Strategy, David Hudson (2014): proposing and funding more use of body-worn camera programs for all police departments in order to promote transparency and accountability; establishing a task force to explore police practices in order to improve police community relations; and lastly, to examine and possibly reform the federal 1033

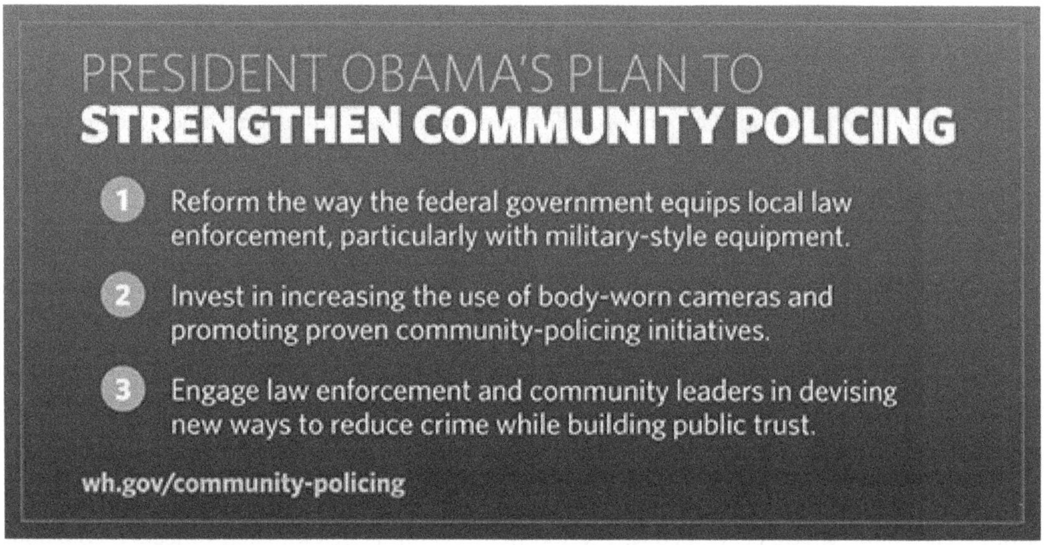

PRESIDENT OBAMA'S PLAN TO
STRENGTHEN COMMUNITY POLICING
1 Reform the way the federal government equips local law enforcement, particularly with military-style equipment.
2 Invest in increasing the use of body-worn cameras and promoting proven community-policing initiatives.
3 Engage law enforcement and community leaders in devising new ways to reduce crime while building public trust.
wh.gov/community-policing

Figure 2.10 President Obama's Plan to Strengthen Community Policing
Source: Hudson (2014)

program, which allows the federal government to grant local and state agencies surplus military equipment and technologies (see figure 2.10). As a result of these steps taken by President Obama, the implementation of the **President's Task Force on 21st Century Policing** was initiated, chaired by Commissioner Charles Ramsey and Professor Laurie Robinson from George Mason University. The committee was also made up of several other prominent individuals from various facets of the country including police chiefs, community advocates, leaders of color, faith-based leaders, criminal justice scholars, and other criminal justice executive members.

The committee came up with six pillars in their proposal for rebuilding the trust between police and the communities they serve:

- Building trust and legitimacy
- Policy and oversight
- Technology and social media
- Community policing and crime reduction
- Training and education
- Officer wellness and safety (Ramsey & Robinson, 2015)

These proposed pillars have been adopted by various police departments around the country. It is important to note that these steps are an ongoing work in progress for some police departments. In explaining the building trust and legitimacy pillar—with the implementation of the body-worn camera program—recent studies have shown that the use of force and citizen complaints have reduced significantly in departments that have implemented this program. In exploring the policy and oversight pillar, it is proposed that police departments should examine their policies to reflect the values of the communities they serve. Policies should be clear and transparent to the community in order to demonstrate accountability and transparency. This also covers data collection on use of force and other police- and community-related interactions. Pillar three, technology and social media usage, should be paramount in police-citizen interactions. This applies both ways wherein police can utilize social media to share information and be transparent, and the community can use social media to reach out to the police department in collaboration with various types of incidents. New technologies and the use of social media (police department websites, Facebook, Twitter, etc.) can also assist police in educating the communities about new policies and provide timely warnings. Pillar four covered community policing and crime reduction wherein it reiterates the importance of community policing. An effective community policing depends on a successful relationship between the police and the community. Without that positive relationship, the concept and original goal of community policing will not flourish. Pillar five presents the importance of training and education. This pillar covered the importance of hiring police officers to reflect the community they are protecting and serving. It is paramount that the police department's internal and external image reflect its population. In addition, officers must be well trained in various cultural diversity trainings and other implicit and unconscious bias initiatives. Pillar five also highlights the importance of education in law enforcement. Studies have shown that officers with a college degree or higher tend to have a positive interaction with the constituents they encounter. Lastly, pillar six explains the importance of officer wellness and safety, as it does not only affect the designated officers, it also affects their peers and the safety of the community they serve. Various police departments around the country have developed safety and wellness initiatives for their officers throughout the ranks of their departments. Some agencies have a mandatory physical training requirements for all officers and others only have these requirements for police recruits and other specialized units such as SWAT teams.

In an effort to rebuild this trust, various agencies should be credited for their continuous efforts in providing excellent research data and resources to both law enforcement and community members. These agencies include the Police Executive Research Forum (PERF), the International Association of Chiefs of Police (IACP), and the U.S. Department of Justice, Community Oriented Police Services (COPS). PERF hosted a ground-breaking event in July 2015, titled "Why Police-Community Relationships Are Important." This was a collective one-day session wherein police officers, police administrators, and community leaders and members discussed strategies for rebuilding the trust between police and the community. The outcome from this one-day session yielded the following recommendations to police agencies:

- Acknowledge and discuss with communities the challenges they are facing
- Be transparent and accountable
- Take steps to reduce bias and improve cultural competence
- Maintain focus on the importance of collaboration
- Be visible in the community
- Promote internal diversity and ensure growth opportunities

These recommendations mirror some of the initiatives provided by the President's Task Force on 21st Century Policing. Regarding the first point, acknowledging and discussing challenges various departments are facing, this initiative is currently being instituted in the majority of police departments as they strive to be transparent. Further reiterating the first point, various discussions between community members and law enforcement officers and administrators should be held periodically. These discussions are geared toward addressing community relations events and issues in order to strengthen the bond between the two entities. Second, being transparent and accountable is mainly the encouragement for using body-worn cameras across every police department. In addition, it's important to help citizens and community members to become aware and educated in police practices. Third, taking the steps to reduce bias and improve cultural competency is also an active initiative that the majority of police agencies are implementing.

Some police departments already have these programs in place wherein officers are mandated to take these trainings on an annual basis. Maintaining a focus on the importance of collaboration and being visible in the community are efforts that police departments can make to become more present within the communities they serve (see figure 2.11). Police are now walking school children to and from the bus stops and participating in outdoor activities with neighborhood members. These are some basic examples of how this initiative is impacting communities in a positive way. Lastly, however, the concept of promoting internal diversity and ensuring professional growth opportunities is admittedly an initiative that the majority of departments are struggling with. Based on the broken trust, most applicants of color are deterred from joining this profession; they are stuck between their personal desires to make a change and their families who tend to provide little or no support for their loved ones to join this profession. As a result, most police agencies are struggling with hiring, recruiting, and retaining members of a diverse class and background. To combat this challenge, many agencies have launched several aggressive recruiting and hiring initiatives all across the country. Their main focus is to have their departments somewhat mirror the communities they serve.

Researcher Tracey Meares (2017) notes an interesting position on the building of trust between community and policing initiatives, expressed in an intriguing article, titled "The Path Forward: Improving the Dynamics of Community-Police Relationships to Achieve Effective Law Enforcement Policies." In her article, Meares explains that it is partial to ask police to tend to socially inevitable problems when they are not social workers. In addition, Meares further notes that although police are available 24/7, 365 days a year, this does not make them social workers. After all, police are not super-human, and like most humans, police can only handle what's realistic in terms of workload. Most importantly, police agencies need to adhere to the fact that all lives are valuable and should

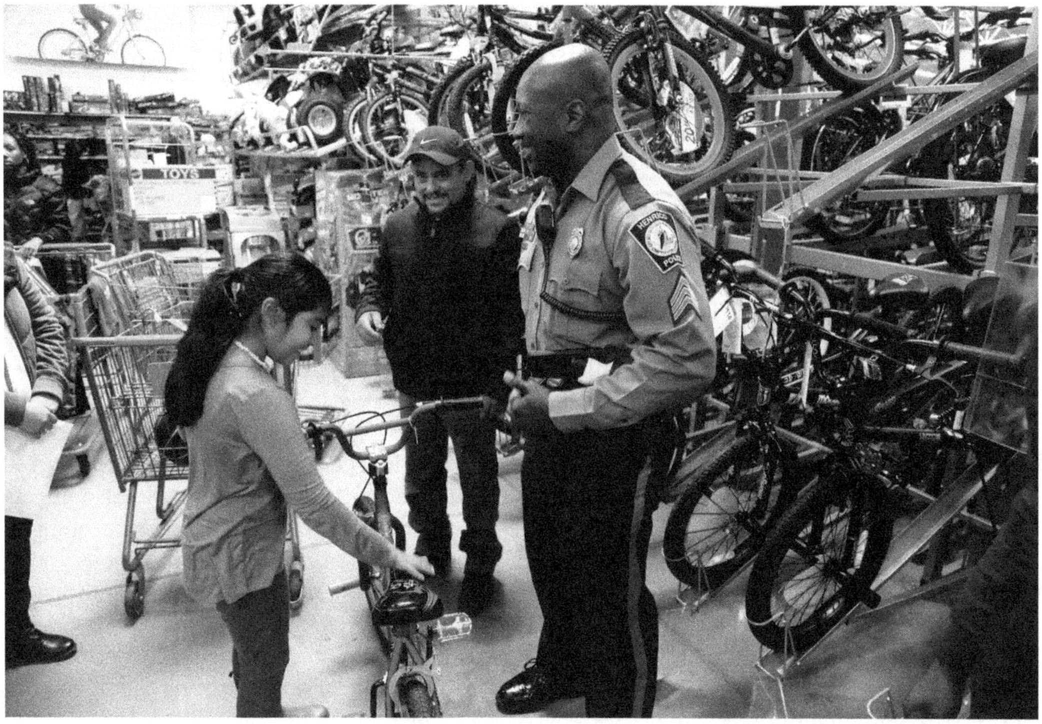

Figure 2.11 Shop with a Cop

strive for further de-escalation techniques, which some departments are currently undergoing (Meares, 2017). There are various embedded notions within this researcher's illustration. Let's explore these further.

In analyzing the first section of Meare's article, which discusses the idea of police being expected to be social workers, it's important to note that most calls for services are funneled through the police department and eventually will be directed to the right channel. However, for incidents that happen during the night and morning hours when all other agencies are closed, it is inevitable for the police to handle such calls dealing with the social well-being of callers and/or related individuals. When police are stretched too thin in their duties and responsibilities, the marginality of error becomes easily apparent, due to being expected to handle too much.

To help resolve this issue, in Denver, Colorado, for example, efforts are now being made to enhance the collaboration between police and social workers. According to an article from FOX Denver by reporter Keagan Harsha (2018), "Colorado Mental Health Professionals Now Responding to 911 Calls," several police agencies in Denver are employing a co-responding strategy wherein they are partnering patrol officers with a social worker to respond to 911 calls. This is a valuable, worthwhile endeavor that demonstrates the close working relationship between the police department and the department of health and social services. As a result of these co-response strategies, the state has reduced the number of mental health-related use of force situations and has referred several individuals to receive appropriate assistance for their mental health conditions. Several other agencies in the United States are also exploring this co-response strategy. The article further noted that the Colorado Department of Human Services plans to support this endeavor financially over the next 3 years.

Additionally, current research shows that the majority of police agencies are exploring more options for less-than-lethal force in order to reduce the loss of lives in various police encounters with community members. Much of the rebuilding focus is placed on police agencies. But, what about the community leaders and community members? What part do they play? They are held accountable as well in this quest for rebuilding the trust between both groups. The next section covers the varied recommendations nationwide in rebuilding this trust initiative between both groups.

Varying Recommendations Nationwide

In addressing the varying recommendations on this important construct in rebuilding community and police relationships, it is important to take a closer look at various periodicals nationwide. For instance, an article written by Stanley Pollack in *The Boston Globe* titled "Building Trust Between Police and Community" highlights an intriguing initiative by the Center for Teen Empowerment by collaborating with the Boston Police Department as a result of the high number of suicides, violence, and unexpected deaths among the youth. The program was so successful in Boston that it was adopted by both the Rochester and Somerville Police Departments. Officers from all three jurisdictions—Boston, Somerville, and Rochester—proudly noted that being in collaboration with this program has changed their perception of how they think about young people (Pollack, 2017). The officers further noted that it gave them a better understanding and challenged the stereotypes they held toward young people. This program is yet another successful example of how a community and police department can collaborate in their efforts to reduce violence and bring about a positive perception of police. To further elaborate on the importance of this trust-building initiative, the U.S. Department of Justice's Office of Community Oriented Policing Services (COPS) listed the internal and external strategies in implementing community trust-building activities. See Box 2.5.

Box 2.5 Implementing Community Trust-Building Activities

ACTIVITIES

Conduct consistent evaluations and review of all employees and immediately address negative behavior and reward positive behavior.

Use some form of early intervention system, not only in Internal Affairs, but to prevent behavior that may lead to an Internal Affairs complaint and investigation.

INTERNAL STRATEGIES

Institute culture-changing policies, programs, and training to solidify the department's core values and ethical principles. Consider developing an Office of Professional Standards to manage these activities.

Develop a comprehensive recruiting plan; recruit and hire people with a service orientation.

Provide continuous training in ethics, integrity, and discretion to every officer from the time he or she enters the police academy through the time of retirement.

IMPLEMENTING COMMUNITY TRUST-BUILDING ACTIVITIES

Conduct consistent evaluations and review of all employees and immediately address negative behavior and reward positive behavior.

Use some form of early intervention system, not only in Internal Affairs, but to prevent behavior that may lead to an Internal Affairs complaint and investigation.

EXTERNAL STRATEGIES

Institute some form of community-oriented policing program to better engage the community.

Develop a citizen's police academy.

Use the media to publicize positive programs and stories about the department.

Hold workshops on subjects of interest to the community.

Conduct a community survey to gauge and enhance public perception.

Proactively involve the public. (U.S. Department of Justice, Community Oriented Policing Services, 2009)

Paul Konz (2016) wrote a contributing article published by the National League of Cities (NLC) titled "Building Trust Between Police and the Communities They Serve." Several major cities' police chiefs and community leaders came together to address this important issue. The outcome of this initiative were five active areas of concern that need work. The areas of concern were as follows:

- Engaging the community in planning and oversight
- Improving training and support for police officers
- Promoting and supporting youth development
- Connecting residents to community resources
- Building relationships between officers and residents (Konz, 2016)

Engaging the community in planning and oversight. In further exploring each of these recommendations, such as the "engaging the community in planning and oversight" recommendation, some police departments are implementing police/clergy advisory boards, citizen police academies, police meetings with faith communities—for example, following any officer-involved shooting (Long Beach, California)—and sharing plans with trusted community partners (local chapters of the NAACP and National Council of La Raza, the faith community), the Community of Trust Committee (Fairfax County, Virginia), and establishing macro-community policing plans (neighborhood safety plans developed with local residents in Seattle).

Improving training and support for police officers. As for the "improving training and support for police officers" recommendation, some of the programs discussed are implicit bias training, de-escalation of force training, cultural competency training (many cities/jurisdictions), changing how officers are evaluated and promoted (Watts, California; Camden, New Jersey), community service in police academy training, training police officers to police one another (New Orleans), and Adopt a Cop programs (churches praying for and/or caring for individual officers in San Jose, California).

Promoting and supporting youth development. In exploring the "promoting and supporting youth development" recommendation, most of the programs highlighted include mentoring, tutoring (Santa Rose, California; "OK" program in Oakland, California; PACER in Camden), PAL, police-athletic leagues, a Chief's Youth Advisory Board (Louisville, Kentucky), police cadet programs (many cities), officer-friendly programs in schools (many cities), and youth/police dialogues (New Orleans, Seattle).

Connecting residents to community resources. Regarding the "connecting residents to community resources" recommendation, some highlighted sections are as follows: mental health clinicians riding with officers (Oakland), mental health officers (Madison, Wisconsin), social workers stationed in police departments (Boston), quality-of-life officers (New Orleans), police/human services/school partnership to divert low-level offenders to services that include school retention strategies (Philadelphia), citation and release (Charleston, South Carolina), and diversion from arrest.

Building personal relationships between officers and residents. Lastly, the "building personal relationships between officers and residents" programs such as pop-up barbecues (Camden, NJ), bike patrols (many cities and states),), police/youth chats (Louisville, KY), Coffee with a Cop programs (several cities and states), Open Up programs (Knoxville, Tennessee), police attending community meetings (many cities and states), police walks with community groups (Long Beach, CA; Boston, MA; Richmond, CA; Seattle, WA), and trust walks (Winston-Salem, NC).

In Konz's article, Terrence M. Cunningham, president of the International Association of Chiefs of Police, expressed his thoughts on trust and bridging the gap between the police and the communities they serve (see Box 2.6).

It is important to point out that the statement regarding acknowledging and apologizing for actions of the past in police mistreating individuals from communities of color goes a great length. This statement is an influential one—it will echo for decades and will act as a foundation in rebuilding these relationships between law enforcement and the communities they serve. The statement made by Terrence Cunningham is powerful; it not only demonstrates transparency and a sense of remorse and understanding for the past incidents described in this chapter, but it also exhibits slow but sure progress in this important quest for rebuilding the relationship between communities and policing. Additionally, as the leader of an international police organization that represents countless numbers of agencies, his views speak for the views of all the agencies he represents.

Box 2.6 Terrence M. Cunningham's Thoughts on Trust

> There have been times when law enforcement officers, because of the laws enacted by federal, state, and local governments, have been the face of oppression for far too many of our fellow citizens. In the past, the laws adopted by our society have required police officers to perform many unpalatable tasks, such as ensuring legalized discrimination or even denying the basic rights of citizenship to many of our fellow Americans. While this is no longer the case, this dark side of our shared history has created a multigenerational—almost inherited—mistrust between many communities of color and their law enforcement agencies. Many officers who do not share this common heritage often struggle to comprehend the reasons behind this historic mistrust. As a result, they are often unable to bridge this gap and connect with some segments of their communities. . . . The first step in this process is for law enforcement and the IACP to acknowledge and apologize for the actions of the past and the role that our profession has played in society's historical mistreatment of communities of color. (Cunningham, as cited in Konz, 2016)

Discussion question: What is the importance and relevance of this statement? Who does it apply to? What are some other recommendations would you make to the president of the IACP in reference to rebuilding community trust?

Chapter Summary

This chapter was indeed a challenging chapter to write as it encompasses several emotions of community members, police officers, high-ranking officials of the U.S. government, faith-based leaders, and college students. All perceptions were presented thoroughly, along with various analytical and methodical research contributions. While there are significant data and research to support the treatment by police toward underrepresented communities, there are currently various measures in place within most police departments to address these issues. It is important to note that work needs to be done on both aspects. Police departments are becoming more transparent, improving legitimacy and accountability toward their policies and procedures. Community members are becoming more involved in police and public safety initiatives thus strengthening this social relationship. The issue of police being expected to be social workers was also addressed by one contributing scholar; this point holds merit as police departments are run on a 24-hour basis and are available to handle all types of calls for service. From the police perspective, once they are stretched too thin, the possibilities of becoming overworked and less tolerant become more probable.

Perception goes a long way, as this chapter presents the various perceptions of policing from the lenses of several groups and sectors. It is important to note that key factors play significant roles in such perceptions—factors such as geographical areas, neighborhood contexts, crime rates, officers' demeanors, and community demeanors. Rebuilding the trust between police and the community is an ever-evolving initiative. This chapter listed several police initiatives that many police and community relations officials are pursuing. Although some of the recommendations for rebuilding trust are different and only pertain to a specific geographic location, most are very similar; as a result, this demonstrates that both groups are working toward one goal.

Discussion Questions

1. Discuss early police practices and current police practices; highlight significant factors that have influenced current police practices.

2. The relationship between race and policing is a prevalent hot topic in current times. List and discuss three initiatives that many police departments and community leaders are exploring to improve the relationship between underrepresented groups and police agencies.

3. Age and gender views on policing are also important concepts. List and discuss three factors that are perceived to have influenced negative perceptions of policing regarding this construct.

4. The media and policing have experienced some turbulent times. However, it has been proven that both sectors can work toward a greater good. List and discuss two ways in which the media and the police can work collectively.

5. List and discuss two advantages and two disadvantages of police militarization.

6. List and discuss three initiatives various police departments are undertaking in order to rebuild trust with the communities they serve.

References

Adegbile, D. P. (2017). Policing through an American prism. *Yale Law Journal, 126*(7), 2222–2259.

Allen, A. (2016). Stop and question campus policing. *Policing: An International Journal of Police Strategies & Management, 39*(3), 507–520. doi:10.1108/ PIJPSM-04-2016-0054

Allen, A., & Jacques, S. (2013). Alcohol-related crime among college students: a review of research and fruitful areas for future work. *Criminal Justice Studies, 26*(4), 478–494.

Bieber, S. (2016). Police militarization in the USA: the state of the field. Policing: An International Journal, 39(4), 586-600. doi: 10.1108/PIJPSM-03-2016-0042

Black Lives Matter. (2013). *Herstory*. Retrieved from https://blacklivesmatter.com/about/herstory/

Blackhurst, P. M. (2013). Examining the Role of Race, Gender, and Class in African-American Police Perceptions in Rural Kentucky [Master's thesis]. *Online Theses and Dissertations*. 151. Retrieved from http://encompass.eku.edu/etd/151

Cheurprakobkit, S. (2016). The impact of race, police experience, and feeling of safety toward the police. *Journal of Police & Criminal Psychology, 2*(2), 55-76. doi: 10.1007/BF02855684

Cochran, J. C., & Warren, P. Y. (2012). Racial ethnic, and gender differences in perceptions of the police: The salience of officer race within the context of racial profiling. *Journal of Contemporary Criminal Justice, 28*(2), 206-227. doi:10.1177/1043986211425726

Dempsey, J. & Frost, L. (2016). *An introduction to policing* (8th ed.). Boston, MA, Cengage Learning.

Dowdall, G. W. (2013). *The role of alcohol abuse in college student victimization*. In B. S. Fisher & J. J. Sloan (Eds.), *Campus crime: Legal, social, and policy perspectives* (3rd ed.) (pp. 184–210). Springfield, IL: Charles C. Thomas.

Ekins, E. (2016). Policing in America: Understanding Public Attitudes Toward the Police. *CATO Institute*. Retrieved from https://object.cato.org/sites/cato.org/files/survey-reports/pdf/policing-in-america-august-1-2017.pdf

English Oxford Living Dictionary. (2017). *Media*. Retrieved from https://en.oxforddictionaries.com/definition/media

Gramlich, J., & Parker, K. (2017). Most officers say they are mistreated by the media. *Pew Research Center*. Retrieved from http://www.pewresearch.org/fact-tank/2017/01/25/most-officers-say-the-media-treat-police-unfairly/

Granados, N. (2016). What is media in the digital age? *Forbes*. Retrieved from https://www.forbes.com/sites/nelsongranados/2016/10/03/what-is-media-in-the-digital-age/#22483c2851ea

Greene, J. R., & Decker, S. H. (1989). Police and community perceptions of the community role in policing: The Philadelphia experience. *Howard Journal of Criminal Justice, 28*(2), 105–123. doi:10.1111/j.1468-2311.1989.tb00641.x
Harsha, K. (2018). Colorado mental health professionals now responding to 911 call. *FOX Denver.* Retrieved from http://kdvr.com/2018/01/09/colorado-mental-health-professionals-now-responding-to-911-calls/
Hobson, J. (2016, July 11). After 9 high-profile police-involved deaths of African-Americans, what happened to the officers? *WBUR.* Retrieved from http://www.wbur.org/hereandnow/2016/07/11/america-police-shooting-timeline
Hudson, D. (2014, December 1). *Building trust between communities and local police.* Retrieved from https://obamawhitehouse.archives.gov/blog/2014/12/01/building-trust-between-communities-and-local-police
Ileto, C. (2017, October 30). Police shoot robbery suspect outside of King of Prussia Mall. *ABC News.* Retrieved from http://6abc.com/police-shoot-robbery-suspect-outside-of-king-of-prussia-mall/2581531/
Johnson, D., Wilson, D. B., Maguire, E. R., & Lowrey-Kinberg, B. (2017). Race and perceptions of police: Experimental results on the impact of procedural (in) justice. *JQ: Justice Quarterly, 34*(7), 1184–1212. doi:10.1080/07418825.2017.1343862
Konz, P. (2016). *Building trust between police and the communities they serve.* National League of Cities. Retrieved from https://citiesspeak.org/2016/11/20/building-trust-between-the-police-and-the-communities-they-serve/
Kraska, P., & Kappeler, V. (1997). Militarizing American police: The rise and normalization of paramilitary units. *Social Problems, 44*(1), 1–18. doi:10.2307/3096870
Lee, J. M., Steinberg, L., Piquero, A. R., & Knight, G. P. (2011). Identity-linked perceptions of the police among African American juvenile offenders: A developmental perspective. *Journal of Youth and Adolescence, 40*(1), 23–37. Meares, T. L. (2017). The path forward: Improving the dynamics of community-police relationships to achieve effective law enforcement policies. *Columbia Law Review, 117*(5), 1355–1368.
National Institute of Justice. (2014). *Perceptions of treatment by police.* Retrieved from https://www.nij.gov/topics/law-enforcement/legitimacy/Pages/perceptions.aspx
National Institute of Justice. (2016). *Race, trust and police legitimacy.* Retrieved from https://www.nij.gov/topics/law-enforcement/legitimacy/Pages/welcome.aspx
NBC Washington. (2017, September 16). *Police: Virginia officer killed 15-year-old boy wielding crowbar.* Retrieved on from https://www.nbcwashington.com/news/local/Juvenile-Dead-After-Officer-Involved-Shooting-444704073.html
Office of Community Oriented Policing. (2015). *Final report of the President's Task Force on 21st Century Policing.* Washington, DC: Author. Retrieved from http://www.cops.usdoj.gov/pdf/taskforce/TaskForce_FinalReport.pdf
Oliver, W. (2006). The fourth era of policing: Homeland security. *International Review of Law, Computers & Technology, 20*(1), 49–62. doi:10.1080/13600860600579696
Pollack, S. (2017). Building trust between police and the community. *The Boston Globe.* Retrieved from https://www.bostonglobe.com/opinion/2017/03/26/building-trust-between-police-and-community/CgxcbptRsCuofjGs2jtPLL/story.html
Potter, G. (2013). *The history of policing in the United States.* Retrieved from http://plsonline.eku.edu/insidelook/history-policing-united-states-part-1
Ramsey, C. H. & Robinson, L. O. (2015). *The President's Task Force on 21st Century Policing.* Retrieved from https://cops.usdoj.gov/pdf/taskforce/taskforce_finalreport.pdf
Sam, B. (2016). Police militarization in the USA: The state of the field. *Policing: An International Journal of Police Strategies & Management, 39*(4), 586–600. doi:10.1108/ PIJPSM-03-2016-0042
Schmalleger, F. & Worrall, J. (2010). *Policing today.* London, UK: Pearson Education.
Sindall, K., McCarthy, D. J., & Brunton-Smith, I. (2017). Young people and the formation of attitudes towards the police. European Journal of Criminology, 14(3), 344–364. doi: 10.1177/1477370816661739
Stein, R. E., & Griffith, C. (2017). Resident and police perceptions of the neighborhood: Implications for community policing. *Criminal Justice Policy Review, 28*(2), 139–154. doi:10.1177/0887403415570630
Terry v. Ohio (1968). 392 U.S. 1, 88 S. Ct
U.S. Department of Justice. (2015). *Why police-community relationships are important.* Retrieved from https://www.justice.gov/crs/file/836486/download
U.S. Department of Justice, Community Oriented Policing Services (2009). *Building the trust between the police and citizens they serve.* Retrieved from https://ric-zai-inc.com/Publications/cops-p170-pub.pdf

Figure Credits

Fig. 2.1: Copyright © 2014 Depositphotos/dechevm.
Fig. 2.2: Copyright © 2015 Depositphotos/lucidwaters.
Fig. 2.3: Copyright © 2004 by Eli Duke (CC BY-SA 2.0) at https://www.flickr.com/photos/elisfanclub/360214806.
Fig. 2.4: Source: https://www.youtube.com/watch?v=2wzNp8Em2mY.
Fig. 2.5: Source: https://6abc.com/police-shoot-robbery-suspect-outside-of-king-of-prussia-mall/2581531/.

CHAPTER THREE

The Career of a Police Officer

Pursuing a career as a police officer involves many steps requiring patience and skill, as well as emotional and physical strength. This chapter will cover the recruiting, retention, academy experience and training, field training process, probation process, the academy lifestyle, and the psychological, physical, and emotional aspects of policing. It describes in detail the selection process from application submission and initial interview to police entrance exams and/or testing. In addition to learning about the author's professional and personal experiences, you will also gain insights into the experiences of other officers, which are also presented in this chapter. The importance of honoring diversity and inclusion in policing (hiring, training, selection process, promotion, discipline, etc.) as well as an exploration of the issues of stress, officers killed in the line of duty, and officer-involved shootings are also discussed in this chapter, yet not always covered in police textbooks.

Learning Objectives

- Outline the basic steps of becoming a police officer
- Understand the field training process and probation period
- Explore diversity and inclusion in policing (hiring, recruiting, and retention)
- Explore the various perceptions of policing from line and executive personnel
- Define the various psychological and emotional aspects of law enforcement
- Understand the emotional and procedural side of officer-involved shootings and officers killed in the line of duty

Chapter Outline

1. A Real-Life Police Scenario for Discussion
2. Considering the Police Career
3. Police and Diversity and Inclusion
4. Perception versus Reality
5. Police Officer Character Traits

A REAL-LIFE POLICE SCENARIO FOR DISCUSSION

from Chernoh Wurie's personal accounts

As I handcuffed a male teenage suspect I'd been chasing on foot to temporarily detain him while I pursued my investigation, I asked him, "Why were you running from me? All I wanted to do was just see what you were doing out this late and why you were walking in this parking lot at 2:30 a.m." I was patrolling a shopping center when I noticed the individual walking through the parking lot. I had stopped to question him, and he took off running.

My first impression was the individual ran because he had done something wrong, so I gave chase. I was in good physical condition. I'm an avid runner and take pride in staying healthy and I knew moments like these were too common in my line of work. Upon further questioning the individual, I determined the juvenile was just scared and didn't want to get charged with a curfew violation. I warned the juvenile about the potential consequences of running away from the police. I also gave him a ride home and informed his parents of what transpired. Later, I charged the juvenile with a curfew violation and informed him of the court proceedings and processes involved.

I returned to my vehicle, leaned back, rolled up my windows, turned the police radio down, and reflected on the incident. "Why did he run from me?" I thought. "I jumped over two fences and entered two different backyards just to stop this individual—all this time, he was just running away for a minor curfew violation charge." Why did I get into this profession? What am I doing to effect change in the minds of youths—why are they so fearful of the police? Why run? What have I got myself into?"

I pondered all these questions. I recalled dreaming about being a police officer when I was growing up. I read detective books and novels and imagined myself solving these crimes and chasing bad guys. I enjoyed talking about crime stories with my friends and family, even though I had little support from my family, who viewed policing negatively and would not support me in my pursuit of this career. Also, my African background didn't support a career in policing. Policing careers in most African nations have been plagued with corruption, bribery, and other negative stereotypes and associations. Regardless, I worked tirelessly to realize my dream. And, many officers, in fact, are now striving very hard to make reformations within their police forces.

Shortly before graduating high school, I began a community-service project with a prestigious police department. After completing the program, I kept in touch with some key people I met during my volunteer service, which led to several paid internship positions with the same department during my college years. The experience provided me with several job opportunities after college. I was already familiar with the work structure, job expectations, the work environment, and the squad I was assigned to in the same department I had interned with. After I was hired as a full-time pre-police officer, I came to the realization that the most valuable experience was my academy training. The academy experience is one of a kind. It's an experience I will never forget. I made lifelong friends through the academy as we shared emotional times together. We also looked out for each other. The academy life was intense, structured, and sometimes jovial. I often used humor to get through hard times and quickly became the jokester of my academy class. This was my coping mechanism to stay calm during tense and difficult times.

One memorable moment occurred during Thanksgiving week, in November of 2005. Some of the county residents had donated a free turkey meal for the police. I was sitting in the back of the room in my assigned seat when I noticed another recruit walking in with a tray on his head, stick in hand, and wearing a very large gown. On the tray was a fully cooked turkey. The recruit was making funny sounds as if he was mocking African hunters upon catching a big game for feasting. I knew exactly what it was and laughed. I also didn't take offense that my fellow recruits were making fun of me and my native land. I was known as the "fast-African" recruit because I excelled in all physical training exercises and assessments. While these were all fun times, the training prepared me with key skills that I would need throughout my career, including the use of firearms, defensive tactics and defensive driving, practical scenarios, use of force, legal updates, and community and citizen engagement exercises. The training was required by the Department of Criminal Justice Services (DCJS) and lasted 28 weeks. I also reflected on the lifelong friends and positive career connections I made during my time working as a volunteer and a police intern.

I smiled and felt as though a weight had been lifted off my shoulders. I now remembered why I entered this profession; I was determined to make a change—to bring about a positive perception of policing.

Considering the Police Career

The police career can be illustrated as somewhat glamourous and fictional, depending on the wide-stream media like Hollywood movies and various fictional police-based crime shows. Popular TV shows such as *NYPD Blue* and *Miami Vice* shaped some of these perceptions in the eighties and nineties. However, currently, real-life shows such as *Live-PD* take the action right to the streets where body-worn cameras and other recording devices are utilized to present the actual duties and responsibilities of a police officer's everyday life. In reality, the police career has various depictions depending on the lenses through which we're looking. For example, the perceptions of high school and college students differ from those of community members, which also differ from the perceptions police officers themselves have in terms of what a "real" police career should look like.

This chapter outlines the various steps in becoming a police officer, various perceptions from the officers themselves, and explores the physiological and emotional aspects associated with the police career. Before we start exploring these important topics, the most frequent question often asked is, "How can one become a police officer in the United States?" Or, "What are the basic steps of becoming a police officer?"

The most common requirements for becoming a police officer are application; police entrance exam; high school diploma or college credit/degree; physical agility; and a medical, psychological, and criminal background check. From a practical standpoint, becoming a police officer goes beyond just meeting the basic requirements. This process is primarily two-fold: First, one must have the emotional intelligence for such a career, and second, one must have the ability to be in tune with his or her own *reasonable suspicion* (as mentioned in chapter 1) or have the capability of developing this concept. These suspicions are mostly supported by their training and experiences.

Many enter this profession without knowing the full intricate details of this career. Therefore, it is wise to conduct thorough research of the profession before initiating the application process. In addition, it is also wise to explore internships, volunteer, and ride-along opportunities before venturing in this profession. By signing up for a ride-along program, one can experience firsthand what the profession entails. However, a ride-along program only lasts for a day and these opportunities are limited to maybe once or twice a year for most agencies. Volunteer programs and internship programs are more advantageous than ride-along programs as they are very detailed and informative. The volunteer or intern is assigned to various sections of the designated police department in order to expose him or her to the different entities within a police department. Once the individual has had extensive exposure to the police department and the career, he or she can decide to start the application process.

Two major characteristics that police applicants should take into consideration are ethical and moral character, and secondly **emotional intelligence**. According to John Dempsey and Linda Frost (2016), police administrators primarily favor individuals with high ethical and moral character. These individuals are viewed as outstanding and exceptional candidates as they can be trusted with positions of authority and higher responsibilities. Having these character traits is a positive addition to the career. Second, emotional intelligence is being able to recognize and balance one's own perceptions and the various perceptions of others while taking these things and the big picture into consideration when making high-impact decisions and while performing conflict resolution and other leadership initiatives (Dempsey & Frost, 2016). This character trait is also very important for applicants to invest in if they are planning to pursue this career. Developing emotional intelligence is a positive initiative as this career exposes the applicant to a myriad of individual personalities and places. It is important for the applicant to have this character trait to be a self-accountable individual when faced with difficult situations and decisions.

The application process can vary depending on the jurisdiction; however, the basic requirements are the same throughout the United States. The next section outlines the basic steps to becoming a police officer.

Application Process

The application process is one of the first initial steps the police applicant must complete. Current research studies also noted that this is one of the stages during which most police departments lose applicants due to screening questions, such as those involving drug use, criminal background, and driving record. The screening questions, depending on the agency, range anywhere from felony violations, serious misdemeanors, extensive traffic violations or demerit driving points, extensive alcohol or recent drug usage or experimentation, poor financial record, and tattoos. It has also been noted by various department administrators that their agencies would receive several applications. However, the majority of the candidates who would pass the initial phase and would be prompted to come in for an oral interview would not show up for unknown reasons.

Depending on the agency, the application process is becoming more simplified wherein applicants can submit their application online instead of printing it out and paying for mailing fees. It has also been proven that with the online migration of police applications by the majority of police agencies, the application process has become more streamlined and simple for applicants. Some agencies have also implemented online application processes at designated recruiting events via an app that allows recruiters to collect applications online while at these events. Recruiters can also conduct pre-screening questions at these events in order to properly retain qualified applicants. The purpose for completing the basic application is to attract applicants' interest and eligibility for the profession. Once they have completed the application, if they pass all the required pre-screening questions, they are invited back to complete a written exam or an entrance test. This topic is covered thoroughly in the next section.

The application step can be somewhat intimidating for those who are not familiar with the process as it asks mostly personal questions about drugs and alcohol usage and frequency. Some questions also ask about the applicants' association with certain people affiliated with gangs, felons, and others who can impede or blackmail the applicants once they become police officers. Some police administrators also noted most agencies receive several applications because of high unemployment rates. Individuals are applying for any and every job opportunity. In addition, some college students are hesitant of this process as they are afraid of being disqualified due to college and university experimentation of drugs and alcohol. The application phase is also a very important phase as it determines the seriousness of the applicant's interest in this profession. The application phase also tests the applicant's character in following through with a commitment. Even though situations are inevitable that will prevent an applicant from pursuing this career, successful completion of this phase demonstrates the applicant's motivation and commitment.

Selection Process

The selection process also can vary per department. However, based on the general guidelines for police officers, the most common steps are listed in Box 3.1. Most agencies will follow these steps in order, although some would have applicants complete several steps in one day in order to address many applicants at one time.

While exploring various criminal justice agencies and departments, several components of the standard selection process for police officers became apparent. Candidates must do the following:

- Complete a basic application
- Write an exam or entrance exam
- Pass a physical fitness or agility test
- Complete a pre-history questionnaire/personal history questionnaire (PHQ) and background investigation
- Undergo psychological testing
- Receive polygraph testing
- Pass an oral board interview

- Undergo a medical exam and drug screening
- Complete a one-on-one interview with the commissioner, chief, or sheriff

Box 3.1 The Hiring Process

The department's recruitment and selection process supports the Prince William County Equal Opportunity and Affirmative Action plans.

The selection process takes approximately 4 to 8 months after the police officer application has been received. Applicants must successfully complete the following phases:

- Online application submission
- Personal history statement
- Conditional offer of employment
- Pre-screen interview
- Physical fitness test
- Polygraph examination
- Background interview and investigation
- Medical and physical examinations
- Psychological examination
- Police ride-along
- Interview with the chief of police or designee
- Final approval by the chief of police

APPLICATION PROCESS

We use a formal application—rather than a resume—in our employment process.

MINIMUM QUALIFICATIONS

Police officer candidates must meet the following minimum qualifications:

- Must be a U.S. citizen
- Must be 21 years of age upon completion of the Prince William County Criminal Justice Academy
- Must be a high school graduate or equivalent
- Must be able to complete the physical fitness requirements
- Vision must be 20/20 uncorrected correctable with the aid of glasses or contacts to 20/40 in the worse eye and 20/20 in the better eye
- Hearing must comply with medical standards
- Valid driver's license at the time of appointment; applicants with six demerits or more are ineligible
- Must not have been convicted of any felony or serious misdemeanor
- No tobacco agreement (Prince William County Government, 2017)

Before explaining the meaning of each step, it is important to list the basic requirements for becoming a police officer that are standard in most agencies. Some agencies have multiple requirements, however, the most common include the following:

- Carrying U.S. citizenship
- Falling within a specified age range
- Attaining a prescribed level of education
- Possessing a driver's license
- Fulfilling fitness requirements

In addition, a history of certain issues or experiences can disqualify an applicant including the following:

- Having extensive tattoos
- Committing felonies
- Committing misdemeanors related to domestic or sexual abuse
- Using illegal drugs
- Acquiring convictions for driving while intoxicated or under the influence
- Making poor financial decisions

Addressing citizenship requirements can vary among agencies. Some strictly abide by this condition, and others allow permanent residents who have applied for citizenship to become officers. If the agency is very much interested in a candidate that is a permanent resident and does not yet possess U.S. citizenship, the agency can explore certain conditional waivers for U.S. citizenship through various state or federal institutions

Age requirements also vary per state. However, the majority of police agencies mandate ages of 21 years or older. They will allow 20-year-old individuals to enter the academy, as long as they are 21 years old by the time they graduate. Police cadets can vary from 14–18 years of age, where the majority of them are eligible to become police officers. The maximum age candidates can enter the academy can also vary per agency. Some agencies do not have a maximum age requirement. As long as the individual can perform well and pass the agility and medical tests, they can participate in the selection process. However, it's not to say that all police agencies have adopted this characteristic. For New York State police, as of 2015, candidates must be under the age of 30 when the application is submitted and 36 by the time of appointment for citizens, and the age of 36 for veterans' applications and 42 when they're appointed.

Educational requirements vary per state and jurisdiction. While some departments are beginning to require applicants to have college credit toward a college degree or have attained an associate's degree before beginning the application process, the majority of agencies still require only a high school diploma or GED equivalent. In recent years, an increasing number of departments have begun leaning toward mandating all incoming officers/police applicants to have obtained a bachelor's degree in any major. With the emergence of criminal justice degrees, the public is now able to gain insight of the profession. Though pursuing a CRJS degree exponentially increases one's knowledge of the criminal justice system and allows students to learn about opportunities beyond policing, the specific major is not among the core requirements of becoming a police officer candidate.

Having a valid driver's license is essential because the majority of the initial patrol officer's duties and responsibilities involve driving. Considering all these requirements, becoming a police officer is very competitive. Frank Schmalleger and John Worrall (2010) in *Policing Today*, noted that during the 1990s, one applicant applied for a police officer's position with the Seattle Police Department and was invited to take the entrance exam with thousands of other applicants. The department was only hiring about 12 officers. Although situations like this occurred in the 90s, it is still common today for smaller agencies to advertise and receive thousands of applicants and only hire a select few.

Despite the continuing competition for positions, police hiring and recruiting has decreased significantly due to some of the issues discussed in chapter 2. In a recent study, researchers examined two major police departments: the Los Angeles Police Department and the Chicago Police

Department. The Los Angeles Police Department noticed a 50% reduction in applications within a 3-year period whereas the Chicago Police Department received 25,000 applications in 1993 and only 1900 in 2000 (Schmalleger & Worrall, 2010). In addition to these alarming numbers, recruiting people of color has become a challenge for almost every police department in the United States. It is tempting to speculate why recruitment levels for police departments have dropped. Perhaps political climates and decisions such as the following have had an impact:

- Wars (recruitment of young men and women for the military)
- Salary an.d retirement benefits (most police agencies are facing high competitions with regard to salaries and retirements with other private employers)
- Federal employment opportunities
- Any negative media coverage of the police which may be dissuading potential candidates from pursuing a rewarding career in law enforcement (Reaves, 2015)

In exploring the basic selection process, it is important to know the similarities and differences between the data most jurisdictions use. According to statistician Brian Reaves (2015) in "Local Police Departments, 2013: Personnel, Policing, and Practices," the percentages that follow indicate the frequency that agencies implement the following aptitude tests:

- Written or aptitude test: 48%
- Personal interview: 99%
- Physical agility testing: 60%
- Polygraph exams: 26%
- Voice stress analyzers: 5%
- Psychological evaluation: 72%
- Drug testing: 83%
- Medical exams: 89%
- Background investigations: 99%

These percentages suggest that most agencies share similar hiring and recruiting processes. The author also utilized the 2013 Law Enforcement Management and Administrative Statistics (LEMAS) to compile this data.

Written exam. The purpose of the written exam is to test the applicants' verbal, written, and comprehension skills. Also, it tests the applicant's ability to think and respond quickly to various scenarios. The written exam is also a form of narrowing the number of finalists from the entire applicant pool. Those who pass this phase are invited to proceed to the next phase, which also varies according to jurisdiction. Some jurisdictions would complete the written exam and an oral board interview the same day (see Box 3.2). As stated earlier, only 48% of police agencies require a written exam. Some have waived this step if candidates possess other qualifications such as military service, college degrees or credits, and so on.

Physical fitness or agility test (PT). The physical fitness or agility test is required to determine the applicant's physical condition. Various local and state police departments were examined to present accurate and similar PT requirements for applicants. Depending on the jurisdiction, most applicants start in a seated position inside a police vehicle, wearing all police equipment (baton, unloaded weapon, ballistic vest, police radio, and other contents on the duty belt.) An instructor will issue various physical commands for the officer to complete. These may include a certain number of the following:

- Push-ups (in 60 seconds)
- Sit-ups (in 60 seconds)

- Squats
- Pull or drag 50–150 pounds human dummy
- Ladder climb (5–6 feet)
- Wall climb (5–6 feet)
- A 1–1.5-mile run in a designated amount of time determined by the jurisdiction

Box 3.2 Advice to Applicants

There is no exact science to preparing for police entrance exams. Some applicants have gone as far as purchasing online tutoring tools or test aids in order to study for their entrance exams. Although some are helpful, applicants should be cautious about these online aids as they can be very misleading or even a potential scam.

Some agencies provide a brief study guide whereas others do not. In general, applicants are expected to know how to read and respond to a scenario using their general knowledge and skills. Some scenarios cover basic math, reading, and writing. Other portions could cover map reading and route interpretations. Some other portions would also cover a memory response column wherein the applicant is provided with a paragraph and a description of an event. Instructors would allow applicants to read the scenario for a couple of minutes, take mental notes, and then respond to a series of questions. Some other written exams would also cover evidence collection techniques, officer safety techniques, and basic laws and regulations by state and county.

The applicant should also review key contributions, accomplishments, and highlights for the specific agency to which he or she is applying in order to be prepared to answer specific questions related to why the applicant is applying to that agency. Lastly, it is also wise for the applicant to know why he or she wants to be a police officer. Most police agencies ask this somewhat generic question during the interview process.

Most jurisdictions will end their testing by having the applicant do a dry fire with both hands separately (left-hand fire and right-hand fire) using an unloaded weapon. (Dry fire—basically pulling the trigger of an unloaded weapon several times in order to determine the applicant's level of trigger and handling coordination when under pressure or stress, using separate hands, one at a time).

Some jurisdictions will not require that applicants wear full officer's gear for these tests but will instead allow workout clothes. Most jurisdictions also have a specific set of requirements for female applicants, which are slightly different from male requirements. For instance, male applicants are required to perform a higher number of sit-ups and push-ups than female applicants. The justification is that males characteristically have more upper body strength. As much as these separate requirements are based on gender challenge equality standards, several jurisdictions are still using them. Some jurisdictions are currently exploring these concepts and have gone to standard PT requirements for all applicants regardless of gender (see Boxes 3.3 and 3.4).

Box 3.3 Advice to Applicants

Agencies also use the PT process to cut applicants from the process. It is wise that all applicants start physical training before getting to this phase. Applicants should be familiar with the PT requirements for the department(s) to which they plan to apply and be ready for the testing. They should visit the department's website and thoroughly study the physical requirements and guidelines covering how to perform these tests. Most jurisdictions would go the extra step to provide instructions on how to perform a complete exercise. Applicants should take advantage of this assistance and other guiding tools available at the jurisdiction websites.

Box 3.4 Advice to Applicants

As mentioned, this is the most time-consuming and expensive portion of the application process. Having some knowledge of the questions ahead of time will greatly benefit the applicants before they apply for a designated police officer's position. Applicants should also be mindful of who they associate with since this information is eventually required for this application. Be familiar with past residences and acquaintances, etc. This step is often difficult for many applicants because they are faced with questions they are not prepared to answer.

Pre-history/personal history questionnaire and background investigation. Most scholars have noted that this phase is the most expensive and time-consuming step of the entire selection process. Along with the pre-history questionnaire, this phase can vary per jurisdiction as well. The questionnaire commonly consists of a 20–50-page document that captures the applicant's entire life history. Some go back as far as birth while others only ask for residency information between 5–10 years of the application. The form also requests information about applicants' close relatives, friends, acquaintances, partners, whether they have a criminal record, and additional personal information.

The reason for this thorough inquiry is because a police officer's duties and responsibilities require trust and accountability. The vetting jurisdiction has to cover all bases to trust the applicant with the responsibility the position demands. The form also requests information about the applicant's financial record and spending habits, debts, employment history, and any criminal court and traffic violations. The vetting jurisdiction stresses these factors as hiring someone with a criminal history would be detrimental to the jurisdiction. Hiring someone with a bad credit report or high spending habits is also a negative factor and may place the applicant at risk of being blackmailed.

Lastly, this form also requests information on the applicants' licensing, certifications, trainings, military experiences, and references. (See Metropolitan Police Department (n.d.) for an example of a pre-history questionnaire form in the City of St. Louis.) Next, see Box 3.5.

Box 3.5 Minimum Fitness Standards for Recruits

"A mandatory physical assessment program is an integral part of the hiring process, as well as part of your career with the Vermont State Police. Our assessment measures the following areas—sit and reach flexibility, bench press, sit ups, push ups, and a 1.5 mile run. You must pass each portion of the test before moving on to the next portion. If you fail one portion, you are done for that testing day.

The minimum standards for the assessments are based on the 50th percentile for a candidate based on age and gender as developed by the Cooper Institute for Aerobic Research.

- An overall fitness level of Superior is attained by: Superior on the run. Any three other fitness areas a superior. Remaining categories 'Good' or above.
- An overall fitness level of Excellent is attained by: Excellent on the run. Any three other fitness areas an excellent or above. Remaining categories 'Good' or above.
- An overall fitness level of Good is attained by: Good on the run. Any three other fitness areas a good or above. Remaining categories 'Average' or above.
- An overall fitness level of Average is attained with a score of Average on the run. You can ONLY score an Average overall with a score of Average on the run.

Videos of various fitness tests are available. These videos were recorded on testing day at the Vermont Police Academy in Pittsford, Vermont." (Vermont State Police, 2017)

TABLE 3.1

MALES	BENCH PRESS	SIT-UP	PUSH-UP	1.5 MILE
20–29	1.06	40	33	11:58
30–39	.93	36	27	12:25
40–49	.84	31	21	13:11
50–55	.75	26	15	14:16
FEMALES				
20–29	.65	35	18	14:07
30–39	.57	27	14	14:34
40–49	.52	22	11	15:24
50–55	.46	17	0	17:13

Psychological testing. This phase is also very informative, time consuming, and conducted at one setting. The applicant is placed alone in a room and is expected to answer 300–600 questions depending on the agency administering the test. Trained psychologists or psychiatrists administer most psychological tests. Modern agencies are transitioning to more focused police hiring and recruiting psychological experts for administering these tests and analyzing the results. This phase is administered to determine the applicant's mental state for the position, measure any biases, and identify any potential for becoming unethical.

A roster of esteemed authors including Kimberly Simmers, an analyst for the Pennsylvania State Police; Thomas Bowers, a clinical psychologist and an associate professor of psychology at Penn State; and Jim Ruiz, retired from the New Orleans Police Department and an assistant professor of criminal justice at Penn State (2003) published an impressive study on psychological testing entitled "Pre-Employment Psychological Testing of Police Officers: The MMPI and the IPI as the Predictors of Performance."

In their study, they identified that the three most common psychological tests used by agencies are the Minnesota Multiphasic Inventory (**MMPI**), the **MMPI-2** (the second edition), and the Inward Personality Inventory (**IPI**). The MMPI is used to deliver a 556-item true-or-false questionnaire. This was originally designed to determine any psychological indications with the applicant (Simmers, Bowers, & Ruiz, 2003). The authors further noted that the MMPI-2 was designed to include several updated questions to determine racial and bias issues, specifically targeted questions toward minorities including members of the LGBTQ community, and other diversity- and inclusion-related topics. Lastly, the IPI was specifically developed to target the law enforcement population and deliver a 310-item and 26-scale true-false questionnaire (Simmers, Bowers, & Ruiz, 2003).

In their conclusion, the authors documented that psychological testing is not only beneficial by helping the department hire the best and brightest; it also serves as protection to other officers and the community they will serve. Furthermore, it is imperative that police administrators continue to use this tool for the police selection process as it helps to distinguish officers who might pose a potential risk. Conversely, it is also vital to distinguish applicants who have a high ethical and moral standard. See Box 3.6 "Advice to Applicants."

Box 3.6 Advice to Applicants

This step can also be nerve-wracking. Unfortunately, there is no practical way to prepare for this phase other than just being authentic. Address the questions thoroughly and truthfully and rely heavily on personal discipline and consistency since some of the questions are posed repeatedly in different formats.

Polygraph testing. As Dempsey and Frost (2016) noted, the polygraph test is conducted to measure the applicant's stress level when asked difficult questions. The test measures the parameters of bodily functions such as pulse, breathing rate, blood pressure, and galvanic skin response. The equipment measures the body's measurements when asked the appropriate questions. Three key factors are dependent on the entire process: the applicant, the machine, and the person conducting the testing.

The applicant's responses are recorded and observed for any stress indications; the machine is calibrated several times prior to the questioning and sometimes during the questioning in order to maintain accuracy. And the person conducting the testing is primarily a trained polygraph examiner who is qualified to ask questions and analyze responses. It is also important to note the Employee Polygraph Protection Act (EPPA), which was signed in to law in June 1988 (Dempsey & Frost, 2016).

This law prohibits private entities from using random polygraph testing or pre-employment polygraph screening. Prior to this law, private entities would perform random polygraph testing for applicants and employees to prevent employee misconduct. However, local, state, and federal employers are exempt from this act. These entities can perform polygraph testing on their applicants and employees for just causes.

However, polygraph testing is not admissible in a court of law because unknown factors can affect results. These factors include but are not limited to applicants' psychological disposition, the presence of drugs or alcohol in their system, and even the polygraph examiner's level of expertise. Despite the likelihood of inaccurate readings, some local, state, and federal agencies still use polygraph testing to eliminate applicants. Regardless of potential inaccuracies, polygraph tests can determine a significant number of truths and lies when used in specific situations.

Frank Horvath and John Reid (1971) are both highly experienced polygraph examiners. Horvath and Reid have performed a number of polygraph tests. They presented an article titled "The Reliability of Polygraph Examiners Diagnosed of Truth and Deception," which discussed a study that consisted of 10 examiners, seven of whom were experienced and three whom were fairly new. Researchers gave examiners several records from polygraph testing. The experienced examiners achieved a higher rate of accuracy in determining the innocence or guilt of examinees based on the polygraph records. Conversely, the inexperienced examiners correctly determined the innocence and guilt based on the records less often. This study reaffirmed that the test examiner's experience plays a big part in the testing results.

Special Agent William Warner (2005) with the Federal Bureau of Investigations (FBI) presented a paper on polygraph testing titled "Polygraph Testing: A Utilitarian Tool." He documented several studies that his division of the FBI's Polygraph Unit in Washington, DC conducted. They conducted several tests per year. Most of the tests yielded positive results. The agents detected deceptions, drew out confessions, and collected information.

Agent Warner further noted that regardless of the debate on this issue, the ultimate goal of administering the polygraph test should be to bring a case to closure, bring a suspect to justice, or

Box 3.7 Advice to Applicants

This testing phase is also an easy step for applicants to get disqualified for being dishonest, deceitful, or extremely nervous. Applicants should always know the details in their pre-history questionnaires because this is the primary source from which examiners will extract information for questions. They should stay confident and be honest. Disclose information that they have listed on their form, even if it could cause a disqualification. Most agencies respect and pursue applicants who are honest rather than deceitful. Applicants should try to compose themselves, try to remain calm, and speak assertively when asked questions.

obtain information for the greater good. Consequently, this tool does serve an important purpose. Polygraph examiners will continue to use the tests to determine truth or deception. Agent Warner is an expert in polygraph testing and has conducted numerous tests—his perceptions on this tool and its use and accuracy are immensely valuable. See Box 3.7.

In addition to polygraph tests, some agencies have started using **voice stress analyzer** machines. This particular tool is less invasive and easy to use. It records the applicant's voice, which the examiner later analyzes to determine whether the applicant experienced any vocal stress during a formalized conversation.

Oral board interview. This step is also somewhat nerve-wracking for some applicants because mostly it involves a roundtable-style interview. Primarily the applicant is taken into a room wherein two or more interviewees would take turn posing questions such as the following:

- Why are you interested in this position?
- Why did you choose this designated agency?
- What is your personal opinion on police use of lethal force?
- How do you address conflict?
- How do you handle difficult physical and emotional situations?
- What are your strengths and weaknesses?

It is advisable for applicants to conduct thorough research on the designated jurisdiction they are applying for in order to be prepared to answered questions relating to why they choose to apply to the designated jurisdiction. These questions are designed to test the applicant's oral communications skills and also to determine their level of comfort when discussing difficult situations such as diversity and inclusion and use of lethal force. See Box 3.8.

Box 3.8 Advice to Applicants

It is advisable for applicants to remain positive, assertive, and to maintain a commanding presence and stature throughout the entire interview. Maintain eye contact and give direct, concise, and informative responses. Refrain from using too many "ums" and "uh-hums," and lastly, do not hesitate to ask the interviewer to clarify the question so you can give the appropriate response.

Medical and drug screening exam. This step primarily covers the applicant's physical ability to perform the duties and responsibilities of a police officer. The applicant is scheduled for a 2-and-a-half-day appointment with the jurisdiction's physician to complete a comprehensive medical examination to obtain information such as height, weight, vision, screening for illegal drugs, urine test, electrocardiogram, blood test, chest X-ray, hearing, and so on. This phase is important because the jurisdiction is focusing on two main goals: short-term and long-term employees.

Medical examination results determine if applicants are at risk of becoming short-term employees and developing a severe illness or disorder that may prohibit them from performing their regular duties and responsibilities, or whether they are prone to injury. For example, some agencies require that all applicants sign a no-smoking policy or tobacco-free policy on and off duty. An agency's main concern is to hire applicants who can perform their duties and responsibilities and retain their careers for the long term.

It is also essential to address the Americans With Disabilities Act (ADA), as this prohibits any employers from discriminating against an applicant or disqualifying an applicant based on his or her disability if he or she can perform the work in spite of his or her disability. Although this concept is somewhat controversial when hiring police officers, an agency can only disqualify an applicant

Box 3.9 Advice to Applicants

This phase is somewhat difficult to prepare for. However, if the applicant exercises regularly, eats a healthy diet, sleeps well, and does not smoke, the medical professional should have no problem clearing him or her for police work. It is also important to contact your primary physician for regular medical checkups. These appointments will enable your physician to identify any issues prior to going through the application process.

with a known disability if it has proper and justifiable documentation or evidence that the applicant cannot perform the regular police duties and responsibilities. Some agencies will compromise by offering the applicant another position in the agency that does not require the regular duties and responsibilities of a police officer. See Box 3.9.

Final interview with senior/higher staff. The content of this phase varies by jurisdiction; some agencies combine this phase with the with the oral board interview. Some would separate and conduct this interview at the very end with the highest-ranking official or officials of the agency. Although it may appear formal, it is a conversation where applicants have a chance to explain why they chose the department, where they see themselves within the department, and what attributes they bring to the department.

Lastly, applicants have the opportunity to reassure the chief/commissioner/sheriff of their moral and ethical character with the promise to become an exemplary officer. See Box 3.10.

Box 3.10 Advice to Applicants

Exude confidence. Understand that this is the easiest phase. Stay relaxed but maintain a commanding presence and posture during the entire interview. Remember to maintain eye contact and prepare to ask detailed questions if given the opportunity. Conduct thorough research on the agency and be prepared to highlight divisions and initiatives that have benefited the police department and the communities they serve.

Academy Lifestyle

The academy lifestyle is unique. Every officer will tell you he or she will never forget his or her academy experiences. This portion of their training is where recruits develop lifelong friendships and relationships. It is understandable that the recruits form bonds as a result of spending countless hours with their peers experiencing some of the most difficult mandated training exercises. The majority of the academy's training is composed of the following evaluating concepts:

- Use of firearms
- Defensive driving

- Defensive tactics/officer survival
- Practical scenarios
- Written exams
- Physical weight and cardio training
- Carson & Staughton (CS) gas
- Oleoresin Capsicum (OC) spray
- Legal updates
- Other forms of mandated trainings

Most jurisdictions are required to follow mandated training standards that their local or state criminal justice departments or public safety divisions or Peace Officer Standards and Training (POST) Department established. Police training is a mandatory requirement to fill the police officer position. It prepares the recruits with all the training possible to handle calls for service after graduation.

Integrity is the key ingredient in police training and employment. Although agencies measure integrity differently, it is important to determine whether academy training affects their integrity levels. Even though the police academy is a mandatory requirement, some researchers have noted that it does not affect the recruits' level of integrity. Conversely, Robert Ford (2003) a researcher from the University of Central Florida published a study titled "Saying One Thing, Meaning Another: The Role of Parables in Police Training."

In his study, he noted that during the early periods of police academy training, some shifts in attitudes and values occur in police recruits (Ford, 2003). According to Ford, these subtle shifts sometimes lead to negative ethical implications as officers' progress in their careers. The researcher interviewed several officers about their academy experiences and how it affected them while they are on the street or patrol.

In this study, most of the police officers interviewed indicated that they were affected in some way by police war stories. Veteran police told police war stories in all settings during training and socialization. Consequently, the police subculture becomes an important part of their lifestyle. Conversely, other researchers presented quite the opposite of these findings. Daniel Blumberg, Luciano Giromini, and Laura Jacobson (2016) conducted a study called, "Impact of Police Academy Training on Recruits' Integrity."

They conducted a study with three police academies in South Carolina's metropolitan area. All three agencies have standardized training requirements, ensuring that each agency is an independent contributor to this study. The researchers focused on measuring whether police training academies influenced recruits' level of integrity. This particular study found that recruit training has little or no influence on police recruits even after graduation. Blumberg and colleagues noted that in all three academies, participants indicated that they entered and completed the academy with high levels of self-reported integrity. In addition, when examining another academy where participants pay their way through, it was also noted that they entered and completed the program with high levels of integrity. From a practical standpoint, the researcher's conclusion supports the theory that individuals pursuing this career have self-discipline and integrity. Therefore, it is quite easy to assume as much.

To further support this point, it is important to examine another study from a different country, in this case, Belgium. Annelies De Schrijver and Jeroen Maesschalck (2015) conducted a study titled "The Development of Moral Reasoning Skills in Police Recruits." The researchers conducted the study at five police academies in Belgium. They discovered that even though the integrity training from the participating academies was somewhat different, the findings were similar. With regards to moral reasoning skills, the study suggested there were no differences in the recruits. The authors surmised that the absence of change in integrity levels probably occurred because the recruits started the academy with relatively high scores (Schrijver & Maesschalck, 2015). In conclusion, most studies have found that police training does not affect the police recruits' level of integrity.

As mentioned earlier, this career path is demanding and honorable. Thus, when pursuing a position, the applicant should be physically, emotionally, and mentally ready for what becoming a police officer entails.

The academy lifestyle varies according to jurisdiction as well. Some academy applicants are only held on a day-to day basis. Others provide a strictly boarding concept where the recruits are not allowed to leave the academy until graduation. Yet other agencies require recruits to stay at the academy from Monday to Friday and allow them to go home on the weekends.

Private police academies are owned and operated by a private entity where recruits have to pay their way through the academy. Other agencies will only pay for the recruits to attend the academy after hiring them.

Academies vary in cost depending on the institution. They all generally follow the same teaching style and curriculum since they are public police academies. Regardless of the living and attendance requirements, the academy lifestyle is a unique experience for every police recruit and officer. They are pushed to the extreme, experiencing various hardships, happiness, sadness, comradery, and sometimes loneliness. It is that one opportunity that every officer gets to prove him- or herself and excel in the rigorous training process.

Field Training Process and Probation Period

Once the officer has completed all the listed steps and has graduated the police academy, he or she is assigned a field training officer to complete one of the final stages of the process. This period also varies per department and can last anywhere from 6 to 24 weeks. The **field training officers** (FTOs), as they are commonly referred to, are well seasoned and experienced officers who are specifically trained to mentor recent graduates from the police academy. Some agencies will assign the FTOs to the recruit while they are still in the academy so the FTO can observe the recruit's performance at the academy and also to solidify the social bond between them.

This phase is the most influential of the officer's career. The more experienced officer (FTO) provides guidance, evaluation, and instructions to bridge the gap between classroom training in the academy and real-life experience in the field. This phase can also be problematic. If the new officer and the seasoned officer don't get along, personality conflicts can arise.

Michael McCampbell, a visiting fellow at the National Institute of Justice, presented a brilliant study in April 1987 titled, "Field Training for Police Officers: The State of the Art." This holistic study explored four police departments San Jose, California; New Port News, Virginia; Flagship, Arizona; and Largo, Florida. Even though the field training programs differed structurally from all the participating agencies, the researcher determined that all the programs shared one goal: to provide tangible guidance, evaluation, and on-the-street and hands-on training. And if needed, they would retrain the new officer (McCampbell, 1987).

In some instances, after training the recruit the first time, the FTO officer may recommend an extension for further training if he or she perceives any deficiencies in the recruit's performance. Furthermore, if there is a personality conflict, the agency can reassign the recruit to another FTO. If that fails and the recruit is still having difficulties grasping the basic foundations, the FTOs may recommend termination.

McCampbell also noted that the FTO program is relatively new and started in San Jose, California in 1972. Some of the findings of his study demonstrated that this program is beneficial not only to recruits, but to the department and the community they serve. The FTO program is also relatively inexpensive, reduces civil liability issues, and provides effective agency operations (McCampbell, 1987).

Conversely, notable police researchers and practitioners Ryan Getty, John Worrall, and Robert Morris (2016), conducted a study titled "How Far From the Tree Does the Apple Fall? Field Training

Officers, Their Trainee, and Allegations of Misconduct." In this particular study, the researchers conducted work evaluating several officers who had completed the Dallas Police Department FTO program and were currently working by themselves.

The study discovered that most of the officers' misconduct or negative allegations against them were a result of their field training associations and experiences (Getty et al., 2016). The study further revealed that FTOs have significant effects and influences on their trainees regarding negative incidents they are involved in the post-field training phase. Additionally, Getty and colleagues added that even though these negative associations are noted for police behavior in the post-field training phase, department administrators are equipped with tools to improve the FTO training program where seasoned officers are trained thoroughly to serve as examples of trustworthy officers who have a high level of influence. These officers are held to a higher standard.

Various agencies are revamping their field training programs to become more effective and reduce any negative association with post officer behaviors. Taking these two viewpoints into account, it is important to remember that FTOs are ordinary police officers themselves. Yet they are placed in new officers' lives to make an everlasting impression. That is why agencies should thoroughly vet officers who expresses an interest in becoming field training officers. They should demonstrate the ability to mentor, a willingness to commit to the program, and a dedication to making a change by positively influencing new officers. Specifically, the FTO should demonstrate his or her tolerance and commitment to fostering a diverse and inclusive agency.

The probation period also varies per department. However, every officer who successfully graduates from the police academy is on a probationary period anywhere from 6 months to a year from the date of hire. During this period, the agency can terminate the officer for a number of issues including jeopardizing an officer's safety, misconduct, and unethical and immoral acts. If any of these problems occur, the new officer would not be eligible for a hearing. Once the officer has completed the probation period, he or she is eligible for a hearing or an appeal process if faced with disciplinary action.

In a nutshell, the termination of officers after probation is much more difficult than when they are on probation. Some agencies also restrict officers on probation from the police vehicles program, residency officer programs, working part-time or off-duty detail work, and any other outside employment. Once they are off probation, they are eligible to perform all these tasks and can apply for specialty units within the department.

Police and Diversity and Inclusion

Based on the topics discussed in chapter 2, most police agencies are initiating diversity and inclusion plans to mirror the diverse communities they serve (see figure 3.1). Before delving into this controversial topic, it is important to know the meaning of **diversity** and **inclusion** and how they relate to policing in hiring, retention, and promotion. Researchers queried several universities to develop a very detailed definition of diversity.

According to the City University of New York (2017), diversity includes primarily demographic and philosophical differences. Furthermore, diversity involves understanding, recognizing, and appreciating other people's differences including race, socioeconomic status, political biases,

Figure 3.1 LGBTQ Outreach and Engagement

age, ethnicity, sexual orientation, gender expression, religious beliefs, political beliefs, and other social and ideological beliefs.

Inclusion, on the other hand, encompasses all aspects of diversity; it is recognizing and empowering everyone regardless of their background, beliefs, and status. Inclusion seeks to promote everyone. In policing, diversity and inclusion can be applicable in three major aspects: recruiting, hiring, and retention. The next sections explain these concepts in detail. To explore current practices agencies are addressing regarding diversity and inclusion, it is imperative to present the case document of the U.S. Department of Justice, Equal Employment Opportunity Commission published in October 2016 titled "Advancing Diversity in Law Enforcement."

It is also important to highlight the police departments that participated in this report and session participants. Police departments from all over the nation including but not limited to Artesia, Atlanta, Austin, Beaufort, Bowie, Burlington, Chattanooga, Colorado's Peace Officer Standards and Training (POST), Colorado State Patrol, Daly City, Detroit, Evanston, Madison, Metropolitan Police Department (DC), and Richmond (CA), participated in the study.

The entities that engaged in the listening sessions are the American Association for Access, Equality, and Diversity; American Civil Liberties Union; Center for Constitutional Rights; Cohen Milstein Sellers & Toll PLLC; Feminist Majority Foundation; Human Rights Campaign; Just Solutions; Levy Ratner, P.C.; Mexican American Legal Defense and Educational Fund; National Association for the Advancement of Colored People; Legal Defense and Educational Fund; National Center for Transgender Equality; National Employment Law Project; National LGBTQ Task Force; National Women's Law Center; Sikh Coalition; the Advancement Project; the Leadership Conference on Civil and Human Rights, and the United Sikhs.

Diversity and Inclusion in Recruiting

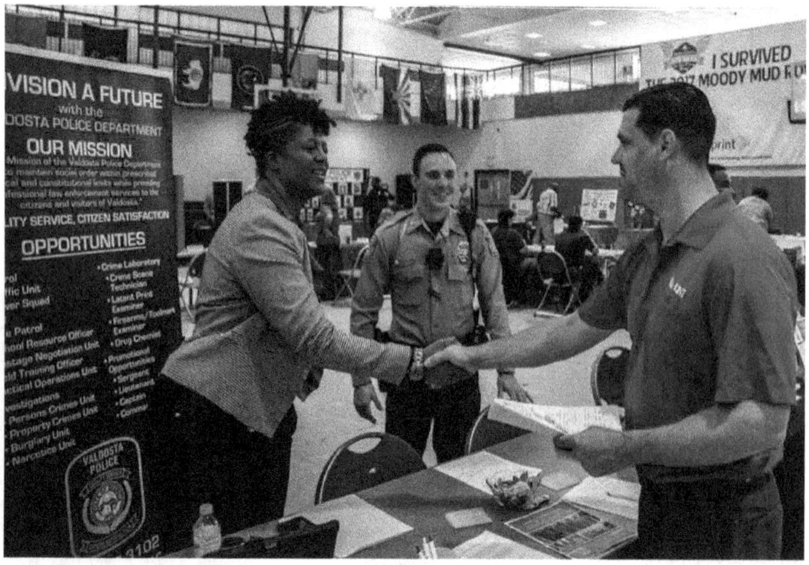

Figure 3.2 Job Fair

According to the U.S. DOJ, Equal Employment Opportunity Commission (2016), there are certain barriers to achieving diversity in police departments. The majority of police agencies have not successfully attracted diverse candidates. There may be legitimate reasons barriers exist. One barrier in particular is **recruitment**: the basic process that involves actively seeking and reaching out to qualified individuals who want to pursue a career in law enforcement. These strategies can involve media advertisements, on-site job fair presentations (see figure 3.2), online advertisements, and movie theater and radio advertisements. One valuable type of recruitment that is not often encouraged or supported is personal recruitment. Personal recruitment requires seasoned officers to seek qualified applicants through and beyond their social networks including places of worship, schools, college classmates, social media, friends, and so on.

For example, a seasoned police officer who is working as an adjunct professor at a university is an excellent conduit for recruiting college students for a police career. The police instructors present real-life knowledge and experiences to their students, thus fostering their interest in law enforcement. Before exploring the proactive measures agencies are taking to increase diversity and inclusion, it is important to highlight the barriers they face. According to the U.S. DOJ, Equal Employment Opportunity Commission (2016), these factors are perceived barriers when recruiting a diverse and inclusive workforce in law enforcement:

- Strained relations and a lack of trust between law enforcement and diverse communities may deter individuals from underrepresented communities from applying for open police positions.
- A law enforcement agency's negative reputation or evidence of unfair operational practices may dissuade applicants from underrepresented communities from pursuing a career in law enforcement.
- Individuals from underrepresented communities may not be sufficiently aware of career opportunities within law enforcement agencies.

Furthermore, the various negative perceptions and encounters between law enforcement and the community breed a lack of trust, thereby reducing the chances that underrepresented individuals develop an interest in this career. The reputation these negative encounters have created is also is a key factor that dissuades underrepresented candidates from pursuing this career.

Police departments have launched many initiatives to improve diversity within their agencies. One strategy they have pursued is partnering with their communities. (Chesterfield Police Department, Virginia; Richmond City Police Department, Virginia; and Henrico County Police Department, Virginia are just a few who attempted this specific strategy.)

Additional promising diversity and inclusion initiatives some departments have undertaken, according to the U.S. DOJ, Equal Employment Opportunity Commission (2016), include the following:

- Proactively recruiting underrepresented individuals in their communities to make potential candidates aware of police career opportunities.
- Building partnerships with various institutions such as educational institutions (colleges, universities, and high schools) with police departments. This avenue provides a medium for a smoother application process once the candidates become eligible for employment. For instance, younger individuals can be thoroughly vetted for pre-employment through internship programs, police cadet programs, police service aid, or police service tech programs. These positions create a positive relationship between young people who are aspiring police officers.
- The U.S. DOJ, Equal Employment Opportunity Commission (2016) noted that effectively and innovatively using social media to relay police activities such as recruiting, partnership functions, and collaborations are critical to building diverse relationships.

Diversity and Inclusion in Hiring

Hiring involves the completion phase in which the agency offers the qualified candidate the position after extreme vetting. This step sometimes boils down to a decision in hiring the best and most qualified candidates regardless of their diversity. Most police departments are only budgeted to hire a specific number of applicants. For example, in a jurisdiction wherein the local government is run by a county board of supervisors, this board determines how many positions can be filled in a given year, depending on the budget. For example, there may be enough funding to hire 10 new officers or deputies. The head of the agency—the chief or the sheriff—has to make the ultimate decision by only hiring 10 qualified applicants. In many cases, the head of the agency is faced with more than 10 qualified applicants and yet is only authorized to hire 10. To best determine the most qualified applicants, the chief or sheriff then has to evaluate applicants based on other relevant factors, including military experience, prior police experience, education, performance during the selection phase, background record, driving record, and commitment to diversity. It is also important to beware of claims of **reverse discrimination**.

Reverse discrimination refers to the unfair treatment of individuals who are classed in the majority class. Perhaps an explanation is warranted. Reverse discrimination involves admissions, employment, or other benefits granted to a group largely consisting people of color even when the member from the majority group is equally qualified or more qualified. For example, let's imagine a sheriff's department that is only authorized to hire two deputies. During the interview process, the department ends up with three finalists—two African American individuals and one White individual—who are all equally qualified for the position.

To diversify the agency, the sheriff decides to hire the two African American candidates for the deputy positions instead of hiring the one White candidate along with one of the two African American candidates. In this scenario which is sometimes very common due to the higher outcry for more minority officers in communities most agencies are exploring the initiative of diversity hiring. It is important to note also that this situation can be somewhat controversial. For instance, if the White candidate inquires from the human resources department or the personnel unit as to why they were not hired, if the agency does not provide a thorough and substantive reason as to their decision, the White applicant would have grounds for a reverse discrimination lawsuit. Therefore, it is worth noting that despite agencies beginning to take positive steps to aggressively diversify hiring within their ranks, they still encounter barriers. However, as noted in the example, the majority of agencies have encountered various barriers. Additional barriers are listed next:

HIRING

- Law enforcement agencies' reliance on inadequately tailored examinations as part of the screening process may have the unintended consequence of excluding qualified individuals in underrepresented communities from the applicant pool.
- Reliance on certain additional selection criteria and screening processes that disproportionately impact individuals from underrepresented communities can also inhibit agencies' efforts to increase the diversity of their workforces.
- Requirements, such as residency restrictions, may limit certain underrepresented communities' representation in law enforcement agencies.
- Length, complexity, and cost of application processes can serve as a deterrent for applicants.
- Law enforcement agencies may be limited in their ability to modify or adjust hiring and selection criteria. (U.S. DOJ, Equal Employment Opportunity Commission, 2016)

In further explaining these barriers, the five key points the U.S. DOJ, Equal Employment Opportunity Commission (2016) listed are very applicable to mostly all police departments that are engaging in this quest for diversifying their agencies. The first step—reliance on entrance exams—is currently being examined by some police departments, that are either eliminating these tests or waiving them if the candidates possess criminal justice or police science-related college degrees. Other police departments have eliminated the police testing exams completely. The second step covers mostly selection processes that are stringent on applicants' backgrounds and prior drug usage. Most agencies are becoming more lenient with candidates' prior drug usage, instead focusing more on the recent (last use) usage rather than the amount and prior usage. This notion was as a result of current research noting that most applicants have experienced using various types of drugs during their teen and young adult years. As a result of stringent drug policies, most agencies are losing qualified applicants who once experimented, have turned their lives around, and want to make a positive contribution to social justice. The last three steps noted residency restrictions and how the cost and length of the selection process can deter underrepresented candidates. Some jurisdictions have lifted residency restrictions and are allowing applicants nationwide to apply to their agencies. The length of the selection process is necessary because police candidates are held to a higher standard. Therefore, the vetting process should be thoroughly completed with no shortcuts. Although some agencies have explored shortening the process, the major processes are still in place for extreme vetting.

An exploration of the promising initiatives taken by most police agencies, according to the U.S. DOJ, Equal Employment Opportunity Commission (2016), reveals the following positive changes:

- Agencies are adopting a holistic view of applicants despite their background and drug use history
- Agencies are willing to work with applicants regarding physical and written qualification requirements, making selection processes more transparent
- Agencies are asking community members to be involved in the hiring process

These steps are all very important in fostering a diversified police agency. Making the process more transparent is key in assisting and encouraging underrepresented communities involving people of color to apply. In addition, involving community members in the hiring process and in decision making builds trust between the agency and the community, allowing the community member to feel he or she is a part of the police hiring process.

Diversity and Inclusion in Retention

Retaining and maintaining police officers from different origins of color is as challenging as it is to hire and recruit them. Most agencies are facing this challenge and are exploring various initiatives to more effectively retain their officers of color. **Retention** in policing refers to the maintenance of individuals to the fullest of their terms and abilities as police officers to reach their fullest potential in promotion or lateral promotion to improve themselves and the departments in which they are employed. Retaining officers of color is extremely beneficial; they can serve as mentors to new officers of color and conduits to officers from colored communities. However, officers of color do face a double marginality wherein they are neither accepted by the community they represent, nor by the department in which they work due to lack of diversity within that agency. Some of the barriers in retaining officers of colors are listed next.

RETENTION

- Individuals may face difficulties adjusting to a law enforcement agency's organizational culture.
- Individuals from underrepresented communities may face difficulties in the promotion process due to a lack of transparency about the process, as well as a scarcity of role models, mentoring relationships, and professional development opportunities. (U.S. DOJ, Equal Employment Opportunity Commission, 2016)

In further explaining the barriers noted by the U.S. DOJ, Equal Employment Opportunity Commission, step one delves into the concept of officers of color facing a double standard wherein they are not accepted in the communities they serve and are also not feeling accepted within their organizations. For instance, a gay or lesbian officer who is rejected by both his or her family due to strict family values and by peer groups due to a lack of cultural and diversity sensitivity will have a difficult time adjusting. The second concept is very accurate wherein officers of color face difficulties in the promotion process as they lack senior guidance and mentorship from senior administration officers of color. For instance, let's say an officer of color tests and scores highly for a sergeant position. The decision is made by the chief of police. However, the chief takes recommendations from the senior staff members who are primarily of the majority class. When this is the case, there will be limited or perhaps even no recommendation for the officer of color when it comes to the promotion opportunity.

As noted by the U.S. DOJ, Equal Employment Opportunity Commission (2016), some initiatives that will be beneficial in pursuing a broader endeavor in diversity and inclusion in police retention should be addressed. These include mentorship and training programs relating to cultural training and diversity initiatives; second, community partnerships; and last, providing incentives for officers of color that will promote a thriving environment for them to stay and pursue their careers. Some agencies have developed various initiatives for compensating officers who speak a second language or can serve as translators during certain detailing and works.

Police and Underrepresented Individuals

For simplicity's sake and the purposes of this book, this section will focus on the most prevalent underrepresented groups, which include female officers, African American officers, Hispanic and Latino officers, Muslim officers, and LGBTQ+ officers.

First, in focusing on women in policing, according to Dr. Brian Reaves (2015), a Bureau of Justice statistician, a total of 11.9% of full-time sworn law enforcement officers in 2007 were female, 10.6% in 2000 were female, and 7.6% in 1987 were female. These numbers are still accurate by today's standards. However, various initiatives have factored into the mix the increase in women in policing, and especially those women holding high-ranking positions.

A concept called **consent decree** has also played a part in this endeavor. A consent decree is a federal court agreement between the court and the police department to cease any suspected immodesties. In this case, the agreement between the federal courts and the police department allow more opportunities to hire and promote women and persons of color within the ranks (see figure 3.3). According to the National Center for Women and Policing (2003), consent decrees are beneficial and can help promote women in policing. However, once these decrees expire, the emphasis on initiatives for hiring and promoting women in policing decreases.

For example, the National Center for Women and Policing (2003), in "The Effect of Consent Decrees on the Representation of Women in Sworn Law Enforcement," noted the Pittsburg Police Department as an example. The department was under a court order from 1975–1991, which stated that for every White male police officer they hired, they were to hire a one African American male, one African American female, and one White female officer. As a result, representation of people of color grew tremendously. However, once the program was listed, the number regressed again. Further studies noted that women in administrative roles nearly doubled during the early 1990s to early 2000s due to various reasons. Factors such as the consent decree was a key ingredient, along with education, lateral movements, mentoring, and personal ambition. Some female police officers stayed at their current organizations and worked their way through the ranks, while others left their positions and sought higher education in law, criminal justice, or public administration and later returned to become successfully elected or appointed as the head of various agencies. Some examples of women in administrative roles in law enforcement include Sheilah Coley, Newark Police Department, New Jersey; Cathy L. Lanier, Washington, DC Metropolitan Police Department; and Kathleen O'Toole, chief of police, the first female police commissioner of the Boston Police Department who later became the chief of police for the Seattle Washington Police Department. These are just a few of the many women

TABLE 3.2 Women and Policing

AGENCY	TOTAL INCREASE IN WOMEN'S REPRESENTATION	DATA PROVIDED	AVERAGE ANNUAL PROGRESS DURING CONSENT DECREE	AVERAGE ANNUAL PROGRESS AFTER CONSENT DECREE
MUNICIPAL POLICE DEPARTMENTS				
Cincinnati (OH) Police	16.2%	1981–2002	0.77%	—
Columbus (OH) Police	4.3%	1982–2002	0.41%	0.19%
Los Angeles (CA) Police	16.2%	1980–2002	0.74%	—
New Haven (CT) Police	14.3%	1984–2002	0.54%	1.11%
COUNTY LAW ENFORCEMENT AGENCIES				
Los Angeles (CA) County Sheriff	2.2%	1991–2002	0.22%	—
McHenry (IL) County Sheriff	12.7%	1995–2002	1.81%	—
Montgomery (MD) County Police	4.0%	1991–2002	0.52%	-0.36%
Nassau (NY) County Sheriff	-0.1%	1995–2002	-0.02%	—
San Diego (CA) County Sheriff	2.1%	1984–2002	0.01%	0.22%
Suffolk County (NY) Sheriff	4.1%	1990–2002	0.34%	—
STATE POLICE AGENCIES				
Arkansas State Police	2.7%	1979–2002	0.12%	—
Florida Highway Patrol	10.9%	1979–2002	0.47%	—
Michigan State Police	4.2%	1990–2002	0.59%	0.12%
New Jersey State Police	3.5%	1975–2002	0.15%	0.06%
New York State Police	6.5%	1979–2002	0.45%	0.13%
Rhode Island State Police	1.1%	1994–2002	—	0.14%
Virginia State Police	1.3%	1989–2002	—	0.10%
Vermont State Police	2.4%	1994–2002	—	0.30%
AVERAGE	6.0%	16.4 YEARS	0.47%	0.22%

Source: National Center for Women & Policing, 2003.

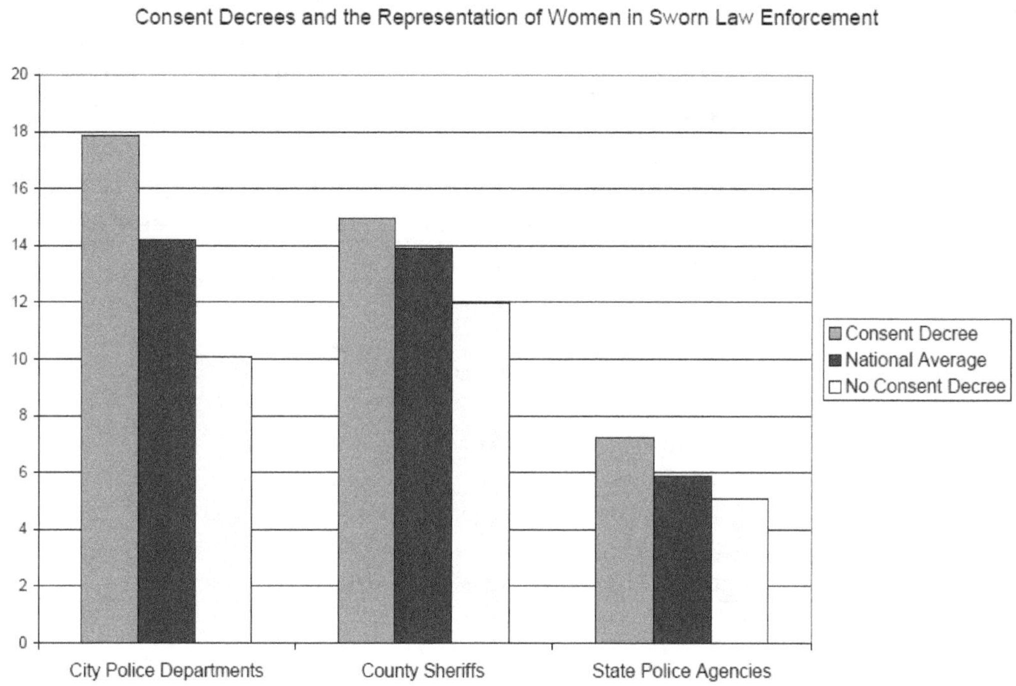

Source: National Center for Women & Policing, 2003.

Figure 3.3 Consent Decrees and Representation of Women

in law enforcement. It is also important to stress that mentoring has increased the number of women in law enforcement as these women in high-ranking positions continue to mentor and encourage newer female police officers.

Additionally, the advancement of African American police officers has come a long way from the days of the slave patrol, when African American police officers were only allowed to drive police cars with the markings "Colored Police Officers" and were only allowed to arrest other African American individuals. It took some brave and groundbreaking initiatives of some police commissioners and chiefs to start hiring African Americans as part of their forces for this number to increase. Chief August Vollmer and O.W. Wilson were big advocates in diversity and pushed to have equality in their police departments. Both African Americans in policing and women in policing have suffered from various factors that have affected their participation in law enforcement, including lack of interest, lack of opportunity or not knowing of opportunities, and lack of support and mentorship from both family members and administration staff. Several key prominent African American police administrators have made it a point to mentor upcoming officers of color. Some of these prominent administrators include Charles Ramsey (Metropolitan Police, DC, and Philadelphia commissioner), Dr. Theron Bowman (Arlington, Texas), and John Batiste (Washington State Patrol). As with women in policing, the majority of these leaders served their tenures and obtained higher education, additional certifications and trainings, and were appointed as heads of various agencies.

To properly cover **Hispanic and Latino officers**, it is important to highlight the difference between the two as they can be commonly misconstrued quite often. Hispanic cultures include Spain and Spanish-speaking origination but do not include Brazil, wherein Latino culture includes Brazil but does not include Spain; it is primarily people from Latin American countries and origins and Hispanics from Spanish-speaking origins. Hispanic is primarily used to refer to the people who speak the language of origin—Spanish (Spain is included but Brazil is not)—whereas Latino refers to the geography and location, which includes Caribbean-Puerto, Cuba, Dominican Republic, South America-Ecuador, Bolivia, Columbia, Peru, and Central America as well as Honduras and Costa Rica, this includes Brazil but excludes Spain (Encyclopedia Britannica, 2017).

In 2007, the number of Hispanic or Latino officers totaled 10.3% of nationwide police officers, according to the U.S. Department of Justice. The low numbers of nationwide officers of color in high-ranking positions is slowly increasing as mentoring and other initiatives are playing a positive role. In addition, incentives and pressures on these officers tend to reduce their tenure as they can be overworked for translating and participating in other community events for their departments. On a positive note, having a higher number of Hispanic and Latino officers is a benefit to a police agency as this population has increased in the last 10 years in the United States. The number of Muslim officers has increased as well. A noteworthy issue that needs discussion is that most Muslim officers primarily have faced various barriers and stereotypical attitudes since September 11, 2001. These issues have encompassed mostly uniform and appearance grievances. Muslim officers have noted that their designated police departments have not supported them in allowing them to wear their traditional head coverings and other traditional Muslim coverings or clothes in honor of their religion. Most of these departments have supported their policies of officer safety issues and public recognition between the community and the officers, and as a result, they are not backing down on their departmental policies regarding uniform policies. Some departments are in support of Muslim officers wearing their traditional head coverings, as they see this as a positive aspect—that community members can relate to these police more closely in the communities they serve, especially if there is a higher Muslim population within the jurisdiction, for instance in New York City.

Another group of underrepresented officers who have faced various barriers over the past couple of decades are officers from the LGBTQ+ communities. Policing has historically been viewed as a masculine profession until women started serving. In addition, some police departments also have a history of discriminating against members of the LGBTQ+ community, causing them to avoid disclosing their sexuality. It is somewhat difficult to pinpoint the actual number of officers representing this community nationwide due to lack of demographic questions specifically identifying gender preferences. Also, some officers may purposefully refuse to put their sexual and gender preferences on their applications in fear of discrimination and other potential stereotypical behaviors by their peers or superiors. Many police departments are starting to support this underrepresented group by creating LGBTQ+ liaison officers or LGBTQ+ outreach units. For instance, the LAPD has a LGBTQ liaison officer, the NYPD has a LGBT Outreach Unit, and the Henrico Country Police Department in Virginia has a LGBTQ liaison officer as well.

Positive initiatives are in place currently for supporting this community of officers. Various research studies are also contributing to the fact that police departments are on the right track in evaluating their training programs in dealing with individuals from this community as well. Tania Israel, Audrey Harkness, Kevin Delucio, Jay Ledbetter, and Todd Raymond Avellar published the research study in (2014) titled "Evaluation of Police Training on LGBTQ Issues: Knowledge, Interpersonal Apprehension, and Self-Efficacy." Another excellent research study was conducted by many of the same researchers as the one previously mentioned (Israel, Harkness, Avellar, Delucio), with Jay Bettergarcia and Joshua Goodman, who published "LGBTQ-Affirming Policing: Tactics Generated by Law Enforcement Personnel" in 2016. These two distinct studies demonstrate that police agencies are seeing higher education's role in improving their training programs in dealing with these communities internally and externally. This will continue to be a controversial issue due to personal biases of various officers. However, with the help of the findings from these studies and the current initiatives that various departments are implementing, members of the LGBTQ+ communities are receiving more representation within various departments, thus fostering promotion and retention within their ranks.

African, Native American, Asian, and other races and ethnicities of police officers may face the same double marginality and barriers as the groups listed. It is particularly difficult for officers of other races to be represented if there is no representation or mentorship within the higher ranks. Secondly, these officers may not be accepted by their family members in pursuing this illustrious career, and as a result, they may feel out of place. Being an officer of color has stringent barriers; these barriers are becoming less and less, however, as more representation and mentorship is being accomplished with higher-ranking officers.

Box 3.11 Perception Versus Reality

A myth and a perception that most officers, and even the community, have is that a policing career is becoming increasingly dangerous, or, that policing is the most dangerous career there is. There is a concept called "paradox of policing" that applies precisely in this section. Paradox of policing is merely wherein several officers are in fear of getting hurt or killed in the line of duty when in actuality the statistics presented by the BJS state that a police officer's career, even though it can be dangerous, is not the most dangerous career. This paradox and phenomenon can be relayed to families and loved ones, and as a result, loved ones would discourage their significant others or children from pursuing this career.

Police Officer Character Traits

When conducting the research for this section, the literature and various police websites revealed words and phrases that accurately describe the character traits of a police officer. Some of the words and phrases used to describe the officer include community oriented, initiative, perseverance, sense of ethics, effective communicator, respect and knowledge of the law, honesty, common sense, problem solver, civility, sound judgement, respect for individuals, controlled temper, thirst for knowledge, teamwork, and commitment to diversity and inclusion.

From a practical standpoint, all of these words and phrases should ideally describe the character traits for every police officer. However, only a few specific words are used repeatedly and are currently applicable to mostly all police departments. The most important words and phrases from the list are **respect for individuals**, which can also be the same as **commitment to diversity and inclusion**, **honesty**, an **effective communicator**, and **thirst for knowledge** in order to adapt to the constant changing times.

As the United States is considered to be the melting pot, communities and jurisdictions are becoming more and more diverse. So, it is imperative that police agencies become more diverse to properly cater to their communities by having their officers commit to diversity and inclusion. Honesty also goes a long way, as many examples have been presented wherein officers are terminated for dishonest acts. Research and practical knowledge have supported the notion that police executives value honesty and credibility. Lies and dishonest actions have no place in policing and these executives would exercise their authority and terminate such individuals immediately who commit such actions in order to protect the reputation of the department. There are also various situations wherein officers have committed serious immoral acts while on duty and off duty. However, some of these officers have been honest and took accountability for their actions and have faced disciplinary measures rather than termination. On the other hand, other officers have been terminated for lying to a superior officer about sick leave, annual leave, the take-home vehicle program, and so on.

As for being an effective communicator, an officer can avert several serious confrontations if he or she is able to communicate effectively with the subject he or she is encountering. Some research shows that effective communication skills have saved many lives. Lastly, the quest for knowledge is also a valuable trait. As times are changing and situations are evolving, it is crucial that the officer always seek further training and experiences to stay ahead of the game.

PERCEPTIONS FROM LAW ENFORCEMENT EXECUTIVES

Several informal conversations were held with various police executives and administrators regarding their perceptions of policing. For this section, executives and administrators will be used interchangeably as they address the same group of police officers. Due to departmental approvals for participation, many of the administrators wanted to contribute; however, they remain anonymous. In addition, they were comfortable with their responses being grouped and presented in themes. Their responses morphed into an excellent theme as many of them have similar perceptions, and these were easy to depict. When asked to list their perceptions on policing, their responses presented four major themes, all surrounding the concept of creating a police relationship between police and the communities they serve: **changing times**, **criticism**, **community policing**, and **individual officers**. Changing times, as mentioned in the character traits section, are inevitable. These administrators noted that every officer should stay ahead of current times by constantly educating him- or herself and staying vigilant. Criticism is also another issue police administrators face, due to their positions. They have to give constructive criticism to their subordinates, and sometimes this is received negatively, therefore causing stress for the administrator. Randy Garner (2010) supported

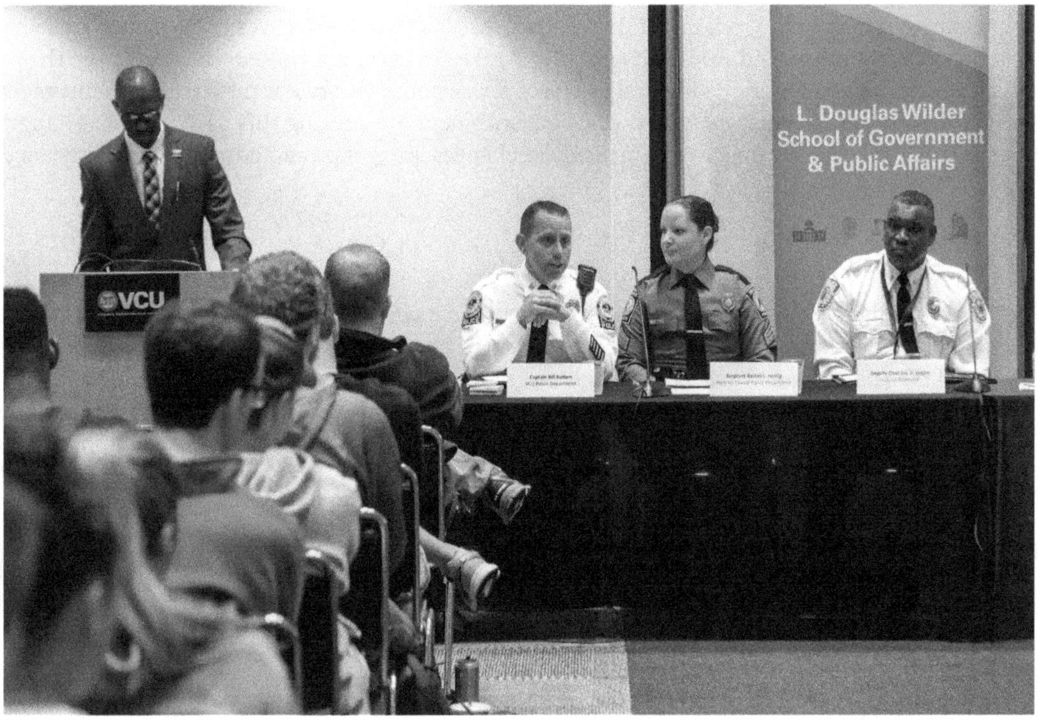

Figure 3.4 Diversity Police Panel

this notion with his study titled "The Impact and Implications of Interpersonal Criticism for Police Executives." The study presented the responses from several police executives regarding their positions, duties, and responsibilities. Criticism was one of the top-listed items they mentioned as an issue relating to their position. Community policing was also emphasized because of the recent negative encounters police and communities have faced. Community policing should be present in order to rebuild that trust. These executives have made it their primary goal to foster a greater community policing strategy for all their subordinates. Lastly, they noted that a change within the individual officers needs to be addressed to foster a greater policing effort for protecting and serving communities. If the officer's inner attitude is disgruntled and burned out from his or her career, his or her productivity and interactions will be greatly affected, thus, yielding a negative relationship between community and policing.

PERCEPTIONS FROM LINE OFFICERS

As with the previous section on police executives, informal discussions were held with officers as well. Again, the majority of these officers wish to stay anonymous and wanted to present their perceptions of policing from their personal experiences. Additionally, their responses also morphed into themes, which are **officer safety**, **officer wellness**, **protectors and helpers**, and **advancement** in order to make changes within their respective agencies. Officer safety is very important—this response was not surprising because every officer is trained to be vigilant regarding officer safety. Most officers' goals are to conduct their work effectively and efficiently and to be able to return home to their families at the end of their shifts; therefore, officer safety was paramount in the conversations. Second, officer wellness is crucial. During officers' police academy training, they are under a strict physical conditioning regimen. However, very few police departments have physical standards beyond academy life, and so officers are on their own. Some officers have made it a point of duty to stay well and take excellent care of themselves. Protectors and helpers were also very important and high in the ranking of their responses. They see themselves as the guardians, protectors, and caretakers, and would do whatever it takes to carry out these roles. Lastly, the theme of advancement was mentioned by only a select few, as not everyone wants to get advancement within their departments. Those who value advancement are seeking this path to make changes within their agencies; the only way to make these changes is to get promoted and effect this change.

Psychological and Emotional Aspects of Law Enforcement

To gather a holistic view on this topic and to understand its importance, it is imperative to examine the work by Dr. Robert T. Muller, (2013) a professor of psychology at York University and also the author of the book, *Trauma and the Avoidant Client*. Dr. Muller published a topic in *Psychology Today* titled, "Toughing It Out: Post-Traumatic Stress in Police Officers." In this article, he talked entirely on the Ontario Provincial Police (OPP) force, which has over 8,000 members. It is important to get a worldwide view beyond just the United States in order to gain a complete understanding of this issue. Muller further noted that officers frequently witness and handle various types of crimes, including homicides, rapes, violent assaults, car accidents, and crimes against children, teenagers, and the elderly. Having been exposed to these types of cases on a continuous level, the officer will become immune and desensitized to these graphic scenes; he also noted that when officers are retired and show any signs of posttraumatic stress disorder (PTSD), they are left to fend for themselves in getting the proper treatment for this illness.

In addition, Muller also noted that the OPP force has many officers and only one full-time psychologist on staff who is primarily screening new applicants only. This trend is also very common here in the United States policing spectra. As mentioned earlier in this chapter, the psychological testing is a requirement for all new applicants; however, it is not required for seasoned officers. Some agencies have explored having a partnership with their community services board or social services members to become available to officers in need of psychological counseling and/or intervention. Some agencies also made it a mandatory requirement for specialized units such as the SWAT team and other highly specialized and tactical teams/units. Muller also noted that officers are somewhat reluctant to come forward when they are having some mental issues because they fear losing their career. This is an accurate statement from a practical standpoint and from current research. An officer takes pride in his or her career, and a history of mental illness or a condition without treatment will prohibit the officer from performing his or her duties and responsibilities. As a result, many are choosing to stay quiet and find other unhealthy coping mechanisms from peers, social stimuli, and family. Most officers confide in other officers, and the conversations flow smoothly and are easily relatable as they have a lot in common being in the same profession. However, modern research notes that the more officers practice supporting inclusion and diversity efforts, the healthier their lifestyles would become. The next couple of sections will cover the details of stress and its association with this career path.

POLICE CAREER AND STRESS

To understand the relationship between officers and stress, it is important to depict a brief example of an officer's assignment. The officer sits in his or her vehicle or station, either patrolling or reacting to the police radio. The proactive officer patrols in search of scenarios that depict police intervention. These scenarios range from robbery in progress, burglary in progress, larceny in progress, motor vehicle theft in progress, and rape in progress, just to name a few. These proactive officers will react to each of these scenarios without hesitation in an instant. The reactive officers who are tied to the radio also face certain types of anxiety as they wait. They may be dispatched to any of these calls, having to immediately cease whatever they are doing and respond in high alert to confront the situation. These constant states of anxiety and ready for action—although effective and advantageous—take a toll on the officer's body physically and mentally. This constant state can also be classed as the **flight-or-fight** response, meaning the body is in a state of reacting to any unknown situation that it's being faced with, whether it is to confront the situation or escape from the situation. Each officer has this unique character trait. As mentioned, exploring these difficult concepts is not a frightening tool or a means to convince young aspirants against pursuing this career. However, it is important to discuss the issues relating to this career in order for aspirants to have a full understanding of what they are embarking on. Police and stress have always been a linkage factor, and various studies have shown that this is a regular trend as officers are progressing in their careers—stress is alongside them due to various factors including **organizational**, **environmental**, **personal life**, and **societal** aspects. These four main factors are the pivotal influential factors of officers' stress during their career. Organizational stress covers the various organizational demands for arrests, citations, promotion, evaluations, compensation, and assignments such as undercover, first-line supervisors, and so on. Environmental factors cover the areas the officers are assigned to work. For example, if they are assigned to a neighborhood that is known for negative stimuli, the officer may or may not be affected by the constant interactions of those they encounter. For instance, if the officer is constantly interacting with individuals associated with drugs and prostitution, studies have shown that the officer is likely to be affected negatively by this interaction. Personal life is basically the close family members and relatives the officer interacts with. Some officers tend to let their occupation affect their personal lives wherein they become too suspicious and paranoid in every aspect of their personal life. For instance, they may develop a suspicious attitude toward their significant others and impose stricter rules and regulations on their children, thus driving a negative relation within their homes. Last, societal and environmental factors are somewhat the same, although societal factors deal more closely with the social status of the officer, who he or she is associating with, his or her friends and counterparts. Officers spend the majority of their time with their peers on and off duty, and these constant interactions have led to officers surrounding themselves with constant talks about police work and interactions with those whom they encounter. Some experts have noted that it is advisable for officers to have friends and peers outside the policing realm in order to have a more balanced societal stimulus. To better understand the types of stress associated with this career, see the next section for further explanation.

TYPES OF STRESS ASSOCIATED WITH THIS CAREER

In order to understand the types of stress associated with the police career it is important to examine Muller's (2013) contribution, that stress is the primary factor that leads to officers' anxiety, addiction, burnout, and depression; these are the primary types of stress police officers face. An article by the National Institute of Justice (NIJ, 2012), titled "Causes of Officer Stress and Fatigue," noted that enduring stress for a long period leads officers to anxiety, PTSD, and depression. In moving forward, it is also important to know the meaning of PTSD and how it relates to police officers. According to the NIJ (2012), PTSD is the psychological condition that prevents officers from moving forward from an event that they witnessed or handled. This sort of "inertia" manifests through lack of sleep, nightmares, increased anxieties, inability to be compassionate, and constantly reliving the event. Furthermore, two major factors were highlighted that cause these types of stress: first, organizational factors, and second, individual factors (NIJ, 2012). Work-related factors involve poor management, inadequate or broken equipment, excessive overtime, rotating shifts, and changes in duties (NIJ, 2012). Individual factors involve family issues, financial issues, health and wellness issues, and second employment to earn more income (NIJ, 2012). In addition, another study by Donald McCreary, Ivy Fong, and Dianne Groll (2017), titled "Measuring Policing Stress Meaningfully: Establishing Norms and Cut-Off values for the Operational Organizational Police Stress Questionnaires" invited several members from the OPP force to contribute to a police stress questionnaire. Six thousand and forty-four invitations were sent out, and only 2,840 participated. Much of the questions covered in the questionnaires encompassed shift work, traumatic events, overtime, occupational hazards, lack of understanding from family and friends, and so on. The findings from this study—although influenced by age, gender, and years of participant service—were similar to the trends here in the United States, according to the presentation from the NIJ. The common themes for stress for most police departments are shift work, traumatic events, family and friends' influences, and occupational hazards. There are many more stressors not documented here, but these are the most common themes based on the research presented. Also, another applicable study by Mark Chae and Douglas Boyle (2013) titled "Police Suicide: Prevalence, Risk, and Protective Factors" highlighted the various causes of stress in law enforcement. The study emphasized five prominent aspects: organizational stress, critical incident trauma, shift work, relationship problems, and alcohol use and abuse (Chae & Boyle, 2013). Last, an intriguing effect of stress on police officers that is usually not talked about is **police suicide**. Police suicide is typically an officer intentionally taking his or her own life, most often with his or her service weapon. It has been noted by experts that stress is a plausible factor to police suicides. To see how prevalent this issue is, a contribution report from Robert Douglas from the National POLICE Suicide Foundation noted that police suicide rates are

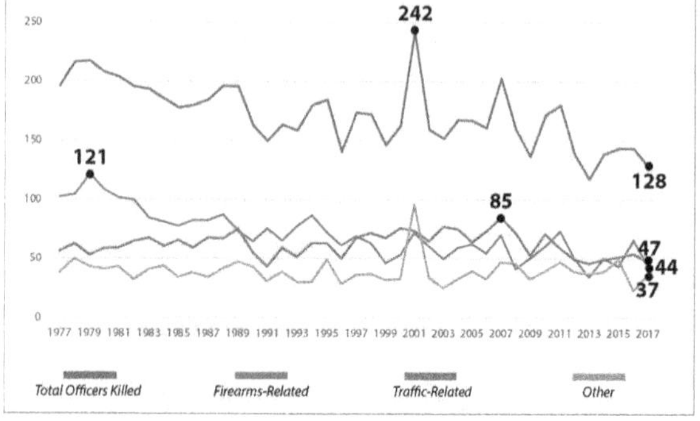

Figure 3.5 Officer Fatalities 1977–2017
Source: RT (2017)

somewhere between 300–400 a year (Kelly & Martin, 2006). The report further noted that stress is a factor that leads to suicide in police officers mainly due to an unsupportive organization and managers, pending retirement, shift assignment, and physical illnesses (Perin, 2007). The next section presents coping mechanisms and alternative assistance for officer stress and also presents warning signs for police suicides.

COPING MECHANISMS AND ALTERNATIVE ASSISTANCE FOR OFFICER STRESS

Coping with stress—primarily police suicides—will be addressed first, and coping for general stress will be addressed second. Mr. Jean Larned (2010) contributed an article in the *Forensic Examiner* titled "Understanding Police Suicide." Larned is a retired police officer for San Antonio, a former special agent for the DEA, and currently a criminal investigations instructor at the FBI national academy. He is also a survivor of a suicide by a close family member. He presented in his article critical warning signs to look for in officers who are exhibiting signs of suicide: talking about suicide; giving direct clues, such as saying, "I do not want to live anymore"; and also giving indirect clues saying, "Life is pointless." Self-isolation, giving away prized possessions, changing beneficiary recipients suddenly, mood changes, and neglecting hygiene (Larned, 2010) are also warning signs. The author also discussed how agencies can be more vigilant in preventing this from happening and listed some helpful concepts, including tracking high-risk officers, access to firearms, getting officers' families involved, training, stress awareness and coping skills, crisis and personal interventions, peer support, and retirement counseling (Larned, 2010). Some might say it is strange to be concerned about pending retirement being a stress factor and thus leading to suicide. The rational is the officer has spent the majority of his or her lifetime as a police officer and has never done anything else. He or she has created social and physical bonds with their peers and the department. The thought of leaving this field has often led to suicide in fear of isolation and boredom. Suicide among police officers is a real threat and therefore needs quick and proactive intervention by agencies. Most agencies are implementing peer groups for intervention and are starting to track high-risk officers to attempt to prevent suicidal thoughts or actions.

To help officers best cope with general stress in policing, the research shows the following themes can be of benefit:

- Making friends outside of police work
- Seeking help through their agency's Employee Assistance programs (EAP)
- Taking advantage of peer support groups, comprised of ranking officers who can be trusted
- Investing in positive social capital such as religious and self-wellness initiatives, and/or closeness with one's family for moral support

Most officers tend to lean on their peers for support, but many of their peers are facing the same stress issues they are facing. So, leaning on peers is not helpful and can create a disgruntled police force and a lack of trust in outsiders.

Most agencies are currently tracking officers' use of force, usage of sick and annual leave, and other misconducts that might indicate any form of suicidal thought or action and are intervening appropriately with programs. Other agencies are also partnering with social services wherein their officers have access to social service agents at any time. Lastly, some are mandating their patrol and specialized officers to attend sessions with a trained counselor at least a couple of times a year, depending on the agency's policy.

POLICE OFFICER INVOLVED IN A SHOOTING

In reflecting on chapter 2, the incidents mentioned regarding the shooting of unarmed African American males were much publicized. Each of these incidents involved an officer discharging his or her weapon, although little publicity was given to the process the officers went through because of their actions. **Officer-involved shootings (OIS)** are not a new concept; they are the process in which the officer made the decision to discharge his or her weapon to disengage or eliminate a potential or perceived threat. The chapter on use of force will cover justifications on use of deadly force and non-justification implications. This section will only focus on the concept of OIS. Usually, when a county or municipal officer is involved in an OIS situation, it goes through several phases.

First, its respective agency's Internal Affairs bureau will respond to assume the investigation. If for any reason there is an indication of the potential of a conflict of interest or bias, a state agency or federal agency would respond to assume the investigation. In some instances, the officer's firearm will be secured for evidential purposes, and in other instances, some agencies will relieve the officer of his or her badge and firearm and will place the officer on a paid administrative leave. Some agencies will place the individual on unpaid administrative leave, depending on the situation. According to Worrall and Schmalleger (2015), after an OIS incident, the officer goes through five major phases: **denial**, **anger and resentment**, **bargaining**, **depression**, and **acceptance**.

The denial phase is when the officer repeats the situation over and over wishing it did not occur. The anger and resentment phase is also very real. The officer becomes very angry and resentful toward the person shot and will ask him- or herself questions, over and over: Why did you make me do this? Why didn't you just listen to my commands? This phase lasts for a short period of time but can be very difficult to get through. The bargaining and depression phases are close together wherein the officer tries his or her hardest to reason with him- or herself to understand what has just happened. In the depression phase, which is closely associated with the bargaining phase, the officer finds no peace after bargaining with himself or herself and just isolates from everyone. This phase can last a while for some individuals without the support of others. Lastly, the acceptance phase, which comes at the end, brings some relief. With the constant media coverage, the officer can revert back to any of the previous phases upon seeing the incident reported on numerous occasions and from various perceptions.

Furthermore, in exploring the phases of OIS, Geoffrey Alpert (2016, a professor of criminology at the University of South Carolina, contributed a piece in *Criminology: Public and Policy* titled "Toward a National Database of Officer-Involved Shootings; A Long and Winding Road." In this article, the expert noted that it is imperative to have a national database for OIS. There are various informational data being collected by the FBI on justifiable homicide; however, these data reported by police agencies are voluntary, and as a result, the FBI cannot accurately track every OIS case. The author further noted that the value of a good database includes accurately tracking the following: the number of incidents in which police officers discharge firearms at citizens; the demographic information of officer(s) and citizen(s) involved; the employing agency; the weapon(s) used; description of injuries; and so on and so forth. Tracking this information is valuable in preparing detailed training programs for police departments in order to prevent or reduce OIS cases.

Alpert (2016 also noted that in OIS cases, it is imperative for the administrators to insist to their training officers that each officer should be held accountable for each bullet fired, meaning the officer must justify each round fired. With this accountability assignment, an officer will examine his or her actions prior to discharging his or her weapon at perceived threats. It is also important to point out that every situation dictates the reason for the officer's action. These officers are trained to confront every possible situation. However, sometimes critical thinking, quick response, and immediate encounter is eminent in order to address the situation. These situations are unfortunate. Some officers go their entire career without discharging their firearms; others have done so numerous times and have gone through all the phases, recovered, and have returned back to work with extensive counseling and therapy sessions. Some departments require their officers to attend a mandatory number of counseling sessions with a trained psychologist for police shootings, and other agencies leave the attendance at the discretion of the officer.

These traumatic events are very real and are being handled in various stages. Several factors that influenced how these events are handled include type of situation, jurisdiction, demographics of the parties involved, media coverage, family and organization support, and self-health and care of the officer.

END OF WATCH: OFFICERS KILLED IN THE LINE OF DUTY

Data for this section was taken primarily from the Federal Bureau of Investigation's (FBI) Uniform Crime Report (UCR) (FBI, 2016), which noted that a total of 118 law enforcement officers were killed during 2016 in line-of-duty incidents. Of those 118, 66 were killed due to felonious incidents and 52 were killed as a result of accidents (FBI, 2016). The report classified the officers as sworn officers with full arrest powers who carried a badge and a service weapon and were from one of the following: city, university and college, county, state, tribal, and federal law enforcement agencies. Furthermore, the report also listed the profiles of the officers to include predominantly White males, an average of 40 years old with several years on the force (FBI, 2016). The felonious circumstances were described as situations mostly wherein some of the officers were ambushed, responding to domestic-related calls, investigating suspicious persons calls, conducting searches, police pursuits, drug-related circumstances, burglary calls, robbery calls, and attempting to arrest a suspect. Fifty-seven thousand, one-hundred-and-eighty officers were also the victims of in-the-line-of-duty, assault-related incidents.

Figure 3.6 Officer Chris Yung and Me

Material on officers assaulted in the line of duty is also rarely covered in current policing literature. The number of such instances is likely far greater than those actually reported, as most officers feel a sense of pride and would not want to appear weak to their fellow officers by reporting that they were assaulted. These numbers for both officers assaulted and killed are quite alarming. As mentioned earlier, these actual events are not depicted here to discourage the recruit from pursuing this career; rather, the intention is to better prepare candidates and inform them of the reality of this career.

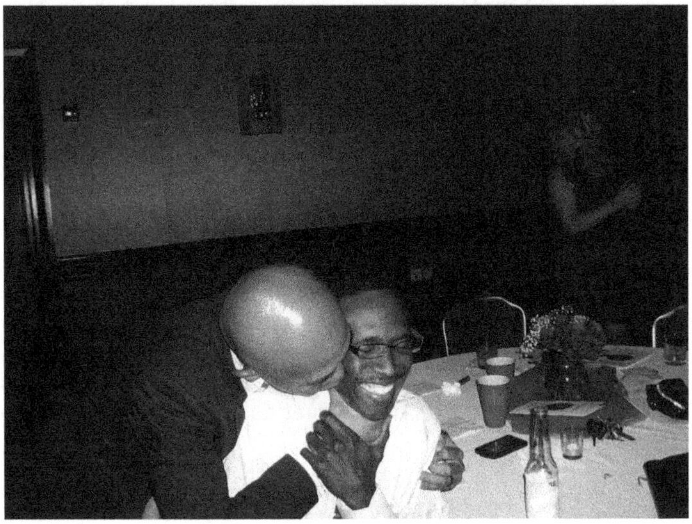

Figure 3.7 Officer Chris Yung Kissing my Face

End of watch (EOW) is a term designated for when an officer is killed in the line of duty. Occasionally, during a deceased officer's memorial ceremony, the designated agency dispatcher will announce his or her badge/unit number at least three times over the radio. The silence on the other end brings about a profound sadness—the chills and stillness that creeps over the mass gathering of police officers from all over the nation neatly dressed in class A uniforms, their faces quiet with teary eyes, is a very sad depiction of the reality of this career.

Chapter Summary

Writing this chapter was especially memorable and bittersweet for the author, as it brings back the academy experiences and the lifelong friendships he has encountered during and after the academy phase. The author reflected on his years of policing, his recruit years, his interactions, confrontations, use-of-force incidents, his commendations, his complaints, his good times, his bad times, and losing a friend who was killed in the line of duty (Officer Chris Yung, Prince William County Police, EOW, December 31, 2012; see figures 3.6 and 3.7). This chapter encompasses the process of becoming a police officer and provides basic tips and advice on how to improve and better prepare oneself for the police selection process. The selection process is an everchanging concept as various agencies are researching how to better attract diversified candidates and also to incorporate fair and equal requirements for all standards regardless of their sex specifically. Some agencies have eliminated the gender-specific recruiting requirements regarding physical agility tests and have adopted an equal point system for all applicants. This field continues to evolve as modern policing improves.

The evolution of policing has grown significantly with women and other groups leading various high-profile, high-ranking agencies. Because of this new leadership evolvement within agencies, younger women and officers hailing from communities that are often largely underrepresented are in a better position for advancement in their careers.

This chapter also covered some very personal and relevant subjects that are often not included in most policing textbooks, subjects such as OIS, how police officers manage stress, and officers killed in the line of duty. The realities of these topics are inevitable and important and should warrant every agency to closely examine its policies on to how to best support officers' stress levels; track high-risk officers; and help officers who are recently separated, divorced, or going through a divorce or who have lost a loved one or are exhibiting any stress indicators. While the burden is on the agency to care for their officers' well-being, it also falls on the individual officer, who must make the change internally within himself or herself and put away any pride and fear in order to get the assistance he or she deserves in dealing with a traumatic event.

As the author wrote this chapter, he reflected on his 10 years of being a police officer and is proud that he sought assistance from peer support, mentorship, social service professionals, and organizational support when he was dealing with multiple traumatic events throughout his tenure. The help is out there and available to officers. An officer's health comes first. Without a healthy officer to perform his or her duties and responsibilities, positive citizen interactions, rebuilding trust between police and community, and organizational goals will be greatly impacted.

Discussion Questions

1. What is the most expensive and most time-consuming phase during the police selection process? What can an applicant do to be more prepared for this phase?

2. What is the purpose of the field training program? List and discuss two advantages and two disadvantages of this phase.

3. Diversity and inclusion in policing was discussed thoroughly in this chapter. List three initiatives agencies are taking to foster this concept within their ranks and the communities. Research and list three prominent police agencies with specific agency initiatives regarding diversity and inclusion (LGBT liaison officers, LGBTQ outreach etc.).

4. Police and minorities were also discussed thoroughly. Pick two underrepresented communities that have faced various barriers in policing and discuss what initiatives have impacted the progress of these groups.

5. List three types of stress police officers face and give two major coping mechanisms that agencies are exploring or offering for their officers.

6. List and discuss the five main phases officers go through after being involved in a shooting.

References

Alpert, G. P. (2016). Toward a national database of officer-involved shootings. *Criminology & Public Policy, 15*(1), 237–242. doi:10.1111/1745-9133.12178

Americans with Disabilities Act (ADA). Retrieved from www.eeoc.gov/ada https://adata.org/learn-about-ada

Blumberg, D. M., Giromini, L., Jacobson, L. B. (2016). Impact of police academy training on recruits' integrity. *Police Quarterly, 19*(1), 63–86. doi:10.1177/1098611115608322

Chae, M. H., & Boyle, D. J. (2013). Police suicide: Prevalence, risk, and protective factors. *Policing: An International Journal, 36*(1), 91–118. doi:10.1108/13639511311302498

City of St. Louis Metropolitan Police Department. (n.d.). *Background questionnaire form*. Retrieved from http://www.slmpd.org/images/hr_forms/commissioned/BackgroundQuestionnaire.pdf

City University of New York. (2017). *Definition for diversity*. Retrieved from http://www.qcc.cuny.edu/diversity/definition.html

Dempsey, J. S. & Frost, L. S. (2016). *An introduction to policing* (8th ed.). Boston, MA. Cengage Learning.

De Schrijver, A., & Maesschalck, J. (2015). The development of moral reasoning skills in police recruits. Policing: *An International Journal, 38*(1), 102–116. doi:10.1108/PIJSM-09-2014-0091

Encyclopedia Britannica. (2017). *What's the difference between Hispanic and Latino?* Retrieved from https://www.britannica.com/story/whats-the-difference-between-hispanic-and-latino

Federal Bureau of Investigation (FBI). (2016). *Law enforcement officers killed and assaulted*. Retrieved from https://ucr.fbi.gov/leoka/2016/officers-feloniously-killed/felonious_topic_page_-2016

Ford, R. E. (2003). Saying one thing, meaning another: The role of parables in police training. *Police Quarterly, 6*(1), 84.

Garner, R. (2010). The impact and implications of interpersonal criticism for police executives. *Applied Psychology in Criminal Justice, 6*(2), 104–113.

Getty, R. M., Worrall, J. L., & Morris, R. G. (2016). How far from the tree does the apple fall? Field training officers, their trainees, and allegations of misconduct. *Crime & Delinquency, 62*(6), 821–839. doi:10.1177/0011128714545829

Horvath, F. S., & Reid, J. E. (1971). The reliability of polygraph examiner diagnosis of truth and deception. *Journal of Criminal Law, Criminology & Police Science, 62*(2), 276–281.

Israel, T., Harkness, A., Avellar, T., Delucio, K., Bettergarcia, J., & Goodman, J. (2016). LGBTQ-affirming policing: Tactics generated by law enforcement personnel. *Journal of Police & Criminal Psychology, 31*(3), 173–181. doi:10.1007/s11896-015-9169-2

Israel, T., Harkness, A., Delucio, K., Ledbetter, J., & Avellar, T. (2014). Evaluation of police training on LGBTQ issues: Knowledge, interpersonal apprehension, and self-efficacy. *Journal of Police & Criminal Psychology, 29*(2), 57–67. doi:10.1007/s11896-013-9132-z

Kelly, P. & Martin, R. (2006). Police suicide is real. *Law and Order, 3*, 93–95.

Larned, J. G.. (2010). Understanding police suicide. *Forensic Examiner, 19*(3), 64–71

McCampbell, M. S. (1987). Field training for police officers: The state of the art. *U.S. Department of Justice, National Institute of Justice*. Retrieved from https://www.ncjrs.gov/pdffiles1/nij/105574.pdf

McCreary, D. R., Fong, I., & Groll, D. L. (2017). Measuring policing stress meaningfully: Establishing norms and cut-off values for the operational and organizational police stress questionnaires. *Police Practice & Research, 18*(6), 612–623. doi:10.1080/15614263.2017.1363965

Muller, R. T. (2013). Toughing it out: Posttraumatic stress in police officers. *Psychology Today*. Retrieved from https://www.psychologytoday.com/blog/talking-about-trauma/201302/toughing-it-out-posttraumatic-stress-in-police-officers

National Center for Women and Policing. (2003). *The effect of consent decrees on the representation of women in sworn law enforcement.* Retrieved from http://womenandpolicing.com/pdf/fullconsentdecreestudy.pdf

National Institute of Justice. (2012). *Officer work hours, stress and fatigue.* Retrieved from https://www.nij.gov/topics/law-enforcement/officer-safety/stress-fatigue/pages/causes.aspx

Perin, M. (2007). Police suicide. *Law Enforcement Technology, 9,* 14–16.

Prince William County Police Department. (2017). *Hiring process.* Retrieved from http://www.pwcgov.org/government/dept/police/pages/hiring-process.aspx https://www.joinpwcpd.org/hiring_process/

Reaves, B. (2015). Local police departments, 2013: Personnel, policies, and practices. *Bureau of Justice Statistics.* Retrieved from https://www.bjs.gov/content/pub/pdf/lpd13ppp.pdf

RT. (2017, December 29). Police fatality rate drastically drops to second lowest in more than 50 years. Retrieved from https://www.rt.com/usa/414503-police-fatalities-decrease-nleomf/

Schmalleger, F. & Worrall, J. (2010). *Policing today.* Upper Saddle River, NJ: Prentice Hall.

Simmers, K. D., Bowers, T. G., & Ruiz, J. M. (2003). Pre-employment psychological testing of police officers: the MMPI and the IPI as predictors of performance. *International Journal of Police Science & Management, 5*(4), 277–294.

U.S. Department of Justice, Equal Employment Opportunity Commission. (2016). *Advancing diversity in law enforcement.* Retrieved from https://www.justice.gov/crt/case-document/file/900761/download

Vermont State Police. (2017). *Minimum fitness standards for recruits.* Retrieved from http://vsp.vermont.gov/employment/fitness

Warner, W. J. (2005). Polygraph testing. *FBI Law Enforcement Bulletin, 74*(4), 10–13.

Worrall, J. & Schmalleger, F. (2015). *Policing* (2nd ed.). Upper Saddle River, NJ: Prentice Hall.

Figure Credits

Fig. 3.1: Copyright © by Henrico County Police Division. Reprinted with permission.

Fig. 3.2: Source: https://media.defense.gov/2017/Oct/23/2001831141/780/780/0/171019-F-VS137-1138.JPG.

Fig. 3.3: Source: http://womenandpolicing.com/pdf/fullconsentdecreestudy.pdf.

Fig. 3.5: Source: https://www.rt.com/usa/414503-police-fatalities-decrease-nleomf/.

CHAPTER FOUR

Law Enforcement Administration

As with most administrative aspects of any organization, law enforcement administration encompasses many levels and categories of duties and responsibilities within both staff ranking and the various agencies. As you explore this chapter, you will find that law enforcement administration can be quite complex, especially when it comes to police hierarchy. In this chapter, you will learn about the hierarchical police organization, including each rank and its function. Our discussion will include the assorted bureaus within the police department, as well as the common organizational charts used for most police agencies in the United States. Finally, you will examine the various levels of policing, including local, state, federal, and private agencies.

Learning Objectives

- Understand the various levels of law enforcement administration
- List and explain the rank structure within law enforcement agencies
- Explore the concept of leadership in policing
- Explore the various divisions and bureaus within a police agency
- Describe the difference between local, state, and federal agencies

Chapter Outline

A REAL-LIFE POLICE SCENARIO FOR DISCUSSION

from Chernoh Wurie's personal accounts

The purpose of the real-life scenario that follows serves to help us clearly explore the police administrative structure. First-line supervisors have one of the most important and active positions within a police department. To be promoted to a first-line supervisor—the rank of sergeant—the officer should have at least 3 to 4 years of active duty experience. The process for most agencies includes a written test at a secured and designated location and an oral response test in front of other high-ranking officers from various departments. Once the officer completes both sections of the test, he or she will be scored and ranked based on the number of participants. Results are mailed to the officer's personal residence and made available to the promotional bodies such as the chief and other high-ranking officers within the department. Some agencies will automatically promote the first two or three ranking candidates; others will leave the discretion to the police chief to select from the top 10 or 20. Each agency has its policies based on promotions. The following real-life example is typical of how stressful this process can be for officers.

Toward the end of every shift, exiting officers waited in line to cash in their paperwork to be dismissed from duty. On November 30, 2012 at 1630 hours, I, too, had neared the end of my shift. Surrendering my collection of the day's summons, parking tickets, and police reports I took notice of my squad mates who had just taken the sergeant's test and were awaiting their results. Much like them, I had been with the police department for more than 6 years and was eligible to take the promotional exam. In fact, I had already done so the day before.

I remembered performing well on the exam, which had included a written portion, a practical scenario portion, and an oral board interview. Throughout the entire process, I had been extra nervous, not about my ability to become sergeant (in that I was confident), but as a result of the panelists whose eyes bore into my back as I left the room. Either they had thought of me as a strong candidate, or not a candidate at all.

Waiting for the supervisor to check my paperwork, I anxiously made a quick phone call to my wife. She assured me that she would check the mail and call me right back.

As minutes passed, an officer named "CJ" was the first to break the heavy silence. He had scored seventh out of 45 test takers. Soon after, at 1650 hours, officer "CM" announced his placement of third out of 45 participants. At 1700 hours, I grew impatient and made my way out the door.

My wife had told me to focus on my driving and to get home safely. What she didn't tell me were my results. Grabbing the letter from my wife as I got home I read the truth in black ink: 40th out of 45 participants. I was devastated. I knew I was a good officer, but my score said otherwise. I had performed well in the written portion but poorly in both the scenario exercise and the oral board interview. I moved on, making a silent promise to try again one day.

Two years came and went. I had performed well on patrol, pursued a master's degree in public administration with a specialization in public safety administration, and completed my doctoral degree in public policy and administration. Juggling my degree requirements and patrol work had been challenging. My supervisors recognized my high performance and had offered me a lateral promotion as the police planner for the chief of police. The position provided me with experience working with police bureaus, which focused on personnel, general orders, and other sectors within the department.

As the 2-year mark approached, I began preparing for the next sergeant test. With the recommendation and support from a very good friend, I focused my attention toward a specific sergeant assessment book in which lied RAF (response, action, and follow-up), the secret to my success.

The concept of the RAF model is basically utilizing the following actions for every scenario: responding to the incident at hand and utilizing whatever you have (whether mental or physical, always with best judgment) to address the situation; taking the appropriate action necessary to effectively attend to the situation; and following up by reaching out to or debriefing the appropriate staff members after the incident. What were the advantages and disadvantages? What was learned? Where can improvements be made in order to address the situation if it were to occur again?

I studied so hard, and it paid off. This time, I received my score in the mail and discovered I'd ranked third out of 40 participants. I asked my wife to read, and then re-read, the score to make sure I understood what it meant. I had received high scores on each assessment and on the written portion of the test. I was a good officer, and now it was on paper.

All ranks within police departments hold testing assessments, and these assessments can vary. With each higher rank comes an even harder test. In totality, these ranks illustrate the structure of a police department. Since the general public is unable to see the working gears of police structures, they often believe officers to be classified as officers of the same rank. In actuality, police departments function very well with a ranking structure.

This chapter will list and clearly define the basic common rank structures. (From Chernoh Wurie's personal accounts.)

Levels of Policing

Forming a police system was inevitable. Early on, European immigrants required law and order only to assure citizens' safety in their rapidly expanding communities. Decades later, policing has since evolved to include numerous levels of hierarchy (federal law enforcement agencies, state law enforcement agencies, local, tribal, and campuses) discussed later on in this chapter. Before delving into these various types of law enforcement agencies, it is important to first revisit the difference between a law enforcement officer and a sworn officer.

According to the Bureau of Justice Statistics (BJS) (2018a), a **law enforcement officer** is an employee of a law enforcement agency or section who is authorized to carry out law enforcement duties and responsibilities. Examples include sheriffs and deputy sheriffs, chiefs, city and county police officers, and law enforcement officers of port and transit authorities. Also included are public university officers and officers at local city and community colleges (BJS, 2018c). Private campus police are excluded as they usually hire and employ their own police officers or private security officers. The **sworn officer** is a concept that is often misconstrued to depict anyone with a badge and a weapon including most private investigators, bail bondsman, and other special police officers. A sworn officer is also authorized to make arrests within the confines of his or her authority while enforcing local, state, and federal rules and regulations.

The number of law enforcement agencies and what they each entail can be quite confusing. To reduce this confusion, let's look at a breakdown of the number of agencies included in the entire United States. Dr. Brian Reaves (2015, a BJS statistician, notes there are approximately 18,000 law enforcement agencies in the United States including 3,000 sheriff's departments, 12,500 local police departments, and 73 federal agencies.

Please see figure 4.1 to depict numbers:

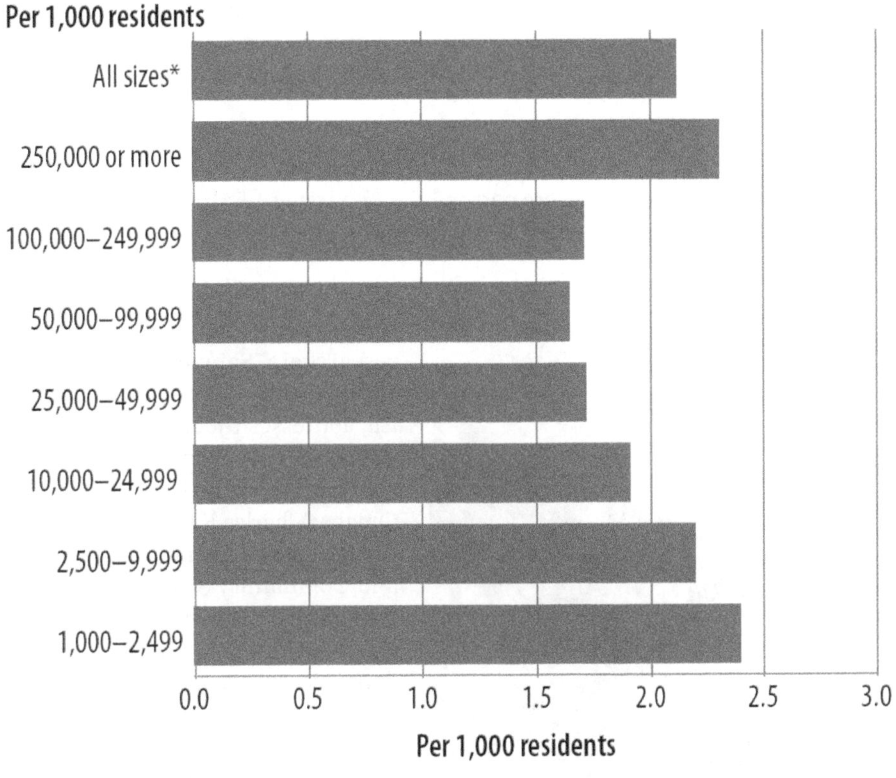

Note: Excludes county and tribal police departments. See appendix table 14 for standard errors.

*Excludes departments serving fewer than 1,000 residents.

Source: Bureau of Justice Statistics, Law Enforcement Management and Administrative Statistics (LEMAS) Survey, 2013.

Figure 4.1 "Average number of full-time officers in local police departments per 1000 residents by size of population served 2013" from "Local Police Departments 2013: Personnel Polices and Practices"

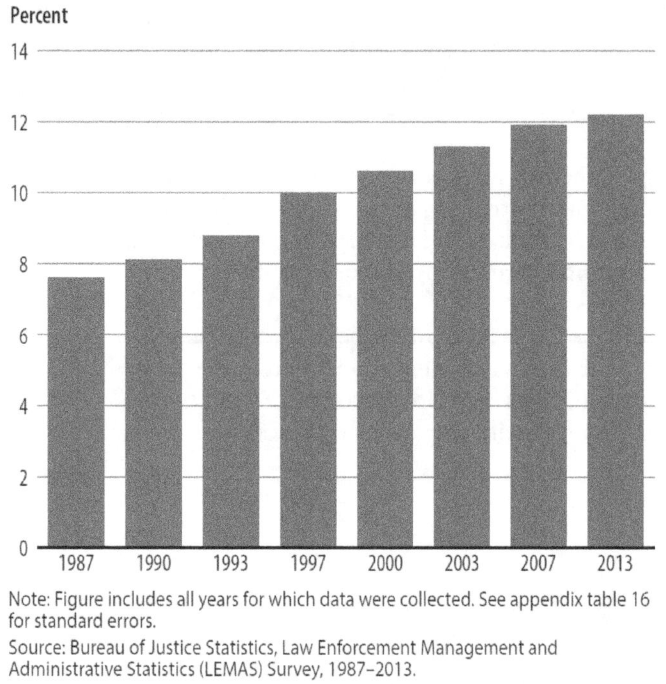

Figure 4.2 "Female representation among full-time sworn personnel in local police departments 1987–2013" from "Local Police Departments 2013: Personnel Polices and Practices"

Source: Reaves (2013)

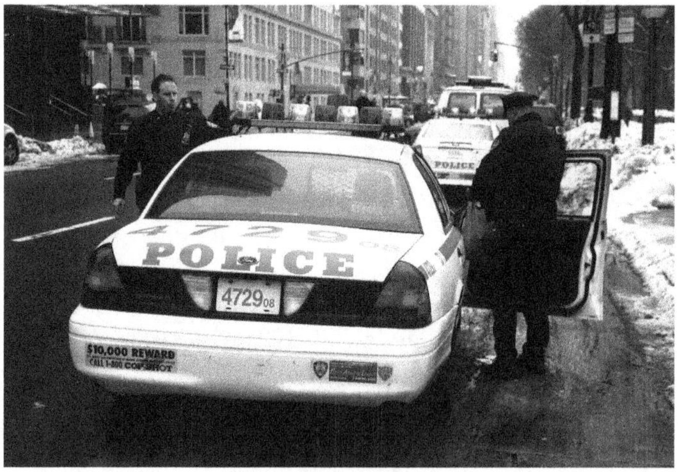

Figure 4.3 NYPD street police

One table depicts the number of law enforcement agencies; the other depicts the number of full-time, sworn police personnel (see figure 4.2).

Before getting into the levels of policing, it is also important to investigate the concept of **police population ratio**, which primarily measures the ratio of police officers to community residents. Usually, the number of officers per 1,000 community residents is the standard ratio. Nationally, the average number of law enforcement officers per thousand citizens is 2.1. This number may vary depending on the size and population of large cities (Walker & Katz, 2018). The ratio is particularly important because the community and the general public need to have a clear understanding of the number of officers needed to protect and serve a specific number of civilians.

Local and Municipal, County Police, County Sheriff

The majority of the material in this section comes from prominent police scholars and researchers. Samuel Walker and Charles Katz's (2018) book, *The Policing in America*, addresses the important intricacies of policing levels. Samuel Walker is a professor emeritus at the University of Nebraska, Omaha. Charles Katz is the director of the Watts Family Center for Violence Prevention and Community Safety and a professor in the School of Criminology and Criminal Justice at Arizona State University. **Local police** departments are comprised of municipal, county police, and county sheriff agencies. Local governments generally operate police departments and include city, town, township, or county (BJS, 2018a). According to Walker and Katz (2018), **municipal police** departments are primarily city police departments. They are the most complex to operate due to factors such as population diversity, the wide range of emergency services, the maintaining of order in large scales, and crime control.

The most notable municipal police departments are the largest: the New York Police Department (NYPD), Los Angeles Police Department (LAPD), Chicago Police Department (CPD), Houston Police Department (HPD), Philadelphia Police Department (PPD), and Detroit Police Department (DPD). Of these, the NYPD is the largest and Chicago is the second-largest police department in the United States (Walker & Katz, 2018).

County police are responsible for order and maintenance within the confines of a designated county. Even though they have some of the same enforcement responsibilities as the county sheriff, their primary roles are different. Some of the primary roles that county and municipal police agencies share include the following:

- Investigating crimes
- Routine patrolling
- Making arrests
- Conducting traffic functions
- Ordering maintenance within their counties
- Preventing crimes
- Educating the public about various laws and infractions
- Conducting community relations
- Presenting cases in court
- Transporting prisoners

Two of the largest county police agencies in the United States are New York State's Suffolk County Police Department and Nassau County Police Department.

Depending on the jurisdiction, the **county sheriff** can perform the same duties and responsibilities as a county police agency. Most jurisdictions have both a county police/city police and a county or city sheriff agency. In jurisdictions without a county or city police agency, the primary law enforcement agency is the sheriff's department. In jurisdictions where both the police and the sheriff are present, the sheriff's primary duties include but are not limited to the following:

- Process serving
- Routine patrolling
- Providing court security
- Securing and maintaining the jail
- Enforcing some traffic enforcement initiatives
- Protecting court officials and witnesses

Lee Brown (1978) identified the four types of sheriff's departments: full-service type, law-enforcement type, civil-judicial type, and correctional-judicial type. The full-service type carries out all duties including law enforcement, judicial, and correctional. The law-enforcement type covers primarily law enforcement duties. The civil-judicial type covers court-related duties and responsibilities. Lastly, the correctional-judicial covers both correctional facilities and court duties and responsibilities but no law enforcement duties or responsibilities.

State Police Agencies

All 50 states have designated state agencies, which are normally classified into two or three categories depending on the jurisdiction. While most jurisdictions only have highway patrol and state police, some also have highway patrol, state police, and investigative services. State police agencies are responsible for enforcing a variety of rules and regulations within the confined area

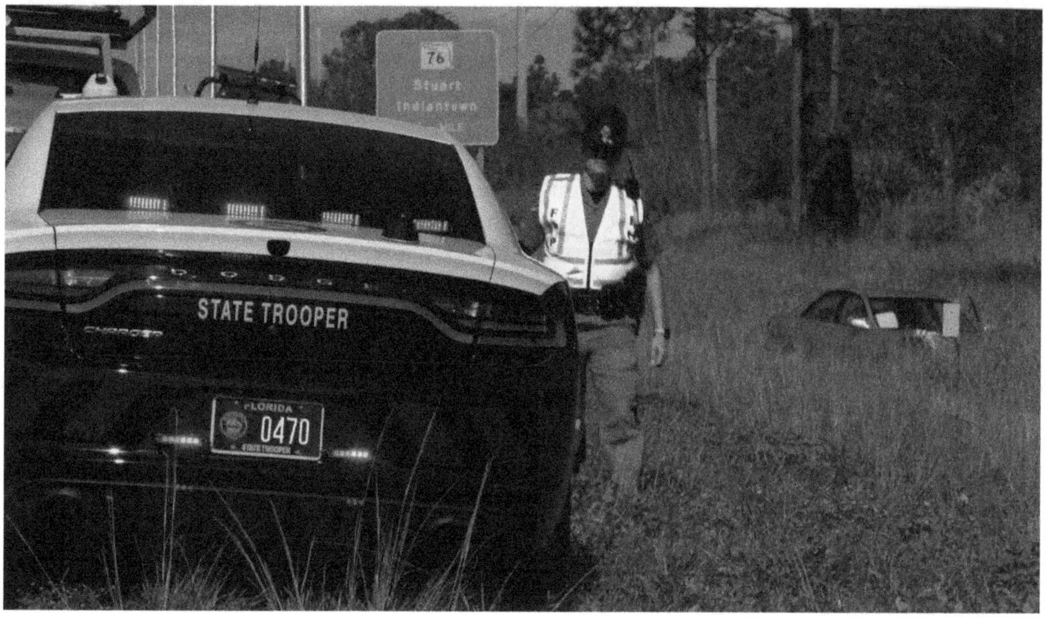

Figure 4.4 FHP ~ Women in law enforcement 15

of the entire designated state. Highway patrols are required to protect, patrol, and enforce traffic infractions on the state highways within the designated state. These patrols are also responsible for protecting the highways from illegal drugs, alcohol, and other illicit substances transported along the state's highways.

According to the BJS, the largest state police agency is the California Highway Patrol and the second largest is the New York State Police. These are followed by the Pennsylvania State Police and the Texas Department of Public Safety. Some jurisdictions have a more centralized function and structure where the agency is called a Department of Public Safety—for example, the Texas Department of Public Safety and the New Jersey Department of Public Safety. These types have a wide array of responsibilities, including investigations relating to the Department of Motor Vehicles and other commercial licensing and business initiatives. Furthermore, criminal investigations are an important function of policing; although they can be broad and encompassing, they are limited to specific bureaus and divisions within a police agency.

Criminal investigations with state police agencies vary per jurisdiction. Some are limited in their capacities to investigate criminal offenses within the state while others have full criminal investigation authority within the entire state. The local and municipal police agencies are authorized to cover the majority of criminal investigations. However, in some jurisdictions the state police agency handles particular alcohol and tobacco violations in addition to plane crashes within their designated state. In addition, some state agencies provide laboratory and forensic processing including ballistics, blood, chemical, bodily fluids, drugs, tool marks, and so on for the local and municipal police agencies. State agencies can also serve as the central hubs for storing criminal data for local and municipal agencies. For instance, the Virginia State Police Department is responsible for maintaining the Virginia Criminal Information Network (VCIN) database. This system stores all criminal information for processed persons, arrested persons, persons with criminal histories, and so on. In some jurisdictions, the state agencies are also responsible for training police recruits and certifying all police officers in that state. Last, if there is a conflict of interest in special investigations such as an officer-involved shooting, an officer killed in the line of duty, or misconduct such as a local or city police department's unethical and corrupt actions, the designated state agency—under these circumstances—will assume the investigation to eliminate further conflicts. Local and state police agencies are closely related and must work collaboratively to achieve public safety.

Additionally, a **mutual aid system** is in place for the majority of local, municipal, and state agencies. This mutual aid system is an agreement between two or more agencies, enabling them to utilize each other's resources in case of an emergency or other necessary situation. For instance, if a local police department is pursuing a robbery suspect who has recently entered a dense vegetation area, and the local police department is a small agency that does not have the necessary resources (a police helicopter, for example) to capture him, the mutual aid system enables the local department to coordinate with their state counterpart to request a police helicopter or other search and rescue personnel (dogs, robots, etc.) to locate the suspect. These collaborations are vital to effectively implement the necessary levels of policing in a designated state.

Federal Law Enforcement Agencies

According to the BJS (2018b), the definition of a federal law enforcement agency is a unit or subunit of the federal government that is responsible for investigating, apprehending, detecting, and preventing various crimes and offenses at the national level. Examples of such federal law enforcement agencies are the Federal Bureau of Investigations (FBI), the United States Secret Service, and the Bureau of Alcohol, Tobacco, and Firearms (ATF). According to Walker and Katz (2018), the terrorist attack against the United States on September 11, 2001 resulted in one of the largest federal government reorganizations in our nation's history. The harrowing events of September 11 also demonstrated that every law enforcement agency should try to be on the same page when protecting the United States against its enemies. These realizations culminated in the passage of the Homeland Security Act on November 25, 2002. This act created the Department of Homeland Security, which is primarily responsible for detecting any illegal acts against the United States. As a result of the Homeland Security Act's passage, a major reorganization was inevitable and implemented, resulting in the two distinct branches of the Department of Homeland Security and the Department of Justice.

Department of Homeland Security agencies:

- Bureau of Customs and Border Protection (CBP)
- Bureau of Immigration and Customs Enforcement (ICE)
- Federal Emergency Management Agency (FEMA)
- Transportation Security Administration (TSA)
- U.S. Coast Guard (USCG)
- U.S. Secret Service (U.S. SS)

(Walker & Katz, 2018)

Department of Justice agencies:

- Drug Enforcement Administration (DEA)
- Federal Bureau of Investigation (FBI)
- Bureau of Alcohol Tobacco, Firearms, and Explosives (ATF)
- U.S. Marshals Service

(Walker & Katz, 2018)

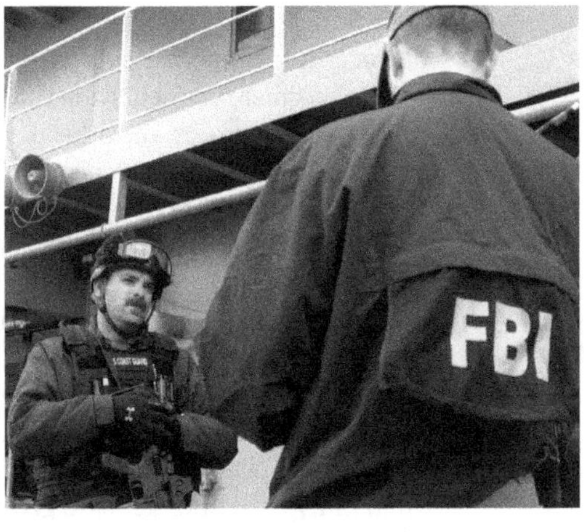

Figure 4.5 FBI and Coast Guard

Each agency is responsible for promoting public safety, public health, liberty, and justice for the United States on the government's behalf. For instance, according to the **Customs and Border Protection** (CBP, 2016) website, the CBP is one of the largest law enforcement organizations in the world with over 60,000 employees. Its primary duties and functions are to

- prevent terrorists and their weapons from entering the United States;
- prevent illegal drugs and illegal persons from entering;
- secure our borders; and
- protect agriculture.

The purpose of the agricultural component is to prevent diseases affiliated with certain foods, plants, and animals from entering the United States. According to the **Immigration and Customs Enforcement (ICE)** website (2017), ICE has about 20,000 employees and three operational directories: Homeland Security Investigations (HSI), Enforcement and Removal Operations (ERO), and Office of the Principal Legal Advisor (OPLA.) This agency covers the majority of duties and responsibilities that the Department of Immigration and Naturalization Services (INS) originally carried.

The **Federal Emergency Management Agency's** (FEMA, 2017) main mission is to prepare for, protect against, respond to, and recover from emergencies and natural disasters. In addition, it is mainly there to support first responders and the citizens to facilitate a fast recovery from mitigating circumstances. The **Transportation Security Administration's** (TSA, 2018) main mission is to protect the nation's transportation channels to promote freedom of movement and for people and commerce. This agency was primarily created after the September 11 attack to improve security and help prevent future terrorist acts.

A number of agencies have housed the **U.S. Coast Guard** in the past. However, it was transferred under the Department of Homeland Security on March 1, 2003. The U.S. Coast Guard's primary duties and responsibilities cover both security and non-security missions. Its six major operational missions are maritime law enforcement, maritime response, maritime prevention, marine transportation system management, maritime security operations, and defense operations (U.S. Coast Guard, 2018). Its homeland security missions include ports, waterways, and coastal security such as drug interdiction, migrant interdiction, defense readiness, and other assigned duties and responsibilities (U.S. Coast Guard, 2018). Last, its non-security missions include marine safety, marine environmental protection and ICE operations, living marine resources, search and rescue, and navigation aid (U.S. Coast Guard, 2018).

Last, we have the **United States Secret Service** (U.S. SS). This agency's initial primary mission was to prohibit counterfeiting of U.S. currency, fraud against the government, distillers who are not conforming to laws and regulations, investigations into the Ku Klux Klan, land thieves, and mail thefts. However, its primary mission currently is to protect the president and vice president, their immediate families, former presidents and their spouses, primary presidential and vice-presidential candidates, foreign heads of states, and other designated federal officials. On March 1, 2003, this agency transferred from the Department of Treasury to the Department of Homeland Security (U.S. SS 2018).

The Department of Justice was the second major agency to split from the bigger conglomerate after the post-September 11 attack reorganization.

The United States attorney general leads the **Department of Justice**. This agency houses several law enforcement agencies including the **Drug Enforcement Administration** (DEA), the **Federal Bureau of Investigations** (FBI), the **Bureau of Alcohol, Tobacco, Firearms, and Explosives** (ATF), and the **U.S. Marshals Service**. The DEA has the critical job of preventing illegal drugs from entering the United States. It focuses mainly on the manufacturing, growth, and distribution of illegal drugs (DEA, 2018). One might ask, "Does the DEA investigate individual offenders?" They can when individual offenders are growing, selling, or distributing illegal drugs at high levels within their criminal organizations.

Figure 4.6 U.S. Marshals escorting prisoner in court

According to the FBI (2018b), their agency has over 30,000 employees consisting of agents, analysts, and other professionals. Its main purpose is to protect the United States from terrorism, cyber-attacks, espionage, and other federal crimes against the United States (FBI, 2018a). It also stresses that both information intelligence and threats drive the FBI's focus. The FBI's original purpose was to investigate antitrust land fraud. Once the crime trends grew more serious and coordinated, the FBI morphed into a primary agency that investigated organized criminals and high-profile cases such as kidnapping prominent figures.

The Bureau of Alcohol, Tobacco, Firearms, and Explosives' (ATF) primary goal is to protect the people of the United States from crimes involving explosives, firearms, arson, and the illegal sale and distribution of tobacco and alcohol products (ATF, 2018). In addition, it also supports other public safety agencies worldwide with situations involving firearms and explosives.

Last is the U.S. Marshals Service, created in 1789 (see figure 4.6). It is one of the oldest federal law enforcement agencies in the United States. The U.S. Marshals Service is primarily responsible for the following federal-related initiatives: judicial security, fugitive operations, asset forfeiture, prisoner operations, prisoner transport, and witness security (U.S. Marshals, 2018).

Several other federal law enforcement agencies exist in the United States, the majority of which are housed separately and include the departments of the following:

- Agriculture
- Commerce
- Defense
- The Army
- The Navy
- The Air Force
- Health and Human Services

All of these divisions have their own federal law enforcement agencies.

Park Rangers

A specialized form of policing that is usually left out in various texts is park rangers. Because **park rangers** fall into various categories, it is important not to classify them under the federal, state, or local categories as they can fall under all three, depending on the state. Most park rangers have full police and arrest powers. The U.S. Department of Game and Inland Fisheries as well as the United States Department of Agriculture are the two primary agencies that largely oversee this section of wildlife law enforcement. According to Parkrangeredu.org (2018), a park ranger's primary duties and responsibilities are to protect national historic sites; protected areas; national, state, and local parks; and wildlife refuges and conservations. Most park rangers attend a specialized academy where they are trained to recognize and enforce federal, state, and local wildlife resources. This section of law enforcement also has a high number of civilian employees comprised of both paid and unpaid volunteers who manage various parks, specifically the visitor centers, and other duties as assigned. Most of the requirements for becoming a sworn park ranger are similar to those for becoming a police officer. However, successful completion of the wildlife and conservatory educational portion of the assessment is required.

Special: Transit, Colleges, Universities

The **transit police** systems cover three major sections of policing including **airports**, **ports**, and **railroads**. The **airport police** departments protect the nation's airports and have the same authorities and duties as local and municipal police departments. Some examples of airport police departments are Los Angeles Airport Police Department, Indianapolis Airport Authority Police Department, and the Metropolitan Washington Airport Authority Police Department (MWAA) covering the Los Angeles International Airport, Washington Reagan National Airport and the Dulles International Airport, respectively. In addition, the MWAA has jurisdiction for the Dulles Toll Highway. **Port authority police** departments provide security and safety for the nation's ports. They also have the same responsibilities and duties as the local and municipal police departments. Some examples are the Delaware River Port Authority Police Department, the Long Beach Harbor Patrol, the Los Angeles Port Police, and the Port of Seattle Police. These departments are tasked with protecting the nation's ports and ensure the smooth and safe flow of people, property, and commercial goods such as cargo entering and exiting the nation's ports. Finally, the **railroad police** department agencies are responsible for protecting the nation's railroads. In addition, their duties include ensuring safe and secure travel for all railroad passengers, personnel, and cargo on railroads and, perhaps most importantly, to prevent terrorist attacks. Examples include the CSX police, Amtrak police, and the Union Pacific Police Department.

The majority of colleges and universities have designated campus law enforcement agencies. Before discussing their roles and regulations, it is imperative to know the definition of this type of law enforcement agency as it is easily misconstrued. According to the BJS (2018c), a campus law enforcement officer is state authorized to prosecute violations on colleges and universities including on-campus and off-campus university properties. Campus law enforcement officers provide quicker response to campus-related criminal incidents. Their authorities vary depending on the state. The majority of these officers are sworn in; those who are not sworn in act as security personnel. All sworn campus law enforcement officers have full police powers that include but are not limited to making arrests, carrying firearms, investigating crimes, detaining suspects, and so on.

Campus police departments are usually considered the understudy, according to Seymour Gelber (1972), a former administrative assistant state attorney in Dade County, Florida. The title of the article is "The Role of Campus Security in the College Setting." The author further noted that the social unrest on college campuses during the 1960s and 1970s necessitated transforming security officers into full campus law enforcement officers with police powers. Over the decades, traditional campus police have also handled mental illness, and natural disasters and have averted terrorist attacks on college and university campuses (Jenkins & Goodman, 2015)).

According to the Bureau of Justice Statistics (2018c), most campus law enforcement officers do have full police authority to include arrest and investigate major crimes. However, several scholars have noted that the lingering perceptions from college students are that campus law enforcement officers are not real police officers and they do not have full police powers.

Native American Tribal Police

For the purposes of this text, the preferred term currently used to characterize what was once described as American Indians is "Native Americans." After all, the label American Indians has a controversial history as well as a negative connotation. The majority of the nation's tribal police departments fall under the Bureau of Indian Affairs (BIA), Office of Justice Services. BIA is currently under the United States Department of the Interior and the Office of Justice Services, which hosts the law enforcement section and is primarily responsible for providing training, support, enforcement, and investigative services. They also preserve peace and protect lives and properties within Native American nations (BIA, 2018). BIA provides these duties and responsibilities for Native American nations that do not currently have their own tribal police departments. In addition, they oversee the departments that have tribal police departments. However, in some instances, these nations are primarily responsible for their own rules and regulations, including their own criminal justice system, with no interference from the U.S. government. As well, the Office of Justice Services is responsible for the enforcement sector within most Native American nations.

It is also important to know a little history about the implementation of Native American tribal police forces. L. Edward Wells and David Falcone (2008) conducted a study titled "Tribal Policing on American Indian Reservations." The purpose of the study was to explore the basic characteristics of Native American police forces at the beginning of the 21st century. The authors pointed out that three major accomplishments led to the implementation of this type of police force: The first was the Major Crime Act 1885; the second was the passage of the Public Law 83-280 (PL-280) in 1953; and the third was the passage of the Indian Self-Determination and Education Assistance Act in 1975 (Public Law-93-683) [2]). The Major Crimes Act of 1885 designated certain crimes under the jurisdiction of the federal government if committed by a Native American within its territory. This act, which was very controversial, is still in place. Public Law 83-280 designates authority to certain states that may take over an investigation of certain crimes committed within Native American territories. This last initiative gives authority to the head of the Department of the Interior and the head of the Education, Health, and Welfare Department to enter into agreements with Native American tribes for the disbursement of grants, financial benefits, and other benefits to federally recognized tribes (BIA, 2018).

In a nutshell, the federal government can still sponsor these tribal police agencies and is largely responsible for their operation even though they may have minimal say in their operations. These contracts can be debatable at times; however, certain laws and regulations are in place to ensure a collaborative initiative exists between the federal government and Native American nations' police departments.

Private Security Firms and Personnel

The private security industry has exploded over the past decades. Professor Robert McCrie (2017), a security operations management expert from the Department of Security, Fire, and Emergency at John Jay College of Criminal Justice, noted in his publication, "Private Security Services Regulations in the United States Today," that after the tragic events of September 11, 2001 and the ensuing war on terrorism, private security industries are in high demand. **Private security** is also essential and can be cost effective. It is important to present a working definition of the private security sector and what it entails. The author explained two distinct definitions for private security. The first is the initial definition, which is "private people protecting private property." Currently, the most favorable meaning for private security is "protection of assets from loss" (McCrie, 2017). The author further elaborated on the type of assets private security firms protect, which encompass anything and everything including people, places, items, merchandize, service, employees, personnel, cash, raw materials—anything that falls within the designated agency's purview.

Another publication, titled "The Bureau of Justice Statistics Statisticians," by Lynn Langton and Brian Reaves, illustrated detailed discussions on private security. This project, managed by Kevin Strom, Marcus Berzofsky, Bonnie Shook-Sa, Kelle Barrick, Crystal Daye, Nicole Horstmann, and Susan Kinsey (2010) and titled "The Private Security Industry: A Review of the Definitions, Available Data Sources, and Paths Moving Forward" presents a holistic understanding of what private security agencies entail. These experts carefully compiled this review to explore the definition of private security and the major components of its intricacies. Strom and colleagues (2010) utilized a definition from the American Society for Industrial Security (ASIS) stating that private security is the nongovernmental, private-sector practice of protecting people, property, and information, conducting investigations, and safeguarding an organization's assets (ASIS International, 2009). The review further noted that private security entails the following sectors and initiatives:

- Physical security
- Personnel security
- Investigations
- Loss prevention
- Information systems security
- Risk management
- Legal aspects
- Emergency and contingency planning
- Fire protection
- Crisis management
- Disaster management
- Counterterrorism
- Executive protection
- Violence in the workplace
- Crime prevention
- Crime prevention through environmental design (CPTED)
- Security architecture and engineering (Strom et. al, 2010)

Both presentations accurately define private security. This sector is essential and helps the public and private sectors assure public safety. In addition, private security can access information from various hard-to-reach private sources. These private sources also hesitate to collaborate with governmental law enforcement agencies. Consequently, private security agencies are useful and necessary when collaborating with the United States criminal justice system.

Rank Structure

For the purpose of simplicity and to avoid redundancy, the concepts span of control, duties and responsibilities, and leadership in policing appear collectively in this section under rank structure. Police officers have varying perceptions of rank structure in policing. Some officers believe their designated agencies have too much power (high ranking) whereas others believe their agencies have too little power (low ranking). Low ranking can hinder the police officer's potential for growth within the ranks. Some community leaders have voiced their opinions that too many ranks within a law enforcement organization can hinder the relationship between the agency and the community because higher-ranking officials are far less likely to interact with their community members. Conversely, others believe higher-ranking officers have more time and resources to attend and participate in community-related events than patrol officers.

This section will cover the rank structure to include the span of control and duties and responsibilities of each rank. Examining the leading police affiliated website PoliceOne.com provides practical knowledge of the meaning and background behind the rank structure. This website is one of the leading law enforcement initiatives in the United States. It provides officers with coverage of breaking news, expert analysis on law enforcement topics, latest career opportunities, fallen officers, product research, help with grants, and online training and learning management (PoliceOne.com, 2018). PoliceOne.com confirmed that the ranking system among law enforcement agencies vary. However, there is a general structure based on the military structure ranking system (see figure 4.7). Most agencies require their officers to serve a minimum of 2 to 4 years at a certain rank to apply for promotion to a higher rank. For instance, a police agency would require a patrol officer to have 4 years of experience prior to applying for a sergeant's position. The process may include a written exam or oral exam, and sometimes an interview with the superior officer in charge (chief, commissioner, sheriff) or designee. A general description of a typical law enforcement agency's ranking structure is as follows:

- Officer
- Corporal
- Detective
- Sergeant
- First sergeant (in some jurisdictions)
- Lieutenant (first and second in some jurisdictions)
- Captain
- Major
- Deputy chief or deputy head
- Assistant chief
- Chief/commissioner/colonel/sheriff

This similar ranking order exists within sheriff's agencies as well with the sheriff as the superior ranking official.

In order to best define rank structure, William R. King (2003), from the Criminal Justice Program at Bowling Green State University, proposed that the literature, "Bending Granite Revisited: The Command Rank Structure of American Police Organizations" provides a scholarly definition. **Rank structure** is the command rank structure of American police organizations, which is also called the chain of command. The formal authoritative format consists of layers in which authorities relegate certain individuals to a structural layer in the top-to-bottom order. The author further presented that rank structures in law enforcement agencies are primarily shown as an organizational chart. The **horizontal** format depicts the number and size of the agency, the specialization units, and how tasks are broken down. The **vertical** element covers the five major sectors: skills, authority, rewards, status, and seniority (King, 2003). See the example that follows of a police department's organizational chart.

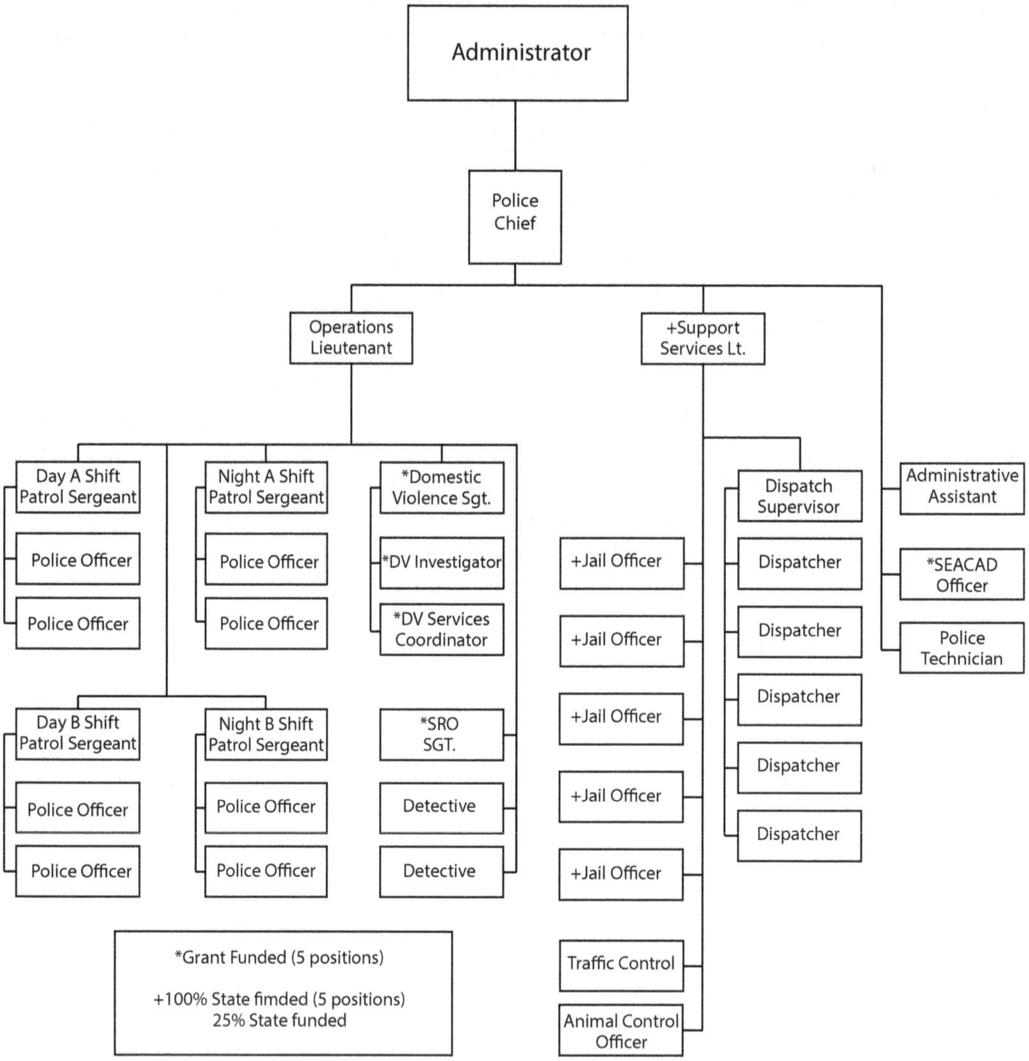

Figure 4.7 Example of a simple law enforcement organizational chart.

Source: City and Borough of Sitka (2005)

Span of Control

What is the span of control? Now that the concept of rank structure of law enforcement agencies is clear, knowing the meaning of the span of control is essential. According to Walker and Katz (2018), the concept of the span of control explains the supervisor's assigned authority allowing him or her to supervise a limited number of subordinates. For example, a police or sheriff sergeant is assigned to a squad or platoon of about 10 to 20 officers depending on the size of the agency. A squad or platoon is the group of officers who are assigned to a specific shift or unit. The sergeant has the span of control over the officers assigned to the squad or platoon.

Most agencies follow a three-shift schedule to provide coverage for 24-hour community protection. The three most common shifts are the day shift, the evening shift, and the midnight shift.

The day shift normally covers time periods from 6:00 a.m. or 7:00 a.m. to 4:00 p.m. or 5:00 p.m. depending on the jurisdiction and the number of hours they allow their officers to work per day. Eight hours, 10 hours, and 12 hours are the most common shift hours. The evening shifts covers from 3:00 p.m. or 4:00 p.m. to 1:00 a.m. or 2:00 a.m. The midnight shift covers from 8:00 p.m. or 9:00 p.m. to 6:00 a.m. or 7:00 a.m., again depending on the agency. Some agencies have rotating shifts where officers will work a day shift for a week and go on break and then upon returning to work, an evening shift. Then after another break, the officers would work a midnight shift. In short, they are exposed to all shifts on a monthly basis. . The positive notion to a rotating shift is that it exposes the officer to the diversity of the varied calls for service within each shift. However, current research has shown that this type of scheduling can negatively impact an officer's productivity and health in later years.

Duties and Responsibilities

This section will discuss the duties and responsibilities for each rank within the law enforcement agency. As mentioned, a general description of a typical law enforcement agency's ranking structure amongst mainly police departments, sheriff's departments, and state police agencies consists of **officer, corporal, detective, sergeant, first sergeant (in some jurisdictions), lieutenant (first and second in some jurisdictions), captain, major, deputy chief or deputy head, assistant chief, and chief/commissioner/colonel/sheriff**. The **police officer**, **deputy**, or **trooper** is the most common level of officer in most jurisdictions. These agents are responsible for enforcing rules and regulations, assigning traffic violations, preventing crime, participating in community initiatives, patrolling, and performing other duties as assigned. The **corporal** position only exists in some jurisdictions. It has some authority, mainly associated with seniority for most jurisdictions. This position may be coupled with an increase in pay for some jurisdictions, whereas in others, it would only count as an increase in status and seniority grade. The **detective** position is sometimes considered an authority status position. In some agencies, the detective position is higher in the hierarchy than a regular police officer. Some agencies have placed the detective position at the same level as their officers, eliminating the rank difference between the two.

The detective is a specialized officer who is trained to investigate specific types of crimes. Most detectives work in plain clothes and only wear department uniforms when attending court or other professional events. There are various types of detectives. Some are part of the street crimes unit and are classified as robbery and theft detectives. Others identify as crimes against children detectives. Detectives are trained in their specific disciplines and can assume major criminal investigations. They also have all the rights and duties of an officer. However, their primary duties and responsibilities are more preventative and reactive (for example, street crimes suppression units, robberies, etc.) and consist of criminal investigations and prosecuting cases in court.

The **sergeant** position comes with a lot of responsibility and is considered a first-line supervisor. It is the most demanding supervisory position in many agencies. Sergeants are responsible for a squad or platoon—mostly, a group of officers in a bureau or section such as the violent crimes unit within an agency. Sergeants are responsible for counseling, training, conducting performance appraisals, serving as liaisons between officers and upper management, and assuming command over major scenes while coordinating resources and personnel. Usually, officers are required to have a minimum of 2 to 4 years of experience to apply for a sergeant's position. The process includes a written or oral exam, participation in a scenario, and an interview with the superior authority in charge.

The **first sergeant** position is held in a few jurisdictions. Some jurisdictions have eliminated this position since it is similar to the sergeant's duties and responsibilities. The only difference is that the first sergeant performs the sergeant's performance evaluation and also acts as a liaison between the sergeant and upper management. First sergeants sometimes hold administrative positions as well, depending on the agency.

The **lieutenant** position is somewhat of an administrative position in most larger municipal agencies. In smaller agencies, the lieutenant has the same authority as a police officer and is considered a working supervisor. Lieutenants answer calls for service, train, conduct evaluations for their subordinates, and also represent members when interacting with upper management. The lieutenants also serve on various committees (finance, use of force, budget, operations, equipment, shift and resource allocations, etc.), investigate civilian complaints about officer behavior or officer complaints against department members, and help the captains operate an entire district, station, or precinct. Additionally, in some agencies lieutenants are responsible for managing and coordinating all efforts and resources and for conducting mutual aid systems during incident command for large-scale incidents. They also supervise sergeants and are sometimes in charge of an entire bureau. This position also requires at least 2 to 3 years of first-line supervisor experience depending on the agency. The exam or testing required to become a lieutenant includes written tests, participating in community events, oral interviews, and interviews with upper management staff. First and second lieutenants are rare, as most departments have eliminated this position due to its redundancy of the original lieutenant's position.

The **captain** position is one of the most administratively demanding positions within an agency because this position heads and manages an entire district, division, or precinct. Captains are responsible for managing the district's budget, represent the agency in community meetings in place of the chief/commissioner/colonel/sheriff, and are also responsible for officers, sergeants, and lieutenants adhering to departmental policies and procedures. In some agencies, this position is the last and final position that can be attained through a promotional process (written exam, various scenario-based exercises, a submission of package that includes training, accomplishments, educational achievements, awards, skills, resourcefulness, etc.). The head of an agency typically appoint positions above a captain. Last, a captain's responsibilities can also include supervising certain civilian employees and hiring specialized civilian personnel.

The **major** mainly supervises the captains and ensures their districts, precincts, or bureaus are running smoothly. The major can also represent the chief, commissioner, colonel, or sheriff at community gatherings and have responsibility for other designated duties as assigned. Majors are also in charge of completing the captain's performance evaluation. This head of an agency usually appoints a candidate to this position.

The next position according to the **American police hierarchy** is the **deputy chief or deputy head**. This position, depending on the agency, is viewed as the third from the head of the agency. In some agencies, it's actually the second from the head. Deputy chiefs or deputy heads are responsible for overseeing majors and sometimes an entire bureau is under their purview. The agency head also usually appoints a person to this position.

Depending on the agency, the **assistant chief or assistant head** is second in charge from the head of the agency. This person acts in place of the head, and some have signature authority if the head of the agency is unavailable. The city, town, or municipal board can also appoint an individual to the assistant chief or assistant head position. The agency head can appoint a person to this position as well. The assistant chief or assistant head can act as an interim head in times of unexpected strife such as death, retirement, or termination of the agency head.

The top of the food chain is the head of the agency, which is typically a **chief of police**, a **sheriff**, a **commissioner**, or a **colonel**. These individuals have a wide array of duties and responsibilities. They are the highest-ranking officers in an agency. They have the final say when hiring officers, making final recommendations regarding officer disciplinary actions, managing the agency's budget and financial initiatives, representing the agency, and providing reports to the community, citizens, local, state, or municipal governmental bodies. The majority of these highest-ranking officers often report to the mayor. The agency head prepares a comprehensive report for the governmental body and is responsible for making promotions, sometimes based on senior staff. Other times, the agency heads promote employees based on their perceptions of the officer. The agency head is also responsible for developing various policies, amending policies, and updating policies and procedures. The local, state, or municipal government often appoints people into these high-ranking positions. With regards to a sheriff, they are primarily elected and only serve a designated term as allotted. Police chiefs can stay in their positions as long as they please, or according to the guidelines outlining retirement age of the designated state and county.

Considering the hierarchy discussed, how much leadership is necessary to effectively run an agency and align its principles with one's community relations and visions? The next section talks about leadership in policing.

Leadership in Policing

How much leadership is too much leadership from the community's perspective? Most agencies are eliminating the typical leadership mentality and portraying an organization where all officers appear equal to their community members. For instance, most agencies would normally require their senior-level officers, from lieutenant to the head of the agency, to wear a white uniform decorated with stripes, bars, and other impressive brass symbols to distinguish their status from the rank and file. This system demonstrates a clear distinction between the officers, first-line supervisors, and the senior staff officers. The Prince William County Police Department in Virginia is one of those agencies that has eliminated the white shirt requirements. Now, all levels and ranks of officers including the chief of police wear the same color of shirt. The stripes and brass are still worn to designate rank within its members, however. Therefore, community members unfamiliar with the rank structure view every officer as a police officer of the same rank. County citizens have viewed this transition as positive.

Before delving deeper into discussion about leadership in policing, it is important to have an accurate definition of leadership. According to the International Association of Chiefs of Police (IACP, 2006), "[L]eadership is the process of influencing human behavior to achieve organizational goals that serve the public, while developing individuals, teams and the organization for future service" (p. 35). To gain a holistic understanding of leadership in policing, it is important to read the literature presented by major scholars regarding this subject. Joseph A. Schafer (2010) from the Department of Criminology and Criminal Justice at Southern Illinois University Carbondale, presented a study titled "Effective Leaders and Leadership in Policing: Traits, Assessment, Development, and Expansion." He distributed surveys to over 1,000 police supervisors participating in the FBI National Academy program, which is open to all police department mid- and upper-level supervisors. This program is one of the most illustrious, informative, and rigorous leadership programs for police managers. Those who graduate from this program feel a sense of accomplishment. Mr. Schafer measured topics such as leader effectiveness, leader development, and assessment of leadership efficacy. The overall findings revealed traits and habits that may be influential factors in personality trait leadership styles. Many participants also noted that hands-on experiences during leadership training are more effective than online, reading, and other leadership learning methods. Last, the majority of participants perceived mentoring and guided experiences as essential in developing effective leaders (Schafer, 2010).

Schafer (2009) presented a previous study titled "Developing Effective Leadership in Policing: Perils, Pitfalls, and Paths Forward." He further noted that insufficient leadership in a police organization can be detrimental to the organization and its personnel (Schafer, 2009). This study used a set of sample participants from the FBI National Academy attendees who consisted of mostly mid- and upper-level police executives. Schafer surveyed the attendees about their experiences and perceptions of leadership. The overarching findings demonstrated that leadership skills are developed through three major methods: **education**, **experience**, and **mentorship** (Schafer, 2009). The author's assessment is considered accurate since current and previous research in leadership in policing echoed these three concepts.

Education is also critical to become a successful and effective police officer. Leaders should educate themselves to stay current with the changing times. Experience also comes with leadership. A 10- to 20-year veteran officer may not have any rank or status; however, he or she would most likely possess the same leadership qualities as any official leader within the police force. These officers' experiences are invaluable and several younger officers are drawn to them for guidance and mentoring. Mentorship, as mentioned earlier in the chapter, is another key method used to develop effective leaders. Some police executives have taken it upon themselves to be more involved in the regular officers' lives. This involvement includes caring for them, riding along with them, interacting with them at roll calls, inviting them out to unplanned and informal lunches, maintaining open-door policies, and encouraging informal conversation between the officers and their police executives. These efforts have proven to increase respect and honesty and to foster leadership within many police agencies. An example can be seen with the Prince William County Police Department where the deputy chief or other high-ranking officials will randomly ride along with a patrol officer to have an open and honest conversation. Although higher-ranking officers view these interactions as informal, some officers perceive these interactions as negative and feel as though they are being watched. However, the majority of lower-ranking police officers have taken advantage of these interactions and voiced their opinions about various departmental issues. Other agencies have started similar interactions between their senior and junior police officers.

Box 4.1 Perception Versus Reality

There is a certain perception that all federal agencies can just swoop in and take over any investigations from county, municipal, or state agencies. While this concept has some merit, there are certain federal guidelines and code sections in place that federal agencies must follow to assume an investigation. For instance, the Federal Bureau of Investigations (FBI) has specific federal authority to investigate violations of congressional assassinations, kidnapping, and assault (Title 18, U.S. Code, Section 351) (FBI, 2018a). Furthermore, the FBI has jurisdiction over limited state offenses including bank robberies, killing state law enforcement officers (28 U.S.C. § 540), crimes against interstate travelers (28 U.S.C. § 540A0), and serial killers (28 U.S.C. §540B) (FBI, 2018a). In addition, the FBI is also responsible for investigating most federal crimes that are not already assigned to another federal agency. The majority of the federal statute violations fall under the FBI's authority. Keeping these circumstances in mind, there is a positive relationship and partnership between most county, municipal, and state agencies that is necessary to work collectively toward reducing crimes against the United States. Police agencies are the first responders; they are more likely to come face to face with an immediate threat against the United States than the federal agencies. As a result of the positive partnership between these agencies and the federal government, it is possible to share information clearly and diplomatically.

Divisions and Bureaus Within a Police Agency

After a thorough look at the nation's law enforcement agencies, the similarities and differences between each department became apparent. Primarily, their organizational structures are very similar and include office of the chief, criminal investigations, patrol or operations bureau or division, support services bureau or division, traffic administration, and the animal control bureau. Larger municipalities have more complex structures and divisions; however, smaller agencies operate within the simple divisions listed. Under the rank structure section graphic that appeared earlier in this text (figure 4.7), police organizational charts portrayed the commonalities of these operations. It is important for each agency to have a designated division or bureau as they cater to various societal, economical, technological, crime prevention, and criminalistics initiatives. The next section explains the duties and responsibilities of these sections and bureaus that are part of a law enforcement agency. It is important to note that the divisions described are the ordinary divisions within most law enforcement agencies; the majority of these have variances in their names and titles.

Office of the Chief

The office of the Chief is also sometimes called the Commissioner's office depending on the jurisdiction. This office primarily houses the chief or commissioner and several other units including internal affairs, fiscal and facility management services, public information, a chaplain program, accreditation and policy, planning and research, and information technology services. This office also receives reports of police misconduct and police commendations. Once a complaint is received, it is forwarded to the department's Internal Affairs unit, who is then responsible for investigating officer misconduct. Some agencies use only sworn supervisors to investigate other officers' misconduct. Some larger agencies include both sworn supervisors and community members on the board to review and make recommendations regarding a complaint. Some agencies only use non-voting or non-decision-making community members. Others have full voting and decision-making community members on the review board during the officer misconduct complaint process.

Criminal Investigations

The criminal investigations division, for the majority of the police departments, houses the following bureaus: special investigations bureau, violent crimes bureau, special victim services bureau, and property crimes bureau. The special investigations bureau includes the following units: narcotics task force, street crimes unit, gang units, and robbery suppression units. The violent crimes bureau handles robbery, homicide, intelligence, and crime analysis. The special victims' bureau covers the following types of investigations: physical abuse, abuse of special victims including children, the elderly (physical, sexual, etc.), and the school resource officers' unit. The property crimes bureau covers various types of property crimes such as burglaries, thefts, fraud, and other white-collar crimes. Depending on the agency, some also place their forensic services bureau under this section.

Patrol Division

The patrol division, sometimes referred to as the operations bureau, houses several units as well. This arrangement may vary per jurisdiction. Regardless, here are the major units within this bureau: patrol squads or platoons, special operations including crash or accident, K-9, traffic or motor, tactical training and response (unit) (TTRU), civil disturbance, honor guard, patrol, search and rescue, community

Box 4.2 Sergeant Leandro Pena

Figure 4.8 Leandro Pena

Most police departments are comprised of an Operations Division, which consists of officers on patrol, and a Criminal Investigation Division. During my 15 years as a law enforcement officer in the state of Virginia, I had the opportunity to work in both divisions. I spent my first 12 years as a midnight patrol officer and 2 years as a Special Victims Unit (SVU) detective within the Criminal Investigation Division. I am currently a sergeant working the midnight shift on patrol.

In thinking about it, I must say that the 2 years that I spent as a criminal investigator have been the most rewarding in my law enforcement career thus far. As a detective, I had the opportunity to work in a unique and elite unit, which helped victims of serious crimes. There is a sense of pride and accomplishment being able to put people who intentionally commit crimes against minors behind bars and hold them accountable for their improper actions.

A lot of people have the idea that solving a crime as a detective is as easy and simple as you see on tv. However, the reality is that it takes a lot of time, dedication, hard work, and perseverance to solve a crime. A criminal investigator faces different twists and challenges with every case that is assigned to him or her. Some challenges are easy to overcome; however, others are more difficult. For example, some of the challenges that I faced during my tenure as a criminal investigator were lack of DNA evidence, language barriers, and uncooperative family members. These are struggles that criminal investigators have to deal with on a somewhat regular basis.

In order to be a good criminal investigator, you need to have a profound understanding of the victim, the offender, and the crime that has been committed. An investigator needs to be able to read between the lines, determine when either the alleged victim or the offender is lying, and use evidence to assist in solving crimes. During an investigation, it is important for a criminal investigator to be fair and unbiased. It is easy to jump to conclusions or form personal opinions about a given case, but a good investigator will thoroughly evaluate and consider all factors in order to properly solve cases. Furthermore, it is critical for a criminal investigator to be humble, to ask for help when needed, and to rely on other criminal investigators' knowledge and expertise in order to solve cases and to accomplish the task at hand. Team work is extremely important when it comes to working on more complicated, complex cases. Criminal investigators also need to have good time and case management skills. A well-trained and knowledgeable criminal investigator knows how to prioritize incoming cases and keeps up with his or her assigned cases. This is very important because if you fall behind on your cases, you will not be conducting a thorough criminal investigation because you will lack the time to do so.

As a criminal investigator, one of the most difficult challenges for me was learning how to not bring the work home with me. This is due to the fact that there are cases that will stay with you for a long time, embedded in your memory. Some cases that hit too close to home or that are extremely severe are hard to forget. Certain cases will make you wonder why bad things happen to good people. Other cases have the potential to give you nightmares or you may encounter difficulty sleeping because you cannot comprehend the pain and suffering that some of the victims went through. One of the most difficult things that I had to experience as a criminal investigator was witnessing the autopsy of a 5-month-old baby who was accidentally smothered to death by his mother while sleeping. For quite some time after I witnessed that, I remember that I would close my eyes and hear the sound of the chainsaw cutting into the baby's skull in order to perform the autopsy. This image did not affect my job or the way I handled my cases, but nothing can mentally prepare you for that. After my shift had ended that day, I remembered going home and holding my son really close to my chest and telling him that I love him. At that time, my son was about the same age as the baby who had died. This is just an example that highlights how being a criminal investigator is a challenging profession at times.

However, despite having to witness difficult things at times, criminal investigations are a vital and crucial part of any police department. Criminal investigators work long hours and, in many instances, sacrifice time away from their families in order to bring closure to the victims' families. A good criminal investigator takes pride in his or her work and strives to do what is needed to solve cases. It's not an easy job, but it's an honorable one, and I would be a detective again in a heartbeat.

relations, court liaison, LGBTQ+ liaison, hostage negotiation, crisis intervention, marine, SWAT, auxiliary, crossing guard, and crime prevention. Some agencies place their animal control section under this division since these officers perform a number of patrol functions during their tour of duty. The patrol division is often viewed as the foundation and backbone of policing since these are naturally the first responders to every situation. They encounter a myriad of incidents and are viewed as proactive, preventative, and responsive to various calls for service. As a first responder, officers tend to move laterally and vertically through the department's ranks due to acquiring a wealth of information and dealing with all sorts of scenarios. Every officer starts from patrol to properly prepare for other sections and divisions inside or outside the agency.

Figure 4.9 Getting ready for patrol

Support Services: Civilian Employees

The support services bureau is the brunt of civilian employees within a law enforcement agency. This bureau entails the following units: **police personnel**, **employee health**, **public safety communications**, **justice academy**, **records**, **evidence and support**, **fleet management**, and **forensics**.

The police personnel unit is responsible for hiring, recruiting, selecting, polygraphing, testing, checking backgrounds, coordinating volunteers, career development, promotional testing, and managing the intern program.

The employee health unit is responsible for the medical and physical examination of all employees including recruits and candidates experiencing the selection process.

The public safety and communications section has various call takers, report takers, police radio dispatchers, and several other civilian personnel.

The justice academy is responsible for both in-service training for officers, recruit training, and outside training programs for other local, state, and federal agencies (firearms, defensive driving, use of force simulations, physical training in cardio, weights, aerobics, defensive tactics, etc.).

The records section hosts all the police reports the officers and other report takers record through the online reporting system. The records section also maintains records relating to traffic summons, accidents reports, parking tickets, and so on.

The evidence and support unit primarily houses all the police evidence seized, acquired, or obtained from various means including crime commission, searches and seizures, safe keeping, and storing. This section also is responsible for notifying officers regarding the dates and outcomes of their seized evidence examinations. Once approved, the majority of the seized evidence is auctioned or released back to the owner under certain circumstances.

Support services has a high number of civilian-trained evidence technicians as well. Fleet management is the section of the agency responsible for acquiring new police, equipped vehicles, maintaining these vehicles, trading these vehicles, and decorating and storing these vehicles for departmental use.

The forensic unit is responsible for all digital, chemical, physical, visible, and invisible processing of forensic evidence using various processes such as fingerprinting, printing photographs, and identifying various types of methods. This section also has high number of civilian employees who are trained to handle, process, document, and recover evidential materials.

Civilian employees are essential to law enforcement organizations because they perform a number of tasks, bring a new set of expertise, and have access to untapped resources that classical police officers cannot do or do not possess. Some of the most common civilian positions within a law enforcement agency are police dispatchers, police call takers, police evidence technicians, crime scene analysists, crime analysts, fiscal and technical analysts, administrative assistants, record keepers, records maintenance employees, data-entry personnel, and police service aids. In almost every law enforcement agency, civilian employees are present to support the duties and responsibilities of the agency. These individuals are thoroughly vetted for their positions because they often work with sensitive information. Therefore, their promise of confidentiality is critical. In addition, most agencies utilize civilian employees with IT, computer technology, crime mapping and intelligence, research and planning, media relations, and community relations initiatives experience. These professionals are sometimes hired to manage or direct certain sections or units such as fiscal and financial services within these agencies. Current research shows that law enforcement agencies that hire civilian employees have increased their productivity and efficiency. One of the only obstacles in hiring civilian employees is that the turnover rates can be exponentially higher. Highly qualified civilian employees tend to migrate from one agency to the other in search of new opportunities. The majority of local and state agencies lose their civilian employees to federal agencies where there's promise of more pay and longer list of benefits. Another factor may be the certain tensions that exist between officers and civilian employees. Officers might not want to take instructions or suggestions from civilian employees, causing stress on both parties. On the other hand, some civilian employees often feel that officers do not value their input. However, both civilian employees and officers bring a myriad of experiences, expertise, and support to the organizational goal and mission. Some agencies have developed valuable organizational structures where collaboration between the two groups has proven beneficial.

Traffic Administration

Depending on the agency, some may have the traffic division as a standalone section whereas others will incorporate it under the patrol or operations bureau. For agencies that have traffic administration as a standalone section, they are typically designated to enforce traffic violations through various means such as aircraft, speed traps, unmarked or unidentifiable police vehicles, motor units, checkpoints, DUI enforcement, parking violations, and other speeding- or traffic-related complaints or issues.

Furthermore, some agencies may also have an accident investigation unit. This unit is responsible for investigating serious or fatal crashes within the designated jurisdiction. They also provide support to state agencies in commercial vehicle inspections at weigh stations. The traffic administration in a law enforcement organization is considered one of the busiest foundational structures as its functions continue to grow to meet societal traffic needs.

Animal Control Bureau

Some agencies have an animal control unit under their operations bureau. Animal Control Bureaus investigate crimes against animals, cruelty laws, capturing and impounding animals, licensing, leash, bites, and dangerous animals. They mainly care for stray animals or other abandoned animals, educate the community about animal laws and policies, and maintain the animal shelter. The sworn animal control officers can enforce laws related to animal violation, licensing, leash, bite, dangerous animals, and any other animal-related laws and policies. These officers can also prepare detailed animal reports for court use or record-keeping purposes.

Animal law is extremely complex. There are various guidelines governing animal law that range from international and federal laws to municipal law. International laws are protected by localized national law enforcement groups and focus on international concerns such as illegal animal trade associated with organized crime. Illegal animal trafficking is one of the largest and most lucrative illegal activities in the world (Convention on International Trade in Endangered Species).

Federal law typically governs wildlife (e.g., the Endangered Species Act). Federal agencies such as the U.S. Department of Game and Inland Fisheries, the United States Department of Agriculture, and the Animal and Plant Health Inspection Service fall under this umbrella. Recently, animal cruelty has become felonious in 46 out of 50 states and is tracked by the FBI.

State animal law often intersects with local or municipal animal law. Usually, state laws govern non-migratory wildlife species or a species within the state. These laws are most frequently associated with gaming, which the conservation police protects in association with the National Park Service or Department of Game and Inland Fisheries.

In some cases, state police or a local law enforcement agency may be tasked with enforcing animal laws. Some jurisdictions have designated animal control officers who may be civilian investigators or sworn law enforcement officers with animal-specific authority. While deputies, police officers, and federal agents may be responsible for enforcing animal laws in addition to their regular duties, designated animal control officers employed by an outside private or municipal agency (even sworn officers) may only enforce animal law. (Personal communication, Krista Shires, January 2nd, 2018).

Chapter Summary

Why are there so many law enforcement agencies in the United States? Do we need that many? This chapter presented the various levels of law enforcement agencies from county, local, state, to federal. Each agency was clearly defined and their unique duties and responsibilities were demonstrated. This chapter discussed the distinction between private security and police, while highlighting key concepts to enhance the reader's understanding of the essential reasons for using private security agencies to protect certain people and properties. The main concept of private security is private people protecting people, places, and properties. The concept of rank structure was also illustrated, with a clear definition as well as an explanation of the duties, responsibilities, and leadership in policing. Also discussed was the concept of developing and sustaining effective leadership, which is imperative in policing. A leader who cannot relate to his or her employees is not fulfilling the mission and goals of the organization. Finally, the divisions and bureaus within a police agency were described, including various offices such as the office of the chief, criminal investigations, patrol division, support services, traffic administration, and the animal control bureau. Each division and bureau was clearly identified and documented to illustrate a clear description of these units and what they entail.

Discussion Questions

1. All the divisions of a law enforcement agency are vital and play a dynamic role in accomplishing the agency's missions and goals. From your reading, which division is considered the backbone and foundation of policing? State two reasons why this division is considered as such.

2. List and describe two major characteristics of an effective police leader. Provide examples from neighboring law enforcement agencies.

3. Provide two major advantages private security officers have over police officers when assigned to patrol or work at private establishments such as apartment complexes.

4. What is a mutual aid system? Provide two concise examples from neighboring jurisdictions where this concept is widely utilized.

5. List and discuss two major reasons why law enforcement agencies employ civilian employees. In addition, discuss the major disadvantages agencies face when employing civilian employees.

References

ASIS International. (2009). *International glossary of security terms.* Retrieved from https://www.ncjrs.gov/pdffiles1/bjs/grants/232781.pdf

Brown, L. P. (1978). The role of the sheriff. In A. W. Cohn (Ed.), *The future of policing* (pp. 227–228). Thousand Oaks, CA: SAGE.

Bureau of Alcohol, Tobacco, Firearms, and Explosives (2018). *About.* Retrieved from https://www.atf.gov/about

Bureau of India Affairs (2018). *About.* Retrieved from http://www.bia.gov/about-us

Bureau of Justice Statistics (BJS). (2018a). *Local police.* Retrieved from https://www.bjs.gov/index.cfm?ty=tp&tid=7

Bureau of Justice Statistics (BJS). (2018b). *Federal law enforcement.* Retrieved from https://www.bjs.gov/index.cfm?ty=tp&tid=74

Bureau of Justice Statistics (BJS). (2018c). *Campus law enforcement.* Retrieved from https://www.bjs.gov/index.cfm?ty=tp&tid=76

City and Borough of Sitka. (2005). *Police organizational chart.* Retrieved from http://sitkapd.com/PoliceOrganizational-Chart.html

Convention on International Trade in Endangered Species of Wild Fauna and Flora. (n.d.). Retrieved March 03, 2018, from https://cites.org/prog/iccwc.php/Wildlife-Crime

Drug Enforcement Administration (DEA). (2018). *DEA Fact sheet.* Retrieved from https://www.dea.gov/about/mission.shtml

Federal Bureau of Investigations (FBI). (2018a). Where is the FBI's authority written down? Retrieved on from https://www.fbi.gov/about/faqs/where-is-the-fbis-authority-written-down

Federal Bureau of Investigations (FBI). (2018b). *About.* Retrieved from https://www.fbi.gov/about

Federal Emergency Management Agency (FEMA). (2017). *About the agency.* Retrieved from https://www.fema.gov/about-agency

Gelber, S. (1972). *The role of campus security in the college setting.* Washington, DC: U.S. Department of Justice. Retrieved from https://www.ncjrs.gov/pdffiles1/Digitization/8966NCJRS.pdf

International Association of Chiefs of Police (IACP). (2006). *Developing leaders in police organizations.* Retrieved from https://cops.usdoj.gov/pdf/workshops/friday/HalsteadHesser.pdf

Jenkins, S., & Goodman, M. (2015), "He's one of ours': A case study of a campus response to crisis. *Journal of Contingencies and Crisis Management, 23*(4), 201–209.

King, W. R. (2003). Bending granite revisited: The command rank structure of American police organizations. *Policing: An International Journal of Police Strategies & Management,* 26(2), 208–230. doi:10.1108/13639510310475732

McCrie, R. (2017). Private security services regulations in the United States today. *International Journal of Comparative & Applied Criminal Justice, 41*(4), 287–304. doi:10.1080/01924036.2017.1364281

Park Ranger. (2018). Park Rangers resources. Retrieved from https://www.parkrangeredu.org/

PoliceOne.com. (2018). *Our mission.* Retrieved from https://www.policeone.com/about/?pgtype=article&region=footer

Reaves, B. (2015). *Local police departments, 2013: Personnel, policies, and practices.* U.S. Department of Justice, Officer of Justice Programs-Bureau of Justice Statistics. Retrieved from https://www.bjs.gov/content/pub/pdf/lpd13ppp.pdf

Schafer, J. A. (2009). Developing effective leadership in policing: Perils, pitfalls, and paths forward. *Policing: An International Journal, 32*(2), 238–260.

Schafer, J. A. (2010). Effective leaders and leadership in policing: Traits, assessment, development, and expansion. *Policing: An International Journal, 33*(4), 644–663.

Strom, K., Berzofsky, M., Shook-Sa, B., Barrick, K., Daye, C., Horstmann, N., & Kinsey, S. (2010). *The private security industry: A review of the definitions, available data sources, and paths moving forward.* Retrieved from https://www.ncjrs.gov/pdffiles1/bjs/grants/232781.pdf

Transportation Security Administration. (2018). *Mission.* Retrieved from https://www.tsa.gov/about/tsa-mission

U.S. Coast Guard (2018). Historian's office. Retrieved from https://www.history.uscg.mil/home/about-us/ U.S. Customs and Border Protection. (2016). *About CBP.* Retrieved from https://www.cbp.gov/about

U.S. Department of the Interior. (2018). *Overview.* Retrieved from https://www.bia.gov/bia/ojs

U.S. Immigration and Customs Enforcement. (2017). *Who we are.* Retrieved from https://www.ice.gov/about

U.S. Marshals Service (2018). *Fact sheet.* Retrieved from https://www.usmarshals.gov/duties/factsheets/overview.pdf

U.S. Secret Service (2018). *Overview.* Retrieved from https://www.secretservice.gov/about/overview/

Walker, S. & Katz, C. (2018). *The police in America: An introduction* (9th ed.). New York, NY: McGraw-Hill Education.

Wells, E. L., & Falcone, D. N. (2008). Tribal policing on American Indian reservations. *Policing: An International Journal, 31*(4), 648–673.

Figure Credits

Fig. 4.1: Source: https://www.bjs.gov/content/pub/pdf/lpd13ppp.pdf.
Fig. 4.2: Source: https://www.bjs.gov/content/pub/pdf/lpd13ppp.pdf.
Fig. 4.3: Source: https://pxhere.com/en/photo/589505.
Fig. 4.4: Source: https://vimeo.com/262863707.
Fig. 4.5: Source: https://media.defense.gov/2007/May/14/2000490990/780/780/0/070511-N-7949W-031.JPG.
Fig. 4.6: Source: https://commons.wikimedia.org/wiki/File:US_Marshals_escorting_prisoner_in_court.png.
Fig. 4.7: Source: http://sitkapd.com/PoliceOrganizationalChart.html.
Fig. 4.8: Copyright © by Suzanne Mendez. Reprinted with permission.

CHAPTER FIVE

Police and Homeland Security

In this chapter, you will gain a thorough understanding of the partnership between police agencies and the Department of Homeland Security. Specifically, our discussion will focus on the initiation and implementation of the 287(g) policy that grants local and state officials the authority to enforce federal immigration laws and regulations. This chapter will also cover the advantages and disadvantages of the policy's implementation and counter-terrorism strategies (both domestic and international), while exploring the various intelligence strategies police departments and the Department of Homeland Security are utilizing to combat terrorism.

Learning Objectives

- Understand a brief history of the 287(g) program
- Understand the levels of partnership between the federal government and local and state agencies
- Examine the benefits and drawbacks of the 287(g) program implementation
- Provide feedback from various perspectives on the 287(g) program implementation
- Illustrate an accurate definition of the Department of Homeland Security
- Provide a detailed explanation of the meanings of terrorism, including domestic and international and cyber terrorism

Chapter Outline

A REAL-LIFE POLICE SCENARIO FOR DISCUSSION

from Chernoh Wurie's personal accounts

In the fall of 2007, I was sitting in a packed room with other police officers for a mandatory in-service training on the new implementation of the 287(g) program in my jurisdiction. The training was a requirement due to the program being implemented in my county; it basically gives local and state police officers the authority to investigate and enforce federal immigration violations.

As I sat back in my chair and digested all the new information about the 287(g) program implementation, I couldn't help the overwhelming feeling I was having as an immigrant myself. I listened to the training instructor and I felt conflicted that I—an immigrant from Africa—was being authorized to enforce federal immigration laws.

Soon after the implementation of the 287(g) program in my jurisdictional county, the immigrant community was becoming increasingly anxious and weary of police presence.

One night, I received a call at 11:30 to respond to a loud party call. Under the noise ordinance in the county, any loud party call after 10:00 p.m. is considered a noise violation.

Calls like this normally require two officers to respond. However, I was the first to arrive on the scene, and I slowly observed the situation before approaching the individuals who were playing the music. Over the radio, I acknowledged my arrival to the dispatcher and made sure my back-up officer was on the way. I observed two individuals sitting on the front porch listening to music and talking loudly. The individuals were of Hispanic origin (I pay keen attention to those who I encounter daily—regardless of race, sex, or national origin). I also perceived that it was a father and son having an evening-on-the-porch conversation, while consuming some alcoholic beverages.

As I approached, I turned my attention to the elder male and advised him, "Sir, I am here due to a noise complaint, would you mind turning your music—"

Before I could say "down," the older male lunged forward, presenting his green card, and throwing it at me. "I am not illegal; I am here legally, you have no right to come here and harass me and my family!"

I kept my calm demeanor and continued to advise the individual that I was not there to inquire on his residency status; I was merely there to keep the peace and to advise him to turn his music down. The individual got very agitated and confronted me, tightening his fists and lunging forward. He was also yelling profanities. At that point, I determined that the individual had been drinking and was being disorderly in public. I briefly advised him that he was under arrest and utilized my pepper spray to affect the arrest. I dispersed two good streams of spray, targeting the individual's face and chest. The individual refused to comply with my commands and retreated into his residence. I radioed in my actions, stating that I had just used chemical force on an individual, but that he had retreated into his residence. The back-up officer arrived. Collectively, we made the conscious decision to enter the residence (knowing we had an arrestee inside) and attempt to arrest the individual.

Upon entering the residence, we located the individual and tried to place him under arrest. He refused again and was pepper sprayed again. Next, his son, who was with him earlier on the porch, also intervened and joined in the commotion while we were arresting his father. Both the father and son were arrested and charged with assault and battery on a police officer and resisting arrest. During the incident, a pregnant female, who later turned out to be the daughter of the arrestee, had witnessed and videotaped the entire scene on her cell phone.

Upon transporting the individuals to the police substation for processing, I asked the elder male, "Why did you get so hostile with me when I was basically just asking you to turn your music down?"

The individual stated, "My friend, it's the new immigration policy; it's got everyone in my community scared and paranoid. We all think the police are out to get us and therefore we have to protect ourselves and our families."

I felt so conflicted hearing this as I transported the individuals to the local precinct for processing. The magistrate asked them how they plead; they both pleaded guilty and had to explain themselves. The magistrate turned to me and asked for my accounts of the incident. I relayed the accounts in concise detail. I also shared that I personally believed there was a greater issue here—a communications or perceptions barrier. The magistrate used his discretion, released both parties on their own recognizance, and issued them a court date. The outcome of the case was very simple; both parties were charged with very minor offenses and did not get any physical jail time. Both were thankful for the outcome and so was I.

As I replayed this scenario in my mind over and over, I could not stop thinking about the fact that I am also a foreigner. What makes me any different from the Spanish or Latino individuals I was arresting and encountering? I struggled with this implementation in its entirety and duration with my jurisdiction. I also modeled my doctoral studies based on this policy, as I saw the crucial need for a human experimental study. I noticed that due to the policy implementation, I found myself in numerous use-of-force scenarios with individuals from the Latino and Spanish community. I also noticed the desertion of houses and schools, a lack of cultural festivities within these communities, and also the fear of policing. I made it a point to study this further and examined the largest foreign population in my jurisdiction, which was the Salvadoran community. I conducted his doctoral dissertation titled, "Exploring the Lives of Salvadoran Families After the

Implementation of the Illegal Immigration Reform and Immigrant Responsibility Act of 1996 Section 287(g)." Upon completing this study, I earned my PhD, continued to work as a police officer, and became a voice in my community and beyond in easing the tensions that existed between the community and the police department in my new role as the police planner. Even though the 287(g) program is still in effect in various counties, it's being practiced minimally due to funding restrictions. I felt positive of my study and my role within this entire process. Because I have gone through several immigration interviews during my permanent residency and citizenship application processes, and although my experiences were very different, I can relate to every foreigner who has gone through these same hurdles.

Police and the Department of Homeland Security

Prior to the tragic events of September 11, 2001, police agencies have had some minor interactions and mutual aid agreements with federal agencies. However, after the events of September 11, 2001, most federal officials started working closely with local and state agencies (the first responders). First responders are primarily the forefront of almost every type of call for service including both domestic and international terrorism. As pointed out in the previous section, this partnership is important because it increases the number of federal agents' eyes and ears when dealing with domestic and international terroristic threats against the United States. For instance, if a person spotted a suspicious individual taking pictures near a nuclear power plant, the witness would dial 911 to notify the local authorities who would then respond to investigate further. The federal government might be notified if there were any further inquiries or suspicions related to the individual such as being on a terrorist watch list. Most local and state agencies do not have access to this database. However, with recent partnerships and agreements, federal agencies are beginning to share such database systems with local and state agencies.

To fully address this section, using various scholarly journals and articles would suffice. However, it is very important to take resources from the practical agencies themselves to demonstrate what they are actually doing as members of this partnership. Primarily Department of Homeland Security (DHS) websites and a subject matter expert from Hillsborough County Sheriff's Office provided the information. According to the DHS (2018b) website "Law Enforcement Partnerships," partnerships at the state, local, territorial, and tribal levels are vital to protect the nation from domestic and international terrorism. The website further lists the following initiatives: the importance of cooperation, building partnerships, and partnership success. In elaborating on the importance of cooperation, over 90% of DHS employees are stationed outside of their national offices to subfield officers in local and state communities to improve accessibility and availability to local and state officials.

To explain the idea of building partnerships, three initiatives are presented in this section: improve communication and share information; enhance the kind of federal resources and support provided to partners through financial means and training; and last, to strengthen analytic capabilities to achieve better awareness of new and improved threats (U.S. DHS, 2018a).

Partnering with local and state agencies has yielded successful investigations and helps detect and prevent terrorism. In addition, DHS initiated the Homeland Security Information Network (HSIN) to share and provide local and state agencies with quick and effective information regarding certain crimes, including weapons smuggling, narcotics trafficking, and gang mitigating. Furthermore, the HSIN also covers Be on the Lookouts (BOLOs), Requests for Information (RFIs), For Your Information (FYI), Intelligence Reports, and other sensitive information sharing (U.S. DHS, 2018b).

To further emphasize the importance of the relationship between police and the federal government, specifically with the Department of Homeland Security, Chief Deputy Jose Docobo (2005) from the Hillsborough County Sheriff's Office presented an excellent article illuminating the topic in titled "Community Policing as the Primary Prevention Strategy for Homeland Security at the Local Law Enforcement Level." The contributor is an expert in his or her field and has several years of experience building sustainable relationships. He listed the following steps to accomplish this partnership and collaboration between the two entities:

- Build and sustain a positive relationship between federal and local authorities
- Nurture community partnerships
- Improve problem solving
- Transform organizations
- Invest in training
- Decentralize decision making and accountability
- Fix geographic accountability and generalist responsibilities
- Utilize volunteer resources to include neighborhood watch programs

Additionally, establishing **volunteers in police services (VIPS)**, **community emergency response teams (CERT)**, medical reserve corps; intelligence gathering; working with the media; business and worship watches; and citizen academies are vital to create long-lasting partnerships between state, local, and federal parties. Forming community partnerships provides several benefits for the local, state, and federal government.

Federal agents were previously viewed as the final response to incidents. People only called them when a big event occurred. However, with such partnerships, agents are placed in local and state communities to provide easy access and information-sharing processes between both parties. The community policing chapter will discuss the majority of these concepts in detail.

However, it is imperative to highlight the importance of the training initiative, CERT, working with the media, and the community partnerships and business and worship watches in this chapter. The training piece provides local and state agencies with state-of-the-art training tools, equipment, and access to locate, identify, and detain suspected individuals or possibly prevent terrorist acts. Involving communities with CERT is also beneficial since groups commonly consist of individuals who have a background in emergency response management or incident command systems. Their knowledge and expertise are critical for emergency response incidents. Partnering of local and state agencies with the federal government provides extra resources and manpower when handling future threats. By involving these members, the hands-on response will be greatly enhanced. In addition, work with the media has also proven beneficial as they can distribute information quickly to large audiences. Although the relationship between law enforcement agencies and the media is sometimes rocky, their partnership is essential. Having the federal government involved also maximizes how much information is distributed to the general public. The media's job is to get the general public's attention. Agencies should be cautious about the type of information they share with the media since the majority of the "cases" are active or can be jeopardized if information gets into the wrong hands. Lastly, using community partners such as business and worship watches are also essential. These additional partnerships create more leverage, access, and information sharing. For instance, if there is a partnership between a local agency and a faith-based organization, information can be shared with the local agency regarding a suspicious issue. The information can then be shared with the federal agency because both agencies have an agreement and have formed a partnership. The same situation applies to business partnerships. Businesses and faith-based coalitions come in contact with a variety of individuals with whom local or state agencies do not. Having a positive dialogue and relationship with these coalitions enables information sharing about suspicious activities with local, state, and federal agencies.

Terrorism: Domestic and International

Before starting the discussion on **terrorism**, it is important to note the operational definitions of this word. Author Mark Burgess (2003), in his paper "Terrorism: The Problems of Definition," used the word *polemic* meaning relating to, or involving strongly critical, controversial, sarcastic, sharp, or incisive argument. Yet these adjectives are all the words used to describe the definition of terrorism. Unfortunately, many readers misunderstand this word in the context of terrorism. Polemic is quite often related to or associated with any devastating incident. Mainstream media adds fuel to the fire as well by presenting every major incident as a terrorist attack. The author uses the term *polemic* accurately when describing the meaning of the word *terrorism*. Later in his paper, he notes three thorough definitions of terrorism from various aspects of the federal government including the Department of Defense, the FBI, and the State Department.

The Department of Defense: Terrorism is the calculated use of unlawful violence to inculcate fear, intended to coerce or to intimidate governments or societies in the pursuit of goals that are generally political, religious, or ideological (Burgess, 2003).

The FBI: Terrorism is the unlawful use of force and violence against persons or property to intimidate or coerce a government, the civilian population, or any segment thereof, in furtherance of political or social objectives (Burgess, 2003).

The State Department: Terrorism is premeditated, politically motivated violence perpetrated against noncombatant targets by subnational groups or clandestine agents, usually intended to influence an audience (Burgess, 2003).

In examining these three definitions, it is important to note that the common theme that resonates within all three is the "[u]se of unlawful violence, to incite or instill fear, against persons, places, things, politically charged, religious, or ideologically incised." Now that three definitions of the word terrorism are provided, we can focus on the two categories: domestic and international.

According to the FBI (2018), domestic terrorism is perpetuated by individuals or groups that are based in the United States and express extremist ideologies that are political, religious, social, racial, or environmental in nature. International terrorists consist of individuals or groups that are inspired or associated by foreign groups to exert their beliefs through various acts of violence against the target country or nation.

Two instances were noted: the December 2, 2015 incident in San Bernardino, California, that left 14 individuals dead and several injured (the federal government classified the event as an act of international terrorism because foreign groups and their ideologies were responsible for such heinous acts); and the June 8, 2014 Las Vegas shooting where an armed couple spreading their warped ideology ambushed two officers (this was classified as domestic terrorism). These incidents happen far too often. Still, it is important to note the difference between the two types of terrorism since they are often confused. The similarity between these two concepts is intriguing as they both describe the motive and perception behind the perpetrators when committing domestic and international terrorism. The actions of terrorists help to shape and promote the creation of new policies and procedures—within local and state agencies—which are designed to combat this threat and to present new strategies for preventing future incidents. Law enforcement agencies are becoming more vigilant daily as more sophisticated terrorists are emerging.

Human Trafficking

Though the partnership between law enforcement and DHS is primarily focused on securing our nation's borders against threat, the threat isn't just limited to terrorism. The Department of Homeland Security also has a large focus on anti-human trafficking efforts and emergency preparedness. Apart from aggressors planning to cause harm to our infrastructure, there is a limitless amount of other dangers such as our own citizens and nature. Human trafficking is a form of modern-day slavery where human bodies are used to attain revenue via the sex trade, labor, and illegal organ extraction, claiming millions of victims every year. Ranked as the third largest criminal activity in the world by the International Labor Organization (ILO), this form of human slavery estimates as a $150 billion global industry (ILO, 2014). Europe and Central Asia are considered major hotspots for sex exploitation whereas California, Texas, New York, Washington, DC, and Georgia are ranked highest in America. Unfortunately, there is no exact number of victims in the United States due to the clandestine nature of the crime. However, in terms of the 40,000 reported victims since 2010, the national average age for labor and sex trafficking victims is 11 to 14 years with 75% being female, of which 25% are underage children (U.S. Department of Labor, 2016).

According to the National Human Trafficking Resource Center's (NHTRC) data breakdown of 2015, 74.5% of all calls made to the center seeking help for victims of trafficking were made by local law enforcement personnel (NHTRC, 2016). More often than not victims of sex and labor trafficking avoid approaching officers with complaints of their abuse due to fear of their handler/pimp, their lack of personal identification, or the strong opinion that no one will believe them. Pimps are also known to play constant psychological mind games with their captives in order to make them fear approaching help by holding their passports captive, by threatening their family's safety, and holding their children hostage. Therefore responding law enforcement officers and federal agents not only have a duty to identify these victims, but also to also protect and provide them with the appropriate resources so that they have access to human trafficking hotlines, rescue organizations, and shelters.

Emergency Response

In 2005, Hurricane Katrina grew from a tropical storm to a category 3 hurricane by landfall, later evolving to category 5 status and claiming 1,833 lives and $125 billion in structural damages spanning from Florida to eastern Texas (Sims, 2007; see figure 5.1). Katrina became the costliest tropical storm in American history and was labeled a disaster. However, the inefficiency of emergency responders dubbed it as a tragedy. In the end, disorientation, lack of planning, inaccessibility to proper equipment, abandonment, and miscommunication caused more damage to the region and its residents than the flooding alone. The downfall of New Orleans began internally, when New Orleans Police Department's sworn officers refused to report to duty. Many made the decision of returning to their families instead of demonstrating the ability to remain resilient in the time of crisis. Those who dutifully remained quickly became overwhelmed as they worked with minimal sleep, minimal resources, and minimal communication, leaving them crippled and unable to perform basic police functions. In hindsight, the response efforts of the NOPD were not acceptable. Hard lessons were learned after Katrina's wake.

Police departments have implemented emergency response plans along with mandatory exercises and training sessions. Operational plans, procedures, policies, and codes have also been designed to ensure effective law enforcement response (Rojek & Smith, 2007). While necessary changes have been made by police departments to prevent the failures experienced during Hurricane Katrina, it is necessary to understand that the impact of a disaster is unpredictable, meaning every level of preparation may never be enough.

Police officers are always the first responders to any calls of distress, whether it's for a fire, robbery, abduction, terrorism attack, or automobile accident. As the first line of defense during disasters, officers must be prepared and equipped to perform tasks that go beyond their everyday duties. Waiting for emergency responders and disaster relief services such as FEMA, the National Guard, the Red Cross, and nonprofit organizations may leave the community in shambles. Therefore, law enforcement is considered the primary point of contact and should perform as such. Officers may be asked to perform search and rescue operations, maintain a safe and secure environment within

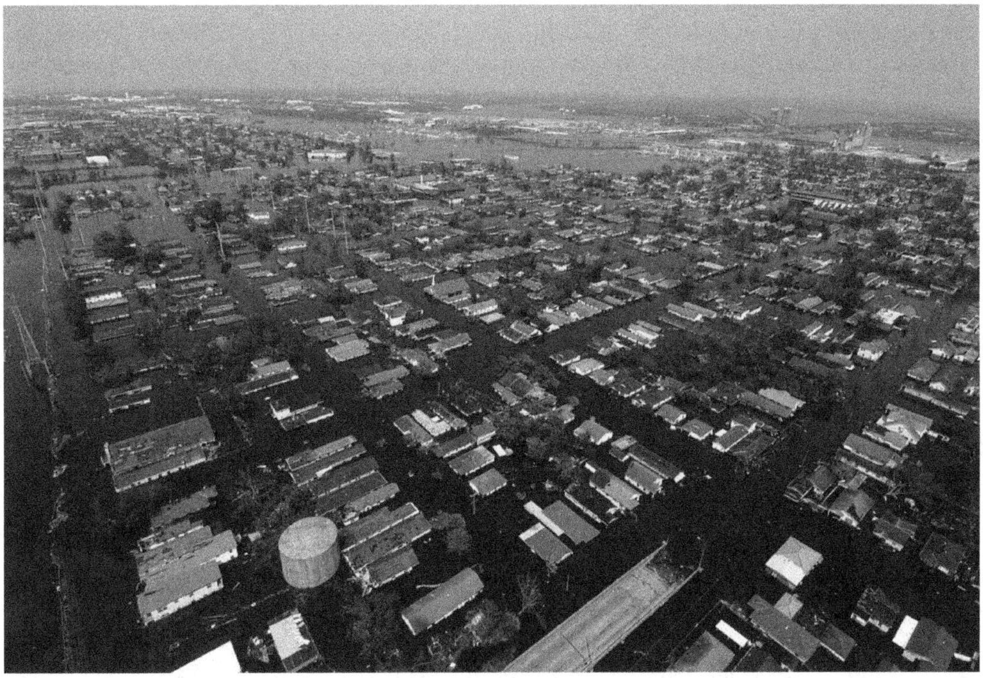

Figure 5.1 New Orleans, Louisiana, after Hurricane Katrina

their community, spread situational awareness, and collaborate with the incident command system to effectively coordinate response activities (Federal Emergency Management Agency (FEMA), 2017). Disasters call for critical decision making, which requires partnerships between multiple jurisdictions as they each bring with them certain specialized expertise. Police officers know their communities best; this serves as valuable information when determining areas of weakness, what supplies to allocate, as well as how to locate members with special needs.

History of 287(g)

To understand the 287(g) policy, it is important to know the program's meaning and background. One of the top priorities for the United States Immigration and Customs Enforcement (U.S. ICE) is to ensure a positive working relationship between local and state agencies.

According to Immigration and Customs Enforcement (U.S. ICE, 2018a), the seedlings of this program took root in 1996 when the pre-existing Illegal Immigration Reform and Immigrant Responsibility Act added the **287(g)** section. This section authorizes primarily local and state employee enforcement or jail officers to perform immigration officer functions through a memorandum of understanding.

This memorandum authorizes the head of ICE to enter into specific agreements that give immigration enforcement authorities to local and state authorities after they complete the basic training under ICE officer supervision. Local and state officers are also selected to form task forces where they can work hand in hand with ICE officers to enforce the **Criminal Alien Program** (CAP). This program primarily monitors and maintains biographic and biometric information, arrests and removes criminal aliens, and incarcerates aliens including those who have evaded identification in the federal, state, and local systems. This program also targets criminal aliens according to arrest and deportation procedures (U.S. ICE, 2018a). CAP's goal is to target illegal aliens who pose a threat to public safety. The requirements for the selected local and state officers to serve in the CAP program are as follows:

- U.S. citizenship
- Complete current background investigation
- Experience in current position
- No pending disciplinary actions

Required training for these officers includes a 4-week basic training at the Federal Law Enforcement Training Center (FLETC) ICE academy in Charleston, South Carolina. A 1-week in-service training is also required for certified local and state officers every 2 years (U.S. ICE, 2018b). According to the American Immigration Council (2017) the main duties and responsibilities for these officers include the following:

- Interviewing individuals to ascertain their immigration status
- Checking DHS databases for information on individuals
- Issuing immigration detainers to hold individuals until ICE takes custody
- Entering data into ICE's database and case management system
- Issuing a notice to appear (NTA)
- Providing the official charging document that begins the removal process
- Making recommendations for voluntary departure in place of formal removal proceedings
- Making recommendations for detention and immigration bond
- Transferring noncitizens into ICE custody (American Immigration Council, 2017)

Last, there are three major models that the policy addresses: the jail enforcement, task force, and hybrid models.

Jail Enforcement Model

In the jail enforcement model, there are jurisdictions where only the correctional or jail officers inquire about the immigration status for every inmate and will make the proper notifications to U.S. ICE if the individual is violating federal immigration rules and regulations.

Figure 5.2 An example of an ICE arrest

Task Force Model

The task force model represents jurisdictions where enforcement officers can inquire about the status of individuals they encounter, issue ICE detainers, and request arrest warrants when appropriate (see figure 5.2). The enforcement officers are mostly field agents and have a wide jurisdiction to cover. These officers have arrest powers for federal immigration violators.

Hybrid Model

The hybrid model is comprised of jurisdictions where both models operate alongside each other. For instance, the Frederick County program has both the jail enforcement officers and the task force enforcement officers. Both the jail officers and the task force officers are trained specifically to enforce federal immigrations violations. However, these officers encounter immigrants in two different settings. The first setting is wherein arrestees are brought into the jails and have to be processed and screened. They would be asked screening questions in order to determine their residency statuses. The other setting is out in the general public or pursuing an active investigation that leads to the direct interaction with an immigrant outside of the jail's confines. The next section covers the local and state enforcement and partnerships of the 287(g) program.

Local and State Enforcement/ Partnership of 287(g)

To accurately depict the participating local and state agencies, U.S. ICE (2018a) provides the following information, included here as Table 5.1, which displays the states, name of agencies, support types, and signing dates for the memorandum.

Currently, ICE has 287(g) agreements with 59 law enforcement agencies in 17 states. ICE has trained and certified more than 1,822 state and local officers to enforce immigration law.

TABLE 5.1 287(g) Results and Participating Entities: Mutually Signed Agreements

STATE	LAW ENFORCEMENT AGENCY	SUPPORT TYPE	SIGNED	MOA
ALABAMA	Etowah County Sheriff's Office	Jail Enforcement	2016-06-08	link
ARIZONA	Arizona Department of Corrections	Jail Enforcement	2016-06-08	link
ARIZONA	City of Mesa Police Department	Jail Enforcement	2016-06-23	link
ARIZONA	Pinal County Sheriff's Office	Jail Enforcement	2016-06-13	link
ARIZONA	Yavapai County Sheriff's Office	Jail Enforcement	2016-06-08	link
ARKANSAS	Benton County Sheriff's Office	Jail Enforcement	2016-06-13	link
ARKANSAS	Washington County Sheriff's Office	Jail Enforcement	2016-06-23	link
FLORIDA	Clay County Sheriff's Office	Jail Enforcement	2017-06-30	link
FLORIDA	Collier County Sheriff's Office	Jail Enforcement	2016-06-13	link
FLORIDA	Hernando County Sheriff's Office	Jail Enforcement	2018-02-27	link
FLORIDA	Jacksonville Sheriff's Office	Jail Enforcement	2016-06-30	link
FLORIDA	Pasco County Sheriff's Office	Jail Enforcement	2017-08-22	link
GEORGIA	Bartow County Sheriff's Office	Jail Enforcement	2018-02-21	link
GEORGIA	Cobb County Sheriff's Office	Jail Enforcement	2016-06-30	link
GEORGIA	Floyd County Sheriff's Office	Jail Enforcement	2018-02-02	link
GEORGIA	Georgia Department of Corrections	Jail Enforcement	2018-02-05	link
GEORGIA	Gwinnett County Sheriff's Office	Jail Enforcement	2016-06-30	link
GEORGIA	Hall County Sheriff's Office	Jail Enforcement	2016-06-23	link
GEORGIA	Whitfield County Sheriff's Office	Jail Enforcement	2016-06-08	link

TABLE 5.1 287(g) Results and Participating Entities: Mutually Signed Agreements (Continued)

STATE	LAW ENFORCEMENT AGENCY	SUPPORT TYPE	SIGNED	MOA
LOUISIANA	East Baton Rouge Parish Sheriff's Office	Jail Enforcement	2017-05-03	link
MARYLAND	Anne Arundel County	Jail Enforcement	2017-06-19	link
MARYLAND	Frederick County Sheriff's Office	Jail Enforcement	2016-08-03	link
MARYLAND	Harford County Sheriff's Office	Jail Enforcement	2016-10-26	link
MASSACHUSETTS	Barnstable County Sheriff's Office	Jail Enforcement	2018-01-25	link
MASSACHUSETTS	Bristol County Sheriff's Office	Jail Enforcement	2017-02-08	link
MASSACHUSETTS	Massachusetts Department of Corrections	Jail Enforcement	2016-06-23	link
MASSACHUSETTS	Plymouth County Sheriff's Department	Jail Enforcement	2017-02-08	link
NEBRASKA	Dakota County Sheriff's Office	Jail Enforcement	2018-01-16	link
NEVADA	Las Vegas Metropolitan Police Department	Jail Enforcement	2016-06-28	link
NEVADA	Lyon County Sheriff's Office	Jail Enforcement	2018-05-04	link
NEVADA	Nye County Sheriff's Office	Jail Enforcement	2017-04-20	link
NEW JERSEY	Cape May County Sheriff's Office	Jail Enforcement	2017-04-10	link
NEW JERSEY	Monmouth County Sheriff's Office	Jail Enforcement	2016-06-08	link
NEW JERSEY	Salem County Sheriff's Office	Jail Enforcement	2016-12-08	link
NEW YORK	Rensselaer County Sheriff's Office	Jail Enforcement	2018-01-30	link
NORTH CAROLINA	Cabarrus County Sheriff's Office	Jail Enforcement	2016-06-28	link
NORTH CAROLINA	Gaston County Sheriff's Office	Jail Enforcement	2016-06-30	link
NORTH CAROLINA	Henderson County Sheriff's Office	Jail Enforcement	2017-02-28	link
NORTH CAROLINA	Mecklenburg County Sheriff's Office	Jail Enforcement	2017-02-28	link
NORTH CAROLINA	Nash County Sheriff's Office	Jail Enforcement	2018-02-02	link
NORTH CAROLINA	Wake County Sheriff's Office	Jail Enforcement	2016-06-08	link
OHIO	Butler County Sheriff's Office	Jail Enforcement	2016-09-30	link
OKLAHOMA	Canadian County Sheriff's Office	Jail Enforcement	2018-01-25	link
OKLAHOMA	Okmulgee County Criminal Justice Authority	Jail Enforcement	2018-01-25	link
OKLAHOMA	Tulsa County Sheriff's Office	Jail Enforcement	2016-06-23	link
SOUTH CAROLINA	Charleston County Sheriff's Office	Jail Enforcement	2016-06-23	link
SOUTH CAROLINA	Horry County Sheriff's Office	Jail Enforcement	2017-06-30	link
SOUTH CAROLINA	Lexington County Sheriff's Office	Jail Enforcement	2016-11-04	link
SOUTH CAROLINA	York County Sheriff's Office	Jail Enforcement	2016-06-28	link

TABLE 5.1 287(g) Results and Participating Entities: Mutually Signed Agreements (Continued)

STATE	LAW ENFORCEMENT AGENCY	SUPPORT TYPE	SIGNED	MOA
TENNESSEE	Knox County Sheriff's Office	Jail Enforcement	2017-06-15	link
TEXAS	Aransas County Sheriff's Office	Jail Enforcement	2017-06-30	link
TEXAS	Burnet County Sheriff's Office	Jail Enforcement	2018-02-02	link
TEXAS	Calhoun County Sheriff's Office	Jail Enforcement	2017-06-28	link
TEXAS	Chambers County Sheriff's Office	Jail Enforcement	2017-07-17	link
TEXAS	DeWitt County Sheriff's Office	Jail Enforcement	2017-06-30	link
TEXAS	Galveston County Sheriff's Office	Jail Enforcement	2017-06-30	link
TEXAS	Goliad County Sheriff's Office	Jail Enforcement	2017-06-26	link
TEXAS	Jackson County Sheriff's Office	Jail Enforcement	2017-01-26	link
TEXAS	Kendall County Sheriff's Office	Jail Enforcement	2018-03-26	link
TEXAS	Lavaca County Sheriff's Office	Jail Enforcement	2017-06-30	link
TEXAS	Lubbock County Sheriff's Office	Jail Enforcement	2016-11-16	link
TEXAS	Matagorda County Sheriff's Office	Jail Enforcement	2017-07-27	link
TEXAS	Montgomery County Sheriff's Office	Jail Enforcement	2017-06-28	link
TEXAS	Nueces County Sheriff's Office	Jail Enforcement	2018-01-18	link
TEXAS	Potter County Sheriff's Office	Jail Enforcement	2018-01-25	link
TEXAS	Refugio County Sheriff's Office	Jail Enforcement	2017-06-28	link
TEXAS	Rockwall County Sheriff's Office	Jail Enforcement	2018-01-25	link
TEXAS	Smith County Sheriff's Office	Jail Enforcement	2017-04-25	link
TEXAS	Tarrant County Sheriff's Office	Jail Enforcement	2017-06-19	link
TEXAS	Terrell County Sheriff's Office	Jail Enforcement	2018-01-25	link
TEXAS	Victoria County Sheriff's Office	Jail Enforcement	2017-07-12	link
TEXAS	Walker County Sheriff's Office	Jail Enforcement	2017-07-20	link
TEXAS	Waller County Sheriff's Office	Jail Enforcement	2017-05-22	link
TEXAS	Wharton County Sheriff's Office	Jail Enforcement	2017-07-17	link
TEXAS	Williamson County Sheriff's Office	Jail Enforcement	2018-02-08	link
VIRGINIA	Culpeper County Sheriff's Office	Jail Enforcement	2018-04-24	link
VIRGINIA	Prince William-Manassas Regional Adult Detention Center	Jail Enforcement	2016-06-23	link
WISCONSIN	Waukesha County Sheriff's Office	Jail Enforcement	2018-02-08	link

Each agency listed has entered into an agreement with the Department of Homeland Security (DHS) while implementing the 287(g) policy. The processes and duration of these agreements are outlined in each memorandum of agreement. Most local and state agencies retain their agreement for about 2 to 3 years and conduct a thorough analysis and evaluation of the program to determine whether they will continue with the partnership or not. The next section outlines the various perceptions of this policy implementation including the advantages and disadvantages.

Advantages of the 287(g) Policy Implementation

As mentioned, enforcement officers have slowly implemented this policy in many jurisdictions. Consequently, several complications have occurred. This section will investigate the advantages and disadvantages of this policy implementation. The Department of Homeland Security (DHS) continues to audit and examine these policies to maintain consistency while also focusing on arresting and detaining criminal aliens. Furthermore, according to United States Immigration and Customs Enforcement (U.S. ICE, 2018a), updated facts noted that some of the advantages for this policy implementation are as follows: increasing public safety by working together with local and state officers to enforce federal immigrations violations; more accurately identifying individuals in custody; providing continuous positive feedback from its partners; and lastly, acting as a force multiplier and covering sparse areas where federal agents are limited.

Explaining these concepts individually allows enforcement officers to focus on public safety while collaborating with local and state officers. Local and state officers are the first responders to make contact with individuals committing federal immigration violations and are at the forefront of almost all types of enforcement services. Therefore, partnering with them is a great advantage and improves the entire outlook of public safety when enforcing immigration violations.

The task force policy is advantageous because it helps to provide a clearer identity of individuals in custody for violating federal immigration laws. For instance, before this policy existed, if illegal immigrants committed crimes, law enforcement charged, arrested, and sentenced them. But the legal system would eventually release them to the U.S. ICE without proper notification about their legal status in the United States. Prior to monitoring various crimes and offenses illegal aliens committed, no one notified U.S. ICE. With the policy in place, correctional officers are specifically trained to identify such individuals, question them about their status, and to eventually notify the U.S. ICE of their charges. U.S. ICE would in turn determine if it is necessary to initiate a deportation process or take custody of incarcerated immigrants after their release. At that point, the correctional officers have to decide whether to initiate federal immigration proceedings. The third benefit is that partnering agencies frequently praise and provide constant positive feedback regarding the policy implementation. Most agencies thoroughly evaluate the policy 2 or 3 years after its implementation to determine whether it is beneficial. Since) U.S. ICE (2018a) revealed that several partnering agencies provided positive feedback regarding this policy implementation, several law enforcement agencies are continuing to renew their partnering agreements with U.S. ICE. Last, U.S. ICE perceives partnering with local and state agencies as a force multiplier that strengthens their ability to enforce federal immigration regulations. It is viewed as a force multiplier due to the number of increased partnerships and memorandum of agreements, thus providing more manpower and resources in combating illegal immigration and targeting violent criminal aliens.

This is an advantage for the U.S. ICE since such agreements guarantee notifications, documentation, and identifying individuals who have evaded them for a while. As mentioned, local and state agents are at the forefront of coming into contact with various individuals. Such contacts lead to further inquiries, and further inquiries lead to identifying these individuals for further legal actions. State and local agents play a vital role in assisting federal agents with their primary tasks and responsibilities. Another advantage not mentioned on the ICE website is that when they partner with local and state agencies, the ICE provides them with federal knowledge, benefits, and training. These benefits sometimes lead local and state officers to a career as federal agents if they choose. However, the majority of these specialized and trained local and state officers must obtain some form of security clearance. Acquiring this clearance is also beneficial to officers' future career aspirations, enabling them to work in the federal agency of their choice.

There is a high turnover rate in these specialized trained officers who are ICE certified because the majority of them transition from their local and state employment to federal employment to pursue increased salaries, benefits, and retirement options. In addition, some scholars and other federal and state constituents have argued that the 287(g) also helps fight crimes and effectively removes illegal immigrants. Therefore, local and state agencies are authorized to enforce federal regulations since they are enforcement agents and acting within the parameters of the U.S. Constitution. Last, when presenting the benefits of implementing this policy, it is important to note Mai Thi Nguyen and Hannah Gill's (2010) study titled "The 287(g) Program: The Costs and Consequences of Local Immigration Enforcement in North Carolina Communities." The study mentioned the public officials' opinions about the program. Note that these perspectives mirror most of the other jurisdictions' perspectives, thus demonstrating that the majority of public officials voted for its passage and implementation.

The researchers posited that the 287(g) allows a multi-agency initiative to combat crime, deterring it holistically. The policy also helps local and state agencies easily identify and start the deportation process of illegal immigrants from various counties. It also helps local, state, and federal agencies to work together smoothly. Finally, the overall goal and mission for this partnership is to make communities safe and to enhance Homeland Security (Nguyen & Gill, 2010). Residents in various counties supported implementing this policy. They viewed it as a way of cleansing their neighborhoods of illegal immigrants, thereby making their streets "safer" for their families. Officials held public forums in several communities where the board of county supervisors and other local and state governmental boards heard countless cries and support for the program. They also heard the countless voices of immigrants against implementing this policy in their communities. However, in the end, the majority ruled and the designated local and state governing bodies adopted the policy, directing their police and sheriff agencies to partner with U.S. CIS. This policy has faced much controversy regarding its implementation. This next section will document how researchers, immigration councils, and institutes discovered the program's disadvantages.

Disadvantages of the 287(g) Policy Implementation

To present a variety of perspectives on the disadvantages of this policy implementation, it is advisable to produce thoroughly reviewed and scholarly articles. This precaution is necessary because anti-immigration groups and councils often have misconceptions about immigration overall. Furthermore, it is important to share thorough and comprehensive studies that capture most of the perceptions of the people the policy impacts directly. To meet this goal, researchers conducted two studies. Lisa Seghetti, Karma Ester, and Michael John Garcia (2009 conducted the first, titled "Enforcing Immigration Law: The Role of State and Local Enforcement." Chernoh Wurie (2012) conducted the second, "Exploring the Lives of Salvadoran Families After the Implementation of the Illegal Immigration Reform and Immigrant Responsibility Act of 1996 section 287(g)."

Seghetti and colleagues completed a comprehensive literature review study where they noted specific problems regarding this issue involving **civil rights**, **detention space**, **impact on communities**, **resources**, and **national security**. When addressing the civil rights implications noted by the authors, they identified three important applicable amendments: the Fourth Amendment, which prohibits unreasonable searches and seizures; the Fifth Amendment, which guarantees due process wherein no person shall be deprived from life, liberty, or property; and the Fourteenth Amendment, which guarantees equal protection of the law for everyone. One may question whether illegal aliens are covered under these amendments because they are neither permanent residents of the United States nor are they citizens. These are questions with which the state supreme courts constantly struggle. The authors also noted that because most of the policy applies to people of color and other underrepresented groups, racial profiling is inevitable when these groups interact with law enforcement officers. Even though various local, federal, and state agencies have implemented stringent rules requiring their officers to complete mandatory cultural diversity trainings, it is still possible for a prejudiced officer to allow racial stereotypes to color their perception and treatment of colored and underrepresented groups.

The second concept noted by Seghetti and colleagues is detention space. U.S. CIS makes several arrests involving illegal immigration and other violations. Housing these individuals has been difficult at times because of lack of space. Living conditions at some of these holding facilities are often chaotic and packed. The third concept noted is impact on communities. Immigrants thrive and dwell in various communities. This particular study revealed that after the policy's implementation at the designated jurisdiction, the immigrants expressed fear, anxiety, and unsteadiness in their former communities. As a result, they do not trust those who are there to protect them. The authors also noted that this policy's implementation impacts resources and national security. Resources are spread too thin. Enforcing this policy requires a lot of resources including but not limited to manpower, supervision, and budgeting from both the federal government and the state or local agencies. In addressing national security, the authors noted that this partnership will force illegal immigrants to go underground and make them difficult to locate, identify, and track.

Wurie (2012) conducted this comprehensive study of the policy's implementation in one of the largest immigrant populations in the county (Salvadorans.) His objective was to explore their life experiences after the policy's implementation. The following affected themes emerged from the study findings: real-estate, education, employment, healthcare, and personal and public safety. Real estate was affected since the county had one of the highest numbers of Salvadoran families. These families purchased houses and were becoming acclimated in their new neighborhoods. However, after the policy's implementation, many left their houses and migrated to other jurisdictions where the policy did not exist. The Salvadoran families left abandoned houses and other structures in their former neighborhoods.

Education suffered because of the Salvadoran families' departures. Several families pulled their children out of the county schools and enrolled them in counties with more tolerant school systems. The Salvadoran's exodus from the county where officials implemented the policy affected all levels of students including pre-kindergarten, kindergarten, elementary, middle, and high schools.

The healthcare system in the county with the implemented policy also suffered after the Salvadorans left. Several medical professionals reported that they were seeing a decrease in the average number of patients. More disturbingly, there were also several in-home deaths because parents were afraid to seek medical attention for their loved ones. They did not want to risk exposure to U.S. CIS and the risk of possible deportation. Last, the majority of participants admitted that they were afraid for their personal safety because they perceived the police as immigration officers. Consequently, they would not report crimes in which they were victims or witnesses. As a result, several crimes remained unsolved and domestic issues continued unreported.

It is important to note that these perceptions come from the participants who were directly affected by this policy implementation. The perceptions from the governmental sides and supporters are also presented. This policy is extremely controversial, as it can have both positive and negative impacts on a community. The positive aspect is that the federal government is tapping into its resources in a force multiplier endeavor and effectively enforcing federal immigration laws. In addition, those who are affected have made the United States their homes or are seeking a better opportunity by expressing their concerns. The recommendations listed in both studies were very similar where education, partnership, and understanding are the key concepts in bridging the relationship and minimizing the discord the policy has caused between local and state enforcement agencies and the communities they serve.

Additionally, it's important to note that a significant number of people did not understand the policy, which many participants confirmed. Most had a profound feeling that police officers would detain and question them for no apparent reason. However, these officers should have provided a reason for stopping anyone. Some law enforcement officers would only inquire about residency statutes if they planned to arrest or actually arrested the individual. To eliminate confusion and growing tension, the majority of the adopted agencies provided educational opportunities where community members could learn about the policy implementation and eliminate any misunderstandings. In addition, partnerships with various community leaders and providing a basic understanding of the policy's implementation has also proven beneficial.

The future of this program implementation depends on the specific need in each community where officials will evaluate whether to continue their partnerships with U.S. CIS. Some have terminated their partnerships due to the negative impact this has had on their communities, while others have terminated their partnerships due to funding and budgeting. In contrast, others have continued to renew their partnerships due to positive feedback from their communities and improving crime statistics in designated neighborhoods.

Box 5.1 Perceptions Versus Reality

When researching for this chapter, two distinct perceptions surfaced. One perception was that most terrorists are foreign nationals. The second perception was that only federal, state, and local law enforcement agencies can prevent terrorism. James Comey addressed the first perception in a FBI article dated November 14, 2013. He noted the frightening reality of the terrorist threats the FBI faces. He proposed that the United States faces an extremely different threat: homegrown violent extremists (HVEs). A good example of HVEs is the Boston Marathon bombers. They acted alone and their ideologies mirrored international extremists. However, they are small and unique cells that are difficult to identify (Comey, 2013). A HVE can be anyone who has a different view from the democratic ideology. Constant communication with extremist views via Internet, phone, or other forms of communication outside the United States fuels the HVE's ideologies. These individuals consist of all races, sexes, and national origins.

The second perception is that only federal law enforcement agencies can prevent terrorism. Fortunately, this belief is a myth. Actually, regular people are most frequently in contact with any terrorist plots far before law enforcement agencies are notified. For instance, the passengers and flight crew of 9/11 Flight 93 fought back and intercepted the targeted location of the plane. Several other documented examples exist where brave citizens are at the forefront of uncoiling terrorist plans.

Strategies for Combating Terrorism: Proactive and Reactive Methods

The fight against terrorism is a constant social, economic, and political battle for the United States. Terrorism threats and actions are becoming more prevalent and combating these actions are at the forefront of the federal government's agenda. As described, forming partnerships with local and state agencies is beneficial because it provides information sharing and easy access to communities and localities for further inquiries and investigations. Before delving into the various prevention strategies, it is important to know the leading agencies addressing this issue.

According to the Office of the Director of National Intelligence (n.d.) website, the U.S. intelligence community is made up of 17 organizations including the following:

- Two independent agencies
- The Office of the Director of National Intelligence (ODNI)
- The Central Intelligence Agency (CIA)
- Eight Department of Defense elements
- Seven remaining departments and agencies including the Department of Homeland Security's Office of Intelligence and Analysis and the U.S. Coast Guard Intelligence
- The FBI and the DEA's Office of National Security Intelligence

The FBI is one of the leading agencies in addition to the Department of Homeland Security. In reality, most local and state agencies have implemented a counterterrorism initiative or endeavor within their department either through a task force, an information-sharing initiative, or cooperation with another larger federal agency. What are these initiatives like? What do they entail? What types of terrorism is the nation facing? These are all important questions addressed in this section.

Jonathan Matusitz and Gerald-Mark Breen (2011) presented a paper titled "A Solution-Based Examination of Local, State, and National Government Groups Combating Terrorism and Cyberterrorism." Although several definitions were mentioned, the authors noted a very simple definition of terrorism that includes violent acts committed by politically charged opponents (Matusitz & Breen, 2011). Even though terrorist acts are evolving every day, to understand the different types, it is best to examine the various categories because they are divided into many ideological approaches. The right-wing and the issue-specific groups (Matusitz & Breen, 2011) include anti-American, Neo-Nazi, anti-Semitic, and anti-federalist clubs. Issue-specific groups include anti-abortion, animal rights, and other environmental initiatives. It is also important to note that the right-wing groups are primarily motivated by political agendas. They are usually extremely violent, execute their plans without regard for anything or anyone, and will not hesitate to commit genocides, homicides, and suicides. The issue-specific terrorists tend to have fewer fatalities than the right-wing groups because their agendas become obvious when they attack targeted victims or entities (Matusitz & Breen, 2011).

In addition to the right-wing and the issue-specific groups, **cyberterrorism** is becoming more prevalent in and outside of the United States. Matusitz and Breen (2011) defined cyberterrorism as intentionally attacking and damaging computers, networks, infrastructures, database systems, and other technologies via electronic means or other network-related mediums. This type of terrorism is particularly important as a majority of the nation's information is stored in various database systems. For instance, cyberterrorists can endanger the public's private medical information if they are able to access a medical healthcare database. A cyberterrorists' goal is to erase the entire database. All information is lost and cannot be retrieved without any backup recovery system in place.

The significant difference between a cyberterrorist and a hacker is very simple. A hacker gains illegal access or entry into a system with the intention to steal, expose, distribute, or compromise the individual's information. Hackers cause less damage and information recovery is still possible after the attack.

In further exploration of cyberterrorism, John Curtis Amble (2012) from King's College London noted in his paper, "Combating Terrorism in the New Media Environment," that the new age of terrorism is slowly migrating toward social media where terrorists have greater leverage, influence, and autonomy to carry out recruiting and other terrorist endeavors. The media lends terrorists the means and opportunity to spread their ideologies and causes. Governmental agencies can examine their strategy and maintain tracking systems on these various groups (Amble, 2012). Many of the threats that are exercised or made against the United States are primarily from emerging countries including Afghanistan, Iraq, Pakistan, and Iran (Matusitz & Breen, 2011). Even though positive relationship initiatives with the United States are underway, it is important to remember they have deployed the most terrorists and suicide bombers who have performed their ideological causes in the United States and worldwide. The authors also mentioned that Al-Qaeda, a militant Islamic organization, is one of the most serious threats to the United States and throughout the world. Various local, state, and homeland security agencies have placed this group at the top of their priority lists since they are one of the most prevalent terrorist groups that target the United States. Their primary goals are fueled with the idea that the United States is interfering with their personal and societal matters within their Islamic states. As a result, they see the United States as their enemy.

The FBI noted recently that three factors have contributed to the emerging threats of terrorism: the Internet, the use of social media, and homegrown violent extremists (HVEs) (FBI, 2018). The Internet is the main source or medium for terrorist groups to broadcast, publicize, and share their ideologies. Social media is another driving force and it's being used to communicate messages and share ideologies with individuals in distant lands for recruitment purposes. Lastly, the HVEs are individuals within the United States who have been influenced by various terrorist groups to carry out their missions and espouse their beliefs in the United States.

Now that we have presented the various types of terrorist threats and motivations, what are the strategies that local, state, and federal agencies use to combat these emerging threats against our nation? The FBI notes there are three important initiatives individuals can take to protect themselves online and in-person: remain aware of your surroundings, refrain from oversharing personal information, and say something if you see something. There are several strategies and combating techniques listed by governmental organizations. However, the simplest strategies noted by the FBI are using the Nationwide Suspicious Activity Reporting (SAR) Initiative (NSI). This initiative is spearheaded by the Department of Homeland Security where the FBI and local, state, and tribal law enforcement agencies collaborate to combat terrorism by sharing, gathering, processing, and analyzing information (FBI, 2018).

Another noted initiative is the community preparedness tools. In this case, local communities such as businesses and faith-based organizations collaborate with their local, state, and federal agencies to accomplish four major goals: connect, plan, train, and report. The connect portion is primarily forming meaningful partnerships to share and maintain information. Planning entails every entity proactively involving communities and agencies. Training, on the other hand, goes along with planning when community members receive updated training from their partners to handle various types of incidents that may occur. Last, reporting is basically urging the community to report anything suspicious to their local, state, or federal agencies. Mostly, they would report to their local and state agencies since these agencies are the first-line responders.

In addition to future strategies and recommendations for combating terrorism, various scholars have also noted specific recommendations. Amble (2012) wrote in his article regarding the terrorist use of new media that several recommendations can be applicable in addressing cyberterrorism. These include providing structural decentralization to allow junior intelligence community members to gain more knowledge regarding the new media usage; developing a centralized strategy to monitor jihadist media sources and medium; and changing human intelligence abilities to suit the new media spectrum (Amble, 2012). Elaborating on the first point, the author emphasizes using young human intelligence analysts as employees to help combat cyberterrorism. These individuals grew up in a technological era and as a result were exposed to various technologies at an early age. Therefore, they can assist in numerous capacities in the fight against cyberterrorism and terrorism in general. In elaborating on the last two points, developing a target central focal point to maintain terrorist media output and changing human intelligence abilities to fit the media spectrum are very much related because the information age is constantly evolving. Agencies have to continually transform their enforcement strategies to fit the current and future perceived threats against the United States.

Matusitz and Breen (2011) posed two important questions related to cyberterrorism and terrorism:

1. Regarding cyberterrorism, can the United States and its supporters craft agreements to support monitoring its citizens' Internet use?
2. And regarding the war on terror, what consequences follow the policy-making process?

These are important questions to take into consideration when attempting to combat terrorism. Terrorism is a nationwide and global issue. Therefore, nations should advise their citizens of the importance and seriousness of this issue. With global awareness, a global agreement and understanding about how to combat terrorism will grow. Ideally, information will be shared freely amongst nations and citizens will live freely and without fear. This scenario is a possibility. However, it will take extraordinary effort, collective agreement, enforcement, and transparency from every nation. The collaboration between local, state, and federal agencies is a positive start in combating terrorism. These initiatives continue to develop and improve in an effort to stay ahead of such threats.

Joint Terrorism Task Force

An effective tool that gained momentum after the 9/11 attacks is joint task forces. Joint task forces are partnerships between allied professionals who work collectively to combat a mutual target. In the realm of homeland security, these professionals can consist of, but aren't limited to, federal, state, local, and tribal law enforcement agencies, as well as private organizations who have goodwill toward the task of preventing or apprehending the target. The most notable joint task force is a JTTF (joint terrorism task force), which focuses on preventative measures against terrorism. First established in 1980 and consisting of only 10 FBI agents and 10 New York Police Department detectives, there are now 184 JTTFs around the country and all are under the umbrella of the National Joint Terrorism Task Force headquartered in Washington, DC.

A JTTF is generally comprised of federal law enforcement agencies such as the Federal Bureau of Investigation (FBI), Bureau of Alcohol, Tobacco, Firearms and Explosives (ATF), Drug Enforcement Administration (ATF), Naval Criminal Investigative Services (NCIS), U.S. Air Force Office of Special Investigations (OSI), and U.S. Customs and Border Protection (CBP). In a classic JTTF arrangement, a number of officers from each agency are pooled together to work on a specific task. This type of grouping can be advantageous since each team member brings different skills, experiences, and information to the table. Federal agents have access to explicit resources that local officials do not. Contrastingly, local officers have extensive knowledge of their communities, which means access to "on-the-ground" intelligence (Wither, 2016). The policing component of a JTTF bridges the gap between law enforcement and the public, which encourages room for increased communication and trust—crucial factors when fighting a war against terrorism.

Homeland Security Versus Citizens' Civil Liberties

The concept of homeland security emerged from the horrific incident that took place on September 11, 2001; the nation has created several federal agencies under this umbrella. Several scholars have noted that the urgency with which this governmental entity was created has impacted the civil liberties of innocent American citizens. This has become a point of controversy as to what is too much homeland protection wherein there are no privacies and everything is made available to the federal government in order to intercept and deter terroristic acts. On the other hand, what is less enforcement for protecting the homeland? Some have noted that less or lack of protection has created a breeding ground for terrorists. This section explores both points of view on the concept of protecting the homeland.

The U.S. Patriot Act

Since the tragic events of September 11, 2001, our government has implemented several laws and policies in the fight against terrorism. Several scholars have noted that in the process of implementing these new policies and laws, civil liberties have been compromised. This section will delve into discussions about the U.S. Patriot Act, the First, Fourth, and 14th Amendments, and the issue and implications of racial profiling.

What is the meaning of the **U.S. Patriot Act**? The acronym stands for Providing Appropriate Tools Required to Intercept and Obstruct Terrorism. Opponents of the act state that it was passed hastily right after 9/11. Supporters have proposed that the various titles and sections of this act have actually saved the nation from terrorist attacks (Congress.Gov, 2012). The various titles and sections covered in this act are as follows:

- Title I: Enhancing Domestic Security Against Terrorism (Sections 102–106)
- Title II: Enhanced Surveillance Procedures (Sections 203–225)
- Title III: International Money Laundering Abatement and Anti-Terrorist Financing Act of 2001 (Sections 312–327)
- Title IV: Protecting the Border
  - Subtitle A: Protecting the Northern Border (Sections 402–427)
  - Subtitle B: Enhanced Immigration Provision
  - Subtitle C: Preservation of Immigration Benefits for Victims of Terrorism
- Title V: Removing Obstacles to Investigating Terrorism (Sections 502–507)
- Title VI: Providing for Victims of Terrorism, Public Safety, and Their Families
  - Subtitle A: Aid to Families of Public Safety
  - Subtitle B: Amendments to the Victims of Crime Act of 1984
- Title VII: Increased Information Sharing for Critical Infrastructure Protection
- Title VIII: Strengthening the Criminal Laws Against Terrorism (Sections 802–817)
- Title IX: Improved Intelligence (Sections 902–908)
- Title X: Miscellaneous (Sections 1002–1016) (Congress.Gov, 2002)

According to the Constitutional Rights Foundation (2018), most of the sections within the Patriot Act are extremely controversial, especially Sections 213 and 215.

- Section 213: Federal district courts may delay warrant notices if the notice may impede the investigation)

- Section 215: Director of FBI or designee to apply for a court order requiring production of certain business records for foreign intelligence and international terrorism investigations) (Congress.Gov, 2002)

U.S. PATRIOT ACT: SECTION 215 EXPLAINED

Based on Section 215, legal authority such as the FBI may be able to seize public library records, bookstores, Internet providers, political groups, churches, universities and other institutions, and businesses if in the midst of a terrorism investigation (Constitutional Rights Foundation, 2018). In exploring Section 213, the Constitutional Rights Foundation allows a federal judge to authorize the so-called sneak and peek in all federal criminal investigations. This initiative is where the designated federal agency may delay notifying the individual being investigated while it is secretly searching the individual's personal records to prevent the destruction of evidence. Some might say this is a violation of the person's Fourth Amendment rights, which prohibits illegal searches and seizures. Others might comment that if the individual is notified, then the propensity of the evidence to be destroyed or disappear is very high. There are many strong opinions about these issues.

The Pew Research Center conducted a public opinion survey in 2013, led by Carroll Doherty, director of the Political Research Center at the Pew Research Institute. In his paper titled, "Balancing Act: National Security and Civil Liberties in Post 9/11 Era," several polls measured people's perceptions of the Patriot Act. Two questions surfaced. The first one was whether they felt anti-terrorism policies would go too far and would restrict civil liberties; the second was whether these policies were adequate enough and were actually protecting the nation (Doherty, 2013). This study occurred in 2010 and about 40% of participants felt that these policies have not gone far enough to adequately protect the country (Doherty, 2013). On the other hand, about 32% of participants stated that these policies have gone too far in restricting the regular individual's civil liberties (Doherty, 2013). Other questions and perceptions included the idea of the government monitoring phone calls and e-mails and the public's willingness to give up some civil liberties in exchange for security. The responses varied. However, most participants noted that many of the measures have not proven to protect the nation from terrorism. It is important to mention that the survey presented here is from a mainstream source and the Pew Research Center conducts many popular public opinion surveys.

From a governmental outlook, the results of the passage of the U.S. Patriot Act have been positive and have deterred several terrorist plots. Several other proponents such as the ACLU and other civil rights advocates have voiced their opinions on this initiative. They, too, have been very vocal in pointing out that this act violates the personal and civil rights of U.S. citizens. Some of the supportive proponents for this act according to the Department of Justice (2018) include that the department's first priority is to protect lives and liberties and to prevent future terrorist attacks on American soil. According to the website, the passage of the Patriot Act has led the way in preventing a number of terrorist plots against the United States. The Department of Justice (2018) further noted that Congress merely took existing laws and policies and retrofitted them to address and combat current and future terrorist plans. Various opinions are presented in this section. Furthermore, others have noted that even though the collaboration between the federal government and state and local agencies has incredible advantages, issues such as 14th Amendment violations and various public safety agencies engaging in racial profiling acts are inevitable.

Further Discussion on Privacy and Racial Profiling

Before delving into this discussion, it is important to know the definition of racial profiling and explain the contents of the 14th Amendment. There are various definitions for racial profiling. However, for the purposes of this text it is advisable to use a definition from the National Institute of Justice (NIJ) whose definition is related to law enforcement and is applicable to this discussion. According to NIJ (2013), racial profiling is defined as when law enforcement targets various individuals on suspicion of crimes based on their race, sex, ethnicity, religion, and national origin. In addition, within the contents of the 14th Amendment, as stated by Cornell Law (2018), the most applicable section of the amendment's five sections is Section 1, which states,

> All persons born or naturalized in the United States, and subject to the jurisdiction thereof, are citizens of the United States and of the state wherein they reside. No state shall make or enforce any law which shall abridge the privileges or immunities of citizens of the United States; nor shall any state deprive any person of life, liberty, or property, without due process of law; nor deny to any person within its jurisdiction the equal protection of the laws. (Cornell Law, 2018)

According to mainstream media, when law enforcement officers work closely with federal authorities, primarily when carrying out terrorist investigations, they tend to focus predominantly on individuals from the Middle East, with a small percent of HVEs. In addition, when federal agencies and local agencies are enforcing federal immigration rules and regulations, they tend to focus mostly on individuals from Latino and Hispanic regions. Take into consideration that there have been cases when individuals feel as though their civil rights have been violated because law enforcement mistook them for terrorists when in reality they are Arab Americans who have no affiliations with terrorists. The same goes for Hispanic and Latino individuals who have been mistaken as illegal immigrants based on their race when in actuality they are Hispanic American or Latino American.

In examining the 14th Amendment in its entirety, it stresses equal protection under the law. Take this account into consideration: If an illegal immigrant becomes a victim of robbery, is he or she guaranteed the same rights as the United States citizen who also becomes a victim of a violent crime? Furthermore, what about illegal immigrants who are witnesses? Are they protected the same as U.S. citizens who are witnesses? Lastly, what about illegal immigrants who are suspects of crimes? Do they have the same equal protection and procedural justice as the U.S. citizens who are charged with violent crimes? According to Wurie (2012), the implementation of the 287(g) resulted in affecting a notable immigrant community in a local agency where the trust was broken between the community and the law enforcement agency. It was established that the policy caused widespread misunderstanding of the policy's implementation within the immigrant community even though the designated law enforcement agency conducted informational and educational sessions. There were several other untouched and unreachable potential victims who became fearful of the policy. Their fear resulted in not reporting violent crimes against them or their loved ones. These scenarios are playing out in many other jurisdictions. Several law enforcement agencies have established community liaison officers for these respective immigrant groups. These officers are responsible for communicating with their communities since they represent these communities personally due to their backgrounds. Other agencies have partnered with local community leaders to provide a greater understanding of immigration rules and regulations to eliminate or reduce fear amongst its members. These agencies have stressed initiatives that protect victims and witnesses regardless of their immigration statuses.

The questions posed are legitimate questions that have been asked by various proponents. It will also be fascinating to pose these questions to young scholars, since these considerations are very relevant to their future careers. The fact remains that federal, local, and state agencies are established to enforce laws and policies. While enforcing these policies, some have made an effort to partner with their local communities to be transparent and inclusive. These endeavors have proven positive on the part of the parties involved. Humanitarian groups are also established to present the voices of those who feel that governmental agencies have treated them unfairly. These concepts are highly controversial. How can law enforcement agencies gain the trust of the communities they protect and still carry out their daily duties and responsibilities?

The U.S. Freedom Act

On June 2, 2015, the U.S. Freedom Act was signed into law by President Barack Obama. The Freedom Act, which stands for Fulfilling Rights and Ending Eavesdropping, Dragnet-collection and Online Monitoring, was formed to renew and revise some expiring provisions from the previous Patriot Act. The titles and sections are as follows:

- Title I: FISA Business Records Reforms (Sections 101–110)
- Title II: FISA Pen Register and Trap and Trace Device Reform (Sections 201–202)
- Title III: FISA Acquisitions Targeting Persons Outside The United States Reforms (Section 301)
- Title IV: Foreign Intelligence Surveillance Court Reforms (Sections 401–402)
- Title V: National Security Letter Reform (Sections 501–503)
- Title VI: FISA Transparency and Reporting Requirements (Sections 601–605)
- Title VII: Enhanced National Security Provisions (Sections 701–705)
- Title VIII: Safety Of Maritime Navigation And Nuclear Terrorism (Sections 801–812)
    - Subtitle A: Safety Of Maritime Navigation
    - Subtitle B: Prevention Of Nuclear Terrorism

Under Title I, the reformed bill stopped the NSA from continuing its system of bulk telephony metadata collection as seen in Section 215 of the Patriot Act. Instead, the data will remain with phone companies, which the NSA can access after obtaining permission from federal court. Under the new bill, permission would only be obtainable if

1. "[r]easonable grounds to believe that the call detail records sought to be produced based on [a] specific selection term . . . are relevant to [the] investigation" (Congress, 2015); and
2. "[a] reasonable, articulable suspicion [that there is an association] with a foreign power engaged in international terrorism or activities in preparation thereof, or an agent of a foreign power engaged in international terrorism or activities in preparation thereof" (Congress, 2015).

Another amendment the new act makes is the ban on pen registers and trap-and-trace devices unless a specific selection term is used for that trap or device. Similarly, it amends the Right to Financial Privacy Act of 1978 and the Fair Credit Reporting Act to require government agencies to also use a specific selection term for national security letters. Recipients of such letters are able to challenge national security letter requests for judicial review.

In terms of FISA, the Freedom Act requires U.S. courts to maintain total transparency of applications—annually submission of total number of FISA applications which have been submitted, granted, modified, and denied.

Much like controversies that arose from the Patriot Act, the Freedom Act faces some scrutiny. Citizens have expressed their disinterest in the government's ability to still procure records with a subpoena. Such a subpoena, when given the title "National Security Letter," is nearly impossible to challenge without absolute proof, leading most cases to be dismissed for lack of formal standing (*CCR v. Obama*). Furthermore, the new limitations to obtaining phone metadata do not cover other scopes of metadata such as e-mails, videos, and social media. The question is, "Has the Freedom Act really done anything for our civil liberties?" According to the both the Patriot Act and the Freedom Act, the NSA still has authority to collect other types of data. Lastly, among the act's most mentionable provisions, Subtitle B of Title VIII prohibits anyone from possessing a radioactive device or nuclear explosive in an attempt to prevent nuclear terrorism within our borders, with the exception of performing activities for the armed forces.

Chapter Summary

There are both advantages and disadvantages to the initiatives mentioned in this chapter. For example, recall the implementation of the 287(g) program in various local and state agencies, which brought about a controversial relationship between these agencies and their localities. Conversely, due to these partnerships, immigration violations were reduced and all other crimes committed by illegal immigrants decreased. Both immigration activists and reformers have valid arguments and can clearly present their perceptions of the initiatives. Some local and state agencies have thoroughly evaluated the partnerships and have terminated the program, whereas others have continued to renew their partnerships. Even though there are various controversies due to this policy implementation, police and the Department of Homeland Security have always been positive allies, and the continuous partnerships can demonstrate a force multiplier for the greater good of protecting the nation from humanitarian atrocities. Local and state agencies are at the forefront of every interaction. They are the first responders. With these partnerships with the Department of Homeland Security, they are equipped with the training, knowledge, and equipment to properly maintain control of major scenes and make the proper notifications in a timely manner.

This chapter also provided a clear definition of terrorism, presenting the types of terrorism along with the major difference between domestic terrorism and international terrorism. As the term *terrorism* is carelessly applied to every negative event, it is imperative to present a concise definition and examples to support it. Exploring the various strategies for combating terrorism is also essential for an introduction to policing textbook as these topics are normally not discussed because they are usually documented under homeland security fields of study. In essence, combating terrorism are initiatives that local and state agencies have undertaken through various task force partnerships with federal agencies. Lastly, a broad discussion on preventing terrorism versus civil liberties is also essential as one might ask, "How much protection is needed when civil liberties are at stake?"

Discussion Questions

1. Describe the advantages and disadvantages of the 287(g) policy implementation in various localities. Research and present two agencies that are currently using this program and two agencies that have terminated it.

2. Define terrorism and document the difference between domestic and international. Provide two example events to support each type.

3. List and discuss two forms of strategies in combating domestic terrorism and cyberterrorism.

4. The last section of this chapter covered homeland security versus civil liberties. Discuss and share your opinions about which is more important. Is it civil liberties or protecting our nation by whatever means? Support your opinion with research or scholarly articles.

5. The U.S. Patriot Act was passed soon after the tragic events of September 11, 2001. Share and discuss your opinions on this act. Does it violate civil liberties? Or it is appropriate and basically reinforcing policies already in place?

References

Amble, J. C. (2012). Combating terrorism in the new media environment. *Studies in Conflict & Terrorism, 35*(5), 339–353. doi:10.1080/1057610X.2012.666819

American Immigration Council. (2017). *The 287(g) program: An overview.* Retrieved from https://www.americanimmigrationcouncil.org/sites/default/files/research/the_287g_program_an_overview_0.pdf

Burgess, M. (2003). *Terrorism: The problem of definition.* Washington, DC: Center for Disease Information. Retrieved from https://www.hsdl.org/?view&did=451434

Comey, J. (2013). *Homeland threats and the FBI's Response.* Retrieved from https://www.fbi.gov/news/testimony/homeland-threats-and-the-fbis-response

Congress.Gov. (2002). *H.R. 3162: Uniting and strengthening America by providing appropriate tools required to intercept and obstruct terrorism* (*USA PATRIOT ACT*) *Act of 2001.* Retrieved from https://www.congress.gov/bill/107th-congress/house-bill/3162

Congress.Gov. (2015). *H.R. 2048: Uniting and strengthening America by fulfilling rights and ensuring effective discipline over monitoring. USA FREEDOM ACT*) *Act of 2015.* Retrieved from https://www.congress.gov/bill/114th-congress/house-bill/2048/text

Constitutional Rights Foundation. (2018). *The Patriot Act: What is the proper balance between national security and individual rights?* Retrieved from http://www.crf-usa.org/america-responds-to-terrorism/the-patriot-act.html

Cornell Law School. (2018). *14th Amendment.* Retrieved from https://www.law.cornell.edu/constitution/amendmentxiv

Docobo, J. (2005). Community policing as the primary prevention strategy for Homeland Security at the local law enforcement level. *Homeland Security Affairs* 1(4). Retrieved from https://www.hsaj.org/articles/183

Doherty, C. (2013). *Balancing act: National security and civil liberties in post-9/11 era. Pew Research Center.* Retrieved from http://www.pewresearch.org/fact-tank/2013/06/07/balancing-act-national-security-and-civil-liberties-in-post-911-era/

Federal Bureau of Investigation. (2018). *Terrorism.* Retrieved from https://www.fbi.gov/investigate/terrorism

Federal Emergency Management Agency. (2017). Law enforcement's role in responding to disasters. Retrieved from https://www.fema.gov/blog/2013-08-12/law-enforcements-role-responding-disasters

International Labor Office. (2014). *Profits and poverty: The economics of forced labour.* Geneva, Switzerland: International Labor Organization.

Matusitz, J., & Breen, G. (2011). A solution-based examination of local, state, and national government groups combating terrorism and cyberterrorism. *Journal of Human Behavior in the Social Environment, 21*(2), 109–129. doi:10.1080/10911359.2011.542986

National Institute of Justice. (2013). *Racial profiling.* Retrieved from https://www.nij.gov/topics/law-enforcement/legitimacy/pages/racial-profiling.aspx

Nguyen, M. T. & Gill, H. (2010). *The 287(g) program: The costs and consequences of local immigration enforcement in North Carolina communities.* Chapel Hill, NC: University of North Carolina at Chapel Hill.

National Human Trafficking Resource Center (NHTRC). (2016). National human trafficking resource center data breakdown. Retrieved from https://humantraffickinghotline.org/audience/law-enforcement

Office of the Director of National Intelligence. (n.d.). Retrieved from https://www.dni.gov/

Rojek, J., & Smith, M. R. (2007). Law enforcement lessons learned from Hurricane Katrina. *Review of Policy Research, 24*(6), 589–608. doi:10.1111/j.1541-1338.2007.00301.x

Seghetti, L. M., Ester, K., & Garcia, M. J. (2009). Enforcing immigration law: The role of state and local law enforcement. *Journal of Current Issues in Crime, Law & Law Enforcement, 2*(1), 41–73.

Sims, B. (2007). The day after the hurricane. *Social Studies of Science, 37*(1), 111–118. doi:10.1177/0306312706069432

Steiner, J. E. (2009). Improving homeland security at the state level. *Central Intelligence Agency.* Retrieved from https://www.cia.gov/library/center-for-the-study-of-intelligence/csi-publications/csi-studies/studies/vol.-53-no.-3/improving-homeland-security-at-the-state-level.html

U.S. Department of Homeland Security. (2018a). *Homeland Security information network–Law enforcement.* Retrieved from https://www.dhs.gov/law-enforcement

U.S. Department of Homeland Security. (2018b). *Law enforcement partnerships.* Retrieved from https://www.dhs.gov/topic/law-enforcement-partnerships

U.S. Department of Justice. (2018). *The USA Patriot Act: Preserving life and liberty.* Retrieved from https://www.justice.gov/archive/ll/highlights.htm

U.S. Department of Labor. (2016). List of goods produced by child labor or forced labor. Retrieved from https://www.dol.gov/sites/default/files/documents/ilab/TVPRA_Report2016.pdf

U.S. Immigrations and Customs Enforcement. (2018a). Delegation of Immigration Authority Section 287(g) Immigration and Nationality Act. Retrieved from https://www.ice.gov/287g

U.S. Immigrations and Customs Enforcement. (2018b). Updated facts on ICE's 287(g) program. Retrieved from https://www.ice.gov/factsheets/287g-reform

Wither, J. K. (2016). The role of the security forces in combating terrorism. Combating Transnational Terrorism, 131–148. doi:10.11610/ctt.ch09

Wurie, C. M. (2012). Exploring the lives of Salvadoran families after the implementation of illegal immigration reform and immigrant responsibility act of 1996 section 287(g) [Dissertation]. ProQuest Dissertations & Theses Global. (1010273089).

Credits

Fig. 5.1: Source: https://www.maxpixel.net/New-Orleans-City-Louisiana-After-Hurricane-Katrina-81669.
Fig. 5.2: Source: https://commons.wikimedia.org/wiki/File:ICE.Arrest_lg.jpg.
Table 5.1: Source: https://www.ice.gov/287g.

CHAPTER SIX

Community Policing

This chapter will cover the various aspects of community policing. Community policing encompasses problem-oriented policing; crime control; critiques of community policing; community views; types of watches—such as neighborhood, business, and religious; and police substations including apartment complexes, businesses, storefronts, and convenient stores. The concept of how much community policing is actually being done or is needed will be addressed as well, along with the need for community justice, which came as a result of the cries of parents and their children who are viewed as offenders based on certain offenses.

Learning Objectives

- Understand the concept of community policing
- Explore the types of community policing and note the various advantages and disadvantages
- Examine the concept of problem-oriented policing (POP) and community-oriented policing
- Illustrate the concepts of crime solving and crime control relating to community policing

Chapter Outline

A REAL-LIFE POLICE SCENARIO FOR DISCUSSION

from Chernoh Wurie's personal accounts

Near the end of August 2010, at 2:30 a.m., I was conducting a routine patrol on one of the major roadways within the county of my jurisdiction. Suddenly, I spotted a dark-colored, four-door sedan speeding along the oncoming traffic lane. I gauged the sedan's speed based on my own current speed, maneuvered a U-turn, and sped up to catch the vehicle. To my thinking, this was an intoxicated driver who was hoping to avoid me. The sedan's driver continued speeding, at around 60–70 miles per hour.

I kept up with the driver as we approached an intersection with a red light. Impatiently, the driver first attempted to make a left turn on the red light, and then proceeded straight ahead to run the red light altogether. Prior to the driver disregarding the red light, I had already established reckless driving charges and had attempted to initiate a traffic stop. I kept the radio dispatcher abreast of my speed and location the entire time while treating this incident as a vehicle pursuit.

I could feel the blood rushing through my system and my adrenaline on high as the driver continued to ignore my attempts for the traffic stop. I followed the vehicle as it made its way to what was then called Potomac Hospital. The driver sped up to the hospital's emergency entrance and finally noticed me in the rear-view mirror.

I cautiously approached the vehicle with my weapon drawn, issuing commands to the driver. I noticed there were two occupants in the vehicle. As I approached the driver's side, I saw that the driver was an older African American lady who was shaking and crying. As she turned to make eye contact with me, I directed my flashlight around the vehicle, perceived there was no visible immediate threat, and holstered my weapon. My attention was then immediately drawn to the person slumped over on the passenger side of the vehicle—an older African American gentleman who refused to make eye contact. I further noticed his t-shirt was covered in blood. When he managed to make eye contact with me, I saw his face was badly swollen and it appeared he had suffered several contusions to his upper facial portions, which caused both of his eyes to be swollen shut. I helped him out of the vehicle and into an awaiting wheelchair. I assisted a triage nurse who ran up and then wheeled him away into the hospital.

Not long after, I learned from the driver that the gentleman was her husband, a very stubborn man who liked to take walks late at night and had apparently been physically assaulted and robbed on this recent late-night walk. He returned home and told his wife that a few kids had assaulted him and had taken his Walkman and wallet. He cleaned himself up and decided to go to bed without reporting the incident. Sometime during the night, his wife had forced him to go to the hospital, which explains the horrid driving to the hospital because he refused to report the incident or to seek medical help.

I stayed in the waiting room and talked with the man's frantic wife to help calm her down and learn a bit of her story. Before we knew it, it was almost 5:00 a.m. The attending physician approached us (the wife gave consent for me to be in the room while the physician disclosed his medical condition) and reemphasized the fact that if he hadn't come to the hospital he probably would have died from brain injury within a couple of hours.

Later that morning, I was able to speak with the gentleman. He was in high spirits and shared that "some little punks pulled one over on [him] and jumped [him]; they took [his] wallet and [his] Walkman." I took his statement, advised him to refrain from taking walks at night, and made him aware of neighborhood concerns about crimes in his neighborhood. Based on the turn of events, I decided not to pursue any traffic charges against the wife for reckless driving and disregarding a red light. I said goodbye to the family at the hospital and promised to investigate the case further. I completed my report, documented everything that happened, and asked several other officers to canvass the neighborhood and to attempt to locate the crime scene.

Not long after, the scene was located. A pool of blood was found, and it was later confirmed that it was the victim's blood. The officers spent several minutes canvassing the neighborhood and produced some witnesses. All the information received plus my report was turned over to our criminal investigations bureau. Several suspects were developed later on and two arrests were made. The suspects ended up being juveniles who were just bored and decided to assault and rob an old man out on a casual walk.

I got home from working the midnight shift that morning and could not stop thinking about the victim, the suspects, and the wife. The actions of the nagging wife presumably saved her husband's life. I was a graduate student during that time of my career, and this confirmed two notions that the research had presented several years ago: that juveniles act on impulse and the elderly are prideful and do not see reporting a crime to the police as an obligated act. Juveniles acted on impulse that night because they were bored, wherein the old man refused to report the incident because he thought he was fine and probably did not trust the police.

Treating community members as family rather than just victims is an important part of community policing. I treated this older couple with respect and care, I took time out of my day to visit them, and I learned about their lives. There are many community policing stories like this involving officers. It is my goal to highlight these reflections as a former police officer and now a scholar and reformer of the criminal justice system.

Early in 2013, I released my first book titled *Impact: A Compilation of Positive Police Encounters*. Several positive police reflections were recorded and presented in this book to demonstrate some of the selfless actions by officers all over the nation. I plan on continuing this endeavor by producing a second one in the not-too-distant future, capturing the positive actions during this chaotic and hostile season between police agencies and the communities they serve. This chapter of this text focuses solely on community policing, highlighting its advantages and disadvantages.

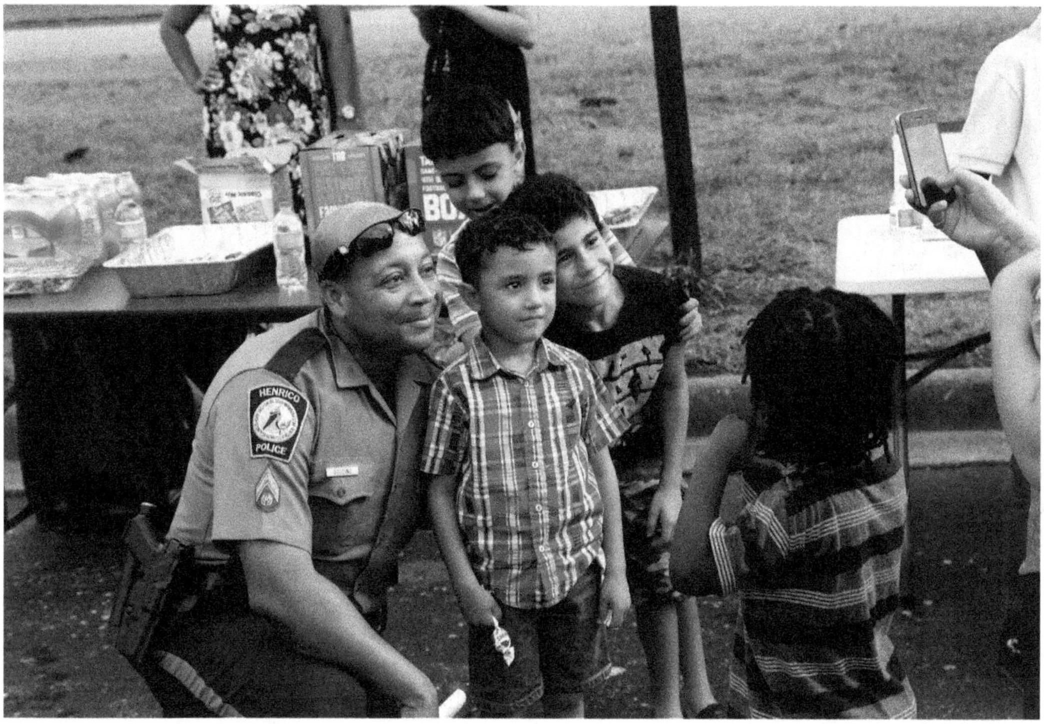

Figure 6.1 Community engagement event, London Towne

Community Policing Definition

Defining community policing is quite simple, as it has been noted to be the same concept as community-oriented policing (COP). Before listing a simplified definition of community policing, let's examine some of the scholarly definitions. For instance, Sutham Cheurprakobkit (2002) published a paper titled "Community Policing: Training, Definitions, and Policy Implications," in which community policing is defined as a new form of policing wherein the police and the community work collaboratively in order to address community problems, such as fear of crime and other neighborhood disorders. The U.S. Department of Justice's Community Oriented Policing Services (COPS Office, 2012) defines community policing as the philosophy that seeks to improve the relationship between the organization and the community they protect, while creating an understanding partnership in proactively addressing community issues such as crime, fear of crime, and social disorder.

The publication by COPS also noted three important key components for the umbrella definition of community policing: **community partnerships**, **organizational transformation**, and **problem solving**. The community partnerships elaborate on the importance of having these meaningful collaborations and a mutual understanding between law enforcement agencies and the community capital they protect and serve. The organizational transformation elaborates on the law enforcement agency's internal structure to be organized and aligned in order to support community needs and partnerships, whether it is by involving community members in various roles or having the community advocate officers within the agency. Lastly, the problem-solving notion stresses the notion of effectively identifying various problems within a community and properly responding to these issues.

Upon stating these definitions of community policing, how can one create a simplified definition? The common themes from the definitions listed are partnerships, collaboration, problem solving, community issues, and fear of crimes. For the purpose of this text, a simplified definition of community policing is a continuous partnership between law enforcement and the community they serve in order to address specific issues and to foster a positive relationship between the two entities. Taking this definition into contextual terms, various police departments are interpreting it in their own ways and incorporating it into initiatives. The next section talks about types of community policing.

Types of Community Policing

Some of the most famous concepts of community policing are having field offices at apartment complexes, the Officer Next Door program, and police substations operating in business complexes, apartment complexes, or similar buildings. Some agencies and jurisdictions are still exploring these forms of community policing, while others have done away with them as they can have some negative implications and unfortunate strings attached by the vendors.

For instance, a newly developed apartment complex would extend an invitation to their local police department stating that they would make available a new apartment unit for an officer to live there rent free. The only thing they ask for in return is that the officer respond to neighborhood calls from their neighbors, take reports, and address any neighboring issues. While this program may seem cost effective for the officer, beneficial to the apartment and the agency, it may be a hazard to the officer's health as he or she would be expected to work his or her regular shift and when he or she is at the apartment resting, he or she would be called on to respond to neighborhood disorders. In essence, the officer would have no time off. This can take a toll on the officer's personal and emotional stress, in addition to causing stress on their family. Most agencies would encourage young officers without a family to participate in such programs. Overall, there are both positives and negatives of such programs wherein both entities can benefit. However, a strict memorandum of mutual understanding should be in place, detailing the officer's duties and responsibilities to avoid businesses overreaching their requests from these Officer Next Door program officers.

Other examples of community policing from various police departments around the country include the Winchester Police Department in Virginia, which has a program called Kids and Cops Camp. Held during the summer, children from ages 9–12 years participate in various activities, such as learning about the police department, and playing kickball, laser tag, and paintball (Winchester Police Department, 2018).

Other examples worth noting are listed by the Ohio Collaborative, Community-Police Advisory Board (2018) and these include community walks in Richmond, Virginia; community-police council in Dayton, Ohio; police iaison officer in Raleigh, North Carolina; community service in Columbia Heights, Minnesota; Teens and Police Service (TAPS) Academy available at various jurisdictions; citizen comment cards in Mound, Minnesota; citizen police academies (multiple jurisdictions); Police Involving Parents programs in Highland Village, Texas; education of the community and private sectors as a tool in advancing community policing (Meth Aware in Little Rock, Arkansas); an elder education seminar in Boca Raton, Florida; Teaching Effective Alcohol Management (TEAM) program in Ocean City, Maryland; a liaison communication project in Bradenton, Florida; and the Serving Our Community initiative in Madison City, Alabama.

Of the programs mentioned, a select few will be discussed, including the **community walks** in Richmond, Virginia; the **community-police council (CPC)** in Dayton, Ohio; the **community service** program in Columbia Heights, Maryland; **citizens police academies**; **Police Involving Parents** program in Highland Village, Texas; and last, the **education of the community** programs to include the Meth Aware, elder education seminar, and the Teaching Effective Alcohol Management (TEAM) program.

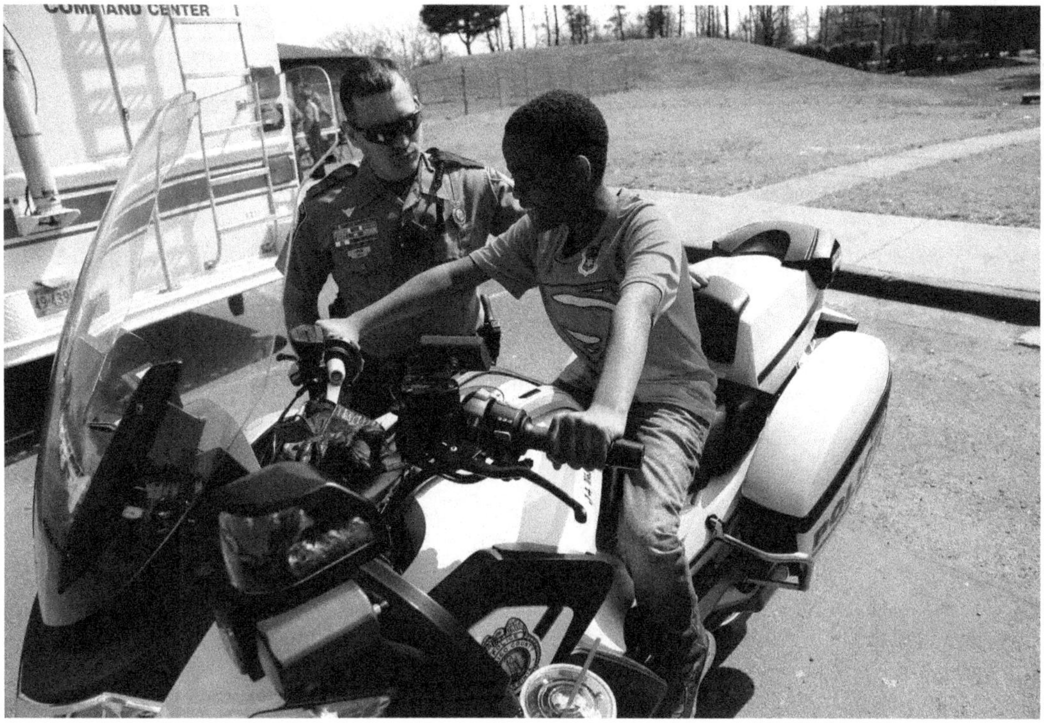

Figure 6.2 Community engagement event, Essex Village

COMMUNITY WALKS

The community walks program, implemented by Chief Bryan T. Norwood, entails the chief and his command staff, including district/precinct commanders, along with other government entities (e.g., public works, social services, public utilities, and local clergy), visiting local communities once a month by knocking on doors to have casual conversations with residents in order to demonstrate the virtual essence of police and community existing together and working together. The original perceptions of police responding to residences are only when they are called. This particular chief was attempting to break that perception by having community residents feel comfortable with their local law enforcement agents and other public service people as a part of their neighborhood community.

COMMUNITY-POLICE COUNCIL (CPC)

The community-police council in Dayton, Ohio, is also worth noting. This council is extremely inclusive, including representatives from all spectrums of the community—from police officers, businesses, community agencies, youth groups, and churches to the local government. The primary responsibilities of this council are to promote safety within the community, change perceptions, and foster a positive relationship between the Dayton Police Department and the community they serve.

COMMUNITY SERVICE

The community service program in Columbia Heights, Maryland, is also noteworthy. In this specific community policing program, officers are required to perform at least 10 hours of community service annually. These services can include working with the community directly in various capacities but

Figure 6.3 National Night Out badge sticker

is not limited to serving food at a local pantry, giving speaking presentations to immigrants, and having an open hour "coffee with a cop" (see figure 6.5). These officers are encouraged to conduct services that align with their skills and interests. The Columbia Heights Police Department was recognized by the International Association of Chiefs of Police (IACP) with a community policing award in 2012.

CITIZENS' POLICE ACADEMIES

Another excellent community policing strategy that numerous police agencies are using is the citizen police academy. The length of these academies varies per agency, anywhere from 5 to 12 weeks. The purpose of these academies is to bring in community members and provide them with several weeks' worth of training scenarios, presentations, exercises, and other applicable materials that are often only provided to law enforcement. The goals of these academies are to be transparent and to show the community what officers face on a regular basis.

The outcomes of the initiatives discussed in this section have been very beneficial for both the agencies and their communities. These initiatives offer a firsthand experience of police officers' duties and responsibilities while also giving community members a clearer understanding of the various units, specialties, divisions, and bureaus that are within the police department.

POLICE INVOLVING PARENTS

The Police Involving Parents program in Highland Village, Texas, is yet another important community policing program. In this particular program, parents, teens, and law enforcement officials partner together in order to address specific reprimands for various teen violations. Due to the success of this program, the IACP awarded the Highland Village Police Department with a community policing award in 2014.

EDUCATION OF THE COMMUNITY

Lastly, the education of the community programs are an endeavor divided into three areas by three different jurisdictions; the Meth Aware program in North Little Rock, Arkansas; the elder abuse seminar in Boca Raton, Florida; and the Teaching Effective Alcohol Management (TEAM) program in Ocean City, Maryland. The Meth Aware program educates community members on the prevalence of the repercussions of methamphetamine. The elder education seminar teaches the elderly population various important topics relating to alcohol, prescription drugs, driving, and various other relevant issues. And the TEAM program in Ocean City, Maryland, focuses mainly on teaching lessons about alcohol-related issues.

The programs we've explored so far in this chapter represent just a small portion of the community policing endeavors most agencies are employing in order to create a positive relationship between their agencies and the communities they serve. Using social media also has become very popular in most agencies wherein the agencies partner with a social medium in order to broadcast important information such as alerts, job announcements, warnings signs, and other related information that is pertinent to the public. This relationship between the media and law enforcement has become quite cumbersome wherein it can be simultaneously positive and negative. Chapter 2 on police perceptions discussed the advantages and disadvantages of the collaboration between law enforcement agencies and the media. In a nutshell, community policing is much needed, but the question is, "How much community policing is too much?" Let's investigate the various views on community policing.

Various Views on Community Policing

The primary duty of law enforcement officers is to twofold: protect and serve. Protecting applies to everyone, mostly the innocent, and at times suspects in special occasions and special investigations. The serving portion has always been a prominent sector of law enforcement. However, serving has been affected by the environmental climate of the decades and the social events that plague them in the United States. For instance, in earlier policing during the political era, politicians controlled law enforcement agencies as they greatly influenced the hiring of police chiefs and the elections of sheriffs. Consequentially, these leaders were indebted to these politicians who helped them acquire their officers, and as a result corruption was easily associated with these agencies. Then there was the reform era wherein various scholars and pioneers such as August Vollmer and O.W. Wilson proposed and changed the perception of policing to become more formalized and professional. Gradually, and up until current times, the community era evolved. This era's evolution stemmed from severe unrest and other chaotic and societal injustices by various parties that have directly influenced the relationship between law enforcement agencies and the communities they serve. Several agencies have embarked on returning back to the professionalism era and to making community policing a primary task.

The question was asked, "How much community policing is too much?" In addressing this question, let's examine the TED (2016) Talk video by Lieutenant Colonel Melvin Russell from the Baltimore Police Department (see figure 6.4). When he was promoted to lieutenant colonel,

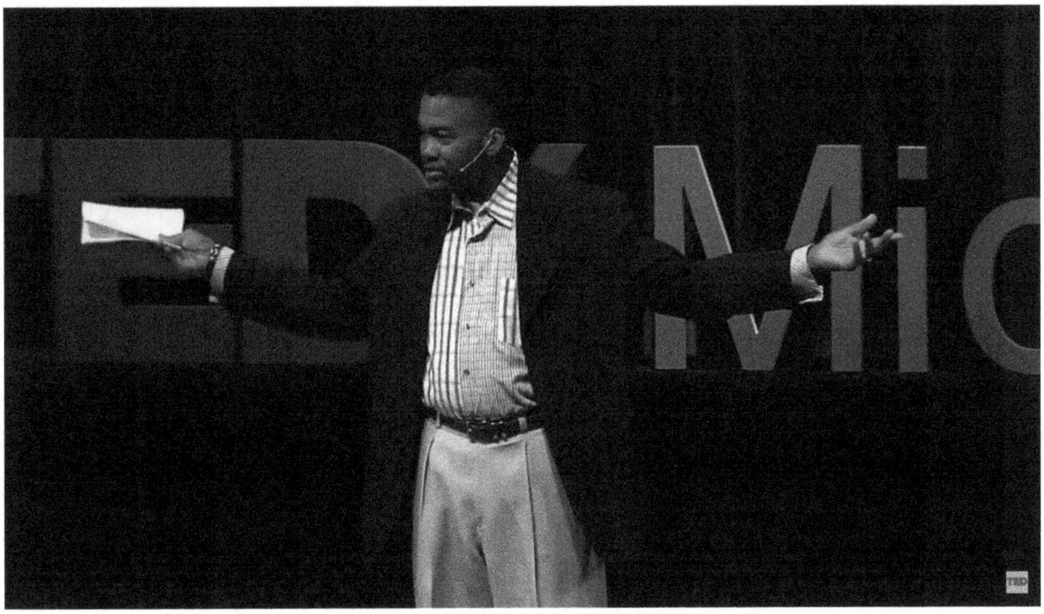

Figure 6.4 I love being a police officer, but we need reform | Melvin Russell

he created the Community Partnership Division, the main goal of which was to bring peace and prosperity in the City of Baltimore.

In his speech, Russell specifically mentioned that technically speaking if his natural body represents a police department, his right arm represents the protecting arm and the left arm represents the serving arm. He further noted that current policing's right arm is becoming too powerful and aggressive whereas the left arm is becoming weaker and weaker. He also noted that current policing strategies are focusing solely on protecting by using various advanced tools in order to keep up with current crime trends and criminals. Focusing too much on the enforcing and protecting arm, the left arm is becoming neglected, thus becoming weaker. This is an excellent analogy as the value of community policing has faced so many varied perceptions.

In further exploring the various perceptions of community policing, it is important to examine the work of the famous police scholars John Worrall and Frank Schmalleger (2016) *Policing*. In this book, the authors note that the extent of community policing covers two distinct possibilities: **structural change** and **attitudinal change**. Structural change applies to the departmental variations both symbolically and physically in order to mirror the concept of effective community policing within their jurisdictions. Attitudinal changes represent the actual officers' personal reactions toward the concept of community policing. The authors further note that most police departments are making symbolic changes to their mission statements and other minor changes in order to adapt to the community policing strategies. However, current research shows that most police departments are becoming more inclusive and are more involving of community members. Rather than just changing their policing and guidelines, they are actually incorporating these methods.

Regarding attitudinal change, recent studies have also shown that officers do not respond well to changes—the majority of them have personal reservations toward their agencies becoming too community involved. Bringing in community members has caused some tension within some police departments. The administrative staff—chiefs, commissioners, sheriffs, and other high-ranking members of police agencies—are the foundation for these community implementations in order for an agency to thrive on fostering these relationships. It's clear that community policing is critical, but the question lingers: How much community policing is too much? What is the medium wherein an agency can meet its community needs by working with them effectively and also still enforce laws, protect its citizens, and control crime? These questions will be surmised at the end of this chapter.

It is also advantageous to examine some critical views of community policing. Worrall and Schmalleger (2016) noted some significant concepts in their community policing chapter that are worth discussing. The authors mentioned that several factors need to be taken into consideration: recent research still showing that African Americans continue to experience negative interactions with the police; citizen satisfaction survey results; and police mind-set for community policing. African Americans and policing have long suffered a negative relationship (refer to chapter 2). Several approaches to mending the broken relationships between these two entities were proposed in that chapter. As a result of these negative relationships, community policing in a perceived African American neighborhood might be somewhat challenging based on the perceptions.

Citizen surveys have also been used to measure the level and effectiveness of community policing. These surveys are disseminated to various communities, and depending on the method, many may choose to respond or not respond. Regardless of the survey outcomes, it is important to examine the sources used to distribute the surveys, the level of participation, and the survey participants. By examining these and making sure that the surveys are distributed equally while reaching all socioeconomic levels of a jurisdiction, an accurate representation would be presented regarding measuring the level and effectiveness of community policing. Last, another critic that is normally associated with the community policing method is the officer's mind-set.

Informal surveys of officers from various departments nationwide reveal that the general theme among police officers is that community policing—although necessary—surpasses the core value of the basic function of traditional policing, which is to fight crime. An agency cannot fight crime and enforce stringent traffic laws when it is actively working to create an effective community strategy. Most police officers tend to view community policing as the agency getting too soft and holding hands with the community. Some administrative staff members also feel this way and therefore tend to be more resistant to the concept of community policing. On the other hand, many command staff members for most agencies have several years of service and have witnessed the evolution of their agencies and are therefore more inclined to adopt community policing strategies.

Back to the earlier questions, "How much is too much community policing, and what is the medium wherein an agency can meet its community needs by working with them and also still enforce laws, protect its citizens, and control crime and yet still working effectively with the community?" To address these questions, it is the responsibility of the agency and its staff to make sure that there is a balance. Encouraging and incorporating community members demonstrates transparency, thus fostering a greater relationship and understanding. The agency should also be cognizant as to how and where members are permitted to participate, as too much involvement can be a conflict if a community member has a negative perception and or an ulterior motive toward the police. Regarding the happy medium, again, this will rely solely on both the agency and the community to work together and involve each other in various endeavors to create a positive relationship.

Box 6.1 Perception Versus Reality

To address the perception-versus-reality segment in this chapter, a depicting example is presented from the Tulalip Police Department (TPD). The TPD is a small tribal police department that is in charge of providing safety and security services to the Tulalip Tribe Reservation. The department only has about 18 officers and responds to hundreds of calls for service. Even though the TPD is not a municipal, local, or state police agency, their primary mission and duties are very similar to those agencies. The TPD produced a document titled "Five Myths of Community Policing." These five myths are listed here:

- Community policing is social work, soft crime
- Community policing is too expensive
- Traditional police work has no place within a community policing environment
- A police agency can adopt full transition to a community policing philosophy in 30 days or faster
- Our department has Community Policing Officers and "real" Police Officers

(Tulalip Office of Neighborhoods, n.d.)

The truth of the matter is that even though these statements are myths, mainstream media often portrays police departments as such. The social work concept has actually been voiced by most officers within various departments. Officers feel as though their jobs are becoming too soft. Being a community-oriented policing department takes time, effort, and work from all those within, along with active community cooperation. Community policing does not mean that a department is becoming soft; it merely means that the department is evolving and is becoming transparent and inclusive toward the communities it serves.

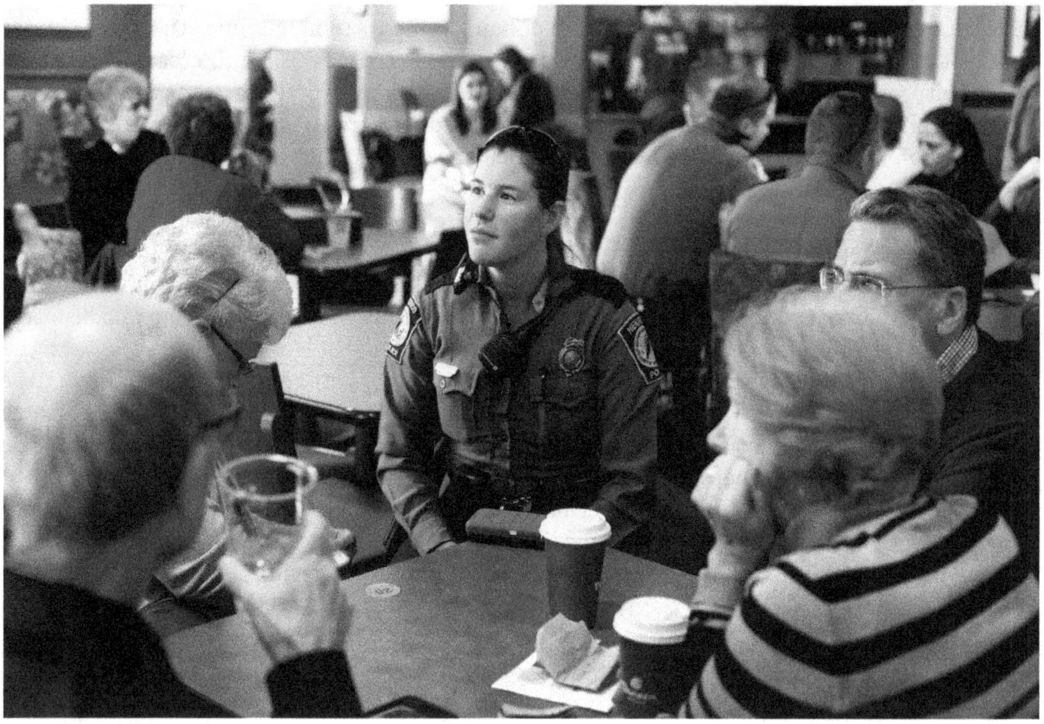

Figure 6.5 Coffee with A Cop

Problem-Oriented Policing (POP)

The concept of **problem-oriented policing** is sometimes depicted as POP and is also often misconstrued as community policing. In actuality, this is a separate concept of community policing. Herman Goldstein (see figure 6.6) is one of the primary pioneers for POP. According to Michael Scott (2016) from the Center for Problem-Oriented Policing in Phoenix Arizona, Goldstein was born and raised in New London, Connecticut. He became quite interested in the daily functions of policing as he progressed in age. According to the author, Goldstein's interest deepened when he was appointed as a staff investigator for the American Bar Foundation survey of the administration of criminal justice (ABF). The study sought to document and understand the daily routines of police officers, prosecutors, judges, and corrections officers (Scott, 2016). During this time, Goldstein rode and observed with several police agencies in Michigan and Wisconsin. The outcome of the study mostly demonstrated that police officers spent the majority of their time interacting with citizens and handling other minor matters in the public rather than actually enforcing the laws. They also found out that a small portion of their daily interactions actually makes it to the courtrooms. Last, as a result of the outcome of the ABF study, the term *criminal justice* came into effect.

Goldstein was also asked by O.W. Wilson to be an executive assistant to him when he was the commissioner of the Chicago Police Department. Goldstein and Wilson sought to revitalize the police department, addressing problem employees, revamping various polices dealing with communities and sub-offices, and dealing with colored and underrepresented communities. Goldstein started to see problems emerging that needed specific attention such as special bureaus to handle street offenses like robbery, vice offences, bicycle theft, and other street-related crimes. Goldstein started crafting the term **POP** to mean addressing specific problems with specific measures and strategies. Instead of addressing all problems with one concept such as community policing,

Figure 6.6 A Conversation with Herman Goldstein

agencies should strive to identify specific problems and target specific resources to address those problems. For instance, the increase of street robberies in certain jurisdictions has prompted these agencies to establish street crimes units or special problems units. These units are solely for suppressing these street disorders. Goldstein summarizes the concept of POP in the following excerpt from his presentation at the International Problem-Oriented Policing Conference in San Diego, California in 2016:

> POP is an approach to policing in which (1) discrete pieces of police business (each consisting of a cluster of similar incidents, whether crimes or acts of disorder, that the police are expected to handle) are subject to (2) microscopic examination (drawing on the especially honed skills of crime analysts and the accumulated experience of operating field personnel) in hopes that what is freshly learned about each problem will lead to discovering a (3) new and more effective strategy for dealing with it. POP places a high value on new responses that are (4) preventive in nature, that are (5) not dependent on the use of the criminal justice system, and that (6) engage other public agencies, the community and the private sector when their involvement has the potential for significantly contributing to the reduction of the problem. POP carries a commitment to (7) implementing the new strategy, (8) rigorously evaluating its effectiveness, and, subsequently, (9) reporting the results in ways that will benefit other police agencies and that will ultimately contribute to (10) building a body of knowledge that supports the further professionalization of the police. (Goldstein, 2001).

For each point listed, discuss specifically whether any neighboring police departments are practicing any of the listed functions.

Similar to community policing, POP has also faced some critics: How much is too much problem-oriented policing? Are police agencies using too much of their resources to address certain problems? For instance, the 1033 program, which allows local and state agencies to utilize excess military gear for police use, can be seen as an example of too much emphasis on problem-oriented policing which will continue to sever the police and community relationships. Police agencies would advise that they are using these specialized tools for enforcing specialized problems. As mentioned in chapter 2, some citizen groups have noted that these programs have created a militarization of the local and state police departments. In a nutshell, police agencies should be cognizant as to what method of enforcement or strategy they propose to address certain problematic issues in order to not be viewed as too powerful or militarized.

In an effort to continue this policy, Herman Goldstein played a key role in creating the Center for Problem-Oriented Policing. This organization is a nonprofit, which is comprised of police practitioners, police researchers, and other university advocates who are all dedicated to promoting problem-oriented policing. The legacy of Herman Goldstein continues, and the concept of POP also continues and is being adopted my numerous agencies nationwide. The benefits of POP demonstrate the effectiveness of police work and the concise distribution of resources allocated to applicable and selected needs.

In a nutshell, problem-oriented policing seeks to address community issues from a holistic approach wherein everything is examined—planning, community reorganization, community watch, citizen's group/advocates, and whether improving living conditions would ultimately reduce crime. See the example from Newport News, Virginia, wherein police used the POP method to reduce crimes in a particular apartment complex. The Newport News Police Department, through its effective use of the POP method, was able to significantly reduce the number of burglaries, robberies, and larceny from autos in a specific geographic location (Eck & Spelman, 1987).

SARA: Scanning, Analysis, Response, and Assessment

Samuel Walker and Charles Katz (2018) presented an excerpt on **SARA** in their text *The Police in America: An Introduction*, which credited John Eck and William Spelman for noting that problem-oriented policing is primarily known for its four stages, SARA: scanning, analysis, response, and assessment. Walker and Katz gave a simplistic explanation for these steps. The **scanning** process is merely wherein officers examine their basic routine duties and beat areas for specific problems. The **analysis** process is after the officers try to identify specific problems. This process is merely based on three guiding principles according to Walker and Katz: the actors, the incidents, and the past responses. In delving a bit more into the analysis process, the actors are the offenders, victims, and other related parties to the issue at hand. The incidents are the physical settings or environments of the scenario, and the past responses are the community input and other initiatives. The **response** process is using both the scanning results and the analysis results to accurately identify a proper response to the designated and isolated problem. Last, the **assessment** process is basically the evaluation process wherein the officers can evaluate their scanning, analysis, and responses to these problems in order to make changes or to note worthiness of such programs (Walker & Katz, 2016). In further explaining the simplicity of the SARA concept, according to the National Center for Justice Planning (NCJP, 2018), scanning is identifying the problem and describing the problem. Analysis is identifying persons involved, documenting the scope and causes, while response is the community involvement and joining on solutions. Last, the assessment process consists of process evaluation and new problem assessment.

Examine all four SARA steps thoroughly and apply them to a specific problem while defining each step and detailing how each step applies to the designated chosen problem.

Citizen Disenchantment

According to Worrall and Schmallegar (2016), one of the primary reasons for community policing and problem-oriented policing is citizens' disenchantment with police services. The authors further noted that underrepresented citizens in particular continue to express dissatisfaction for police who would come in and out of their neighborhood without having much sensitivity regarding how to interact with them. Furthermore, the recent incidents noted in chapter 2 regarding the shooting of unarmed African American males from 2014 to 2017 has magnified this distrust between police and the underrepresented communities, thus fostering the enhanced push for community policing. In addition, citizen disenchantment is not only applicable to widely underrepresented communities; it is applicable to anyone who has had a negative experience with the police. For instance, in a community where several arrests have been made in order to effect problem-oriented policing, that specific community will have a negative and a positive perception of the police. Some community members who are directly affected will have a negative perception of the police while those who are not directly affected will have a positive perception, noting that the police are effectively performing their duties and responsibilities. Citizen disenchantment can be applicable to a specific community that has moderate social disorder wherein the police department will respond with saturated policing (responding in larger-than-usual quantities in order to address a specific problem). Another perception this concept presents is that community members have noted they believe that the police departments are just performing the so-called community policing strategies as a check box to make their agencies look good to the public, but that they do not actually care about their neighborhoods. Several community members have expressed this notion at various community meetings. It is important to note that jurisdictions wherein the police have already established positive relationships with their communities, well before issues arise between both entities, may still have solid foundational relationships.

This concept is real and it's affecting several police agencies. How can it be addressed? The recommendations that came from President Obama's Task Force on 21st Century Policing made several suggestions on how local and state agencies can mend this issue, listing local government, law enforcement, and communities; all three should work accordingly. Under the local government section, it is recommended that listening opportunities with the community are implemented, citizen surveys on police perceptions are conducted, and the root causes of crime are recognized and addressed (COPS Office, 2015). Under the law enforcement section, it is recommended that police agencies constantly review and update use-of-force policies and also include community members in the process. Additionally, it was recommended that agencies examine their hiring practices and involve community members in the process. Last, under the community section, it is recommended that they engage with law enforcement in various aspects, make an effort to participate in police perceptions surveys, and actively work with law enforcement agencies on various applicable issues (COPS Office, 2015). The listed recommendations are just an excerpt from the full listing (COPS Office, 2015). A successful examination and admission of these recommendations would result in a positive and cultivating perception between the police and the community. It will be a process and can take time; however, it is doable.

Rapid Response to Calls for Service and Preventive Patrol Versus Community Policing

Community policing and problem-oriented policing have been exploited in the study of policing. It is important to know the similarities and differences. To address this comparison, it is important to know the meaning of the following terms: **rapid response**, **calls for service**, and **preventive patrol**.

RAPID RESPONSE

According to Richard Larson (1990) from the National Center for Community Policing School of Criminal Justice at Michigan State University, in his paper "Rapid Response and Community Policing: Are They Really in Conflict?" when an agency is operating in a rapid response note, it is viewed by the community as lazy. Even though this article is over 20 years old, it is still applicable to the concept of community policing. The outcome of the article presents the perception that officers only get out of their cars in order to respond to an incident or for meal breaks, that officers spend the majority of their time in their vehicles and are only responding to various incidents that they're dispatched to or if they observe something (Larson, 1990).

Larson further noted that this situation can be compared with the medical term *rapid response* wherein several ambulances are waiting for an incident to happen before they can respond and there are no preventive health care measures being taken. The community sees the police who are operating in a rapid response mode as useless to the community because they are entirely reactive, rather than preventive.

CALLS FOR SERVICE

The term *calls for service* in primarily the situation that is being generated based on the incident. These are varied incidents that require some form of police interaction between a citizen and the police agency. This can be a wide variety of scenarios such as traffic accidents, domestics, serious felony or misdemeanor incidents, driving while intoxicated or driving under the influence, assaults, and other disorderly incidents.

PREVENTATIVE PATROL

Preventive patrol on the other hand focuses on thwarting the crime before it happens through various means. Szynkowkski (1981) gave some very good details in his article titled "Preventive Patrol-Traditional Versus Specialized." He defined preventive patrol as the use of uniformed officers constantly being present patrolling a specific area whether by foot, bicycle (see figure 6.7), or vehicle in order to demonstrate their presence. He further noted that preventive patrol operates on five goals: (a) deterrence of crime, (b) apprehension of criminals, (c) recovery of stolen property, (d) satisfaction of public demands for services unrelated to crime, and (e) development of a sense of security and confidence in law enforcement agency (Szynkowkski, 1981).

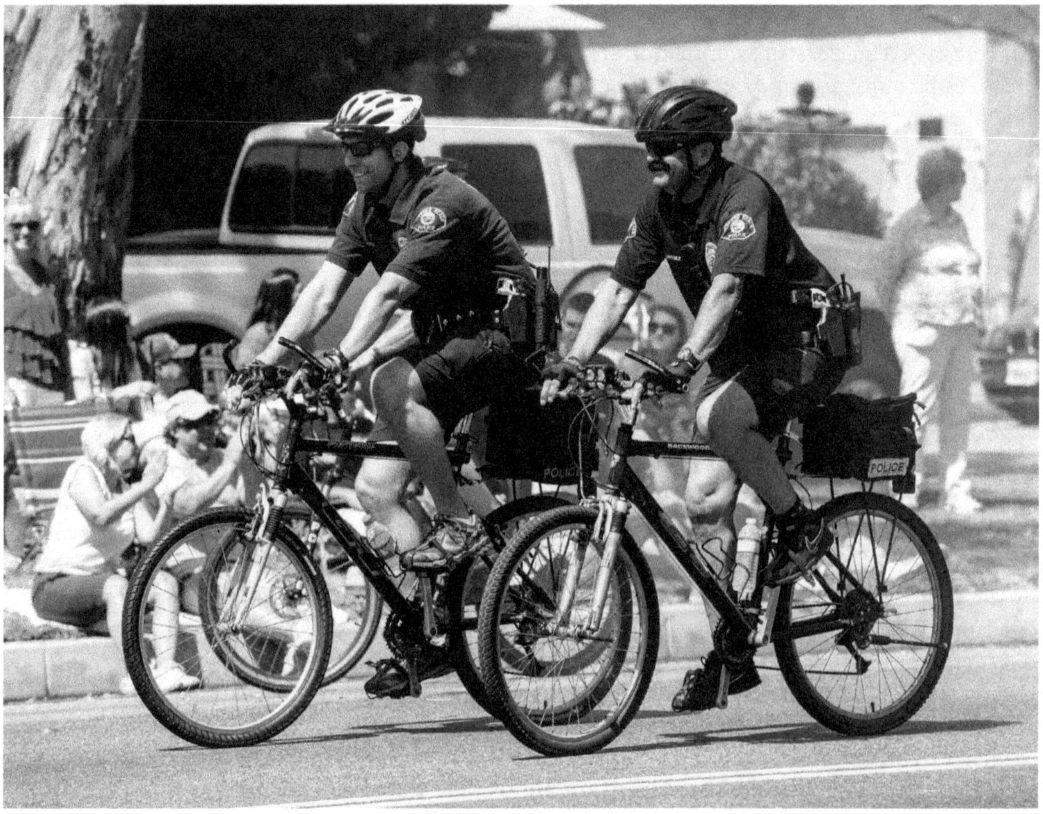

Figure 6.7 Torrance Police bike patrol

Rapid response was employed earlier in police history due to the constant demand for police to respond and handle certain calls for service by the community. The agencies sprang into action and implemented rapid responses. There are a lot of factors that call for these responses—the time the officer receives the call; the time the officer takes to mentally prepare for the call; the actual responding to the call, taking into consideration the time to get there and distance of the call; and how the officer actually handles the call. All these concepts are embedded into rapid responses to calls for service. Preventive response tends to focus mostly on deterrence wherein an agency will deploy or saturate a number of officers at a problem area in order to deter an ongoing issue or to prevent an incident from happening. Community policing demonstrates the collaborative endeavor between both the community and the police department. However, with the rapid response to calls and preventive patrol, there might be a conflict, and this conflict will prevent a negative perception for the police department. Agencies should have a proper balance for the overarching community policing concept while still conducting rapid response when needed and utilizing preventive patrol when requested. This will be a difficult transition and implementation in order to work collectively; however, it is doable with the collaborative efforts from both entities.

Does Problem-Oriented Policing Work?

John Dempsey and Linda Frost (2016) noted in their text "An Introduction to Policing" that there are several positive examples of problem-oriented policing nationwide. The authors also surmised that the concept of community policing and problem-oriented policing have merged over the past few years to form the concept community-oriented policing. Some examples of community-oriented policing can be seen with the California Highway Patrol (CHP) and the San Marcos Police Department in Texas. In the example of the California Highway Patrol, the agency was noticing a higher number of fatalities involving farm vehicles transporting farm workers to and from various locations. Due to relaxed regulations on farm vehicles there were limited or no safety laws or regulations in place. In addition, due to language barriers, reaching this population was somewhat difficult, thus adding to more of the problem of increased fatalities. The CHP took an active role in addressing this issue by working collaboratively with the state legislatures and were able to influence one or more safety regulations for farm vehicles. The agency also took an active role in enforcing these policies and providing an educational program called the SAFE (safety and farm vehicle education) program (CHP, 2002). The agency utilized the SARA method to scan, analyze, respond, and then assess their response to the problem. Based on their publication, their response lowered the number of farm vehicles significantly (CHP, 2002).

Another prominent example of community-oriented policing can be seen with Texas State University and the San Marcos Police Department. According to Dempsey and Frost (2016), in 2007, the San Marcos Police Department received over 2,800 calls for service relating to noise complaints. The agency and the community, along with the university officials formed the Achieving Community Together (ACT) program to address this issue. According to the Department of Housing and Residential Life website, the ACT program is a collaborative effort between the City of San Marcos and Texas State University (2018) and is designed to address issues such as noise, parking, unkempt property, and trash. The educational aspect was part of the initiative wherein the agency and the community came together to educate the various individuals who were violating the noise ordinances. In assessing the ACT collaboration after its implementation, it was noted that this endeavor was beneficial as it reduced the high number of noise complaint calls for service.

In examining these two scenarios it is important to note that education was the common theme between both initiatives. Both agencies and community liaisons were determined to work collaboratively and in the end used means other than arrests and other traditional methods to effect a change in the community. These initiatives demonstrate that education can be perceived as the successful key ingredient to most community-oriented programs.

Racial Profiling

The term *racial profiling* is fairly new. In order to talk about this term and its applicability to policing and community policing, it is important to know its history. This term has been used loosely over the past decades. However, it started surfacing during a federal lawsuit in New Jersey's Superior Court between 1994–1995, charging New Jersey state troopers for stopping only persons of color (African Americans and Hispanics). To summarize, the defense stated that their clients were only stopped because of their race; therefore, they were racially profiled. After several arguments, the presiding judge agreed with the defense and ruled that the troopers were indeed stopping individuals based on their races. The presiding judge then dismissed several drug charges and rulings that the stops were biased and violated the individuals' 14th Amendment rights. This was one of the groundbreaking cases that set the tone for the racial profiling notion, according to Christopher Baxter (2014) with the New Jersey Politics website. Several other high-profile cases where officers used lethal force options and took the lives of certain individuals from underrepresented communities have morphed into the umbrella term racial *profiling*. In addition, several incidents occurred in a neighboring state of New Jersey, New York, where the New York City Police Department was performing the stop-and-frisk program (wherein the department stops and temporarily details individuals due to basic suspicions of drugs, weapons, and other illegal substances). The premise behind these programs is to reduce crime. However, there have been several federal and state lawsuits filed against many state agencies noting that their officers were racially profiling individuals and their stops were based on the races of the individuals they stopped. This concept is extremely controversial; before exploring its delicate nature, let's present a simple definition for it. According to the National Institute of Justice (NIJ, 2018), racial profiling by law enforcement is defined as the practice of targeting various people in suspicion of crimes committed based on their race, ethnicity, religion, or national origin. The American Civil Liberty Union (ACLU, 2018) defines racial profiling as the discriminatory practice by law enforcement officials of targeting individuals for suspicion of crime based on the individual's race, ethnicity, religion, or national origin.

The two definitions outlined are practically the same. How complex is this issue? A short scenario is as follows: Police officers are flooded with suspects and other be-on-the-look-out (BOLO) information during their briefings prior to starting their patrols. Hypothetically, if they are given five BOLOs for robbery suspects in a particular area, four out of the five suspects are males of color, which include African American or Hispanic males. Upon receiving these suspects' information, they are equipped with the mind-set that any individuals who resemble these suspects should be stopped and questioned.

Stopping someone who resembles the original suspect and questioning him or her is still within the framework of the officer's duties and responsibilities. However, when racial profiling is taken to the next level where the officer stops every underrepresented individual with the notion that he or she is a suspect of a crime or looks and acts suspicious is when this notion can become very problem oriented. So, racial profiling can be both useful and problematic. How so? It can be useful in terms of hot calls when police are looking for a felony or other serious offender, and once the offender has been confirmed to be an underrepresented individual, the police tend to have a somewhat narrowed focus of whom to look for. As mentioned, this concept can be problematic, as officers who already have a preconceived notion on race and have personal biases may react negatively and would perceive every underrepresented individual as a suspect. This notion can affect their judgement from the start of the interaction with the individual and, quite often, these interactions do not end well.

The concept of racial profiling should be thoroughly examined by any agency that is currently using it in order to reiterate the fact to officers that stopping someone solely based on his or her race, country of origin, and religion without any proper justification would result in serious repercussions. Also, implementing cultural diversity and other inclusive training for officers might strengthen the mind-set officers have toward minorities and how they may act in various underrepresented communities.

Community Justice

This concept is also fairly new within the criminal justice system. Worrall and Schmalleger (2016) gave a very simple definition for this concept in their textbook. Although **community justice** is the custom-fit crime control initiative wherein the community and the various systems such as police, courts, and corrections come together collectively to address specific issues, the authors note that these three systems—police, courts, and corrections—cannot address these issues (including drugs and other juvenile issues) alone. A collective effort is needed. For instance, in addressing teen and other youth issues, a specific court should be implemented called the "teen court" wherein the community and the courts work actively in order to deter problem teens from engaging in certain behaviors. These courts also are notorious for actually using teenagers in their proceedings as they want to reiterate the notion of being judged by their peers as a form of influential and deterrence factor. In addition, in addressing drug problems, various drug courts were to be implemented to only hear drug cases. Both the drug courts and teen courts are actually in use by various jurisdictions.

In further examining the concept of community justice, David Karp and Todd Clear (2000) published a compelling chapter in *Boundary Changes in Criminal Justice Organizations* called "Community Justice: A conceptual framework." David Karp is an assistant professor of sociology at Skidmore College and Todd Clear is a distinguished professor at the John Jay College of Criminal Justice. Both scholars noted in their publication that community justice is an active endeavor wherein community organizations, citizens, and the criminal justice system can work collaboratively in addressing specific issues. In a sense, it is similar to community policing; however, this is a broader term for greater partnerships on a greater scale.

The authors also proposed that an ideal community justice system entails five key elements:

- community justice operates at the neighborhood level
- community justice is problem solving
- community justice decentralizes authority and accountability
- community justice gives priority to a community's quality of life; and
- community justice involves citizens in the justice process.

(Karp & Clear, 2000)

Community Justice Operates at the Neighborhood Level

In explaining each concept, the idea that community justice operates at the neighborhood level simply means lifting all traditional meanings that are defined by local governments, state governments, and municipalities. In community justice terms, jurisdictions and boundaries are viewed as spaces rather than actual boundaries, which will limit the community's participations in the designated program.

Community Justice is Problem Solving

Community justice in problem solving basically refers to actually analyzing each incident as a problem and trying to solve it. For instance, a typical crime or offense starts with the offense, an arrest, trial, sentencing, appeal, or incarceration. However, under the community justice model, the incident would be viewed as a problem, and necessary steps to resolve the problem would include examining the location and the offense, why it happened, how it can be prevented from happening again, what the individuals could learn from their actions and assessing the solutions used to solve the problem, how effective the solutions are, and so on.

Community Justice Decentralizes Authority and Accountability

The third concept of community justice decentralizes authority and accountability and refers to the traditional notion that the criminal justice system is a sort of hierarchy. However, in the community justice model, several community members including police administrators and business administrators work together to address an issue. There is no hierarchy or reporting to a higher authority. Most of the reporting on program outcomes is provided to citizens' groups and other community advocates. For instance, the National Night Out program that is being conducted by several agencies (see figure 6.3) involves law enforcement leaders and officers along with community members such as apartment owners and neighborhood watch coordinators coming together to have an open celebration in which community members feel comfortable to share things with criminal justice officials.

Community Justice Gives Priority to a Community's Quality of Life

The fourth concept of community justice gives priority to a community's quality of life. The primary goal for these programs is to improve the quality of life for communities. By focusing on specific issues and dedicating their full attention to providing favorable and effective strategies, the outcomes will result in improved quality of life within the designated communities.

Community Justice Involves Citizens in the Justice Process

Community justice involves citizens in the justice process. Most scholars would agree that feeling included speaks volumes when it comes to decision making. When the community is involved in the justice process a certain level of comfort is achieved. This level of comfort also morphs into transparency between the community and its governmental officers (police, courts, corrections, and so on).

Some have criticized the use of community justice and have labeled it as being too soft, similar to the perception of community policing. These criticisms mainly stem from traditional ideas wherein convention dictates the formation and outcome of justice processes. In a nutshell, a traditional approach is basically the "old school" way of doing things—where the police departments make the decisions without seeking the input of the community members who they serve. However, encouraging community justice and allowing community members to become involved in the justice process can be beneficial to some jurisdictions. These ideas support a structure and framework, and they may work for some aspects of community issues; however, involving the community in all processes creates a feeling of comfort and openness between the community and the justice systems.

Chapter Summary

This chapter explores community policing in its entirety. Community policing is a concept that can be, at times, controversial, yet some agencies have implemented various community policing programs since their inception and others are actively implementing these programs currently based on community and public demands.

Based on these programs, some critics have noted that community policing is merely to appease the public, yet the communities and the agencies are not actually passionate about their implementation. As mentioned, if the agency leaders and officers are not passionate about the implementation, then it will only be implemented at face value. Real passion for community policing can bring positive changes to communities and would enhance existing relationships.

This chapter also covered the various types of community policing, various views and perceptions of community policing, problem-oriented policing, the SARA method, racial profiling, and community justice. Problem-oriented policing has also proven beneficial for most police agencies as they are continuously implementing these programs.

Box 6.2 Implementation of Community Policing

Five ways stakeholder groups can implement the Task Force's recommendations

LOCAL GOVERNMENT

1. Create listening opportunities with the community. 2. Allocate government resources to implementation. 3. Conduct community surveys on attitudes toward policing and publish the results. 4. Define the terms of civilian oversight to meet the community's needs. 5. Recognize and address, holistically, the root causes of crime.

LAW ENFORCEMENT

1. Review and update policies, training, and data collection on use of force and engage community members and police labor unions in the process. 2. Increase transparency of data, policies, and procedures. 3. Call on the POST Commission to implement all levels of training. 4. Examine hiring practices and ways to involve the community in recruiting. 5. Ensure officers have access to the tools they need to keep them safe.

COMMUNITIES

1. Engage with local law enforcement; participate in meetings, surveys, and other activities. 2. Participate in problem-solving efforts to reduce crime and improve quality of life. 3. Work with local law enforcement to ensure crime-reducing resources and tactics are being deployed that mitigate unintended consequences. 4. Call on state legislators to ensure that the legal framework does not impede accountability for law enforcement. 5. Review school policies and practices and advocate for early intervention strategies that minimize involvement of youth in the criminal justice system (COPS Office, 2015).

As mentioned previously, community policing and problem-oriented policing have slowly merged into the concept of community-oriented policing, which is basically addressing the same goals as community policing and community justice. With the issue of racial profiling, this concept continues to be controversial; however, with proper attention and training, it can be applicable to certain scenarios. Box 6.2 shows how community policing can be implemented and carried out. These recommendations were geared toward three main entities: local government, police, and communities. It is truly impressive that the Task Force recommendations addressed these various entities rather than making them a one-way directive. This demonstrates the notion that all entities have to put in the work and do so collectively. Therefore, the burden falls not only on the police agencies or the communities they serve, it should encompass all levels of governments. All units—including but not limited to police, courts, corrections, juvenile justice, community, and parents—have to contribute and fully participate in order to create the desired positive relationships. Having the mentality that all entities can benefit from working together versus working as separate islands of their own making will create a profound understanding and appreciation for each entity's existence.

Discussion Questions

1. Research three neighboring police agencies and present three community policing initiatives implemented by each agency. State the positives and negatives of each program listed, based on varying perceptions.
2. What is the difference between community policing and problem-oriented policing? Give two examples of each type.
3. What does SARA stand for? List two municipal agencies nationwide that have successfully implemented this program within their agency.
4. What is racial profiling? List two positive outcomes of this concept and two negative outcomes that can come from this concept.
5. Community justice has been advocated to be beneficial to all entities within a jurisdiction (police, courts, community, corrections, etc.). List and describe three positive or beneficial outcomes from the implementation of these programs. Feel free to use any jurisdiction or locality to explain your responses.

References

American Civil Liberties Union (ACLU). (2018). *Racial profiling: Definition*. Retrieved from https://www.aclu.org/other/racial-profiling-definition

Baxter, C. (2014). Timeline on N.J. state police struggles with racial discrimination. *NJ Politics*. Retrieved from https://www.nj.com/politics/2014/01/timeline_of_nj_state_police_struggles_with_racial_discrimination.html

California Highway Patrol (CHP). (2002). *SAFE: A safety and farm vehicle education program: Reducing farm labor vehicle collision*. Retrieved from https://popcenter.asu.edu/sites/default/files/library/awards/goldstein/2002/02-07(W).pdf

Cheurprakobkit, S. (2006). The impact of race, police experience, and feeling of safety on attitude toward the police. *Journal of Police & Criminal Psychology, 21*(2), 55–67.

Community Oriented Policing Services Office. (2012). *Community policing defined*. Retrieved from https://ric-zai-inc.com/Publications/cops-p157-pub.pdf

Community Oriented Policing Services Office. (2015). *President's Task Force on 21st Century Policing implementation guide: Moving from recommendations to action*. Washington, DC: Author.

Dempsey, J. & Frost, L. (2016). *An introduction to policing* (8th ed.). Boston, MA: Cengage Learning.

Eck, J. E., & Spelman, W. (1987). Problem-solving: Problem-oriented policing in Newport News. *Police Executive Research Forum*. Retrieved from https://www.ncjrs.gov/pdffiles1/Digitization/111964NCJRS.pdf

Goldstein, H. (2001, December). *Problem-oriented policing in a nutshell*. Paper presented at the International Problem-Oriented Policing Conference. San Diego, CA.

Karp, D. R. & Clear, T. R. (2000). Community justice: A conceptual framework. Boundary changes in criminal justice organizations. In C. M. Friel (Ed.), Criminal justice, Vol. 2 (pp. 324–368). Retrieved from https://www.ncjrs.gov/criminal_justice2000/vol_2/02i2.pdf

Larson, R. C. (1990). *Rapid response and community policing: Are they really in conflict?* National Center for Community Policing, School of Criminal Justice, Michigan State University. Retrieved from https://www.ncjrs.gov/pdffiles1/Photocopy/134978NCJRS.pdf

National Center for Justice Planning (NCJP). (2018). *Scanning, analysis, response, and evaluation (SARA) problem solving model.* Retrieved from http://www.ncjp.org/index.php?q=strategic-planning/justice-applications/sara-problem-solving-model

National Institute of Justice (NIJ). (2018). *Racial profiling.* Retrieved from https://www.nij.gov/topics/law-enforcement/legitimacy/pages/racial-profiling.aspx

Ohio Collaborative Community-Police Advisory Board (2018). *Examples of community-policing engagement.* Retrieved from http://www.ocjs.ohio.gov/ohiocollaborative/links/Examples-Community-Police%20Engagement.pdf

Scott, M. S. (2016). Pioneers in policing: Herman Goldstein. *Police Practice & Research, 17(6)*, 582–595. doi:10.1080/15614263.2016.1148339

Szynkowkski, L. (1981). Prevention patrol: Traditional versus specialized. *Journal of Police Science and Administration* 9(2), 167–183.

TED. (2016, February 3). I love being a policeman, but we need reform, Melvin Russell [Video file]. Retrieved from https://www.youtube.com/watch?v=IfjIotVUpbc

Texas State University. (2018). *Off-campus housing: ACT and ACT ally.* Retrieved on from http://www.reslife.txstate.edu/OffCampusLiving/ACT.html

Tulalip Office of Neighborhoods. (n.d). *Five myths about community policing.* Retrieved from www.nwtemc.org/blockwatch/5MythsAboutCommunityPolicing.doc

Walker, S. & Katz, C. (2018). *The police in America: An introduction* (8th ed.). Dubuque, IA: McGraw-Hill Education.

Winchester Police Department. (2018, June 13). *Winchester Police to hold 17th annual Kids and Cops camp.* Retrieved from http://winchesterpolice.org/winchester-police-to-hold-17th-annual-kids-cops-camp#

Worrall, J. & Schmalleger, F. (2016). *Policing* (2nd ed.). Columbus, OH: Prentice Hall.

Figure Credits

Fig. 6.1: Copyright © by Henrico County Police Division. Reprinted with permission.
Fig. 6.2: Copyright © by Henrico County Police Division. Reprinted with permission.
Fig. 6.3: Copyright © by Henrico County Police Division. Reprinted with permission.
Fig. 6.4: Source: https://www.youtube.com/watch?v=IfjIotVUpbc.
Fig. 6.5: Copyright © by Henrico County Police Division. Reprinted with permission.
Fig. 6.6: Source: https://www.youtube.com/watch?v=XNS9d7Vqhno.
Fig. 6.7: Copyright © 2013 by mark6mauno (CC BY 2.0) at https://www.flickr.com/photos/mark6mauno/8754976155.

CHAPTER SEVEN

Police Personality and Police Culture

This chapter will cover the stress factors involving police work. These encompass, but are certainly not limited to PTSD, police suicide, and juggling responsibilities and pressures of family, friends, and social networks. We will also explore the definition of police culture and police subculture, along with police mind-set.

Learning Objectives

- Understand the concept of the police subculture
- Explore the thin blue line and the code of silence concepts in policing
- Examine statistics and other related concepts of officers killed in the line of duty
- Explore the emotional facets of officers killed in the line of duty
- Explain the basic stages officers go through after losing their peers in the line of duty

Chapter Outline

A REAL-LIFE POLICE SCENARIO FOR DISCUSSION

from Chernoh Wurie's personal accounts

It is important to note that fictional names and locations were used in this scenario in order to adhere to the internal investigation process at the time and disposition of the incident described.

On a cold, 37-degree winter night in December of 2009, an officer received a call at 9:30 p.m. about a man standing on his back porch, wielding a handgun. The neighbor advised the dispatcher that the man possibly had mental issues and had threatened to harm himself.

Upon responding to the call, several officers formed what is called a "perimeter," wherein officers surround the house in strategic positions in order to have a vantage point of the individual. Officers Smith and Jones were assigned to take a position on the rear portion of the residence. As they took their position, they could clearly see the individual on the back porch pacing back and forth saying, "I can see you PO PO; come and get me." Officer Smith was equipped with his service weapon and a less-lethal shotgun that shoots bean bags. Officer Jones was equipped with his service weapon and a regular shot gun that shoots both slug and buck shot rounds. The officers took cover behind some very thick trees and continued to observe the individual as he continued to pace back and forth with the weapon in his hand. The officers radioed their position to the incident commander and advised him of the individual's actions. They were told to stay put and address any potential threatening movements (which means to use lethal force if the subject poses any threat to himself and/or others).

At any given moment, the man on the porch could turn the weapon on himself and or turn it toward the officers. The officers pointed their weapons at the subject, continuing to observe his actions and movements. Although darkness can make seeing difficult, this was an advantage to the officers as the darkness of the wooded area where they were positioned provided good coverage, while the individual was visible because the porch lights were on. Simultaneously, a trained negotiator was called out. Upon his arrival, the negotiator maintained a very long and positive rapport with the individual.

As the negotiations continued, Officer Smith noticed Officer Jones was swaying back and forth, almost losing his balance. Officer Smith asked Officer Jones several times if he was okay; he responded that he was just cold. The temperature outside continued to drop. Officer Jones then began to vomit and could not stand up. Officer Smith reached over, removed Officer Jones' shotgun, and told him to sit down. Officer Smith was worried about his partner and could not radio his condition because the radio was being used to maintain communication with the individual on the porch with the gun. As Officer Smith reached over to assist Officer Jones, he could smell alcohol on his breath. Officer Jones acknowledged that he had been drinking prior to his shift. Officer Smith knew Officer Jones was going through personal battles with depression, separation from his spouse, and other financial issues.

Officer Smith managed to cover his position and his colleague's position while the situation concluded. The negotiator was able to persuade the individual to step outside without incident. He was then arrested and transported to the station for processing and a scheduled mental evaluation. Officer Smith also assisted Officer Jones back to the station. There, Officer Smith was faced with the decision to either report his good friend's misconduct of being intoxicated while on duty or to cover up the incident and privately confront him, advising him to seek help in dealing with his personal issues. Officer Smith decided to inform his immediate supervisor who was also familiar with Officer Jones's issues. Officer Jones was placed on an administrative leave and referred to the Employment Assistance Program for further help.

Eventually, Officer Jones returned to work. He was grateful to Officer Smith for reporting him and admitted that he probably would have continued down the same sad path had Smith not intervened.

Understanding the Concept of the Police Subculture

This real-life police scenario is only a small glimpse of what officers face on a regular basis regarding tough decisions involving their colleagues. One officer was faced with the decision of exposing his friend, putting his friend's job at risk. In some situations, both officers would keep quiet, and the situation would be dealt with personally or through professional assistance. The point of this story is to depict that no matter the situation, officers are human, too. This chapter delves into the personal side of police officers and their culture, which we will refer to as police subculture.

In examining this concept of police subculture, Steve McCartney, a retiree from the Vancouver Police Department, and Rick Parent (2015), an associate professor at Simon Fraser University School of Criminology, contributed a chapter in police subculture in their book *Ethics in Law Enforcement*. In their chapter, the authors surmised the concept of police subculture precisely. They noted that in the midst of the negative perceptions of current policing due to the "**us-versus-them**" mentality, cynicism and loyalty are still prevalent within this illustrious culture., . The us-versus-them mentality is the notion that police officers classify themselves into an elite force that is deemed to be the most respectable, most dangerous, and most community-serving profession. This mentality can be taken into a negative context when officers feel that everyone who is not a police officer is against the police. Certain bonds and relationships that exist between officers help them to cope with difficult situations during the course of duty. McCartney and Parent (2015) further noted that these positive, shared values are not limited to support, empathy, teamwork, understanding, and other facets connected to handling posttraumatic stress disorder and other job-related issues. See Box 7.1, which outlines positive and negatives aspects of police culture.

Box 7.1 Police Culture: Positive and Negative Attributes

The following table outlines both positive and negative attributes within the police culture.

TABLE 7.1 Police Culture: Positive and Negative Attributes

POSITIVE ATTRIBUTES	NEGATIVE ATTRIBUTES
Safety	Cynicism
Camaraderie	Close-mindedness
Empathy	Biases
Support	Prejudice
Caring	Non-scientific tactics
Teamwork	Overly conservative
Loyalty	Loyalty
Sacrifice	Alienated
	Suspicion
	Authoritarianism

Source: McCartney and Parent (2015)

In exploring Box 7.1 depicting the positive attributes and the negative attributes of the police subculture, it is evident that a deep-rooted mentality exists within this construct. One might ask the question of whether police officers are born with the culture mentality of the us versus them or if they are trained to have this mentality. Norman Conti (2010), in his article "Weak Links and Warrior Hearts: A Framework for Judging Self and *Others* in Police Training," noted that an ethnographic study based on an American police academy revealed that the police mentality was present in the recruits at an early age. The researchers were finding that the majority of police officers were entering the profession because it was their dream career. Similarly, other researchers have also supported this notion, providing the basis to say that most police officers are driven toward this illustrious career due to personal drive and ambition.

As we continue to examine the concept of police subculture, it is important to know its definition as well as the other major attributes that comprise this concept, including the historical aspect, current perceptions, and the thin blue line and code of silence concepts.

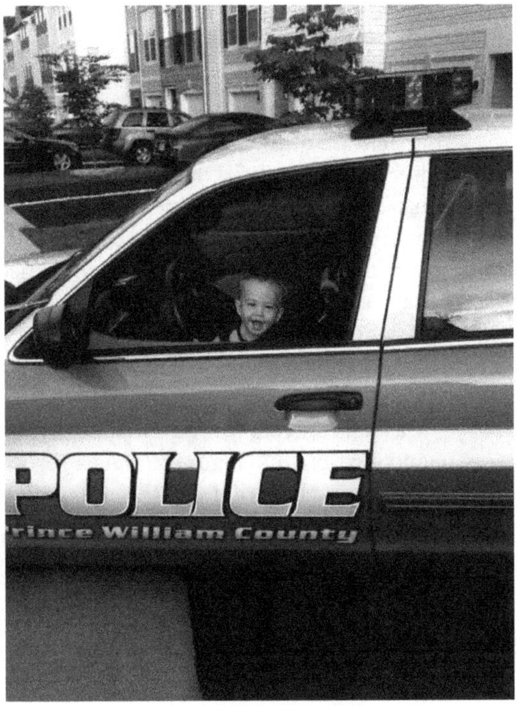

Figure 7.1 Community policing

Definition of Police Subculture

Pulling from a collection of scholarly articles and other textbooks, the most common definition for the **police subculture** is the collection of specific norms, values, characteristics, and lifestyles held by a certain group of individuals (police officers) that is different from the conventional societal standards. In expounding more on this definition, these values and norms are easily shared amongst these individuals because they spend a lot of time together during their tours of duties working peculiar hours, in designated assignments, in life-or-death situations, and also in handling various personal and professional incidents. Officers spend the majority of their time with other officers, thus having a close-knit relationship; as a result, the us-versus-them mentality naturally thrives in this type of setting. For instance, most shifts are divided into three categories—dayshifts, evening shifts, and midnight shifts. The day shifts cover anywhere from 6:00 a.m. or 8:00 a.m. to 4:00 p.m. or 5:00 p.m. This may vary per agency. The evening shift covers anywhere between 1:00 p.m., 2:00 p.m., or 3:00 p.m. to 9:00 p.m., 10:00 p.m., 11:00 p.m., or sometimes 12:00 a.m., depending on the agency. The midnight shifts range mostly from 7:00 p.m., 8:00 p.m., 9:00 p.m. to 5:00 a.m., 6:00 a.m., or 7:00 a.m., depending on the agency. Each agency has a squad or a platoon—a group or set of officers who are assigned to the patrol division and supervised by a sergeant and lieutenant. Some agencies may have several sergeants per squad or platoon depending on the size of the agency. As noted, officers within a platoon or squad may be assigned to patrol certain beat areas as their primary patrol areas; their solidarity sometimes spans from their beat mates to their platoon or squad mates. Some researchers have noted that the traits of the police subculture are very specific and are classified as secrecy, loyalty, honor, clannishness, and support. This solidarity can have both a positive and negative impact. It can be positive wherein police officers can count on each other for support, life-saving scenarios, compassion, understanding, and accountability. However, it can be negative in cases where police officers are only reaching out to other police officers who have similar mind-sets and understandings, thus closing their perceptions of the outside world; as a result, the notion of us-against-them mentality flourishes in police systems.

To solidify this idea even further, Mark Malmin (2012), a seasoned police officer, detective, hostage negotiator, and court bailiff in San Francisco, noted in his article "Changing Police Subculture," in the *FBI Bulletin*, some key points to be considered. The three major points to take away from his article are **officer training periods and academy mind-set, officers relying on others for support, and administrators and officers' changing mind-set**. The author is a veteran officer who has held numerous positions within his former department, and as a result, is well versed in police subculture. He noted that recruits enter the academy with a minimal mind-set of policing where they are exposed to other seasoned officers who are academy instructors and are sometimes overly hard on recruits in order to prepare them for the realities they will face upon graduating. These instructors also rely mostly on their experiences, sometimes presenting unrealistic perceptions for the recruits who are soon to graduate from the academy.

Upon graduating, these officers are also being trained during their field training periods by seasoned officers who also impart their experiences and knowledge coupled with mandated policies and curriculum (Figure 7.2). As a result, the recruit is being exposed to the realities of the job in addition to the training officer's personal and professional experiences. Some agencies are implementing policies wherein the recruits, upon graduating, are exposed to several training officers at different shifts in order to get a wide variety of experiences. Other agencies are only assigning their recruits to one field training officer (FTO).

The second point Malmin highlighted is that officers rely on other officers for support. For example, let's take the SWAT team members into consideration. This elite group of officers undergoes an advanced training and selection process in order to be on this team. They handle high-risk situations that often end in a traumatic event for those involved. How do these officers handle stress and deal with traumatic events? Most rely on other officers' support to analyze and decompress

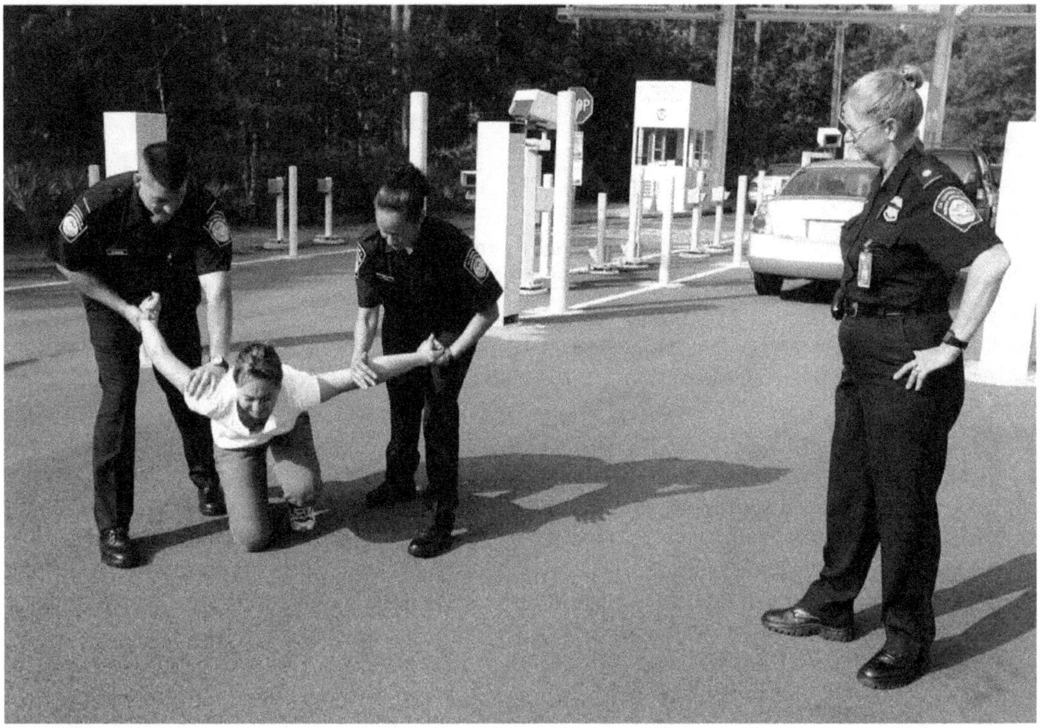

Figure 7.2 CBP Field Operations Academy, arrest

after such situations. Malmin also notes that some agencies mandate their officers seek professional therapeutic assistance after such events. However, some do not seek such help, but instead lean on other officers for moral support. The author further added that supervisors and administrators should not settle for the meager answer when they ask their subordinates "Are you okay?" and they say, "I am fine." They should take the time to interact one on one with their officers and get to know them personally in order to build a trusting relationship. They should encourage peer support and other professional assistance outside the realm of the agencies.

Last, the author suggested that in order to address the negative concepts associated with the police subculture, administrators and officers should shift their mind-set. Various researchers have found that officers resist change; yet, changing the culture starts within the agencies. Administrators and supervisors should encourage their officers/subordinates to maintain social capital relationships outside the department such as those relationships with religious organizations and community organizations and recreational organizations and to participate in initiatives other than just the police department.

Many police agencies are implementing a wellness program—a unit dedicated solely to the wellness and longevity of the officers' lives. These units cater to provide support to officers for physical health and trainings, nutritional health and initiatives, peer support, therapeutic assistance, and many other applicable initiatives. Officers are far too concerned with not getting their next promotion or losing their jobs if they seek professional therapeutic assistance (Malmim, 2012). The truth is that many who have taken advantage of such services have noted how beneficial these sessions can be. It would behoove officers to share these insights with new recruits and mid- and later career officers, that seeking assistance would not hurt their careers. It is important to note that police administrators and line officers are striving to make positive changes to the entire notion of the police subculture by encouraging officers to invest in outside activities. As mentioned, the police subculture can be perceived as a double-sided concept wherein it has its advantages and disadvantages. This will be explored further in the chapter summary.

Examining the Historical and Current Aspects of the Police Subculture

In exploring the basic understanding of the police subculture, it is important to know the history of this construct. The police culture has existed since the inception of the traditional police. Some policing scholars have suggested taking into consideration the early 1960s, when, due to the social climate and other societal norms, there was a negative perception of police and their interactions with African Americans. Some historians have classified the 60s as the decade that changed a nation, wherein civil rights leader Martin Luther King Jr. was assassinated, the Civil Rights Act was passed, President John D. Kennedy was assassinated, and the civil rights protests all changed the nation. These significant events not only changed the nation but changed policing, specifically between the police and the African American communities. The police deployed all resources in addressing the civil rights protesting taking place all over the nation (see figure 7.3). This negative relationship between African Americans continued into the late 1980s and improved for a little while. However, as mentioned in chapter 2 of this book, current relationships and perceptions are mirroring that of the earlier times of policing upon examining the recent traumatic events between the police and mostly African American males. One might ask the question, "Are the negative perceptions during the early 1960s affecting today's police subculture and minority communities?"

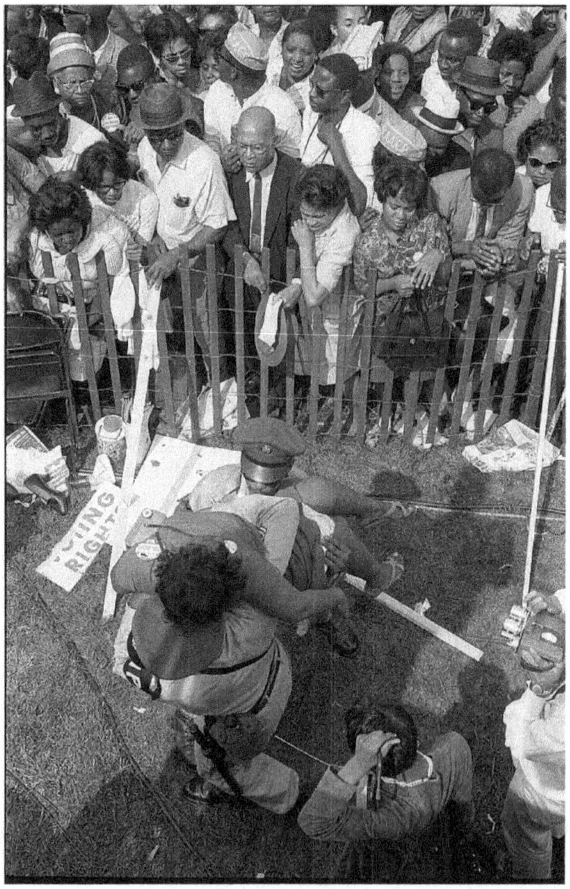

Figure 7.3 Civil rights march on Washington, DC fence

This is definitely a question to ponder as both the police and the communities are striving to improve their relationships. The recruits who are being incorporated into policing are being exposed to this police subculture—both the positive and the negative aspects—and are being exposed to seasoned officers who share their personal perceptions on various entities. Most police agencies are exploring the historical aspects of the police subculture and are implementing ways they can learn from it and recruit ethical and moral officers within their forces. Many agencies are strengthening their recruiting efforts and improving their diversity in hiring (age, sex, gender identification, social class, religion, ethnicity, etc.) in order to be more inclusive and representative of the communities they serve. In learning from past experiences, ethics and diversity plays a key role in what departments are moving toward; as a result, the police subculture will be more comprehensive.

Further delving into the historical concepts of the police subculture, let us examine a study conducted by Steve Herbert from Indiana University in 1998 titled "Police Subculture Reconsidered." In this particular study, the researcher immersed himself into the Los Angeles Police Department and conducted several personal observations, riding along with selected supervisors, line officers, and other specialized units. Upon completing his field observations, he listed six normative orders that made up the entire police subculture context—the law, bureaucratic control, adventure/machismo, safety, competence, and morality. Before explaining these applicable orders, it is important to note the meaning of normative order. The normative order is viewed "as a way of highlighting the cognitive and reflective activities of human agents in defining situations, and it opens an analytic window onto social conflict by elaborating a variety of orders and potential contradictory tendencies" (Herbert, 1998, p. 352-360). This is definitely a complicated definition and concept. To boil this down to its simplest form, it is the concept that covers the human reactions, societal norms, and police officers' responses to various scenarios.

THE LAW

In addressing the law aspect of the normative orders in the police subculture, the author contended that the law can be ambiguous at times to enforce, and officers are often less supervised, thus having a tremendous range of discretion when enforcing the laws and regulations. Oftentimes, enforcing the law is clear and to the point in serious offenses. However, some situations fall in the gray area, thus giving the officers the choice to enforce and conform like others or to choose a lesser action at their discretion. The laws are a basic function for police officers; therefore, some choose to stay solely with enforcing the law to its fullest, leaving no room for discretion; some may refer to this as the "letter of the law."

BUREAUCRATIC CONTROL

The second normative order is bureaucratic control, which is the concept of having something in place that guides the police structure. It is what upper management uses to direct the organization and other issues within the agency. However, with these guidelines in place each officer has a unique set of interpretations and responsibilities depending on his or her job description. The researcher continued to provide an example wherein he rode with a patrol officer who responded to a group of day laborers and cleared them from loitering on a street corner. The researcher also rode with a patrol sergeant who drove by the same individuals who were perceived to be loiterers and barely said anything to them. The researcher suggested that each officer, even though he or she has full police powers, has have two different sets of responsibilities. One officer responds to the complaints of the residents and the other is only responsible for the behaviors of his subordinates. These defined and specific sets of responsibilities can put officers on a two-path course of police subculture wherein the first path for line officers is to stick to their peers and the second path for supervisors is to stick to managerial-level peers as their social friends. The same goes for all the other designated units within a police organization—mainly, officers define their social network based on their assignments and units.

Some police administrators have noted that academy mates tend to continue a lifelong friendship and social network in many cases.

ADVENTURE/MACHISMO

The third normative order, adventure/machismo, is clearly characterized in those police agencies where officers are classified into two main categories—"hardchargers and station queens" (Herbert, 1998). The hardchargers are officers who are not afraid of anything and who often place themselves in at-risk situations including life and death. These officers are very aggressive, and they have an innate attitude toward at-risk situations and low regard for death or grave injury. These officers are sometimes viewed as the "Dirty Harry problem," meaning the ends justifies the means (officers may feel that their actions even though illegal would justify the outcome of the incident). The author noted that the other type of officers are normally classified as a "station queens" and are viewed as officers who tend to stay away from the street-related calls, as they feel more comfortable handling incidents inside the station wherein their lives would not be at stake or threatened. In circling back to the "hardcharger" mentality, it is important to note that many recruits upon graduating feel the compulsive notion to become the hardcharger in order to fit into this new culture; in a sense, they are indoctrinating themselves into this illustrious career and culture.

SAFETY

The next order described by Herbert is the safety normative order. Safety is paramount in police work; therefore, it plays an important role in forming the mentality of the police subculture. The researcher described observing the **roll calls** or **briefings** prior to the officers starting their shifts and also would observe officers after the end of their shifts. Roll calls or briefings are usually held in a classroom or conference room with the shift/platoon officers and the supervisors where officers receive their assignments, vehicle numbers, information on stolen equipment, and other related information including wanted persons and persons of interest. This can also vary per department. However, most commonly the roll calls and briefings are forms of sharing information, acknowledging other officers, and addressing community complaints and other related activities. The researcher specifically noted that the supervisors value safety, and as a result they would reiterate "stay safe out there" at the end of every roll call or briefing. Another instance wherein safety is reiterated is at the end of every shift, when officers would revel over the fact that they made it through a shift safely and are going home to their loved ones. The particular bond over this notion, as during the shifts, is that officers collectively go through various situations ranging from fights, disorderly calls, suicides, fatal accidents, homicides, police shootings, vehicle pursuits, and others.

COMPETENCE

Competence is another normative order Herbert observed. This order elaborates on the notion that a strong sense of pulling one's weight, of competently fulfilling one's responsibilities, thus shapes police culture (Herbert, 1998). This normative order speaks greatly toward the police subculture as officers are judged on their ability to handle calls by themselves, without requiring additional officers. This notion tends to make officers become more susceptible to scrutiny by other officers if they require too much assistance in their assigned areas.

For instance, an officer is assigned to patrol and respond to calls in a specific beat area. On several occasions, other officers are called by the dispatcher to respond to the original officer's area to handle calls for service. Because they were alerted by dispatch, the other officers will deem that the original officer cannot pull his or her weight. This order can be double-sided as well, as being too overly competent and not wanting others' assistance can cost the officer his or her life or the life of others, because he or she becomes so prideful and wants to handle everything by him- or herself in his or her designated area. Frequently, senior officers recognize the new officers who might be trying to do too much on their own and intervene and assist them without being asked to help. This demonstrates the everlasting bond that exists between police officers that is part of the subculture—the unspoken call for assistance.

MORALITY

The last normative order described by the researcher is the **morality** order. Herbert (1998) denoted that most police officers with the department that he studied in the LAPD see their professions as falling into the category of the fight between good and evil. Officers are not just enforcers of the law; they are also individuals who are selected to correct the wrongs of mankind. This perception covers both people and places wherein police officers call certain individuals *"bad guy," "knucklehead," "idiot," "terrorist," "asshole," and "predator"* (Herbert, 1998). Regarding areas, officers refer to them as *"dirty"* if they are problematic areas that are known for drugs and other illegal activities. These officers have the mind-set that they have to clean up the impurities that stain the morality of the cities they protect, to clean up the areas that are deemed dirty. This mentality has plagued the police subculture for quite some time.

Current police subculture has not changed much since this study was conducted. Most often, the police subculture has a negative association. However, the police subculture depicts several examples wherein officers have relied on this culture to assist each other during stressful times. For example, due to the current negative perceptions that exist regarding policing, police officers normally rally together in order to compete in social events such as the annual polar plunge, the Special Olympics, and a 9/11 run and stairclimbing competition. These are just a few of the team-building events police officers partake in to build up and encourage each other. Although only police seem to participate in these events, which can make police feel isolated from the public, these opportunities continue to build their bond among each other and their families. Other agencies have included community members in some of these activities in order to break the police subculture mentality.

In examining current trends of the police subculture, a controversial term—the "**Ferguson effect**"—has come about. This term was coined shortly after the fatal shooting of Michael Brown by Officer Darren Wilson in Ferguson, Missouri. This concept is based on the idea that crimes have spiked in major cities and the killing of police officers has spiked after the incident between Officer Darren Wilson and Michael Brown. It is important to note that this concept is somewhat controversial as several studies have been conducted and have found no evidence validating this theory. One study in particular was published in 2017 by Edward Maguire, Justin Nix, and Bradley Campbell, titled "A War on Cops? The Effects of Ferguson on the number of U.S. Police Officers Murdered in the Line of Duty." The scholars used time-series analysis from the Officer Down Memorial Page pre-Ferguson and post-Ferguson data for officers killed in the line of duty and surmised that there were no significant spikes or evidence to note that the Ferguson effect is a factor relating to officers. As a result of the Ferguson case, some officers have feared being in the spotlight like Officer Darren Wilson and have turned away from various encounters. In fact, some have been seriously injured and have even lost their lives in trying so hard to avoid becoming the next Officer Darren Wilson.

Although it can be difficult to quantify this action, the current police subculture is shaping itself more toward community policing as it works to rebuild the trust that has been severed between the police and the community. Some officers favor the current efforts police agencies are making in order to rebuild their community's trust; while others do not, suggesting that police agencies are becoming too soft. Regardless of the current and historical perceptions of the police subculture, one thing is certain: The mind-set is shared by many and the profession is a close-knit one that is hard to penetrate by an outsider. This is where the concepts of the thin blue line and the code of silence emerge. The next section discusses these concepts regarding police subculture (Maguire et al., 2017).

Thin Blue Wall of Silence and the Police Code of Silence

The blue wall of silence and the police code of silence are practically similar in meaning and are used interchangeably, depending on the audience. For the purposes of this text, the term *police code of silence* will be used primarily to discuss this concept. The **police code of silence** is a symbolically constructed phrase by officers wherein they protect each other from superiors and outside individuals from various complaints regarding wrongdoings and other misconduct. This bond is sometimes unspoken and is expected to be upheld by every officer regarding the other within his or her precinct, platoon, squad, unit, or sometimes externally for officers at outside agencies. In exploring this concept further, two important questions need to be investigated. First, **"Is this concept real?"** And second, **"Is this concept still present in modern-day, 20th-century law enforcement?"**

In addressing the first question regarding the realness of this concept, it is important to note two major commissions: the Christopher Commission and the Mollen Commission. The Christopher Commission was formed in 1991 by the city mayor Tom Bradley shortly after the Rodney King–Los Angeles Police Department incident. The Mollen Commission was formed in 1994 by City Mayor David Dinkins shortly after several NYPD officers were arrested by Suffolk County police for several misconduct activities relating to selling illegal substances (Weisburg & Greenspan, 2000).

The similarity between both commissions is that they were formed after several complaints were launched against both police departments regarding officers not reporting or handling complaints properly. Both commissions found several instances wherein both agencies did not properly handle complaints. Both made several recommendations, mostly pertaining to the reporting process and the accountability initiatives of these agencies when these reports were being made. It is important to note that the concept of the police code of silence played a key role in both the findings of these commissions. Both commissions changed police history and related to the Wikersham and the Knapp Commission, as referenced in chapter 1.

To further explore the validity of this concept, a research study titled "Decoding the Code of Silence" was published in 2018 by Sanja Ivkovic, (a professor at Michigan State University), Maria Haberfield (a former lieutenant of Israel National Police and a professor at John Jay College), and Robert Peacock (a doctoral candidate at Michigan State University). The research was impressive and holistic as it surveyed more than 600 police officers between 2013 and 2014 from various Midwest and East Coast portions of the United States. Officers were provided with several scenarios regarding misconduct issues, and the researchers measured three constructs: the seriousness of the scenarios, the appropriate and expected discipline, and the willingness to report. The scenarios covered the following: free meals/gifts from merchants; failure to arrest friend with felony warrant; theft of knife from crime scene; unjustifiable use of deadly force; supervisor offering holiday for errands; officer striking arrestee; verbal abuse of motorist; cover-up of police DUI and accident; auto body shop five percent kickback; false report of drug possession; and sergeant failing to halt beating of child abuser (Ivkovic, Haberfield, & Peacock, 2018).

The findings of this study were multidimensional, as it presents various responses depending on the seriousness of the action relating to the misconduct. Most officers reported that they would adhere to the code of silence when it comes to minor police misconduct such as verbal abuse, acceptance of small gifts, and police DUI and accident. Only a small number indicated that they would adhere to the code of silence when it comes to serious police misconduct such as stealing from a crime scene, abusing deadly force, and falsifying police reports (Ivkovic et al., 2018). Furthermore, the researchers noted that line officers are more likely to adhere to the code of silence than supervisors, who have an obligation and responsibility to report. Some supervisors are caught in the middle of whether they should report or cover for the line officer as they have personal tithes such as academy classmates and social relationships. Last, the research presented facts that the police code of silence is the least likely to provide protection for officers in extreme cases (Ivkovic et al., 2018). Several factors should be taken into consideration according to the outcome of this study: the demographic of the participants, the level of understanding of code of ethics, the years of service, ranking and status of the officers, and several other influential factors. The researchers cleverly noted that even though the findings of this study presented various factors demonstrating the police code of silence, it is important to note that it cannot be generally applicable to every police department, as each department can be unique in its own special way.

Another work that can be used to demonstrate the realness of the police code of silence concept is a publication titled "Police Attitudes Towards Abuse of Authority: Findings From a National Study" published in 2000 with the National Institute of Justice. The researchers surveyed 925 randomly selected police officers from 121 various police departments and explored questions on police abuse of authority—mostly relating to use of force, what was observed, where it was observed, and how it was handled. Even though the study explored several themes and patterns with police abuse of authority, it is important to note that the researchers concluded there were varied opinions on the difficult question of whether officers should report other officers for wrongdoings and other misconduct (Wiseburg & Greenspan, 2000). The researchers pinpointed that the officers surveyed responded that most of their decisions came down to two concepts: behavior and attitudes. Most officers do not believe in wrongdoings and other police misconduct. However, often, they do not report these instances when colleagues are involved. The code of silence has its advantages and disadvantages; it presents officers with various dilemmas, and throughout their careers they are faced with instances wherein their professions and personal relationships are at stake.

When it comes down to the code of silence, it's fair to say that greater than three-quarters of police surveyed admitted they do not accept this as an essential part of the mutual trust necessary to effective policing. However, about one-quarter of those surveyed agreed that whistle-blowing is not worth it, while more than two-thirds claimed that police officers who report episodes of misconduct are likely to be stonewalled by their colleagues, and more than half of those surveyed agreed that it is not uncustomary for police officers to completely ignore or downplay other officers' poor behavior (Wiseburg & Greenspan, 2000).

In examining this section from the study by the NIJ (National Institute of Justice) researchers, the primary outcome is that most officers who decide to report misconduct are given the cold shoulder; therefore, they may not feel obliged to report wrongdoings and misconduct and will instead sweep it under the rug, so to speak (Wiseburg & Greenspan, 2000).

Taking into consideration these two research studies, it is safe to say that the police code of silence is a real concept. However, in moving forward to the next question, "Is this concept still applicable in today's law enforcement?" the two studies depicted here varied from time span to demographics and participants/officers. Regardless of these discrepancies, the outcomes are similar, demonstrating that in addressing the second question there has not been much change in the concept of the police code of silence in the current law enforcement era. The NIJ study was conducted over 20 years ago, whereas the "Decoding the Police Code of Silence" study was more recent (conducted during 2013 to 2014). Furthermore, in order to explore the question on whether this concept is applicable in current times for the purpose of this book, current times will include the year 2000 to the present.

John Hein, a criminal justice instructor for American Public University, who has also spent over 35 years in various civilian, law enforcement, and federal agencies, wrote a thought-provoking piece in 2016 on PoliceOne.com, titled "What is the Cost of the Code of Silence?" A good reputation can be difficult for a police officer to develop, but extremely easy to lose. The author used his professional and personal experience to say that the code of silence must be eliminated, as this concept destroys an officer's reputation, which he or she has spent years developing. The author also acknowledged that this concept is real and is present in current-day law enforcement practices. He presented the example with the Chicago Police Department and the shooting of Laquan McDonald in October 2014. After the shooting, the incident was investigated internally by an investigator who advised that the shooting was justifiable. The report was signed and approved by several other commanding officers within the police department (Hein, 2016). Further details

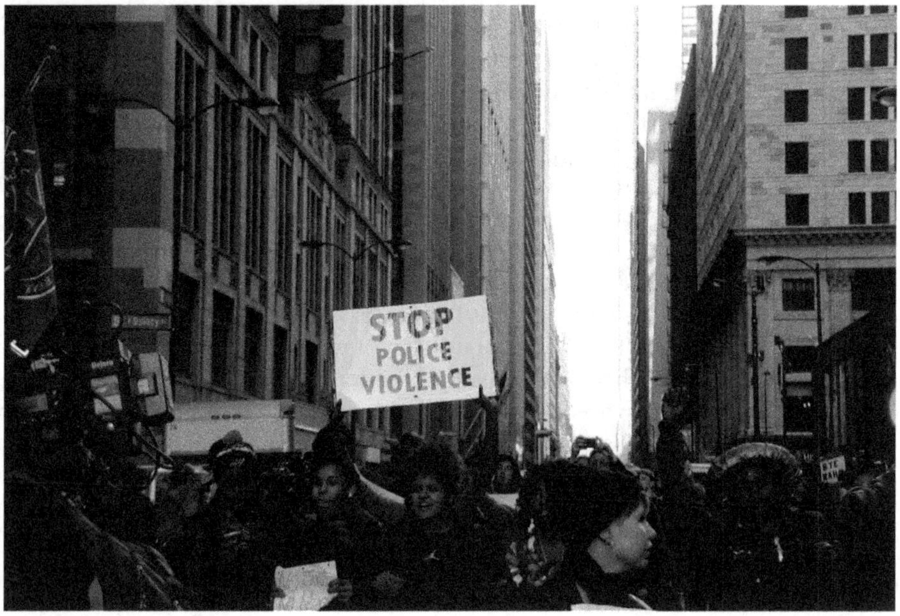

Figure 7.4 Protest, Chicago, December 2015

showed that the incident was captured by a dash camera and the footage was not released to the public for over a year after several complaints, outcry from the community (see figure 7.4), and a federal court order. The camera footage negates the perception of the officer wherein he stated that Laquan McDonald lunged toward him in a threatening manner. It also showed that he was shot several times while he was lying down and facing away from the officer and only one officer discharged their firearm during the entire time (several others were on the scene and witnessed the entire incident). The author further noted that this is a clear example of the code of silence—several witnessed the shooting, and several supervisors up the chain of command signed off on the incident as a justifiable shooting. Deeper investigations on the federal level found the officer guilty of second-degree murder and 16 counts of aggravated battery. As a result of this incident, the police superintendent and several other officers were terminated for attempting to cover the incident.

In analyzing this scenario, it is easy to say the department was withholding information and was adhering to the code of silence. However, from internal examination, it is the practical procedural operations of a police department for most shootings to be investigated, determine whether they are justifiable or not, and then forward the case up the various levels of the command structure within the department (sergeants, lieutenants, captains, majors, assistant chiefs, deputy chiefs, and then finally the chief or commissioner). This is practiced in most police agencies, as most of their investigations are done internally. Several agencies are starting to examine and include outside agencies to investigate police shootings. Are outside agencies guaranteed to be fair in their investigations? Or are all police agencies, regardless of their locality or jurisdictions, still obliged to adhere to the code of silence? This is a question that will remain in the minds of many as the criminal justice system continues its ever-changing reformation based on past and current events relating to police misconduct.

Are all police agencies biased or is there some level of accountability when it comes the levels or policing such as local, state, federal, and so on?

Fair and Impartial Policing

In the wake of recent times and the negative perceptions police agencies are receiving regarding their interactions with their communities, several agencies have embarked on implementing **fair and impartial policing (FIP)** training for their members. FIP is a rigorous several hours of implicit and explicit bias awareness training conducted by executive- and national-level instructors who are experts in this field. This concept was developed by Dr. Lori Fridell, a professor of criminology at the University of South Florida, and Anna T. Laszlo, who is the director of training and the curriculum designer for FIP. Both advocates have extensive knowledge in police research and initiatives and were very passionate in addressing the biases that exist within the policing realm. As a result, they developed this training, and it has been recognized nationwide and implemented by several police departments. The trainings consist of several levels, which are applicable to almost every level and rank within every police agency. The trainings are designed for recruit and patrol officers, first-line supervisors, mid-management, command or command/community trainings, and the train-of trainer (TOT) program (Fair & Impartial Policing, 2018). The FIP training is administered by experts who have been vetted thoroughly and have been trained by the developing experts for several hours in order to be certified to instruct this training to their peers. One might ask, "Why it is administered to various levels of law enforcement officials?" It is administered to patrol officers as they are the forefront of citizen contacts, as most of their time is spent interacting with the community members in their assigned areas. It is also administered to first-line supervisors, as these officers also are responsible for a diverse set of officers in their span of control and being culturally aware is necessary in dealing with their officers. In addition, these first-line supervisors are also responsible for handling complaints made by community members. The FIP training ensures that these supervisors are equipped with the necessary tools to receive and handle such complaints from various individuals. It is also administered to mid-level management officials and command-level officials as they also handle citizens' complaints and officer complaints within their respective agencies. The training equips these managers with the proper tools of dealing with other high-ranking supervisors and high-ranking community members regarding various situations involving their personnel. Furthermore, prior to developing this concept of FIP, the researchers from FIP noted that most of the nationwide discussions surrounding biases boils down to two major concepts: race and ethnicity. The researchers focused on implicit and explicit biases as a justification and a much-needed concept in policing. A simple definition of explicit biases are negatively known and self-recognized reactions or instances toward certain groups, sex, cultural, age, gender expression, religion, and beliefs. For example, racism is a form of explicit bias.

Whereas implicit bias, according to the Kirwan Institute for the Study of Race and Ethnicity (2015), refers to the attitudes or stereotypes that impact our understanding, actions, and decisions in an unconscious manner. It's the notion that biases exist within the individual and manifest within him or her wherein he or she is perceiving or subconsciously negatively reacting to a particular group, age, sex, gender expression, class, religious belief, and so on. For instance, the institute noted that a few characteristics that can be classified as implicit biases are that they can be pervasive; that implicit and explicit biases are related but distinct mental constructs; that they do not necessarily align with our beliefs or favor our own group; and that implicit biases are malleable. Taking into consideration that the policing career is very intricate with several layers, implicit and explicit biases are a natural character trait of citizens, and police officers are regular citizens themselves. FIP seeks to explore these traits whether consciously or subconsciously. These training programs are geared toward presenting officers with the knowledge, skills, and capabilities to deal with a myriad of situations when dealing with individuals from diverse backgrounds and beliefs.

Box 7.2 Retired Assistant Chief Clarence Hunter

Figure 7.5 Clarence Hunter

My journey in law enforcement has spanned over 29 years and two different police departments in Virginia, the Richmond Police Department and the Henrico County Police Department. After serving six years on active duty in the U.S. Army, I started with the Richmond Police Department in 1990. During my time in Richmond, I saw firsthand the destruction crack cocaine was doing to families that lived in the inner city and surrounding jurisdictions. With the cocaine epidemic rising and the homicide rate following suit, law enforcement used aggressive tactics to help community members that were living near well-established drug corners. I was part of a strike force unit that routinely placed four officers together who "jumped out" on drug corners, searching for drugs and weapons. My only focus was tackling the problem, with little vision of connecting to the community I served. As officers we were recognized for the number of felonies, cocaine, and gun arrests that we made, and were proud of the difference we were trying to make. Establishing positive, long-term relationships with the community was not a focal point during this difficult time.

Today, as a retired assistant chief from the Henrico County Police Department, I reflect on my policing focus in the early nineties. I am still very proud of the men and women I worked with in my early days in law enforcement, as we policed in a way that was needed to combat the rising violence that was associated with crack cocaine.

In today's policing environment, we are once again faced with another drug epidemic-opioids. We are seeing the negative impact the drug is having on our communities and crime rates. Today's law enforcement officers are focused on addressing the problems opioids are causing. From my perspective, our willingness in law enforcement to work with all stakeholders has been a change from my early years. These stakeholders include those in the mental health profession, treatment centers, and families of the addicted.

Our success in law enforcement will continue to hinge on our relationships with community members. As I stated earlier, in the beginning, I did not have a vision on how to connect with those in the community. What I have learned is that with every encounter we have with a citizen, each officer can shape how the public views law enforcement. The way we interact, our body language, our choice of words and most importantly our actions, all matter in each instance. We are shaping how people perceive those in a police uniform and their willingness to work in partnership to address issues that arise.

To improve these interactions with our communities, the Henrico County Police Department adopted Fair and Impartial Policing as our model for implicit bias training. The program was designed by Dr. Lorie Fridell, a professor at the University of South Florida. Dr. Fridell has authored several books and has worked extensively with numerous policing agencies to provide science-based implicit bias training. One of the highlights of my career has been the opportunity to work as one of her national instructors. Training with police departments on a national level and providing this training has been most rewarding. In law enforcement, like any other profession, we carry biases because we are human. If we fail to recognize this, it may impact our relationships with our communities and have a detrimental effect on how we police. Through science-based implicit bias training, we can learn to manage our biases and improve the relationships with our citizens in every circumstance we may encounter them.

Box 7.3 Perception Versus Reality

The varying public perception that most police officers are killed in the line of duty and that this occupation is the most dangerous profession in the United States is not always accurate. According to the National Alliance of Mental Illness (NAMI, 2018), nearly one-quarter of officers think about suicide at some point in their lives. Additionally, more than 140 officers committed suicides in 2017, which is more than the number of officers killed in the line of duty that year. Based on preliminary online research of various credible sources, it is noted that the police officer profession is somewhere in 13th or 14th place when it comes to the top 25 most dangerous professions in the United States. Logging and fishing-related work were listed as the two most dangerous professions in the United States. Too much emphasis is placed on the job itself while little attention is given to the reality of the prevalence of police officer suicides. Several agencies are actively looking into improving the moral, professional, and personal attitudes of their officers on a continual basis. This next section covers intricate details on police officer suicides and health-related problems relating to their duties and responsibilities.

Officers Killed in the Line of Duty

Law enforcement officers are slain every year in the line of duty. According the Uniform Crime Report (UCR), 46 officers were killed on the job in 2017 (UCR, 2017). The deaths are often left to weigh heavily on family members and fellow officers, who must continue on even in the wake of tragedy. Several other resources are worth noting in presenting the actual numbers of officers killed in the line of duty. The reporting mechanisms normally classify the incident as a "fallen officer" or "officer down." Some of these outlets are the **Officer Down Memorial Page**, the **National Law Enforcement Officers Memorial Fund** page, and the **PoliceOne.com** page. Most of these pages are nonprofit organizations run by prior officers or regular concerned citizens. Most of these organizations share a similar purpose—they present the heroic nature of officers killed in the line of duty, sometimes including officers who died due to illness or other related injuries.

As a coping method, some officers who have lost colleagues in the line of duty develop a sense of cynicism or aggression and disdain for the public; this can negatively impact the relationship they have with their community. Many agencies take steps to combat this and other potential concerns, which may arise from work-related trauma. The Federal Department of Health and Human Services provides federal law enforcement officers with counselor hotlines for both employees and their families, including prevention and awareness training for stress management and suicide prevention, and critical incident stress management (CISM) following an officer's involvement with a critical event. Many state and local agencies have adopted this model of officer assistance (U.S. Department of Health and Human Services, n.d).

In addition, the U.S. Office of Justice Systems offers a vicarious trauma toolkit through their Office for Victims of Crime (n.d.) for emergency responders and other victim service workers who come into contact with other people's trauma. The law enforcement toolkit provides departments with checklists and guidelines for creating proper training protocols, health and wellness practices, healthy work environments, and effective leadership after a traumatic event.

Coping Mechanisms and Coping With Stress

In addition to the CISM and the vicarious trauma toolkit, several other resources are available for police officers who have witnessed traumatic incidents. Most police agencies are mandating that their officers and specialized units meet with community services or mental health professionals on a daily basis in order to discuss personal and confidential issues. Several factors contribute to police officer stress. Homer C. Hawkins, clinical social worker and affiliate of Michigan State University, conducted a study in 2001 titled, "Police Officer Burnout: A Partial Replication of Maslach's Burnout Inventory." In Hawkins's experiment, he examined over 452 sworn police officers from four different police departments covering cities comprised of 65,000 to 240,000 people in the United States. His study was focused mainly on police burnout and the relationship between emotional exhaustion, depersonalization, and personal accomplishment on the job. The study also took into account the participants' race, age, sex, religion, marital status, educational level, length of time on a particular assignment, and length of time in law enforcement. The results of the findings yielded the following: Married officers had higher emotional exhaustion than non-married officers, female officers had lower depersonalization scores, and White officers had higher depersonalization and emotional scores (Hawkins, 2001). He also discovered that length of time of service is directly related with emotional exhaustion.

This study is relevant to this topic of discussion dealing with police stress. It is impressive to see that variables such as sex and other demographics were taken into consideration as these are important influencing factors regarding police stress. The major factor that has one of the highest impacts is length of time in law enforcement. Most officers would exert stress after being on the force after several years. It is also important to note other factors affecting stress. However, before addressing these factors, several scholars have noted that stress is classified as either periodic or intermittent in policing (Tsai, Nolasco, & Vaughn, 2018). These three professors—Lily Chi-Fang Tsai (University of Maryland, Eastern Shore), Claire Nolasco (Texas A&M University, San Antonio), and Michael Vaughn (Sam Houston State University)—published a study in 2018 titled "Modeling Job Stress Among Police Officers: Interplay of Work Environment, Counseling Support, and Family Discussion With Co-Workers." The researchers noted that since stress is perceived to be either periodic or intermittent, it is caused by various incidents or situations. For instance, in addressing **intermittent** stress, officers are exposed to incidents such as high-speed chases, gun-fighting, domestics, and other fatal vehicular accidents. On the other hand, **periodic** stress occurs over time as the officer faces situations that are repeated or similar to other situations, thus creating an image or perceived understanding of the issue—for instance, arresting someone for the possession of illegal drugs. Another added factor is chronic organizational stress (Tsai et al., 2001). In exploring these reasons further, it is important to note the difference and list examples of each stress type—periodic, intermittent, and chronic organizational stress. **Chronic organizational** stress occurs when officers are exposed to the constant demands and structure processes by their designated agencies. Such demands have been noted to take a toll on officers' health and wellness as they vigorously work their entire career to uphold and meet these demands. Such demands can vary by agency and can include some of the following; driving under the influence (DUI) arrests, traffic tickets, criminal and drug arrests, and meeting community demands. As mentioned earlier, police officers respond to a myriad of incidents involving humanity at its absolute. Responding to these traumatic events year after year, over time exposes them to internal stress and sometimes to external stress wherein it affects their personal characteristics.

As police departments nationwide implement certain coping mechanisms, it is wise to adhere to the notion that every officer is responsible for him- or herself and his or her actions. Prior researchers have noted that police job stress stems from the dangers of police work, police work environment and peer support, work-family conflict, and chronic organization stress (Tsai et al., 2001). However, the current and most prevalent research is pointing toward ranking status of officers and organizational stress. With ranking officers, the researchers noted that ranking or serving officers face more stress as they are constantly under pressures of making tough decisions that are directly related to their officers and community members. These decisions weigh heavily on the decision makers. Organizational stress is also inevitable as officers are under constant stress of organizational changes in structure and policies. These changes also weigh heavily on officers as most of them do not like change (Tsai et al., 2001).

Further coping mechanisms are focused on the police leadership and administration to secure effective trainings on delivering safe and practical decisions when disciplining their subordinates. In addition, researchers also identified that police agencies should constantly explore stress-related workshops, team building exercises, ways to improve communications, and peer mentoring and support initiatives for their employees. In addition, it was noted that officers might be more willing to write or express their emotions if given the opportunities in varied settings without any judgement or ridicule. Last, even though gender did not predict much of a change in police officer stress, agencies could start providing specific gender-based support services wherein both male and female officers can seek the appropriate support they need for coping with stress. As mentioned earlier in this chapter, officers tend to gravitate toward their police peers; breaking this cycle by providing outside support could help to mitigate the one-sidedness of a close-minded peer support group. In addition to police stress, once stress builds up and is not addressed, it leads to depression and ultimately police suicides. The next section talks lengthily about police suicides and its causes, along with providing some suggested remedies.

Police Suicides and Health Concerns

Before we delve into this concept, let's first review the definitions for the terms that will be used, including mental illness, depression, and posttraumatic stress disorder (PTSD). According to the National Institute of Mental Health (NIMH, 2017), mental illness is defined as any mental behavior or emotional disorder. This definition can vary depending on the condition and seriousness of the disorder. The institute also defined suicide as death caused by a self-directed injury with the purpose of inflicting death. The concept is classified into two related terms: suicide attempt and suicide ideation. Suicide attempt is the non-fatal, self-inflicted injury attempt with the intention of taking one's own life. Suicide ideation is the thinking and considering of the possibility of committing suicide (NIMH, 2017). Posttraumatic stress disorder is defined as a disorder that can develop after exposure to a serious or potentially traumatic event. Some related events include violent personal assaults, natural or human-caused disasters, accidents, combat, and other forms of violence (NIMH, 2017). Additionally, some first responders have military experiences—creating added career-related posttraumatic stresses depending on their military service and assignments.

Researchers from the Ruderman Family Foundation—Miriam Heyman, PhD, Jeff Dill, MA, NBCC, and Robert Douglas, DCC—published a white paper for the foundation in 2018, titled "The Ruderman White Paper on Mental Health and Suicide of First Responders." The study focused solely on the fact that police and firefighters are more likely to die by suicide than in the line of duty. The researchers noted that in 2017, 140 police officers and 103 firefighters died from suicides, while 93 firefighters and 129 police officers died while performing their duties (Heyman et al., 2018). The researchers further documented that these suicides resulted from mental illness, such as depression and PTSD.

The numbers mentioned are indeed astounding. It is simple/easy to think that these first responders are killed by suicides rather than their own occupations, thus fostering more research and exploration into this ideation. So, what is causing officers to commit suicide?

Another study was conducted by Mark Chae and Douglas Boyle, published in 2013, titled "Police Suicide: Prevalence, Risk, and Protective Factors." In this innovative study, researchers used a best-evidence synthesis approach to locating the best, immediately available literature and research on this subject. Upon completing a comprehensive study, researchers discovered that five major concepts were associated with the suicide ideation: **organizational stress**, **critical incident trauma**, **shift work**, **relationship problems**, and **alcohol use and abuse** (Chae & Boyle, 2013).

ORGANIZATIONAL STRESS

In elaborating on these findings listed by the researchers, it is evident that each plays an important role in police stressors. Organizational stress entails the fact that almost all police agencies are operated on a hierarchical administration and structure. As a result, every officer is guided by a set rules and policies, which can sometimes refer to general orders or standard operating procedures. Although rules and regulations are necessary for the smooth functioning of an agency, adhering to so many rules and regulations can create stress. Second, supervisors are under a lot of stress as they are responsible for managing several subordinate officers in addition to completing their evaluations. Furthermore, the researchers noted that disciplinary measures can also weigh heavily on the officers being disciplined and the ones delivering the decision to the types of disciplinary measures. Also, when they researchers examined gender and police stress, they discovered that female police officers are more likely to be emotionally affected by calls relating to abuse or children who have been beaten and are more likely to exert higher stress levels when exposed to domestic-related calls for service (Chae & Boyle, 2013).

CRITICAL INCIDENT TRAUMA

Critical trauma incidents were explored earlier in this chapter. These events play a key role in the officer's lives, and include vehicle accidents involving their colleagues, losing their colleagues in the line of duty, losing their colleagues due to illness, losing the life of a victim, and losing a loved one.

SHIFT WORK

Regarding shift work, since police agencies provide services on a 24-hour basis, they are required to be available all the time. Thus, their shift work has to cover the 24-hour period. Many officers work rotating shifts, which means an officer works all three shifts on a rotating schedule in a month instead of permanent shifts. Due to stress on the officers' bodies from working three various shifts on a rotation (days, evenings, midnights), they have eliminated rotating shifts and have implemented permanent shifts. (These are the schedules that officers can work entirely without switching to other shifts. For instance, an officer's permanent shift can be the day shift; therefore, he only works the day shift).

RELATIONSHIP PROBLEMS

In addressing relationship problems and alcohol use and abuse, researchers presented a clear picture as to how these play a part in police stress. The stress of police work can permeate into officers' personal lives, thus affecting their relationships with their partners, family members, and close friends.

ALCOHOL USE AND ABUSE

Alcohol use and abuse is a global coping mechanism for the stressful situations police officers experience all over the world (Chae & Boyle, 2013). Most officers view seeking mental health and other personal care and support as negative and weak; many are afraid to seek such assistance as they fear they may lose their weapons or their livelihood such as their employment. In their reports, researchers listed some promising programs that have helped various northeastern police departments. These include the Police Organization Providing Peer Assistance (POPPA) and the Cop2Cop program. Both of these programs are well known and have proven valuable to New York and New Jersey City police departments. These programs deliver personal care, support, and follow-up for officers in need by other officers as well as social and psychological professionals. These programs require commitment and dedication from the officers seeking help. Overall, the research shows that constant follow-up and one-on-one support from officers and by officers is proven to reduce police suicide-related events.

Law enforcement personnel are especially prone to depression, posttraumatic stress disorder, and anxiety, which increases the risk of suicide (Johnson, 2016). Johnson also notes that many officer suicides go undocumented, as fellow officers may often alter the scene in order to save face for the family of the deceased. The stigma surrounding mental illness in law enforcement is so prevalent that officers will go out of their way to tamper with evidence. Johnson (2016) notes that this very stigma is what causes officers to avoid seeking treatment in the first place. Police officers are supposed to be brave pillars of the community, for whom no job is too tough. This is wholeheartedly true. However, it does not mean that officers go unaffected by the events they experience. Fear of being found unfit for duty, reassignment, the "blue wall of silence," and a feeling of lack of agency support are all cited as reasons officers stay quiet about their mental health and their concern for their comrades (Johnson, 2016; NAMI, 2018).

HEALTH CONCERNS

Police officers in the United States spend a lot of time sitting in their vehicles. From cruising to paperwork, the patrol car becomes a home away from home. For this reason, officers experience many of the same ailments as truck drivers and office workers do, such as low back pain, sciatica, and obesity. To break up these extensive lengths of inactivity, police officers experience intense periods of extreme mental and physical stress multiple times throughout their shift. The erratic hours and busy schedule of a police officer leave little time for meal planning or exercise. Long shifts result in little sleep and constant fatigue, which puts great strain on the entire body. A study of police officers in Buffalo determined that officers are more likely to be obese (40.5% of officers vs. 32.1% of the normal population in Buffalo); have metabolic syndrome, also known as pre-diabetes (26.7% of officers vs. 18.7% of the normal population in Buffalo); and experience depression (12% of officers vs. 6.8% of the normal population in Buffalo) (Hartley et al., 2011).

Because of their high-stress job, it is a commonly held belief that police officers have a higher divorce rate than civilians. The American Community Survey conducted from 2011–2013 interviewed citizens from all manners of employment. Included were law enforcement officers. While the national average for divorce was 19.7%, the rate of divorce for law enforcement personnel was 16.08% (Aamodt, 2016).

Chapter Summary

Several research studies were presented in this chapter to demonstrate the existence of the police subculture. However, one related study that was not mentioned, which has an alternative outcome, was conducted by John Cochran and Max Bromley (2003) from the Department of Criminology, University of South Florida, titled "The Myth(?) of the Police Sub-Culture." The researchers cleverly used advanced statistical techniques such as cluster analysis (selecting officers in the same group who are more similar to each other than those in other groups) and discriminant function analysis (where the DFA classifies unknown individuals and their classifications into a specific group such as sex and background) to sample Hillsborough County, Florida, Sheriff's Office (HCSO) in order to establish the taxonomy of policing (Cochran & Bromley, 2003). The results demonstrate the existence of three types of deputies: the sub-cultural adherents, the normal, and the COP cops. These three deputy types were documented as the types of cultures present within the organization sampled. The sub-cultural adherents were the closest to a police sub-culture, whereas the COP cops were more police community relations oriented, and a small percent were labeled as the normal, meaning that this group was not associated with any aspect other than just doing their jobs (Cochran & Bromley, 2003). The researchers further noted that even though there was a small percent of the existence of the police subculture, the overarching concept of this theory can be strictly dependent on the jurisdiction. This study was conducted with a sheriff's department. Sheriffs are primarily elected and held accountable by the communities they serve; therefore, their responsibilities are mainly focused on community policing and welfare.

The thin blue wall of silence, sometimes referred to as the police code of silence, was also explored, and several examples were presented. Various actions by officers going above and beyond to cover up another officers' wrongdoings can lead to extreme corruption and thus falls under the negative construct of police subculture. On a positive note, officers do lean on each other for comfort, understanding, and sometimes through life-changing circumstances. Because of these collective experiences, officers share a special bond that holds them together for a very long time, often until retirement.

The fair and impartial policing training initiated by Dr. Lori Fridell is slowly making its way across the nation. This training, which initially began in the Northeastern states' police agencies, educates officers on how to handle their implicit and explicit biases while interacting with individuals they come across on a daily basis.

Last, officers killed in the line of duty, police suicides, and coping mechanisms are extremely important in this profession. Some agencies are making this information available to their police recruits at the forefront of their trainings in order for them to be aware of the complexities and realities of the profession they have chosen. Some recruits may end their training process after learning such information and its possibilities; others may persevere and continue with their trainings, seeking guidance from seasoned officers. Seeking guidance from seasoned officers can be viewed twofold: First, if the seasoned officer is bitter and disgruntled, then that behavior and attitude may be passed on to the recruit or trainee. Second, if the seasoned officer is a hard charger, then that attitude and demeanor will be passed on to the recruit or trainee. Very often a recruit or trainee will emulate several attitudes and demeanors and form his or her own self-identity, which is of key importance in this profession. Most agencies are assigning their new recruits/trainees to field training officers with various shifts/platoons in order for the recruit/trainee to be exposed to diverse attitudes. Other agencies attempt to match the recruits/trainees with seasoned officers who have similar attitudes in hopes that they will work collectively and effectively during the field training process. As mentioned, the field training process is one of the most important phases of the new recruit's/trainee's employment process; it shapes who he or she will become for his or her entire career as a police officer. In relation to coping with stress, several coping mechanisms were mentioned. Most importantly, officers should strive for more positive social connections outside of the police department in order for them to turn off the constant police officer mentality, which can take a stressful toll on officers and their personal social networks.

Discussion Questions

1. The **us-versus-them** mentality has been noted in several policing texts. Conduct a thorough online research effort and present two scenarios to demonstrate this concept.
2. According to the article by Steve Herbert (1998) titled "Police Subculture Reconsidered," six normative orders were listed. Select three of these orders and explain their respective meanings as they relate to current policing styles and ideologies.
3. The blue code of silence and the police code of conduct are very similar and have been used interchangeably. Complete a thorough online search and present one scenario depicting a negative example of the police code of silence. For instance, an incident wherein several officers covered for other officers during an external investigation.
4. What is the main purpose of the Fair and Impartial Policing training program? List four benefits/advantages of this program to police agencies.
5. In reference to coping with stress and police work, list and describe four coping mechanisms that police officers can turn to in times of stress.

References

Aamodt, M. G. (2016, September). Law enforcement divorce rates: An updated analysis. *Conference: Society for Police and Criminal Psychology*. Retrieved from https://www.researchgate.net/publication/308750553_Law_Enforcement_Divorce_Rates_An_Updated_Analysis

Chae, M. H., & Boyle, D. D. (2013). Police suicide: prevalence, risk, and protective factors. *Policing: An International Journal 36*(1). 91–118. doi: 10.1108/13639511311302498

Cochran, J. K., & Bromley, M. L. (2003). The myth(?) of the police sub-culture. *Policing: An International Journal, 26*(1), 88–117.

Conti, N. (2011). Weak links and warrior hearts: A framework for judging self and *others* in police training. *Police Practice and Research, 12*(5), 410–423. doi:10.1080/15614263.2010.536726

Fair and Impartial Policing. (2018). *The #1 provider of implicit-bias-awareness training for law enforcement in North America.* Retrieved from https://fipolicing.com/

Hartley, T. A., Gu, J., Baughman, P. J., Violanti, J. M., Andrew, M. E., Fekedulegn, D., & Burchfiel, C. M. (2011). Health disparities in police officers: Comparisons to the U.S. general population [Abstract]. *National Center for Biotechnology Information, 13*(4), 211–220. doi:10.1037/e577572014-379

Hawkins, H. (2001). Police officer burnout: A partial replication of Maslach's burnout inventory. *Police Quarterly, 4*(3), 343–360.

Hein, J. (2016, September 22). What is the cost of the code of silence? A good reputation can be difficult for a police officer to develop, but extremely easy to lose. *PoliceOne.Com*. Retrieved from https://www.policeone.com/investigations/articles/223697006-What-is-the-cost-of-the-code-of-silence/

Herbert, S. (1998). Police subculture reconsidered. *Criminology, 36*(2), 343–370.

Hyeman, M., Dill, J., & Douglas, R. (2018). Ruderman white paper on mental health and suicide of first responders. (Ruderman Family Foundation White Papers. Retrieved from https://issuu.com/rudermanfoundation/docs/first_responder_white_paper_final_ac270d530f8bfb

Ivković, S. K., Haberfeld, M., & Peacock, R. (2018). Decoding the code of silence. *Criminal Justice Policy Review, 29*(2), 172–189. doi:10.1177/0887403416680853

Johnson, S. (2016, December). Investigating barriers to mental health care in law enforcement officers (Doctoral dissertation). East Tennessee State University, 2016. *Digital Commons*. Retrieved from https://dc.etsu.edu/cgi/viewcontent.cgi?article=4568&context=etd

Kirwan Institute for the Study of Race and Ethnicity. (2015). *Understanding implicit bias. Ohio State University.* Retrieved from http://kirwaninstitute.osu.edu/research/understanding-implicit-bias/

Maguire, E. R., Nix, J., & Campbell, B. A. (2017). A war on cops? The effects of Ferguson on the number of U.S. police officers murdered in the line of duty. *Justice Quarterly, 34*(5), 739–758. doi:10.1080/07418825.2016.123620

Malmin, M. (2012). Changing police subculture. *FBI Law Enforcement Bulletin, 81*(4), 14. Retrieved from https://journal.media/police-subculture

McCartney, S, & Parent, R. (2015). *Ethics in law enforcement.* Victoria, British Columbia: Creative Commons. Retrieved from http://opentextbc.ca/ethicsinlawenforcement/

National Alliance on Mental Illness. (2018). *Law Enforcement Officers.* Retrieved from https://www.nami.org/Find-Support/Law-Enforcement-Officers

National Institute of Mental Health. (2017). *Mental illness.* Retrieved from https://www.nimh.nih.gov/health/statistics/mental-illness.shtml

Tsai, L. C. F., Nolasco, C. A. R. I., & Vaughn, M. S. (2018). Modeling job stress among police officers: Interplay of work environment, counseling support, and family discussion with co-workers. *Police Practice & Research, 19*(3), 253–269.

U.S. Department of Health and Human Services. (n.d.). Law enforcement medical operations program. *Federal Occupational Health.* Retrieved from https://foh.psc.gov/whatwedo/EAP/Law/LawAssist.asp

U.S. Office for Victims of Crime. (n.d.). *The vicarious trauma toolkit.* Retrieved from https://vtt.ovc.ojp.gov/tools-for-law-enforcement

Weisburd, D., & Greenspan, R. (2000). *Police attitudes toward abuse of authority: Findings from a national study.* Washington, DC: Office of Justice Programs.

Figure Credits

Fig. 7.2: Source: https://commons.wikimedia.org/wiki/File:CBP_Field_Operations_Academy-arrest.jpg.

Fig. 7.3: Source: https://commons.wikimedia.org/wiki/File:Civil_rights_march_on_Washington,_D.C._fence.jpg.

Fig. 7.4: Copyright © 2015 by Daniel X. O'Neil (CC BY 2.0) at https://commons.wikimedia.org/wiki/File:Protest,_Chicago,_December_2015_(23611780470).jpg.

CHAPTER EIGHT

Police Dishonesty and Police Deviance

Policing is an illustrious and exciting career, and due to its autonomy and discretion, officers have a lot of leverage in handling various situations and scenarios. As a result of the high discretion level and autonomous work life, officers face some of the most unethical incidents. Because they are human beings, officers may find themselves enticed by corrupt behaviors and activities. This chapter will explore the various types of police corruption, reasons for police corruption, signs of police corruption, and police misconduct. This chapter will also cover police ethics, codes, values, and morals.

Learning Objectives

- Understand the concept of police corruption
- Explore the different types of police corruption
- Examine the reasons for police corruption and ways to identify police corruption
- Understand the concept of police code of conduct and the peer accountability process

Chapter Outline

1. Police Corruption
2. Perception Versus Reality
3. Examining Police Behavior
4. Exposing Police Deviance
5. Combating Police Corruption
6. Chapter Summary
7. Discussion Questions

A REAL-LIFE POLICE SCENARIO FOR DISCUSSION

from Chernoh Wurie's personal accounts

The time was 2115 hours, and the on-duty sergeant was wrapping up his roll call briefing for the midnight shift about crimes in our assigned areas, DUI enforcements, and other items of note. Normally, during roll call, the entire squad of about 15 to 20 officers sits in a classroom-style setting and receives instructions, beat or area assignments, police cruiser assignments, and other facts for their shift. As the sergeant spoke, I couldn't wait to head to my patrol vehicle and to my favorite late dinner spot, Chick-Fil-A, which closed its drive-thru window at 2200 hours (and sometimes earlier). My traditional order was a strawberry milkshake, large French fries, and sometimes a chicken sandwich. On this particular night, I was craving all three items. As soon as the sergeant finished his instructions so we could hit the streets, I ran downstairs and loaded my police cruiser for duty—police duty bag, a less-than-lethal-force weapon, and my taser, and marked on the radio that I was in service. I left the police station lot at about 2140 hours and made it to Chick-Fil-A right before closing. The cashier in the window gave me a very big smile and took my order, which amounted to about $10. However, since I was a police officer, and in uniform, and on duty, I received a 50% discount, bringing my total down to about $4 or $5. I was content with this gesture and thanked the cashier. She responded, "My pleasure," and I was on my way.

Nothing exciting happened that night. However, it dawned on me that I had been going to Chick-Fil-A for as long as I could remember while on the force, and never once thought of it as something that could be considered a form of police corruption. This practice was very common among other officers and other businesses who would offer on-duty officers half-priced meals as long as they dined in their establishments in order to show the uniform presence. Needless to say, I came to the realization that this could be perceived in the eyes of others as a form of police corruption. Although I did not stop going to Chick-Fil-A, I limited my visits there.

As an officer, some establishments insisted on offering me half off my meals; I respected their decisions and accepted.

Another common situation where this concept of police discounts comes into play involves apartment complexes wherein police officers receive reduced rent in exchange for parking their vehicles on the property and making themselves known to the community in order to deter crimes. Can this also be perceived as a form of police corruption? In examining these two concepts closely, there are legitimate reasons for these establishments to partner with police agencies and offer such incentives. This chapter explores the various types of corruption, special incentives, and how these situations can be perceived by those outside the spectrum.

Police Corruption

The history of police corruption (or police misconduct) has been associated with policing since its inception. Some of the famous words and phrasings connected with this concept include violating public trust, abuse of power, personal gains, falsifying evidence, sexual misconduct, perjury, fixing, shakedowns, theft, payoffs, and ticket fixing.

In revisiting the eras of policing—the political era, the professional era, and the modern era—we can see that each era influences the concept of police corruption today. The political era (the first era) was extremely corrupt as policing was in its earlier stages. Everyone was involved in its policies with less rules, regulations, and requirements, and the politicians made decisions on who to hire and retain as an officer. The reform/professional era was also somewhat corrupt. However,

Figure 8.1 Diversity and inclusion Panel

brave individuals such as August Vollmer and O.W. Wilson started the transformation of policing and developed several professional standards, many of which are still being used today in some agencies. The modern era is often referred to as the most tumultuous time of policing due to the severed relationship between the police and the communities they serve. All three of these eras directly influence police corruption. The foundational aspects of policing were originally viewed as corrupt by many. During the reform era, some endeavors such as various commissions (discussed later on in this chapter) were established to address widespread police corruption. And during the modern era, many people view policing as mirroring its past negative perceptions, especially when considering the political and reform eras, despite the strides made by police agencies to rebuild their relationships.

Definition of Police Corruption

Police corruption or **police misconduct** is defined as simply improper behavior or any intended wrongdoing by an officer (Merriam-Webster, n.d.). Maintaining good conduct applies to officers while they are on duty and off duty, as they are expected to adhere to their oath of office at all times. In order to get a holistic and universal definition of police misconduct, it is important to look at international scholarly articles relating to this topic. For instance, George Chak man Lee (2018) posited in his article "Police Corruption: A Comparison Between China and India," that in order to be considered a clear definition of police misconduct, it must contain the following: bribes, embezzlement, nepotism, cover-ups for police misconduct, and abuse of power. Furthermore, Roebuck and Barker (1974) gave a series of listed notions that can be viewed as police corruption:

> 1. Corruption of authority is when an officer receives something due to their position but is not actually transgressing the law, such as accepting a free cup of tea or a meal from a restaurant owner. 2. Kickbacks are when an officer accepts payment for referring business to companies or individuals. 3. Opportunistic theft is basically the theft of materials from those that have been arrested or even victims at the scene of an accident. 4. Shakedowns are when an officer elicits a bribe for not following through with a criminal proceeding. 5. Protection of criminal activity is when an officer is paid to ignore illegal business oriented crimes such as prostitution or drug dealing. 6. The fix is where police officers undermine police investigations or proceedings by ignoring or losing evidence for a fee. 7. Direct criminal activity is when a police officer commits a crime for personal gain. 8. Internal payoffs refer to when officers barter for privileges such as a change in shifts, promotions, and transfers. 9. Flaking/padding involves the planting of evidence in order to gain a conviction. (Roebuck & Barker, 1974, internal citations omitted)

Taking into consideration these various definitions of police corruption, it is imperative to recognize that they all seem to cover the same concepts. For the purpose of this text, the definition of **police corruption** is a single or collective intentional wrongdoing of a person or persons who holds police authority while on or off duty. This definition can vary, depending on the action by the participating officer. Various types of police corruption exist.

Types of Police Corruption

Although several types of police corruption exist, we'll narrow this topic down for the purpose of this text. Let's examine the works of Julian Roebuck and Thomas Baker, which was originally presented in 1974 and titled "Typology of Police Corruption." This article lists eight types of police corruption—**corruption of authority**, **kickbacks**, **opportunistic theft**, **shakedowns**, **protection of illegal activities**, **the fix**, **direct criminal activities**, and **payoffs**. All of these, despite the number of years that have passed, are currently applicable to today's law enforcement. Before delving into each corruption type, three police misconduct examples are provided, courtesy of Lieutenant Robert H. Garrett (2015) with the Criminal Justice Institute SLES Session XLV. These examples depict the exact meanings of police misconduct.

> 1. A Tennessee patrolman forced a woman to perform oral sex on him. Hamilton County Sheriff's patrol officer Willie Marshay Greer, 33, pulled a woman over for speeding at 1:00 a.m., and after running her name through a database and discovering she had an open warrant for arrest, offered to "strike a deal." "I could let you go, but you'd owe me," the woman said Greer told her. Greer then forced the woman to perform oral sex on him while handcuffed (Essert, 2014).
> 2. A Chicago cop sodomized a man they wanted to turn into a drug informant. Angel Perez, a 32-year-old Chicago man, is suing the Chicago Police Department after accusing several officers of beating him and sodomizing him with a gun to force him to cooperate as a drug informant in 2012. According to a report in VICE, "One of the officers 'inserted a cold metal object, believed to be one of the officer's service revolvers, into the plaintiff's rectum.' The complaint continued: 'The two officers laughed hysterically while inserting the object and Sergeant Cline joked, 'I almost blew your brains out'" (Essert, 2014).
> 3. King City police officers were arrested in a corruption scandal. The highest-ranking officers in the King City Police Department for years targeted the city's most vulnerable residents, essentially stealing their cars for profit, District Attorney Dean Flippo said. In what is likely the most widespread case of official corruption in Monterey County history, six King City police officers, including the former and acting chiefs of police, were arrested on felony charges on Tuesday, and four of them were accused of conspiracy, embezzlement, and bribery. The owner of a local tow truck company, the brother of the acting chief, was arrested in the scheme, which involved impounding the cars of mostly unlicensed drivers, then selling them when the cars' owners were unable to pay towing and storage fees (Hennessey, 2014).

Before delving deeper into the types of corruption, let's explore the term **corruptor**. A corruptor has various meanings; some corruptors have even been depicted as fictional characters in the Marvel Comics. However, in reference to police corruption, a corruptor is any one or business that seeks to make personal gains and agreements with a police agency in order to get first-hand referrals in return for gratuities and other forms of gifts for the referrals by police. These are legitimate business persons mostly.

CORRUPTION OF AUTHORITY

The first type of corruption is listed as **corruption of authority**; according to Roebuck and Barker (1974) this type of corruption is twofold. The first section falls under things that come with the profession that do not particularly violate any departmental policies. For instance, free meals, alcohol, entertainment, sex, and so on, which may be provided to the officer by the corruptor who just likes the police. However, the officer's authority then becomes corrupt when accepting such gifts. Another section of this type of corruption involves situations where the corruptor is a business who pays officers for property protection without proper documentation of the agreement.

The authors gave two distinct examples here as well: first, when businesses pay officers who arrest robbers or burglars in their establishments for arresting the perpetrators, and second when bounty hunters act as the mediators between the police and the arrestees. Here, police notify the bondsmen when an arrest is made and the bondsmen pay the police as an appreciation and an unspoken agreement for the common understanding of helping each other. Some corruptors' actions are intentional. However, upon accepting these contributions such as free meals and other discounted merchandise, their authorities have become corrupt (Roebuck & Barker, 1974). It is important to note that some departments have strict policies prohibiting officers from accepting any sorts or types of gifts. Some regulate the various forms and types of gifts their officers can accept or not accept.

KICKBACKS

Kickbacks, on the other hand, are a very direct method of police corruption. This type of corruption encompasses the act wherein the officer accepts something in return for referring the people he or she interacts with on a daily basis to reputable assistance agencies such as ambulances, towing companies, funeral homes, bondsmen, attorneys, taxi cabs, and several other human services companies (Roebuck & Barker, 1974). These companies are reputable and are anxious to use police-referred police services, and in return for their business, they will provide kickbacks to the referring officers. A simple example of this can be wherein an officer responds to a crash scene, properly works the scene, and then calls the towing company that has a separate unofficial agreement to respond and tow the crash vehicle. In return, the officer gets a direct payment for calling that specific towing company. It is also important to note that several agencies are addressing this by having reputable partnerships with these human services companies with an agreement in place, wherein a random pick system is generated from a list of agreement-binding agencies in time for referral services. These companies do not pay anything to the departments, although some are required to pay other incentives to the locality or jurisdiction but not directly to the agency. These agencies are considered reputable because they have met the standard requirements set forth by the department regarding human safety.

OPPORTUNISTIC THEFT

The third type of corruption is opportunistic theft, which entails stealing from arrestees, victims, crime scenes, and unprotected properties. According to the authors, this type of corruption does not include any corruptors; it only involves the officers as they are the ones performing the illegal acts. The police profession is extremely independent wherein officers are not directly supervised on a daily basis. Officers come in contact with deceased victims at crime and burglary scenes, and they confiscate immense amounts of contraband and related items. Officers who are corrupt or prone to misconduct behaviors are more likely to take items from crime scenes for personal gains, keeping a portion of confiscated contraband, and in some cases selling it for profit or for personal use. For example, these officers might steal expensive valuables at burglary scenes and document the items as stolen.

SHAKEDOWNS

The fourth type of corruption described by the authors is shakedowns. This type of corruption is where the officer witnesses a certain violation involving the offender and consequently accepts a bribe or something in return for not citing, charging, or arresting the violator. This type of corruption is most common in traffic and criminal-related offenses. For instance, an officer witnesses or observes someone driving erratically. The officer pulls the person over based on reasonable suspicion that he or she is intoxicated. Upon performing field sobriety tests, the officer determines probable cause that the individual is intoxicated. As he or she attempts to arrest the individual, the individual offers to pay the officer in order for the officer to release him or her and have him or her call someone for a ride or take a taxi cab. Once the officer accepts this type of bribe and turns a blind eye to this incident, it is considered a shakedown. This also happens with drug dealers and prostitutes wherein undercover officers observe these violations and accept myriad forms of payments ranging from money, sexual favors, drugs, and other related discounts.

PROTECTION OF ILLEGAL ACTIVITIES

The fifth type of corruption is the **protection of illegal activities**. This type of corruption covers a wide range of illegal activities from various spectrums, including prostitution, taxi-cab services, illegal drug transactions, gambling establishments, escort services, illegal sales and transportation of alcohol, and trucking companies operating outside of their normal routes or failing safety standards for operating. Most of these are legitimate businesses, and these types of corruptors are careful and pay heavily for police protection. This type of corruption involves several officers within a police department, including higher administration. The corruptors compensate the police departments to not perform their regular duties and responsibilities in the specific locations of these illegal activities. For instance, a trucking company that pays off a police department in order for its specialized accident investigations unit not to stop and inspect its trucks for safety violations is a notable example of protection of illegal activities. Another example is an escort service owner who pays off the police to not enforce or investigate prostitution within a certain location if it is illegal in that jurisdiction.

THE FIX

The sixth type corruption is **the fix**, which basically covers two major concepts. The first concept is the fixing of traffic tickets in order to prevent traffic violators from going to court or accumulating negative DMV driver demerit points on their licenses. The second concept is the arrangement between the arresting officer and the corruptor to fix the case through whatever means necessary in order to prevent the corruptor from getting a criminal charge and possible jail or prison time (Roebuck & Barker, 1974). For example, if a business owner gets pulled over for a speeding violation, if issued a traffic citation, the report would negatively affect the company's insurance policy. The owner of the company calls and makes a special arrangement with the officer or the officer's immediate supervisor in exchange for some benefit with the business. The officer then gets instructed to advise the prosecutor that the driver has complied with the law and to drop the citation charge. The case gets dropped due to the officer and his immediate supervisor fixing the traffic citation.

Other examples of fixing criminal cases mostly involve undercover officers who personally witness illegal activities by the corruptor. The corruptor then approaches the officer and offers a deal/something in return in order for them to make the case go away. The undercover officer then tampers with evidence in order to document that there is no evidence, or limited evidence, to prosecute the corruptor. The authors further noted that these incidents are so common and minor that other officers who are aware of them choose to ignore them or support it. Some departments react harshly to these types of offenses while others provide counseling and minor punishments for these violations. It is important to note that each agency handles such violations according to their general standard operating procedures or general orders.

DIRECT CRIMINAL ACTIVITY

The seventh type of corruption is **direct criminal activity**. This type of corruption involves no corruptor. This is where the officer or officers decide to commit criminal activities on their own—knowing patrol schedules and times and when and where there is a lack of police presence, giving them the opportunity to perform burglaries and other robberies. For instance, a corrupt officer who knows the vacation schedule of a particular family may decide to break into the residence and steal items while on or off duty. Another example can be an officer who gambles and is in a lot of debt, so he or she decides to put on a mask and rob a bank at the opportune time where there are no security guards or police patrolling the vicinity. Roebuck and Barker (1974) affirmed that these types of corruptions are harshly dealt with by various departments and include federal criminal prosecution and termination. Police officers who are charged with serious offenses while they are in the commission of the duties and responsibilities vested upon them are mostly prosecuted in federal courts. In addition, even other officers do not tolerate these types of behaviors, including those who may be involved in other forms of minor corruption; they despise those officers who commit such crimes while on or off duty.

INTERNAL PAYOFFS

The last type of corruption mentioned by Roebuck and Barker (1974) is **internal payoffs**. This type of corruption mostly involves police officers paying each other for special favors such as promotions, suitable area or beat assignments, special holidays and days off, and other favorable scheduling fixes. Roebuck and Barker (1974) posited that this type of corruption is easily manifested within larger police agencies as it includes several individuals benefiting themselves by getting something in return for looking out for other officers. This level of corruption does not only cover monetary givebacks, it also covers sexual favors wherein a seasoned supervisor would ask for sexual favors from a newer officer who is seeking recognition for reassignment or promotion. Other examples include officers directly paying supervisors for certain favors such as days off, favorable shift and area assignments, and so on. Some ask for reassignments to areas where they can get kickbacks and then give a portion of these kickbacks to their supervisors for granting them the assignments. This type of corruption is also harshly dealt with by other officers and is extremely intolerable from a departmental standpoint. Officers who are caught in such actions also face termination and are sometimes criminally prosecuted.

As mentioned in the descriptions of the types, each agency has policies and standard operating procedures on police corruption. Police agencies and their members are becoming vigilant in detecting and reporting police corruption, as explained in the next section.

Other forms of police corruption are internal corruption and police brutality. Internal corruption covers a wide range of actions by several officers, including lower and upper management. These actions can go on for months or years, as they get covered up by various respected members of the agency. A specific instance could be a special relationship that exists between certain members of an agency involving promotions, benefits, and other favorable acts being conducted within the agency and amongst officers for something in return. These actions could include sexual favors, monetary gifts, or other gifts or incentives.

Police brutality, on the other hand, mostly includes outside individuals such as prisoners, victims, witnesses, and others who are not affiliated with the police department wherein police officers would use the more-than-usual or necessary force in arresting, interacting with, interviewing, or interrogating someone. Police excessive use of force or using unnecessary force will be covered in later chapters. However, it is important to acknowledge here as it pertains to police corruption. It becomes police corruption when an officer uses unnecessary force or excessive force to effect an arrest or apprehend someone, even though there is substantial evidence to demonstrate that the use of force was unjustified. Corruption comes into play when the officer's supervisors, including the agency head, document the incident as "justified" in order to protect the reputation of the officer and the department.

Police sexual misconduct is another form of police corruption that we do not hear much about. According to the International Association of Chiefs of Police (IACP, 2011), "Addressing Sexual Offenses and Misconduct by Law Enforcement" executive guide, the definition is as follows:

> Sexual misconduct by law enforcement is defined as any behavior by an officer that takes advantage of the officer's position in law enforcement to misuse authority and power (including force) in order to commit a sexual act, initiate sexual contact with another person, or respond to a perceived sexually motivated cue (from a subtle suggestion to an overt action) from another person. It also includes any communication or behavior by an officer that would likely be construed as lewd, lascivious, inappropriate, or conduct unbecoming an officer and violates general principles of acceptable conduct common to law enforcement.

It is important to note that the authors of this document were experts ranging from psychologists, chiefs, upper police administrators, probation and parole officials, and other victim witnesses' advocates. The document also listed 10 forms of police sexual misconduct, which include but are not limited to the following:

- Sexual contact by force (rape or other sexual assault)
- Sexual shakedowns (sexual favor for not arresting or citing a citizen)
- Gratuitous physical contact with suspects (inappropriate or unnecessary searches or frisks just to satisfy sexual need of officer)
- Officer-initiated sexual contacts while on duty (sex with victims/known persons while on duty)
- Sexual harassment of colleagues/coworkers (unwanted approaches/repeated unwelcomed approaches toward colleagues/coworkers)
- Engaging in citizen-initiated sexual contact while on duty (having sex with citizens while on duty)
- Sexual behavior while on duty (masturbation, viewing pornographic images, or sexting while on duty)
- Voyeuristic actions that are sexually motivated (looking into windows at citizens for sexual pleasuring)
- Unnecessary contacts/actions taken by officers for personally and/or sexually motivated reasons (unwarranted callbacks to crime victims, making traffic stops to get a closer look at the driver, etc.)
- Inappropriate and unauthorized use of department resources and/or information systems for other than legitimate law enforcement purposes (using CAD/RMS to run victim's information to know his or her personal welfare)

The experts of this publication duly noted that these forms of police misconduct sometimes go unnoticed or unreported because victims do not report the incidents due to fear of the officer, experiences involving trauma, retaliation, feelings of humiliation, a perception that they may not be believed, and a perception that the agency won't do anything to the officer even if the report is validated. As a result, many victims choose to stay silent (IACP, 2011). Lastly, these incidents are difficult to measure and gauge, as most officers who are under such investigations would opt to resign in leu of termination, and they would in turn get another position from another jurisdiction where they may continue their actions (IACP, 2011). Consequently, reporting these incidents is crucial. The next section discusses strategies for reporting incidents involving corruption for victims and other officers.

Reporting Police Corruption

Reporting incidents of police corruption—whether the events involve sexual misconduct or fall under the eight types of police corruption noted—should occur as the incidents are being tracked, measured, documented, and addressed in order to prevent further occurrences by police agencies. According to the IACP (2011), reporting and investigating these incidents falls under four categories; **reports and complaints, the investigation, dispositions,** and **victims.**

REPORTS AND COMPLAINTS

Filing a police complaint is a very serious action. Therefore, various agencies have policies in place for this process. According to the IACP (2011), when reporting such complaints, those making the report should ensure that their concerns are presented as comprehensive, accessible, fair, thorough, and transparent. It should be comprehensive wherein when a complaint is made an agency should have a detailed process in place in order to investigate. It should be accessible to potential victims wherein it is formalizing and easy to complete, rather than be an overwhelming burden for the reporting party. It should be fair wherein the reporting party should feel as though their complaint is being handled in an orderly, honest, and serious manner. It should be thorough to ensure accuracy, accountability, and follow up. Lastly, it should be transparent wherein the reporting party should be kept in the loop, particularly during the investigations (IACP, 2011). Most agencies have a very streamlined process in place wherein anyone can make a complaint. Once the complaints are filed in person or online, a quick response is necessary in order to assure the reporting party that the investigation has ensued. Prompt measures should be taken in order to protect the victim's identity as well as prevent retaliation from other officers (or their associates) who may be involved.

THE INVESTIGATION

Depending on the complaint, investigation methods and strategies may vary. Whether it is a sexual misconduct case or one of the listed eight types of police corruption, the investigation agency should address the following standards. Once the complaint is received in person or via e-mail or other electronic means, it should be assigned to a police supervisor. Some agencies have a specialized unit that investigates police officers' misconduct called an Internal Affairs unit or bureau. This unit is mainly comprised of police supervisors and/or police investigators who can carry out various types of investigations. The IACP (2011) noted that all complaints require an administrative investigation.

There are two types of investigations—an administrative investigation and a criminal investigation. The administrative investigation is mainly an internal investigation conducted by the department wherein the officer is not charged criminally or the complaint does not arise to a criminal matter. A criminal investigation is wherein the complaints require a criminal investigation and if the outcome of the investigation determines that the officer did commit the act, he or she will be charged criminally. The IACP (2011) also noted that both investigations are extremely important in most complaints, because in some instances, in order to maintain the integrity of the agency, the department head will seek the expertise, manpower, and resources from a neighboring jurisdiction to take primary role in the investigations. For instance, in a high-profile sexual misconduct case involving an officer and a reporting party in a local police agency, the agency head may seek guidance from the state police agency to intervene in the criminal investigation if the complaint rises to that level.

It is important to note that both administrative and criminal investigations can be conducted separately, and agency leaders should maintain a solid wall between the investigations. Both parties should be kept apprised of the incident and there should be clear and utter transparency for both the reporting party and the officer involved. The officer's rights as in ***Garrity v. New Jersey*** should also be upheld. In the *Garrity* case, the Supreme Court ruled that police officers and other public officials have the right not to self-incriminate in administrative investigations with their agencies. In simple terms, an officer can refuse to answer any questions during an administrative investigation if he or she feels he or she is being forced or coerced—that if he or she does not answer, he or she will be terminated. This violates their Fifth and 14th Amendment rights.

It is also important to note that all investigations should be victim centered in order to provide assurance and confidence in order for future reporting parties to feel comfortable and to trust the reporting mechanisms within the police agency. Once the investigation is initiated, the investigator assigned will interview both parties involved and any other involving parties and make a decision as to whether the complaint is valid. There are four main dispositions for any such complaints: unfounded, exonerated, not sustained, and sustained (IACP, 2011). Unfounded means that the allegation was thoroughly investigated, and no evidence was found or identified to substantiate the complaint. Exonerated means that the incident did take place. However, the situation was lawful and according to departmental policies. Not sustained means that there was inadequate evidence to either prove or disprove the complaint. And lastly, sustained means that the evidence was adequate enough to prove the complaint. These dispositions are noted by the FBI's Uniform Crime Report mainly for administrative investigations wherein the complainant and the officer involved should be notified in writing. At the end of a criminal investigation—once a criminal violation has been noted—the complainant should be notified in writing as well, along with the county prosecutor or the commonwealth attorney, who should be notified for charging options. The complainant may be advised to seek private counsel or police union representation as well for representation for any criminal proceedings. Whether it is a criminal or an administrative investigation, almost every police agency has a guide in its complaint process and its channels. Several agencies are currently examining their policies in order to make their complaint process more streamlined for reporting. These efforts are being undertaken due to agencies being proactive in addressing reporting parties' needs while preserving the agencies' integrity and reputation, and upholding the officers' rights.

Effects of Police Corruption

The effects of police corruption can be far reaching on various levels for the parties involved, and also for those not involved. Popular criminal justice scholars have noted that the most common forms of police corruption are social, political, economic, and personal. In order to explore the holistic severity of the effects of this concept, let's examine a scholarly article that was published on the opposite continent of the United States—in Ghana. Justice Tankebe published the article, "Public Confidence in the Police: Testing the Effects of Public Experiences of Police Corruption in Ghana." In this piece, Tankebe (2010) posited that one of the most important concepts that is affected is the social aspect wherein due to a corruption incident, the public loses trustworthiness in the police. This effect will last for a long time until the agencies strive to regain trust from the communities they serve (Tankebe, 2010). Trustworthiness is a concept that is difficult to build between a community and the agency that represents that community. Once that trust has been established, any report of corruption can quickly destroy it. The second affected form is the political aspect. Once a corruption incident has been reported and has affected the social spectrum, it quickly makes its way to the political realm where other surrounding agencies and governmental bodies may start limiting their social and political interactions with said agency. As with the social aspect, the agencies would have to rebuild their relationships.

The economic realm ties in closely with the political realm wherein various costs of police corruption are examined. Samuel Walker and Charles Katz (2018) noted the six costs of police corruption in their policing text, which are described as follows:

- Corruption imposes high costs on the agency, the criminal justice system, and the society
- Corruption protects other criminal activities
- Corruption undermines the effectiveness of the criminal justice system
- Corruption undermines the police professionalism
- Corruption is a secret tax as these actions go unnoticed and taxes are not being paid for such services because they are illegal
- Police corruption undermines the public trust

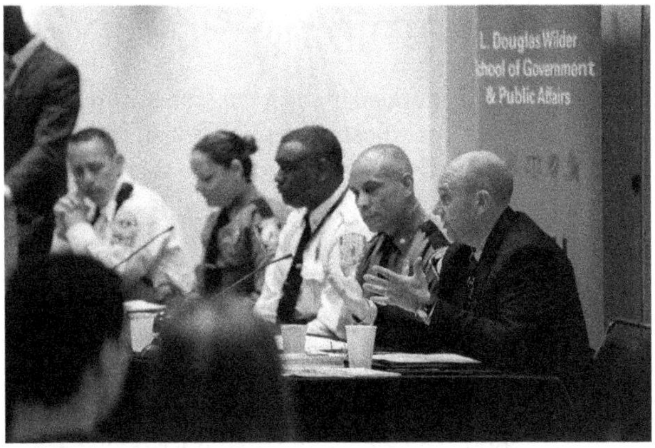

Figure 8.2 Police leaders tackling diversity and corruption issues in policing

As we can see, these effects of corrupt policing affect the inner core of everyone, mainly those who are involved in the field, but also those who are not.

The last realm (and sometimes the most affected) is the personal realm. Not only would the officer's agency face ridicule in the social and political realm, it would be shunned personally by other police officers. As mentioned in previous chapters, police officers thrive on their social relationships with peers and on peer accountability. Officers could suffer personal losses in their friendships as a result of police corruption incidents. They could also suffer personal family losses wherein close intricate family members shun them due to their actions. Eventually, some officers may even lose their spouses (and if children are involved, the family dynamic would be disrupted) in separation and divorce.

Box 8.1 Perception Versus Reality

A perception of police, from the outside looking in, may be that all police officers think alike and therefore have the tendency of being corrupt. Based on the research presented, even though officers think alike, they act differently to different situation. So it is false to make a broad justification to say that all cops have a tendency for corruption based on this notation. . Although there have been a large number of police corruption cases amongst officers, and we've seen wide scales of this issue, it is important to note that the particularistic perspective also holds true. This means that each officer has his or her own mind-set and can make decisions of his or her own volition. It is of no shock to assume that officers face a higher degree of instances where they are placed in the position of being corrupt due to discretion, lack of oversight, and independence. However, with the use of body-worn camera systems being slowly implemented in most major police agencies, this tendency can be reduced as the use of such devices creates transparency. An example was also included in this chapter to denote that officers within a specific unit do, of course, think differently, and can therefore make individual judgements. Classifying all officers as the same and prone to making similar misconduct actions is fairly false. There are several instances of untold stories in which officers have displayed acts of kindness toward their community members and most often toward a stranger. These actions are merely based on the officer's personal judgement and character.

Examining Police Behavior

As mentioned in the police subculture chapter and the perceptions of policing, it's clear that various types of officer perceptions exist. However, for the purposes of this textbook, only two types will be covered and are applicable to this chapter—the universalistic and the particularistic perspectives.

Universalistic Perspective

This type of view posits that all officers are similar and exhibit similar characteristics. In examining this further, this statement can be viewed in two dimensions. First, there are various similarities among officers due to their common training and education. Officers spent several hours in the police academy and also post-police academy in order to maintain their certifications during in-service training. As a result, these trainings and daily interactions provide them with a common mentality on things that they may encounter daily. In addition, because they spend several hours a week with other officers in the same beat, area, platoon, or squad, they develop a universalistic mind-set wherein they would have the tendency of thinking and acting in a way that is similar to their peers.

On the other hand, some specialty units tend to view other officers as if they are not doing "real" police work. For instance, a member from the Tactical Training and Response Unit (TTRU) would view the work of community officers as "not real police work" due to their daily assignments. The TTRU members are constantly engaged in training and high-risk responses—including those with hostages, serving felony warrants, and barricade incidents—whereas the community officers are in the communities daily, interacting with community members and creating valuable social relationships with these communities. Each unit is performing its duties and responsibilities very well. However, because their roles are completely opposite, each team can view the other from a different point of view, thus introducing the individualistic perspective.

Particularistic Perspective

This type of view posits that officers have individual characteristics and make decisions on their own without any outside influences or similar thinking as their peers. As mentioned, officers from different units can think differently than their peers, just as regular citizens living on the same street can think differently than their neighbors, and so on. In reiterating this under this perspective, it's important to examine officers within their assigned platoon/unit/squad.

A platoon normally has about eight to 10 officers assigned to work a shift who are supervised by a sergeant. This number may vary depending on the size of the department. All the officers within that platoon have a similar mind-set to a point. However, not all of them may be interested in traffic enforcement or issuing traffic citations on a daily basis. Some officers within that same platoon are more interested in making community contacts and interacting with business and resident owners in order to show their police presence, while others within that platoon are more interested in driving under the influence (DUI) enforcement. In addition, within that same platoon there will be some officers who aspire to become detectives or investigators. Therefore, these officers would opt in and volunteer to take criminal-related calls wherein they can perform minor investigations in order to build their skills for applying for a detective or investigator unit position. Even though there are many units within a police agency, officers within a platoon may exert their passions and interests in what they like to do best while still carrying out their regular duties and responsibilities, ranging from DUI enforcement, traffic violations, drug enforcement, thefts, and other criminal and non-criminal related interactions.

When dealing with police corruption, it is important remember that the universalistic and particularistic perspectives play a big role as they justify the notion that officers can think and act alike, and they can also think and act individually. These perspectives are relevant because most corruption cases involve one officer or a group of officers.

Some examples of police corruption can be found in the Box 8.2.

Discuss the following situations/ people:

- Miami River Cops (1980s);
- Rampart Division Scandal (1990s) LAPD
- According to NEWSONE (2011) top five most corrupt U.S. police officers of all time are Robert Gisevius, Kenneth Bowen, and Anthony Villavaso, Jon Burge, David Mack and Rafael Perez, Josept Miedzianowski, Louis Eppolito and Stephen Caracappa.

Exposing Police Deviance

Although there are several ways to expose police deviance, for the purposes of this text, we will focus mostly on the famous police commissions that helped expose police corruption: the **Wickersham Commission** and the **Knapp Commission**.

The Wickersham Commission

Due to the widespread complaints of police corruption during the political era and into the reform era, President Herbert Hoover appointed a special committee in 1929 to examine and investigate any form of corruption across the United States criminal justice agencies. The committee was originally called the National Commission on Law Observance and Education and gained its name after the appointed Attorney General George W. Wickersham. In addition to the head of the committee, there were 10 other members from various local and state institutions who held positions such as the dean of Harvard Law School and the president of Radcliffe College. The committee examined all aspects of the criminal justice system, including police and prosecuting procedures, causes of crime, and probation and parole guidelines. Upon completing the investigations, the committee published a widespread report known as the "Lawlessness in Law Enforcement." According to policing scholars, this publication shocked the nation as it revealed widespread police misconduct, bribery, entrapment, falsifying evidence, illegal wiretapping, and extensive use of the "**third degree**," which means the use of coercion by any means while interrogating a suspect to obtain confession.

The Wickersham Committee found that police departments across the country were using this method of interrogation. In addition, Sam Walker, a famous police scholar, mentioned in his book *Popular Justice* that prior to the Wickersham report, police detectives in Cleveland would starve suspects, depriving them of food and water during interrogations. In San Francisco, officers would physically abuse suspects in the patrol wagon as a sign of what was to come when they got to the police lockup, and several other serious abuses occurred at the hands of police in order to coerce suspects to confess.

Furthermore, the committee also uncovered several injustices within the correction and courts systems involving prosecution, probation, parole, sentences, unfair dealings, and especially the rise of plea bargaining. Even though the times were difficult during this committee's investigations (the Great Depression and alcohol prohibition was strongly impacting daily life for nearly everyone) the committee still completed its investigations by interviewing several key, high-level parties such as judges, police officers, prosecutors, jail administrators, and social workers. Once the outcome was published, many agencies were forced to reform their policies and to take a harder look at their dealings with the communities and people they served.

The Wickersham Committee was instrumental as it was one of the first established commissions to examine corruption within all forms of governmental agencies, specifically the criminal justice system. David Hanson noted in his article "Wickersham Commission: Pro-or Anti-Repeal? You Decide" that the major concepts covered within the committee's report included the following:

- Proposals to improve enforcement of criminal laws
- Enforcement of the prohibition laws, criminal statistics, prosecution
- Enforcement of deportation laws
- The child offender in the federal system of justice
- Progress report on the study of the federal courts, criminal procedure, penal institutions, probation and parole, crime and the foreign born, lawlessness in law enforcement, cost of crime, causes of crime, and police

As presented, these recommendations were truly inclusive and encompassed the entire system of government.

The Knapp Commission

Even though the Knapp Commission is similar to the Wickersham Commission, they have significant differences, such as their members' formation and their initiations. The Knapp Commission formed as a result of allegations brought forward by former NYPD Officer Frank Serpico and Sergeant David Durk. A famous Hollywood movie, *Serpico*, is based on Frank Serpico's character, played by Al Pacino. As compared to the Wickersham Committee, which was nationwide, the Knapp Commission was mostly focused on investigating police misconduct within the NYPD. According to Frank Schmalleger and John Worrall (2010) who noted in their book, *Policing Today*, the Knapp Commission was established in 1970 by Mayor John Lindsay due to an article that was published in the *New York Times* detailing specifics of widespread police corruption by the NYPD—initiated by Frank Serpico. The mayor appointed Judge Whitman Knapp to serve as the chair of the five-member committee.

Roberg, Novak, Cordner, and Smith (2005) noted in their book *Police and Society* that the committee found several instances of police misconduct within the NYPD. One example was gambling. Plainclothes officers would be assigned to gambling establishments, and these establishments would pay a substantial amount of money monthly to certain precincts wherein officers would split these proceeds in exchange for their presence and protection of these establishments. Furthermore, the authors noted that the committee identified two types of officers—**grass eaters** and **meat eaters**. Grass eaters are officers who receive small gifts and other gratuities in exchange for minor deviance acts for their personal gains, such as a free meal for dining in a restaurant to show police presence. Meat eaters, on the other hand, are officers who engage in serious acts of deviance behaviors such as protecting a gambling institution for substantive money in return. These types of officers actively seek illegal and alternative opportunities in order to receive financial or other favors for their personal gain.

In addition, the Knapp Committee made several recommendations. A few of these are as follows:

- Commanders should be held accountable for their officers' dealings
- Commanders should properly file key proactive reports demonstrating they are aware of police corruption and are preventing it
- Internal affairs units should be created for every precinct
- Undercover operatives should be immersed within each precinct
- Robust screening and selection standards for officers moving through the ranks should be increased
- A complete reform within the police subculture should be initiated

These recommendations were made to the NYPD. Taking into consideration their history of police corruption, they have amended several policies and procedures in order to address these recommendations. The NYPD is one of the largest police agencies in the nation, so it is prone to fostering police corruption. However, with effective policies, greater accountability, oversight, and transparency, the agency can almost eliminate all tendencies of police corruption. The next section presents strategies for combating police corruption.

Combating Police Corruption

Combating the issue of corruption is not an easy task as corruption stems from everyday activities and police work continuously to be autonomous. However, there are some positive recommendations that can help agencies work closely with their officers and strive even harder to prevent misconduct within their ranks. Even with maximizing the use of the body-worn cameras, not all specialty units wear these cameras, other than patrol officers. Various forms of corruption are always being identified. One of the best ways to deliver meaningful recommendations for combating corruption is to examine the International Association of Police Chief (IACP) document on police corruption. This is a good place to start as it comprises the opinions of police scholars from both a theoretical and a practical standpoint, from actual practitioners who are passionate about ridding this issue from their agencies. Some of the major recommendations proposed by the IACP (2011) include **considering a policy (law enforcement authority and agency authority), examining hiring standards for officers, continuous training for new and seasoned officers, evaluations and early intervention systems, establishing and strengthening internal affairs units, rewarding good officers, and the use of database systems to recognize corrupt officers from preventing them from becoming police officers at other agencies.**

Creating a Policy to Combat Corruption

Considering a policy or implementing a policy is one of the most important steps police agencies can take in combating corruption. Several agencies have implemented steps and have also updated their policies to reflect modern culture as both times and police work. Law enforcement authority deals with the issue that officers arrest and transport suspects on a daily basis. The majority of agencies have implemented policies prohibiting officers from performing on-duty sexual contact with their arrestees even if it is consensual. These policies cover any acts while on and off duty and for using any departmental properties such as buildings or vehicles. The second coverage is agency authority under establishing a policy. The IACP noted that agency leaders should be vigilant in mandating these policies, establishing these policies, and making sure these policies are consistent across all systems. The other recommendation in combating police corruption is examining hiring standards. Even though bad officers can make it through the hiring process, agencies should reexamine their hiring practices by thoroughly examining every candidate in order to eliminate any bad apples. Candidates for hire or lateral transfers who are certified officers seeking employment at another agency due to termination, separation, retirement, family lifestyle, relocation, and several other reasons should be carefully reviewed.

Promoting In-Service Training to Combat Corruption

Another recommendation for combating police corruption is training. Officers go through a tremendous number of hours during the police academy and also after the academy. Agencies have increased their in-service training curriculum to include integrity tests that measure officer's discretions with various scenarios to see if officers make the right or more feasible choices. These responses are then reviewed by either their supervisors or by external training parties who are contracted by police agencies. Officers also learn a lot from their field training officers (FTOs). Agencies have examined pairing new officers with multiple FTOs in order to give them a wide variety of exposure to police attitudes.

Integrity Tests

In addressing seasoned officers, agencies have established mandatory integrity tests for seasoned officers on an annual basis. Their responses and scores are reviewed by external parties depending on the agency. Some are reviewed by internal members in order to determine if the officer is showing any signs of police misconduct. These tests cover a variety of scenarios that expose the officers to various decision-making strategies. Some are a pass or fail while others are a simple "write up a response for the scenario." Some agencies have noted that these tests have been beneficial within their agencies as a tool to remind officers of the complexities of their duties and responsibilities.

Evaluations and Early Intervention Systems (EIS)

Another recommendation is the evaluations and early intervention systems. According to the IACP (2011), early intervention systems are beneficial in preventing problem behavior and in monitoring and identifying officer misconduct through communications and other evaluation systems. Supervisors can collect and evaluate several electronic messages from cellphones and computers in vehicles, and they can even speak with colleagues to determine if there are any patterns in a particular officer's behavior that may indicate any form of past, present, or future police misconduct.

Internal Affairs Units/Internal Affairs Bureau

Another formal level of addressing police misconduct and complaints are the formation of Internal Affairs units or bureaus. The concept of police internal affairs units or bureaus are well established in most police departments. Some agencies are creating separate units to house this section of investigations and some are relocating it under the office of the chief as it works closely with the police chief. In order to create more transparency, some agencies are even creating this unit by bringing together several outside departmental and civilian members, along with internal members in order to have a broader representation. Some agencies have questioned the loyalty and honesty of these units as the majority of them are made up of officers as well. The notion of the thin blue line, as discussed in the previous chapter, may apply wherein officers may have the tendency to cover for other officers' misconduct. Some agencies have addressed this seriously by having a strict and rigorous process for officers who express interest in these units by requiring stress tests, several scenario-based exercises, personal and professional background checks, and reference checks. Personnel files are also taken into consideration for such positions as an investigator within these units.

REWARDING GOOD OFFICERS

Rewarding good officers was another recommendation made by the IACP. Most officers take pride in their daily duties and responsibilities and several agencies have the "officer of the month" or "officer of the year" program, along with various other community awards wherein community members can vote for an officer to be recognized for his or her outstanding efforts. Although these simple actions will not always prevent police misconduct, they lessen the chances of officers getting involved in misconduct behaviors when they are compensated and recognized appropriately. This incentive also covers compensating officers on a regular basis for outstanding work; as a result, they will not look elsewhere for an alternative means of financial gain.

A SYSTEM-WIDE DATABASE TO DETER CORRUPTION

Last, the IACP proposes that a system-wide database should be created wherein officers who have been terminated for police misconduct are placed on a list so that other agencies can look and verify their records before rehiring them. The issue as it stands is that some officers are found guilty of police misconduct administratively by an agency and are given the chance to resign in lieu of termination. These officers are primarily not entered into a nationwide system, and as a result, another agency can rehire them without knowing their internal dealings within the other agency. Some agencies do a thorough background investigation of lateral transfers as they are on heightened alert that officers separate from agencies for various reasons. These are just a few of the recommendations made by various entities including the IACP and the police researchers, Sam Walker and Charles Katz.

Chapter Summary

This chapter covers the definition and types of police corruption. It is important to note that the terms *police* corruption and *police misconduct* are used interchangeably. The types of police corruption are quite expansive, and we've discussed several in this chapter. Some agencies may classify certain types of incidents as police corruption based on their policies and procedures. Reporting police corruption and exploring the effects of police corruption were also discussed in this chapter. The reporting of this issue can be quite difficult as victims tend to see themselves as not credible or that they will not be taken seriously. Approaches to alleviate the issue of police corruption were presented in this chapter along with discussions about how agencies can make their reporting standards easier and more victim centered. As mentioned earlier, the effects of police corruption not only affect officers but everyone around them, including on a social, personal, political, and economical level.

Basic police behavior—specifically the universalistic perspective and the particularistic perspective—were also discussed at length in this chapter. In addition, we explored two main police commissions—the Wickersham Commission and the Knapp Commission. Several other commissions exist, such as the Mollen Commission, which was initiated in 1992 by Mayor David Dinkins who appointed Milton Mollen to chair the committee. Like the Knapp Commission, this committee was also appointed to examine widespread corruption in the NYPD in the early 1990s. Last, this chapter covered combating police corruption. The fact remains that police corruption is a rampant problem in most agencies, especially larger police agencies. However, smaller agencies can also have instances of rampant police corruption, and sometimes these instances go undetected for several months—and even years.

It is important to note that the views expressed here address most police agencies, and it is also important to note that several of these agencies are currently working very hard to improve their policies to cover both minor and major acts of police misconduct. Combating corruption is a continuous work-in-progress initiative for police agencies.

Discussion Questions

1. List and describe the most common types of police corruption.
2. Reporting police corruption can be very troublesome for the victims involved. Based on your readings, what are some strategies police agencies are taking in order to make their reporting processing more streamlined?
3. List and describe three effects of police corruption.
4. What is the difference between universalistic and particularistic perspectives? Provide examples of each.
5. What is the difference between the Wickersham and the Knapp Commissions? What are the outcomes of each commission?
6. List and describe three effective strategies and recommendations for police agencies and police administrators to combat police corruption.

References

Buttle, J. W., Graham Davies, S., & Meliala, A. E. (2016). A cultural constraints theory of police corruption: Understanding the persistence of police corruption in contemporary Indonesia. *Australian & New Zealand Journal of Criminology, 49*(3), 437–454. doi:10.1177/0004865815573875

Essert, M. (2014). 7 *huge cases of gross police misconduct made news this week.* Retrieved from https://www.mic.com/articles/79011/7-huge-cases-of-gross-police-misconduct-made-news-this-week

Garrett, R. H. (2015, November 13). Police misconduct and corruption. Retrieved from https://www.cji.edu/site/assets/files/1921/policemisconductandcorruption.pdf

Hanson, D. (2019). Wickersham Commission: Pro-or anti-repeal? You decide. *Alcohol Problems and Solutions.* Retrieved from https://www.alcoholproblemsandsolutions.org/wickersham-commission-pro-or-anti-repeal/

Hennessey, H. S. V. (2014, February 25). King City policy officers arrested in corruption scandal. *Monterey Herald News.* Retrieved from https://www.montereyherald.com/2014/02/25/king-city-police-officers-arrested-in-corruption-scandal/

International Association of Chiefs of Police (IACP). (2011). *Addressing sexual offenses and misconduct by law enforcement.* Retrieved from https://www.theiacp.org/sites/default/files/all/a/AddressingSexualOffensesandMisconductbyLawEnforcementExecutiveGuide.pdf

Lee, G. C. M. (2018). Police corruption: A comparison between China and India. *Journal of Financial Crime, 25*(2), 248–276. doi:10.1108/JFC-10-2017-0096

Merriam-Webster. (n.d). *Police misconduct.* Retrieved from https://www.merriam-webster.com/dictionary/misconduct

NEWSONE. (2011). *The top 5 most corrupt U.S. police officers of all time.* Retrieved from https://newsone.com/1551885/top-5-corrupt-police-officers/ Roebuck, J., & Barker, T. (1974). A typology of police corruption. *Social Problems, 21*(3), 423–437. doi10.2307/799909

Roberg, R., Novak, K. & Cordner, G., & Smith. B. (2005). *Police and society* (3rd ed.). Los Angeles, CA: Roxbury.

Schmalleger, F. & Worrall, J. (2010). *Policing today.* Upper Saddle River, NJ: Pearson Education.

Tankebe, J. (2010). Public confidence in the police: Testing the effects of public experiences of police corruption in Ghana. *British Journal of Criminology,* 50,(2), 296–319.

Walker, S. (1998). *Popular justice: A history of American criminal justice* (2nd ed.). New York, NY: Oxford University Press.

Walker, S. & Katz, C. (2018). *The police in America: An introduction* (9th ed.). New York, NY: McGraw Hill Education.

CHAPTER NINE

Police and Evolving Technology

The technological trend is ever changing. Law enforcement should stay current and be vigilant in combating technological crimes. This chapter will identify the various technologies in use today such as body-worn camera systems, computer-aided dispatch (CAD), automated license plate readers (ALPRs), social media and police, Google Glass, brain fingerprinting, integrated automated fingerprint information systems (IAFIS), police drones, and many more.

Learning Objectives

- Identify and understand various police technologies relating to all types of investigations
- Explore computer-based systems in policing
- Examine the legal and applicable aspects of new police technologies

Chapter Outline

A REAL-LIFE POLICE SCENARIO FOR DISCUSSION

from Chernoh Wurie's personal accounts

At the start of my shift, I signed out my less-than-lethal shotgun and Taser from the police armory, checked my mail, and went out to the parking lot. I inspected my cruiser, making sure I had the supplies I needed for the road. I got in the vehicle and turned on the computer-aided design/dispatch (CAD), signaling to the police dispatcher that I was beginning my tour of duty.

The CAD is one of the modern technologies used by most police agencies. The computer enables officers to receive visual addresses, directions, warnings, warrant and wanted checks, lookouts, criminal histories, suspicious activities, calls for service, and other messages from fellow officers along with the dispatchers. The dispatcher acknowledged my check-in by saying my unit number, 1380. My vehicle was also equipped with an ALPR (automated license plate reader) system connected to my computer. The ALPR has two high-resolution cameras mounted on the back of the cruiser, spaced apart from each other. Once activated, they take pictures of the license plates of vehicles in the area surrounding the cruiser and transmit them to the computer to check for stolen vehicles. I had been trained on this equipment and have used it on several occasions.

As I left the police station, I drove to Interstate 95 to capture license plates of vehicles entering and leaving the county. It is assumed that car thieves will try to transport a stolen vehicle as far away from the jurisdiction where they are stolen, in order to prevent apprehension or recognition by the victim. I positioned my cruiser so I could capture several license plates as they entered the county. About 30 minutes into my proactive stolen vehicle lookout, an older, light green Honda Civic zoomed past me at high speed. Sure enough, I got a notification with a high-pitched beeping on my computer and an audible voice, sounding the words "Alert: stolen vehicle, stolen vehicle."

The ALPR is a basic system, containing a database of license plates belonging to stolen vehicles, suspicious vehicles, and other vehicles of interest. Every time the

ALPR captures a license plate, it runs it through the database and sends the operator an alert if there is a match.

Upon receiving the alert, I shifted into pursuit mode, activating my lights and sirens. I also notified the dispatcher that I received a stolen vehicle hit on my ALPR and was in pursuit of it. The dispatcher confirmed the stolen vehicle, which had been reported stolen 2 days earlier.

I noticed the vehicle was about three cars ahead of me. It was evident the driver had noticed me and was trying to evade capture. Two of the three vehicles got out of my way and I was only one vehicle away from the stolen vehicle. With a loud siren and several high-pitched "move out of the way" commands, the third vehicle moved, and I was right behind the stolen vehicle. I pursued the vehicle for about 5 miles when I was joined by several other officers. It was earlier in the morning, traffic was light, and our speed did not exceed more than 50 mph. The stolen vehicle eventually crashed into a utility pole, where a young male driver exited the vehicle and attempted to evade us on foot.

I liked running and was in great shape, so I immediately gave chase and apprehended him a short distance from the vehicle. The 16-year-old driver was arrested and transported to the police station where he was charged with grand theft auto, evading police, and reckless driving.

I was thankful no one else was injured, as police pursuits can be very dangerous. The vehicle was also recovered, and the owner and his insurance agency were notified.

I was also grateful for the ALPR system that notified me of the stolen vehicle. Newer technologies are emerging in policing every day; this chapter covers just a fraction of these technologies police agencies are evaluating and using to stay ahead of the ever-changing criminal spectrum. Some new technologies are even too new to appear in this chapter; others might be omitted for security reasons.

Technology and Policing

To be effective, police agencies need to stay ahead of the ever-changing technological evolution. Ryan Cotter (2017) noted in his work "Police Intelligence: Connecting the Dots in a Network Society" that intelligence-led policing is the gold standard in 21st-century policing. Even though this study was focused on Ontario, Canada, it is applicable to the United States and globally, as intelligence-led policing is refining the concept of traditional policing.

Some believe this is breaking with tradition, whereas others consider these new-found enforcement, investigation, and proactive measures a step forward, a responsive approach to the nation's outcries for less use of lethal force by police. Information sharing, aided by technology, is what leads to effective prevention, enforcement, and investigations, particularly when dealing with multiple jurisdictions (Cotter, 2017).

Intelligence-Led Policing (Strategic and Tactical)

Intelligence-led policing was first introduced in Great Britain in the early 1990s, when repeat offenders and incidents were plaguing the cities. Intelligence-led policing came about mainly due to the constant criticism of the reactive nature of the police at the time and the lack of trust in policing related to using new technologies (Cotter, 2017). This type of policing is merely the use of information sharing and resources in order to prevent specific types of problems from reoccurring.

The Bureau of Justice Assistance (BJA) paper "Intelligence-Led Policing: The New Intelligence Architecture" offers a simple definition of intelligence-led policing and also notes the two types of intelligence: strategic and tactical. The authors noted that in order to define the term *intelligence*, it is important to know its common misunderstandings.

One common mistake pointed out by the authors is that people may refer to "collecting intelligence" instead of "collecting information." They explained, "The intelligence is not what is collected, it is what is produced after collected data is evaluated and analyzed" (BJA, 2005).

Another important concept that is commonly misunderstood is the difference between strategic and tactical intelligence. Strategic intelligence is the wide-range utilization of manpower and resources that are allocated during the information gathering phase. Tactical intelligence is directly related to the success of an investigation (BJA, 2005). Tactical intelligence is used in immediate investigations that are shorter in time, whereas strategic intelligence is used in long-term or extended investigations. In its simplest form, strategic intelligence is the planning phase wherein various resources are explored in order to carry out an investigation, whereas tactical intelligence is the actual and physical carrying out of the plans laid out by the strategic planning process.

Let's explore some examples. In Great Britain's policing history, several complaints were made to the police services about certain thieves who were repeatedly carrying out burglaries. Police began strategically allocating resources in the targeted areas in order to disrupt these specific offenders.

Intelligence-led policing also made its way to the United States in the early to late 1990s, when crime analysis units would analyze a wide range of information received from various means and strategically disseminate this information to patrol officers, detectives, and other agencies. Authors of the BJA (2005) also noted that intelligence-led policing has succeeded in the United States in part due to the development of fusion centers.

Fusion centers are multi-agency facilities where agents from neighboring agencies work collectively, with high levels of information sharing. Their goal is to prevent, investigate, and enforce specific incidents such as sexual assaults across state lines, illegal drugs and misuse of prescription drugs, terrorism, and other interjurisdictional crimes/offenses. There are several fusion centers in the United States that are actively working together to address incidents like these. As technology evolves, the fusion centers are where police agencies can work closely together and ensure that information is appropriately shared at all levels.

Body-Worn Camera Systems

What are body-worn cameras (BWCs; see figure 9.1)? They have been around since the introduction of the video camera. However, BWCs gained prominence following the final report of the President's Task Force on 21st Century Policing, which identified five pillars of modern-day policing: building trust and legitimacy; policy and oversight; technology and social media; community policing and crime reduction; and training and education (President's Task Force on 21st Century Policing, 2015).

After this report was published, several agencies started embracing all of the pillars, but some focused mainly on building trust and legitimacy. Agencies interpreted this as needing to be transparent with the communities they serve; as a result, they started seeking funding for implementing body-worn camera programs in their jurisdictions.

Additionally, in the article "The Impact of Law Enforcement Officer Perceptions of Organizational Justice on their Attitudes

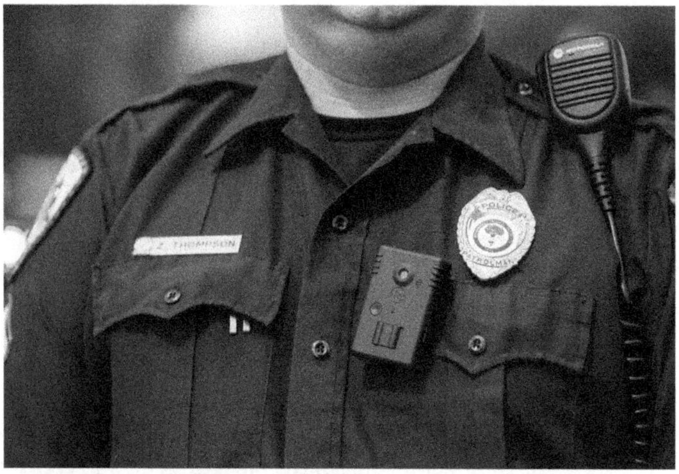

Figure 9.1 Body camera

Regarding Body-Worn Cameras" Michael Kyle and David White (2017) from Southern Illinois University Carbondale noted that major civil unrests as a result of controversial police shootings has prompted police to ensure more transparency by using body-worn cameras.

One of the major sellers/vendors of body-worn camera systems is Axon, which currently contracts with multiple agencies. The BWC is basically a recording device mounted on officers as part of their uniform; some are placed on their chest and others are placed on their shoulder strap or eyeglasses. The device is equipped with a microphone that captures audio and a small camera that captures visuals.

According to the International Association of Chiefs of Police (IACP), BWCs are used to provide an accurate record of police arrests, citizens' interactions, and all other critical incidents an officer faces while on duty. The information obtained from BWCs will help officers in documenting evidence, establishing probable cause or reasonable suspicion, investigating a crime scene, and providing courtroom testimonies, as well as education, training, and evaluation (IACP, 2019a).

Since 2014, the IACP has published various model policies for agencies when implementing this type of program. These model policies cover purpose, policy, and procedures. The purpose section documents the reason for the memo in detailing guidelines for agencies to follow in addition to a reason and justification for the program implementation. The policy section covers the guidelines to ensure consistency among agencies using the device. Last, the procedures section covers logistics such as when and how to use the BWC, restrictions on using the BWC, storage, and supervisory responsibilities (IACP, 2019a).

Restrictions on using the BWC may differ by department, such as those that cover specialized populations, places and locations, or have confidential missions. The IACP listed four restrictions, but this list, which includes the following, can be more robust depending on the agency: communicating with other officers without the permission of the head of the agency; communicating with undercover officers and informants; communicating during break and on personal activities; and communicating in locations where personal privacy is expected, such as restrooms and locker rooms.

Most sellers of body-worn camera systems have advised agencies that the device only activates when the officer initiates it. However, there are options wherein it can be automatically initiated due to the activation of a signal word or radio communication, and so on.

It is also important to examine what researchers note about the pros and cons of the BWCs. Three major pros are that they improve public safety and police interactions, provide accountability and transparency for police agencies in complaints and even commendations, and increase the public trust in law enforcement. Some cons that have been noted by researchers are that they are costly and not versatile, they invade citizens' rights of privacy and constitutional rights, and they may alter the officer's typical responses as they are aware of being "watched." Not all of these cons have been proven, however.

Storage is also another point to note when it comes to the implementation of BWC programs. Because these systems will be recording daily or used predominantly during the officers' daily work schedules, special consideration must be given to securing the proper amount of storage needed for such data. Many agencies are exploring cloud storage, which is an online secured storage database owned primarily by private companies. Agencies are also concerned with the security and accessibility of such data, as online information can be vulnerable to computer hackers. Some advantages of using the cloud storage system are that its users can easily access its content as long as a network is available, and this type of storage device has the capacity to hold a larger amount of data than conventional storage systems. Agencies are taking special precautions in contracting with major sellers to guarantee security and accessibility of the recorded data.

Kyle and White (2017) posited that much credit should be given to the officers who wear BWCs. As they tackle some of the most difficult and controversial scenarios, these officers are expected to uphold the law and act according to their training and experience while being judged, not only by the judicial system and police administrators, but also by the general public.

Seasoned officers may express their displeasure with wearing BWCs, as they find it harder to naturally perform their duties while being constantly watched. They fear that their autonomy and discretion are being taken away from them. Newer officers, who are trained in the police academy to wear and operate the device without knowing any other way, are mostly in favor of it, as they become accustomed to wearing it routinely.

Another justification for the use of this device was noted by the Police Executive Research Forum (PERF, 2015) as a result of the shootings of Michael Brown (MO), Eric Garner (NY), Walter Scott (SC), and Freddie Grey (MD). Based on these tragic events, police administrators became concerned that their agencies had lost legitimacy from the communities they serve, and several have invested in the BWCs program.

Kyle and White (2017) surveyed 201 law enforcement officers from four major police agencies in the midwestern and southern United States, measuring officers' perceptions on organizational justice and on BWCs. The researchers used a structural equation model and found that law enforcement perceptions of organizational justice are an evident factor affecting their attitudes toward BWCs.

What does this mean, in actuality? Let us start by explaining what organizational justice is. In this case, it is the way an officer views how the police organization treats him or her—fairly or unfairly—in light of various incidents. In this study, it was evident that line and level officers view the implementation of BWCs as too swift and too reactional to public outcry. The officers surveyed clearly noted their frustrations about the swift implementation of this policy and also shared how they felt unheard regarding their concerns about the program. It is speculated that officers react negatively to change. A swift change that may cause officers lose the autonomy of doing their jobs can cause some officers to react passively, while causing other officers to react proactively—perhaps even leaving the force to pursue another career.

In short, arguments can be made as to the advantages and disadvantages of body-worn camera programs. A majority of the larger police agencies have implemented BWCs, and others are still in testing phases. It's within each agency's discretion whether to use BWCs. However, all agencies have an obligation to the communities they serve. If these communities demand transparency through BWCs, then the designated agency is obligated to explore them. Some agencies—due to the outcry of their community members and the call for transparency— are made to implement this program by consent decree, which is a court order stating that they must implement the program. A recent example occurred within the Newark Police Department (2019) wherein the Department of Justice discovered several instances that surmounted to unconstitutional policing. Therefore, a consent decree was put in place in order for their agency to be more transparent by using the body-worn camera program.

Police Drones

Police drones, also known as unmanned aerial vehicles (UAVs), are being used by some agencies. The perceptions among citizens about the use of these devices are mixed.

Before delving into the public's perceptions of UAVs, it's important to know the basic functions of the device. UAVs are simply free-flying devices that range in size and are not controlled by a pilot but rather by a digital stick or a remote control. The device can provide real-time pictures of a large area, and some capture sounds and other data. They can be connected wirelessly and relay information back to the user who is monitoring it on a projector or screen.

Miliakela Heen, Joel Lieberman, and Terance Miethe from the Department of Criminal Justice at the University of Nevada, Las Vegas published a resonating study in 2018 titled, "The Thin Blue Line Meets the Big Blue Sky: Perceptions of Police Legitimacy and Public Attitudes Towards Aerial Drones." The study pointed out that UAVs have been useful to law enforcement, especially in specific instances like crowd management, accidents and crime scenes, hostage situations, and other high-risk incidents. UAVs give law enforcement the ability to enter locations and domains that are too hostile or dangerous to send in an actual officer.

The researchers noted two examples wherein unmanned devices were used to end or assist in dangerous situations. During an active shooter incident, the Dallas Police Department used an unmanned robot to deliver and detonate explosives that disabled the gunman.

Another example was the Orlando "Pulse" nightclub shooting in 2016, where an active shooter entered the club and killed several individuals inside. The attending law enforcement agencies utilized unmanned robots to search the crime scene for explosives, based on intelligence reports.

Even though these newer technologies may benefit police agencies, sometimes they are not well received by the public. Some may say that the police are becoming too militarized, as unmanned aircrafts and vehicles/robots have been primarily used by the military to detect explosive devices. The results by the study conducted by Heen and colleagues (2018) revealed mixed perceptions on this concept. Some members of the public indicated support for UAVs when used for search and rescue operations, tracking down runaway criminals, and controlling illegal immigration.

The perceptions were further broken down into two parts: proactive enforcements and reactive enforcements. Most study respondents supported police using UAVs in both proactive and reactive enforcements, like preventing crimes from happening and responding to search and rescue calls or to an active crime scene. Most of the opposition toward law enforcement use of UVAs centered on surveillance of ordinary citizens—proactive surveillance—which may be viewed as a violation of privacy. Both sides of the argument have some merit. As mentioned in the discussion over body-worn cameras, various agencies are exploring these newer technologies with an eye on transparency, efficiency, and accountability to their communities.

Brain Fingerprinting

Another scientific method that has assisted police investigations since the early 1990s is brain fingerprinting. This was developed by Dr. Lawrence Farwell, a neuroscientist.

Dhiraj Ahuja and Bharat Singh from YMCA University of Science and Technology in India published a paper titled "Brain Fingerprinting" in 2012. The researchers presented the history, definitions, and concepts of this technology. They described the process invented by Dr. Farwell: A small cap-like device is worn on the subject's head and connected to a computer to read his or her brain waves. The device reacts to a unique brain wave pattern when it encounters a familiar stimulus (Ahuja & Singh, 2012). When the subject who is hooked up to the machine is asked a question, the device focuses on the remembrance or familiarity of an item, object, location, scene, occurrence, or person based on the brain wave pattern and sends a signal wave pattern to demonstrate knowledge of the investigation.

As the experts noted, there are four steps in the brain fingerprinting process: brain fingerprinting crime scene evidence collection, brain fingerprinting brain evidence collection, brain fingerprinting computer evidence analysis, and brain fingerprinting scientific results. The researchers argued that there are some problems with this technology, as it only measures and detects activities or provides knowledge about what is being investigated. It does not detect "intent," and intent is what is mostly needed to prove certain crimes.

The results of brain fingerprinting may prove that the subject was at the scene. However, the results do not prove that the same subject committed the offense. He or she could also be a witness or a victim.

Finer details and specifics could be asked of a subject in order to better ascertain his or her type of involvement in the incident. For instance, Dr. Farwell used the device in 1999 to assist police in investigating a sexual assault and murder involving suspect James Grinder. Grinder was allegedly accused of raping and killing a 25-year-old female victim. Using the brain fingerprinting test, Dr.

Farwell was able to measure the brain waves of James Grinder and determine that he had knowledge of the crime scene and crime itself. Grinder was asked specific questions about the incident that no one would know except the victim and the perpetrator. He confessed to the crime several days after the brain fingerprinting.

According to Ahuja and Singh, there are seven major limitations with this type of technology. The first is that the device only detects what information is in the subject's brain, not how it got there. Second, it only detects information and not "intent." Third, it cannot be used for general screening. Fourth, the device detects information but cannot identify lies. Fifth, it depends on the subject's memory. And sixth, it only depicts the information that is included in the probe stimuli-questions asked. Last, it is no substitute for common sense or good judgement investigation (Ahuja & Singh, 2012).

Dr. Lawrence Farwell, Drew C. Richardson, and Graham M. Richardson also contributed an informative paper on this topic in 2012, entitled "Brain Fingerprinting Field Studies Comparing P300-Mermer and P300 Brainwave Responses in the Detection of Concealed Information." As they described brain fingerprinting, it simply detects concealed information stored in the brain by measuring brainwave responses. The researchers studied behaviors in 76 people, across four types of people who have experiences with the following real-life events: felony crimes, real crimes with real consequences, knowledge unique to FBI agents, and specialized expertise such as explosive (EOD/IED) devices.

The results of the tests were stunning, as they yielded little or no errors, specifically noting that accuracy, validity, and reliability depend on following the methods outlined in the discussed study. The results of the study demonstrated the accuracy of the device in detecting knowledge of the various individuals and their connections to what was being explored. Cases where there were deliberate experiments to determine memory and knowledge of incidents were positive wherein the participants' brain memory signals proved that they had knowledge of certain events. Also, individuals who had no knowledge of certain incidents had no brain memory activities, thus showing that the tests were primarily accurate.

It is speculated that some agencies at the local, state, and federal levels have examined brain fingerprinting, some have used it, and some are piloting it today. Brain fingerprinting has been piloted by several federal agencies, including the FBI, CIA, DOD, and Secret Service. However, it was stated that they found limited applicability for their daily duties and responsibilities (U.S. General Accounting Office, 2001). Clearly, more experience with brain fingerprinting is needed in order to best determine its usage in law enforcement.

Google Glass

Google is the most popular website in the world. It connects users in different ways and collects and presents Internet search information customized by an individual's location and needs. The owners of this massive website saw the opportunity to provide information along with accurate location updates in an even smaller device. They came up with Google Glass, which is a pair of eye glasses that visually collect information in the wearer's periphery. The glasses transmit real-life information to a smartphone or computer.

This device is being tested by several police departments in Massachusetts, California, and Georgia, including Byron Police Department and the NYPD. The device works primarily through facial recognition. If information about a specific person has already been entered (into a police database system such as a criminal history information network), and this person becomes visible in the Google Glass, the device will display this information to the officer by detecting the person through facial recognition only if a picture of this person was uploaded into the police database originally. It has also been useful in identifying terrorists and other wanted and special interest individuals (Envisage Technologies, 2014).

Figure 9.2 Google Glass

As explained in this article from Envisage Technologies, wearing the device leaves the officer's hands free to carry a weapon or work and document a crime scene. The device works similar to the body-worn cameras. However, Google Glass provides several more features such as location and time stamps, facial recognition, and communicating with the officer (see figure 9.2). It also moves naturally with the officer's face since it is designed to follow the officer's viewing path.

Envisage Technologies (2014) presents some of the benefits: (a) keeping officers' hands free so they can carry out their duties (searching, arresting, apprehending someone, etc.), and (b) allowing the information collected in this database system to be shared between agencies. For example, regarding the seriousness of an offender and providing a virtual image of the subject with warning histories about his or her past interactions (e.g., a violent offender etc.) can be shared with the officer prior to their arrival or making contact with the subject. Sharing this information with other agencies is invaluable, especially for officer safety concerns.

Also, in 2014, Yesenia Duran published an article titled "Google Glass Finds Its Way Into Law Enforcement." She interviewed two officers from the Byron Police Department who tested Google Glass; one was a sergeant and the other was a K-9 officer. Both said the device was easy to wear and that they had no obstructions getting in and out of their vehicles while making traffic stops, conducting minor investigations, interacting with citizens, or during their firearms training (Duran, 2014).

The testers noted a few negatives about the device. Since the device is placed on top of the right eye, if someone is left-eye dominant, it can be more difficult for them to use.

Another negative issue was battery life. Because most officer shifts are 10 to 12 hours long, the testing officer shared concerns regarding the battery life of the device, for example would the battery life last for that long? It was determined that the device should explore a more effective and substantial battery power or supply in order to meet the officer shifts demands. Also, not every police department issues their officers cellphones. To use Google Glass, some officers would have to use their personal cell phones, and this would use up their personal storage space. This concern was also expressed by the testing officers. However, in order to eliminate this concern, most agencies issue their police officers a cell phone for departmental usage. These phones can be linked to the device in order to provide a mobile display and accessible information in a wider transmitting medium. Access to Google Glass will remain a concern for small agencies who do not issue their officers work cell phones.

Finally, some citizens may have concerns about an officer simply looking at their faces and receiving all kinds of personal information. This could seem like an invasion of privacy and individual rights. There are not many reports that agencies are actively using Google Glass; however, the technology is being tested and its use is likely to expand in the future. More research is needed for police agencies to best understand how and when to use Google Glass.

Social Media

Social media is basically the collection and sharing of information through various person-to-person networks and platforms. Despite the negative perceptions about police using social media, the tool has more benefits than negatives. Some of the major examples of these platforms include Facebook, Twitter, Google+, Wikipedia, LinkedIn, Reddit, and Pinterest. More are being developed and will be readily available by the publication of this textbook.

How can police use these mediums to their advantage? According to an article on PoliceOne.com (2019), social media—mostly Facebook and Twitter—are being used by officers to reach each other, other police departments domestically and internationally, and their communities.

Chief Benjamin Bliven from the Wausau (WI) Police Department published an article with the *FBI Law Enforcement Bulletin* in 2018 titled "Perspective: Impact of Positive Stories Through Social Media." In the article, Biven shared several examples of how his agency is using social media to put a positive influence on current rhetoric about police. He noted that several unfortunate events in recent years have negatively affected the relationships between police and the communities they serve. Social media has played a role in spreading these incidents.

On the flip side, police departments can use social media to show the positives of policing, too. Bliven says negativity spreads like wildfire on social media, sometimes to the detriment of officer safety. He urges police leaders to spread positive messages through social media in order to show the human side of policing.

Bliven gave several examples about how to do this, including some from his own police department. The examples included police giving a tour of the department to a Cub Scout troop; officers stopping in at a children's school performance to say hello; a diabetic officer meeting with young children suffering from the disease who are worried they cannot accomplish their dreams; troopers volunteering their time to build a ramp for a man who lost a leg; a deputy explaining the job of a K-9 to a child; a trooper playing ice hockey with a group of kids; sheriff's office employees volunteering their time on ski patrol; and the list goes on (Bliven, 2018).

Another example from his department was sharing a very humiliating BWC video of one of his officers slipping and falling on ice twice in one day, showing that police have a sense of humor, too. Bliven noted that the reaction to this video was quite positive, as the community appreciated seeing the realness and humility of the officer. Bliven challenged other police departments to use social media as a force to spread positive stories about policing.

Another concept that swept the nation's police agencies during 2018 was the "lip sync challenges" going viral on social platforms, where different agencies would challenge each other to a lip sync battle. Some would include their entire departments in high production music videos, with officers dancing and singing on social media for the world to see. Several agencies in the United States engaged in these battles, again showing that cops are humans, too.

Another benefit of using social media for law enforcement is that it can help identify and locate suspects, victims, witnesses, and other persons of interest. Information moves very quickly through social media. Agencies are using Facebook, Twitter, and so on to seek information from the public and even offer rewards for providing information. Several cases, including cold cases, have been solved using social media and several victims and other persons of interest have been identified. (Have students research the Golden State Killer, and how this cold case was brought back to life and solved, perhaps in part due to *I'll Be Gone in the Dark* author Michelle McNamara's (2018) presence on social media, and investigative DNA testing.)

As mentioned with all other new technologies, there are pros and cons. Some agencies have policies governing officers' personal use of social media. Negative or other derogatory comments by officers on social media outlets can be used against them in administrative matters.

Futuristic Police Vehicles

The future of police vehicles is ever changing, so this section will only cover the major features that agencies are looking for in new or futuristic vehicles. A publication by the Government Fleet (2019) titled "The Next Generation of Patrol Vehicles" listed some basic features needed: **engine technology, self-autonomous features, officer safety features, connectivity,** and **space efficient features.**

Police vehicles have to function on all terrain, with robust safety features, the latest technology, and efficient use of space. Critics have noted that the more sophisticated police vehicles get, the more militarized policing gets, which is slowly taking away its protecting and serving duties.

Several agencies came under fire from community members when they responded with SWAT and other tactical vehicles that resembled war tanks for crowd control during some protests. Most agencies are becoming more sensitive to this issue; however, they are going to put officers' safety as paramount in all deployment.

Engine technology is also important. To be considered "police equipped," a vehicle must have a high-powered engine to be able to transport heavy equipment and pursue fleeing criminals driving ever-faster civilian vehicles.

A second must-have feature is that it be semi-autonomous. Officers perform a variety of tasks in their vehicles—some consider it their office. So, a well-equipped vehicle should have some self-driving capability while taking into consideration speed and safety measures. Features such as GPS, cruise control, an automatic braking system, four-point sensing, and warning systems when close to objects or changing lanes are vital.

Officer safety features are also a must. Some agencies are exploring bulletproof vehicles and other security features to protect officers from ambushes.

Another officer safety device is a locking or security system that prevents the vehicle from getting stolen when left running idle, or a push mechanism that only the trained officer knows to push before the vehicle can be operated.

Connectivity is also a key feature. As mentioned earlier, Google Glass, body-worn cameras, and other electronic devices may be used in the vehicle, and many of these systems require the use of Internet, intranet, or another secured network. Agencies are investing in high-connectivity vehicles so that their officers can access and process information swiftly and efficiently.

Space efficiency is also another must. Officers may be assigned several weapons such as a rifle, a shotgun, a less-than-lethal shotgun, a battering ram, and other equipment needed that takes up storage in their vehicles. Some agencies invest in a racking system for storing this equipment. A police vehicle is essentially an officer's office space, where he or she spends the majority of his or her shift. Having a spacious and well-equipped police cruiser is a vital to the job and enables the officer to perform his or her duties effectively.

Thermal Imaging Devices

Thermal imaging devices come in various sizes—some are handheld and others are mounted in aerial vehicles, camera tripod stands, small planes, or in helicopters. They are useful for scanning a large area in order to detect a suspect hiding under the cover of a dense object. The imaging device detects heat and other body particles and projects it on the designated screen. Ron LaPedis (2018), a security expert for over 25 years, noted in a piece in PoliceOne.Com the features of police thermal imaging devices, that these devices can give police enhanced detecting capabilities only if they get the high-quality products and a strong manufacturer behind the products. He also noted that they can also be used in locating illegal growth operations wherein heat or other light sources are used to produce the plants. The device can pinpoint the area and project the heat source origination. He further noted that the most capable devices should be able to detect various temperature ranges, have several fields of view, have a high-resolution camera, perform repeatability wherein it can show the same object even if viewed from multiple locations, operate with accuracy in depicting locations and images, and perform image overlay wherein it can project one image at a time and provide a good overlay of images to cover a holistic picture/image (LaPedis, 2018). Available software and learning how the device stores and transmits evidence are also key things to consider when purchasing these devices. These devices are also used for search and rescue missions, crime scene searches, and locating individuals with special needs or accommodations such as missing children or senior citizens.

Box 9.1 Perception Versus Reality

The Hollywood movie *Robocop* has been portrayed as a fantasy version of the future police officer, but this perception may be getting stale now that newer technologies are emerging every day in policing and crime fighting. Technologies such as brain fingerprinting, futuristic police vehicles, police drones, body-worn camera systems, and Google Glass, are just a few of the newer technologies that are being tested by various policing agencies.

The goal is to protect the public, ensure officer safety, and be able to respond to any and all foreseeable situations that require police involvement. Ideas such as flying police vehicles and building the police officer of the future are currently being tested by various agencies. Think about unmanned aerial vehicles (UAVs) and police robots that can go into any situation to locate explosives or eliminate an armed subject who has barricaded him- or herself inside along with hostages. What used to be a fantasy in policing is now becoming a reality. This chapter gives but a glimpse of how technologies are changing modern-day policing.

Documents and Records Management Systems (RMS)

A broad range of records management systems (RMS) exist today, and at the top of this list are computer-aided dispatch systems (CAD), used in the daily operations of police agencies and which we will delve into shortly. According to the FBI's Manual of Law Enforcement Records (U.S. Department of Justice,1984), RMS is an agency-wide operating system that makes it possible to store, retrieve, archive, manipulate, retain, and view records, information, and documents.

Although this manual (U.S. Department of Justice, 1984) is quite old, it lists the basic law enforcement records management systems that are still in use today by various agencies, including the following:

- Computer-aided dispatch systems (CAD)
- Integrated automated fingerprint identification system (IAFIS)
- Next-generation identification (NGI)
- Interstate Identification Index (III)
- National Crime Information Center (NCIC)
- Law enforcement National Data Exchange (N-DEx)
- National Instant Criminal Background Check system (NICS)
- Uniform Crime Reporting (UCR) program
    - Summary Reporting system

- National Incident-Based Reporting system (NIBRS)
- Law Enforcement Officers Killed and Assaulted (LEOKA) program
- Hate Crime Statistics program

Why RMS? Law enforcement agencies are held to a high standard in storing accurate, effective, and useful information in order to maximize officer safety, increase investigation potential through the sharing of information, and enhance public safety within the communities they serve. The primary items stored or maintained in RMS include personal information such as full names, AKAs, addresses, other personal characteristics, evidence data, property data, arrest and incident reports data, permits, driver licenses and registrations, and crime statistics (NIBRS, 2002).

Computer-Aided Dispatch Systems (CAD)

Before delving into documents and other record management systems, let's first talk about CAD systems, which are computer-aided dispatch systems. These systems are widely used by police, fire, EMS personnel, and also other private agencies. CAD is a dispatching system that has a variety of functions, including call taking, resource management, location verification, unit status management, dispatching, and call disposition. These systems are primarily linked with mobile data computers (MDC) in displaying texts and other useful information to the users (NIJ, 2003). According to the NIJ (2003), a historical aspect of this system came about with proper documentation, participation, and joint suggestion from individuals from a variety of law enforcement agencies, organizations, and private industries, including Law Enforcement Information Technology Standards Council (LEITSC), the International Association of Chiefs of Police (IACP), the National Sheriff's Association (NSA), the National Organization of Black Law Enforcement Executives (NOBLE), and the Police Executive Research Forum (PERF). From this council, the standard functional specifications for law enforcement CAD systems was implemented. Some of the major purposes for these systems as noted by the council were that the CAD systems were instrumental in rapid response time and system reliability—two features that are crucial to calls for service. The CAD system also supports "be on the lookout" (BOLO), call placement for future incidents, location history regarding officer safety, and other hazards at designated locations. NIJ (2003) also mentioned that CAD systems can handle the following: law enforcement dispatch, CAD systems for administrators, support services, call management and management reporting, interfaces, EMS dispatch, fire dispatch, intelligence transportation, and properties. Overall, CAD systems are used by multiple agencies, primarily for their easy accessibility and convenient means of communication with neighboring agencies.

Integrated Automated Fingerprint Identification System (IAFIS)

The integrated automated fingerprint identification system (IAFIS) is housed by the FBI Criminal Justice Information Services (CJIS). IAFIS collects 10 fingerprint cards electronically supplied by all police agencies in all 50 states. Information in IAFIS is supplied by local, state, federal, tribal, and non-criminal agencies along with some international agencies with certain agreements and partnerships in place (U.S. Department of Justice, 1984).

The publication by DOJ also noted that there are three main basic types of reasons for fingerprinting someone and running their prints through IAFIS: fingerprinting an individual who is charged with a crime; fingerprinting a job applicant as required by local, state, federal, or other authorities; and voluntary fingerprinting supplied to CJIS for future personal identification (e.g., also for children as required by the Missing Children Act).

The IAFIS is normally used by various law enforcement agencies to run fingerprints received from the other agencies through its originally stored crime scene fingerprints database and known criminal fingerprints database. The purpose of this process is to secure a match or to clear a background check for someone for employment or other related requirements.

Next-Generation Identification (NGI)

Next-generation identification (NGI) is being explored to replace the IAFIS (FBI, 2019a). It has far more capabilities and features than the IAFIS and has become the world's largest biometric and criminal history databank. NGI is considered to have multimodal functionality, which means it continues to evolve and advance as technology advances.

Some new capabilities of the NGI are advanced fingerprint identification technology (AFIT); an enhanced version of the IAFIS and the Repository for Individuals of Special Concern (RISC); and a searchable database that responds quickly in yielded searches for officer safety concerns when they are dealing with individuals with special concerns or issues that may pose harm to themselves or the officers they encounter. Various cautionary information can be entered into this system, and officers have quick and easy access to this information regarding violent offenders. The latent and palm prints component of NGI is an enhanced viable record management system that is more rigid and detailed in reading, recording, and presenting responses in a timely manner. It is a more robust and efficient fingerprint database system that is more inclusive of both fingerprints and palm prints. The rap back provides notifications to authorized agencies about individuals in positions of trust such as teachers, caregivers, or individuals who are under investigation or criminal justice supervision. The interstate photo system collects photos received by law enforcement during processing, such as facial shots, scars, marks, or tattoo and other symbols.

The cold case/unknown deceased component of NGI uses various criminal, non-criminal, and civil searches in order to provide association or clarity to a case or cases that is or are unknown or has or have gone unsolved for some time. It forms a correlation between the newly entered information and the old information that was stored regarding a case and then cross-checks it to determine any similarities or identifications. Once a match is noted, the appropriate parties are notified to either reopen or reexamine the case. This system provides the law enforcement community with enhanced database systems in order to form a link for their investigations.

Interstate Identification Index (III)

The Interstate Identification Index (III) is one of the largest name-based systems housed by the FBI and CJIS agencies. Federal and state agents have special authority and access to this database; they can check names of individuals who are being investigated, arrested, or are of special interest through the system. If a match is located, a special request is made to send transmission to the requesting agency with authorized permission.

National Crime Information Center (NCIC)

The National Crime Information Center (NCIC) is often considered the lifeline of law enforcement (FBI, 2019b). NCIC is housed by the FBI and is a place where all criminal justice agencies can enter information for access by all other criminal justice agencies nationwide. It has 21 "files," or components, including seven property files and 14 persons files.

The files are labeled as follows: article, gun, boat, securities, vehicle, vehicle and boat parts, license plate, missing person, foreign fugitive, identity theft, immigration violator, protection order, supervised release, unidentified persons, protective interest, gang, known or appropriately suspected terrorist, wanted persons, national sex offender registry, national instant criminal background check system (NCIS) denied transaction, and violent person.

The NCIC is one of the largest criminal database systems in the nation. Individual states also have their own criminal information network systems, such as VCIN, Virginia Criminal Information Network; MCIN, Maryland Criminal Information Network; and DELJIS, Delaware Criminal Justice Information Systems.

National Data Exchange System (N-DEx)

Another program that is housed by the FBI is the National Data Exchange system. This program allows agencies to share, link, analyze, and search information online across jurisdictional boundaries. Agencies around the nation deposit various types of information in this system, including booking reports, incident and arrest reports, pretrial investigations, supervised released reports, photos, calls for service, and regular field contact on interaction reports (FBI, 2019c). Various requesters can benefit from this system such as analysts, corrections personnel, detectives, patrol officers, pretrial, parole, probation officers and dispatchers, and communications officers. It helps agencies from around the nation to connect the dots and quickly locate various types of information about a suspect or a person of interest.

National Instant Criminal Background Check System (NICS)

The FBI also houses the National Instant Criminal Background Check system (NICS). It was created upon passage of the Brady Handgun Violence Prevention Act (1993), which federally mandated background checks for firearms purchases within the United States. The NICS instantly checks the criminal history of an individual who is attempting to purchase a firearm at a U.S. gun store.

This system works in partnership with federal firearms licensees (FFLs), who have access to it and can check an individual's background and criminal history before completing a gun sale (FBI, 2019e). If an individual is denied the purchase due to information contained in the NICS, a note is added to his or her record in the system in order to prevent him or her from buying a gun from another location or dealer.

Uniform Crime Reporting (UCR) Program and National Incident-Based Reporting System (NIBRS)

The Uniform Crime Reporting program was started by the International Association of Chiefs of Police (IACP) in the early 1920s, when police executives expressed interest in developing a concise and effective uniform crime reporting procedure across all agencies (FBI, 2019d). The FBI was tasked with housing, collecting, and publishing the nation's crime statistics, based on voluntary reporting from agencies. Agencies at the local, state, tribal, and federal level, as well as universities and colleges, report crime statistics to the FBI UCR on a daily basis.

There are four major data collection strategies: the National Incident-Based Reporting system (NIBRS), the Summary Reporting system (SRS), the Law Enforcement Officers Killing and Assaulted (LEOKA) program, and the Hate Crime Statistics program. In the future, the system will also start collecting national use-of-force data. All of the data collected in UCR is useful to law enforcement administrators and executives, students of criminal justice, all media outlets (including social media, TV, news), and the general public. Law enforcement administrators also use this information to address their crime rates in order to examine effective strategies moving forward for protecting their communities. This information is vital to police administrators, especially in their strategic plans for future goals and initiatives for their agencies. For instance, if the information gained from UCR indicates that the crime rate in a designated jurisdiction has increased, then the administrator would address or adopt new strategies in order to lower crime rates within his or her jurisdiction for the next or upcoming years. It is truly a useful compilation of statistics that is beneficial in all aspects of policing and beyond.

ShotSpotter

This newer device is currently being used not only by police and criminal justice agencies, but by other private agencies as well. In the simplest terms, it is a program that uses algorithms, artificial intelligence, and advanced sensors to detect and alert police of gunfire in a location or area. Highly sophisticated outdoor sensors are placed outside at specific locations to detect sounds that are similar to gunfire and triangulate the sound location through high-powered GPS systems to identify the location of the sound. This program is available not only to police but also to private agencies wherein it is used for real estate, neighborhood watch programs, and other environmental studies initiatives. It operates in three ways: First its detection and location, second for classification, and third for notification. The detection and location are the crucial portions as it has to capture the data and analyze it to separate all other noises and vibrations to isolate the sound of the shot and pinpoint a location. The second step is fine tuning and removing all obstructions from the pulse. Lastly, once it's determined that it is a gunshot, first responders are notified (ShotSpotter, 2018). This system is highly sophisticated when it comes to identifying the exact location of gunfire with a highly equipped GPS system. ShotSpotter has helped law enforcement agencies and other private agencies narrow down problem areas and to properly allocate their resources. ShotSpotter is currently being used in several U.S. cities including Louisville, Chicago, and Cincinnati.

Automated License Plate Readers (ALPRs)

The automated license plate reader/recognition system is used to capture vehicle plate registration information using character recognition software, sending the data to a screen for officers to read and analyze. The officer can access additional information about the individual associated with the license plate that is projected onto the screen, such as whether there is an indication or warning regarding this person.

"Vehicles of interest" are entered into the ALPR system on a daily basis, including stolen vehicles, stored vehicles, towed vehicles, missing vehicles, and so on. Once a license plate is captured and sent to the officer's screen, it is then run through the database. If a hit/match is made with a stolen vehicle, the ALPR notifies the officer and provides a description of the vehicle.

Many people have expressed concerns that this system could violate privacy as it operates by running random vehicle license plates as they are simply encountered out in public. According to the IACP, several agencies are addressing policies to protect the privacy of citizens pursuant to United States Code 18 USC § 2721-2725, which prohibits the release and use of certain personal information from state motor vehicle records. Officers are careful as to how they access this type of information and how it is being used and disseminated, as they can easily violate the U.S. code and statute. ALPRs are used by several police agencies and are still being improved to meet the demands of users while also protecting the privacy of the communities these agencies protect.

New Technologies

In addition to these legacy technologies, some newer systems are currently being used or piloted by various agencies. Following are some of the most popular programs.

Verizon Connect Networkfleet is mainly used to provide networking capabilities for radio and other communications devices. Omigo has case management, crime scene management, a criminal database, field reporting, incident mapping, and investigations management features. Command Center Software Suite by Motorola Solutions and Column Case Management both have all the capabilities of Omigo. Mark43 Platform has all the capabilities also except for crime scene management. Investigations and Incident Software by Resolver has all the capabilities except crime scene management and criminal database.

Rhodium Incident Management has only incident mapping capabilities; SmartDraw legal edition has only crime scene management and evidence management. D4H Readiness and Response has only field reporting and incident mapping, and Presynct OnDemand has only case management, field reporting, incident mapping, and investigation management (Capterra, 2019).

Less-Than-Lethal Force Technologies

Some members of the public have been asking for police officers to be equipped with other use-of-force options beside firearms when dealing with resisting subjects. This section talks about the use for force—its definition and applications—and explores the various technologies that agencies are using and exploring to reduce death or risk of killing aggressive individuals.

Definitions

The first thing to understand is the terminology: use of force, lethal force, less-than-lethal force, excessive force, and the use-of-force continuum. Use of force is the amount of effort used by the officer to arrest or control an aggressive or combative individual. Lethal force is also known as deadly force, and it is that level of force that may cause serious bodily injury, incapacitation, or death to an individual.

Prior to the ***Tennessee v. Garner*** case, officers could use deadly force to stop a fleeing felon suspect. This U.S. Supreme Court case prohibited the use of deadly force by an officer, unless the officer felt that their life and/or the lives of others were in danger. After this case, several agencies added the word "violent" before the "fleeing felon" clause in their departmental policies. In this way, police are prohibited from using deadly force unless they have probable cause that the individual is violent and poses a threat to him- or herself, the officer, or others.

Less-than-lethal force is any force used to control or arrest a resisting or combative individual that would not reasonably result in death of the suspect. This includes tools like pepper spray, Tasers, extended batons, non-lethal projectiles, pepper balls, and so on. Excessive force is the more than the expected force used in an arrest or to control a subject, as outlined on the use-of-force continuum.

Use-of-Force Continuum

In real life, officers have to make split-second decisions in various scenarios, including highly dangerous ones. The use-of-force continuum refers to the various levels of force that an officer may use, based on the level of threat an individual may pose (see figure 9.3).

Take the example of an officer responding to a scene of an irate individual who is not posing any threat and has not displayed any weapons but is very upset. The officer may view this situation as a verbal encounter and use verbal skills to deescalate the situation. But in a split second, if the individual displays a weapon, putting him- or herself and the officer in danger, the officer may revert to a firearm or other less-than-lethal equipment, depending on the weapon that was displayed by the individual.

Mesloh, Henych, and Wolf (2008) published a report for the U.S. Department of Justice titled "Less Lethal Weapon Effectiveness, Use of Force, and Suspect and Officer Injuries: A Five-Year Analysis." They said that the use-of-force continuum is the nexus between the officer's perception of the individual's resistance level during the interaction and the most appropriate responses to be delivered by the officer.

While use-of-force levels change rapidly, officers are trained in this while at the academy and on the job through in-service training, in order to stay current on appropriate and effective techniques and strategies to use with resistant or combative individuals.

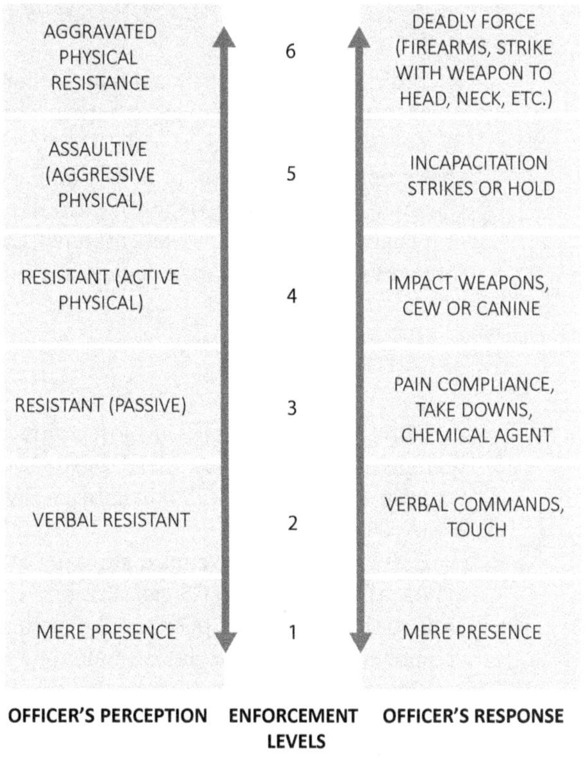

Figure 9.3 Use of Force Continuum

Conducted Energy Devices (CEDs)

The Taser is perhaps the most well-known example of a **conducted energy device (CED)**. It was invented by NASA aerospace scientist Jack Cover, after he read a book by Thomas Swift that featured an electric rifle shooting invisible bullets charged with lightning. Cover developed the Taser in the late 1960s to help law enforcement use less-lethal forces when interacting with combative and resistant individuals. He titled the device "TASER," after his inspiration for the device: Thomas A. Swift Electric Rifle.

The device consists of either a handgun or rifle structure with two needle darts that are designed to penetrate the skin—even through clothing—and deliver up to 50,000 volts of electricity. Once the device is connected with the subject through darts or probes attached to a thin wire, the electricity delivers the shock.

The shock causes involuntary muscle contractions that may result in serious injuries, for example from a fall (NIJ, 2008). The positive aspect of this device is that it incapacitates the subject for a period of 3–5 seconds, giving the officer time to control the offender and ensure he or she does no further harm to him- or herself or anyone nearby. However, the devices must be deployed with training. Agencies have extensive policies regarding when to deploy the Taser, where to aim it, and whom to use it on. These are necessary in order to prevent death or permanent incapacitation via a fall or other serious injuries. Physical and mental conditions are to be taken into consideration when deciding whether to deploy this device. In addition, they are only work as designed within a certain distance.

There are also touch or contact stun guns that can be used to deliver a much smaller dose of electricity.

Directed Energy Weapons (DEWs)

According to the NIJ (2011), a directed energy device or weapon uses microwaves, particle beams, or lasers to destroy or damage its target. They are mostly used by the military to shoot down enemy drones or other perceived threats. The type of force these devices deliver is similar to a blunt force that stops its target without bodily damage. Blunt-force trauma are any non-penetrable trauma that may cause a serious or non-life-threatening injury to its target. Blunt force objects are usually non-sharp, rugged, flat, molded, rounded, thick, heavy objects that are capable of delivering a blunt-force trauma. These types of devices are expensive and have only been explored by some agencies.

Chemicals

According to the NIJ (2011, the most common chemical weapons are oleoresin capsicum (OC) spray, tear gas, and stink bombs. All of these chemicals are used to temporarily incapacitate an actively resisting or aggressive individual, by causing sensitive irritation to the eyes, nose, lungs, or other exposed cavities.

Several agencies have used and are currently using these tools. A majority of police agencies expose their recruits to CS gas, also known as tear gas, and OC spray while they are at the academy, so that they can experience the feeling before using it on a subject. The CS gas has chemical components (chlorobenzylidene malononitrile) that irritate the nasal, breathing cavities, and lungs, making it very painful to breathe and causing extreme crying due to burning of the interior of the eye cavity. OC spray (pepper spray) also acts in a similar fashion; however, it mostly has oleoresin capsicum as the active ingredient. OC/pepper spray causes irritation, crying, and temporary blindness of the subject when used properly. Chemical weapons have been proven effective, depending on the situation. They are mostly used for crowd control and other individual encounters with combative subjects. Policies and procedures are in place for all the agencies that use these agents in order to protect the officer and public.

Distraction Devices

Many agencies' specialty units use distraction devices such as laser dazzlers, bright lights and noises, and flashbangs (NIJ, 2011). These are mechanisms that divert the individual subject's concentration while other resources and manpower are being stealthily deployed to detain or arrest him.

Vehicle-Stopping Technology

Agencies are also using various devices to stop or disable a fleeing vehicle. According to the NIJ (2017), some of the most common technologies are tire-deflator devices, electronic discharge devices, electromagnetic radiation devices, directed energy devices, and remote tracking of fleeing vehicles.

Tire-deflator devices target vehicles moving at a high rate of speed and use spikes spread across the road to deflate and disable the tires. The electronic discharge devices can be used very close to the target and disable the vehicle's electronic capabilities. The electromagnetic radiation devices are used to target the ignition and fuel pumps of a vehicle, in order to keep it from moving forward. Directed energy devices also target the vehicle's electrical systems, resulting in a complete shutdown. Remote tracking of fleeing vehicles is also instituted. These are all tested devices that have been used by federal agencies and some local and state agencies that have access to them. In some jurisdictions, there is a concept known as **mutual aid** where, during emergencies and other events, there is an agreement between agencies to lend resources and manpower to each other. Mutual aid covers the following: vehicles, helicopters, planes, manpower, and so on. With the remote tracking of vehicles, agencies have witnessed several deadly crashes and also have risked the public in various types of collisions while pursuing fleeing vehicles. The remote tracking of vehicles is an alternative to vehicle pursuits in order to reduce civilian casualties as a result of police pursuits. Remote tracking devices work swiftly and quietly by precise actions and planning on the agency's part.

As agencies pilot technologies like the remote tracking system, they learn to make improvements that make them less dangerous, for example, "tagging" the vehicle in order to track it, which can be done by firing small particles of GPS pellets or nodules on the targeted vehicle that send its location back to the agency every couple of minutes. The NIJ has funded several agencies to pilot this technology, with some positive results. It is important to note that these devices all have risks and other effects that agencies are taking into consideration as well, in order to protect the public they serve and their officer's safety.

Barriers and Blunt Force

Barriers and blunt force involve using various types of obstructions and projectiles such as nets, foams, and other physical barriers often used in control. These devices help agencies maximize their presence and take control of an area or a situation with less risk of problems.

Legal Aspects of Technology and Policing

Various parts of the U.S. Constitution and U.S. Supreme Court decisions are interpreted to govern how technology can be used in policing. The following chapter will cover several legal aspects of policing. For this chapter, we will discuss only the Fourth Amendment to the United States' Constitution, which is one of the most critical amendments for U.S. law enforcement to understand. The Fourth Amendment to the U.S. Constitution prohibits "unreasonable" searches and seizures by police or any governmental body. People, places, and property are protected. The Fourth Amendment provides that no warrant authorizing a search or a seizure shall be issued without "probable cause," supported by an affirmation or oath from an appropriate official.

Box 9.2 Fourth Amendment

The right of the people to be secure in their persons, houses, papers, and effects, against **unreasonable searches and seizures**, shall not be violated, and no Warrants shall issue, but upon probable cause, supported by Oath or affirmation, and particularly describing the place to be searched, and the persons or things to be seized. (Cornell Law School, 2019)

When deploying any of the technological devices described in this chapter, proper justifications should be in place before arresting someone, attempting to stop him or her, or searching him or her. Proper justifications include securing a search warrant or having reasonable suspicions. In order to obtain a search warrant, the requesting officer should demonstrate a reasonable suspicion or probable cause. Reasonable suspicion conveys the concept that the individual or vehicle has just committed a crime, is about to commit a crime, or will be committing a crime. Whereas probable cause conveys the actual evidence that a crime has been committed, the physical evidence is needed or justified before a search warrant is issued.

The key words here are "seizing" and "searching." The various technologies discussed earlier are used mainly to effect an arrest while seizing someone. Some of these devices are used while searching for information, such as surveilling individuals to obtain information for possible criminal charges. Most agencies have legal requirements and certification trainings on a daily basis so that their officers stay current on the laws that govern their daily actions. These trainings are administered with contracts in place with defense attorneys who are currently practicing or have practiced these types of cases. Agencies also have policies in place to guide their officers in conducting legal searches and seizures. This helps the agencies focus on their job and avoid unnecessary civil litigation for violating citizens' rights.

Chapter Summary

As mentioned in the beginning of this chapter, policing technology is an ever-changing concept. In order for police agencies to detect, prevent, and address future emerging crimes, they must stay ahead of criminal and other evasive or deceptive motivations by various individuals or entities. While most of the basic and recurring technological devices were discussed in this chapter, there are many more being tested and developed today.

Intelligence-led policing and its strategic and tactical measures were thoroughly presented along with police drones, brain fingerprinting, Google Glass, social media, police vehicles, and thermal imaging devices. Some of these devices are extremely sophisticated and some are not; some have a lot of logistical hurdles to overcome before being deployed and some are very simple to use.

In addition to documents and records management systems and less-than-lethal force technologies that are also equally prevalent in policing, this chapter listed some of the most basic information delivery systems used by law enforcement such as IAFIS, NGI, III, N-DEx, NICS, UCR, NIBRS, and ALPR.

With regard to less-than-lethal force, comprehending the meaning of related concepts is important to understanding when, why, and how officers use force. Many agencies train their officers to respond to various situations with a level of force. In addition, use-of-force continuum and other less-than-lethal force options were discussed in this chapter.

It is important to note that with newer technologies in policing comes new accountability and reporting requirements. These systems are being developed to protect human lives and reduce the number of lethal force incidents that involve police.

While these systems are not perfect, they provide options for law enforcement to use when dealing with dangerous individuals. Cost, training, and legal concerns will determine the deployment of such technologies. Many state and local agencies are seeking funds from the federal government to be able to use these new technologies.

Discussion Questions

1. Define the concept of intelligence-led policing. Explain the difference between strategic and tactical intelligence policing.

2. Select three of the technological devices described in this chapter and discuss their advantages and disadvantages in policing.

3. What is the "use of force continuum"? How can this concept be improved?

4. Discuss three potential risks that officers and agencies face when deploying conducted energy devices (CEDs).

5. Describe the ALPR system and discuss how it could potentially undermine privacy rights.

References

Ahuja, D. & Singh, B. (2012). Brain fingerprinting. *Journal of Engineering and Technology Research, 4*(6), 98–103. doi:10.5897/JETR11.061

Bliven, B. (2018). Perspective: Impact of positive stories through social media. *FBI Law Enforcement Bulletin*, 13–18.

Bureau of Justice Assistance (BJA). (2005). *Intelligence-led policing: The new intelligence architecture*. Retrieved from https://www.ncjrs.gov/pdffiles1/bja/210681.pdf

Capterra. (2019). *Law enforcement systems*. Retrieved from https://www.capterra.com/sem-compare/law-enforcement-software?gclid=EAIaIQobChMI5ayyrMbu3wIVA4rIChıeZQDHEAAYASAAEgJBofD_BwE&gclsrc=aw.ds

Cornell Law School. (2019). *Legal Information Institute: The Fourth Amendment*. Retrieved from https://www.law.cornell.edu/constitution/fourth_amendment

Cotter, R. S. (2017) Police intelligence: Connecting the dots in a network society. *Policing and Society, 27*(2), 173–187. doi:10.1080/10439463.2015.1040794

Duran, Y. (2014). *Google Glass finds its way into law enforcement. Hendon Media Group*. Retrieved from http://www.hendonpub.com/resources/article_archive/results/details?id=5007

Envisage Technologies. (2014). *Police departments begin testing and training with Google Glass*. Retrieved on from https://www.envisagenow.com/police-departments-begin-testing-and-training-with-google-glass/

Farwell, L., Richardson, D. & Richardson, G. (2012). *Brain fingerprinting field studies comparing P300-Mermer and P300 brainwave responses in the detection of concealed information. Cognitive Neurodynamics, 7*(4), 263–299. doi:10.1007/s11571-012-9230-0

Federal Bureau of Investigation (FBI). (2019a). *Services: Next generation identification (NGI)*. Retrieved from https://www.fbi.gov/services/cjis/fingerprints-and-other-biometrics/ngi

Federal Bureau of Investigation (FBI). (2019b). *Services: National Crime Information Center (NCIC)*. Retrieved from https://www.fbi.gov/services/cjis/ncic

Federal Bureau of Investigation (FBI). (2019c). *Services National Data Exchange (N-DEx) system*. Retrieved from https://www.fbi.gov/services/cjis/ndex

Federal Bureau of Investigation (FBI). (2019d) *Services: Uniform Crime Reporting (UCR) program*. Retrieved from https://www.fbi.gov/services/cjis/ucr

Federal Bureau of Investigations (FBI). (2019e). *Services: National Instant Criminal Background Check System (NCIS)*. Retrieved from https://www.fbi.gov/services/cjis/nics

Government Fleet. (2019). *The next generation of patrol vehicles*. Retrieved from https://www.government-fleet.com/279703/the-next-generation-of-patrol-vehicles

Heen, M. S. J., Lieberman, J. D., & Miethe, T. D. (2018). The thin blue line meets the big blue sky: Perceptions of police legitimacy and public attitudes towards aerial drones. *Criminal Justice Studies, 31*(1), 18–37. doi:10.1080/1478601X.2017.1404463

International Association of Chiefs of Police (IACP). (2019a). *Body-worn cameras*. Retrieved from https://www.theiacp.org/resources/policy-center-resource/body-worn-cameras

International Association of Chiefs of Police (IACP). (2019b). *Automated license plate recognition*. Retrieved on from https://www.theiacp.org/projects/automated-license-plate-recognition

Kyle, M. J., & White, D. R. (2017). The impact of law enforcement officer perceptions of organizational justice on their attitudes regarding body-worn cameras. *Journal of Crime and Justice, 40*(1), 68–83. doi:10.1080/0735648X.2016.1208885

LaPedis, R. (2018, August 10). *How to buy thermal imagers. PoliceOne.com*. Retrieved from https://www.policeone.com/police-products/police-technology/thermal-imaging/articles/477958006-How-to-buy-thermal-imagers/

McNamara, M. (2018). *I'll be gone in the dark: One woman's obsessive search for the Golden State Killer*. New York, NY: HarperCollins.

Mesloh, C., Henych, M. & Wolf, R. (2008). *Less lethal weapon effectiveness, use of force, and suspect and officer injuries: A five year analysis*. Retrieved from https://www.ncjrs.gov/pdffiles1/nij/grants/224081.pdf

Newark Police Department. (2019). *Consent Decree and Planning Division*. Retrieved from https://www.npdconsentdecree.org/city-of-newark-consent-decree

National Institute of Justice (NIJ). (2003). *Standard functional specifications for law enforcement computer aided dispatch (CAD) systems*. Retrieved from https://it.ojp.gov/documents/leitsc_law_enforcement_cad_systems.pdf

National Institute of Justice (NIJ). (2008). *How conducted energy devices work*. Retrieved from https://www.nij.gov/topics/technology/less-lethal/pages/how-ceds-work.aspx

National Institute of Justice (NIJ). (2011). *Less-lethal technologies*. Retrieved from https://www.nij.gov/topics/technology/less-lethal/pages/welcome.aspx

National Institute of Justice (NIJ). (2017). *Technology for pursuit management*. Retrieved from https://www.nij.gov/topics/law-enforcement/operations/traffic/Pages/technology-developments.aspx

National Incident-Based Reporting System (NIBRS). (2002). *Handbook for acquiring a records management system (RMS) that is compatible with the National Incident-Based Reporting System (NIBRS)*. Retrieved from https://www.waspc.org/assets/CJIS/trainingmanualsandreference/nibrs_handbook_rms.pdf

Police Executive Research Forum (PERF). (2015). *Critical issues in policing series: Re-engineering training on police use of force*. Washington, DC: Author.

PoliceOne.com. (2019). *Social media for cops*. Retrieved from https://www.policeone.com/social-media-for-cops/

President's Task Force on 21st Century Policing. (2015). *Final report of the President's Task Force on 21st Century Policing*. Retrieved from https://cops.usdoj.gov/pdf/taskforce/taskforce_finalreport.pdf

ShotSpotter. (2018). *ShotSpotter technology*. Retrieved from https://www.shotspotter.com/technology/

U.S. Department of Justice. (1984). *Law enforcement records management systems (RMSs) as they pertain to FBI programs and systems*. Retrieved from https://www.fbi.gov/file-repository/law-enforcement-records-management-system.pdf/view

U.S. General Accounting Office. (2001). *Investigative techniques: Federal agency views on the potential application of brain fingerprinting*. Retrieved from https://www.gao.gov/new.items/d0222.pdf

Figure Credits

Fig. 9.1: Copyright © 2016 by Ryan Johnson (CC BY-SA 2.0) at https://commons.wikimedia.org/wiki/File:Bodycam-north-charleston-police.jpg.
Fig. 9.2: Copyright © 2013 by Loïc Le Meur (CC BY 2.0) at https://commons.wikimedia.org/wiki/File:A_Google_Glass_wearer.jpg.
Fig. 9.3: Source: https://www.researchgate.net/figure/Force-Continuum_fig3_261985229.

CHAPTER TEN

Legal Procedures and Professionalism in Policing

This chapter will primarily cover the legal aspects of policing, including key amendments to the United States Constitution (Second, Fourth, Fifth, Sixth, and 14th). In addition, this chapter will also document the U.S. Supreme Court's role in regulating the police, the basic exclusionary rule, issues dealing with probable cause and reasonable suspicion, police traffic stops; investigative detention, search warrant procedures and exceptions, search and seizure, applicable U.S. Supreme Court cases, and the *Miranda* ruling.

Learning Objectives

- Identify various applicable amendments to policing
- Explore the U.S. Supreme Court cases relevant to daily police work
- Examine the difference between the exclusionary rule and the fruit of the poisonous tree doctrine
- Understand the importance of police accountability and accreditation

Chapter Outline

1. A Real-Life Police Scenario for Discussion
2. Police and the Law
3. Exclusionary Rule and Fruit of the Poisonous Tree Doctrine
4. Perception Versus Reality
5. Professionalism of Policing
6. Chapter Summary
7. Discussion Questions

A REAL-LIFE POLICE SCENARIO FOR DISCUSSION

At 10:45 p.m. on October 3, 1974, it was dark and cold in the small neighborhood in Memphis, Tennessee, when two police officers responded to a residence for a burglary call. Upon arrival, the officers separated; one checked the front perimeter of the residence, and the other checked the rear. The officer checking the rear of the residence illuminated the backyard with his flashlight and saw a young, Black male crouching beside a 6-foot chain link fence. The officer presumed that the individual was the suspect, advised the man to "halt," and identified himself as an officer. He believed the subject was unarmed, as he did not observe any weapons being displayed.

After initially heeding the officer's warning to halt, the suspect attempted to flee the scene by jumping over the fence. The officer fired his weapon and struck the suspect in the back of the head; he was transported to a nearby hospital and then pronounced dead. Later, it was determined that the individual was 15-year-old Edward Garner. Upon examining the items recovered from Garner, officers discovered $10.00 and a woman's purse—possibly items from the burglary.

Preliminary investigations found that the shooting was "justifiable" under Tennessee law and the police department's policy, which was that an officer can use any means necessary to stop a fleeing felon. If the officer has given notice or warning to the subject and the subject flees or aggressively resists during an arrest, the officer is permitted to use any force necessary to effect the arrest.

Garner's family brought a lawsuit against the city and the police department, and the district court held that the officer's actions were justifiable under state law. The case was then appealed to the U.S. Court of Appeals for the Sixth Circuit, which reversed the lower court's decision. The appeals court determined that Tennessee law failed to define the use of deadly force to effect an arrest of a fleeing subject.

Several agencies across the country had been operating under this type of policy, and officers had been trained that it was justifiable force to shoot an unarmed individual who had just committed a felony offense and was attempting to flee.

This chapter delves into the complexities of policing and the law. This short, real-life scenario sums up the famous Supreme Court case *Tennessee v. Garner*.

This case played an important part in the laws and policies that govern police use of force and current police interactions with the citizens they encounter. It was ultimately determined by the court that it was unjustifiable to shoot someone without proper justification or cause if he or she is merely a fleeing felon. There have to be other reasons, such as the individual possesses significant threat to themselves or others. After the outcome of this case, many police agencies have revamped their procedures and policies on police use of force to include adding the words or phrases "eminent threat or danger" and "significant threat or danger" to their use of force policies (Legal Dictionary, 2019).

Police and the Law

There are various laws that guide police work. However, for the purpose of this chapter, we will focus on the most applicable amendments to the United States Constitution: the Second, Fourth, Fifth, Sixth, and 14th. All of these amendments have major relevance for policing.

Second Amendment

> *A well-regulated Militia, being necessary to the security of a free State, the right of the people to keep and bear Arms, shall not be infringed.*

There has been much debate and controversy over the Second Amendment. Many activists consider the "right to bear arms" one of the most important rights enshrined in the U.S. Constitution.

Some critics, though, have said that this amendment undercuts the rights of people of color. They cite recent police shootings of African Americans as evidence. These points are worthy of debate by criminal justice scholars. But how does the Second Amendment apply to policing?

Most jurisdictions or states allow their residents to openly carry a firearm, as long as it is visible and registered as part of an "open carry" initiative. If someone is lawfully carrying a firearm and it is visible to the public, many times law enforcement officers are called by a concerned citizen. If they respond, they will interact with the individual exercising his or her Second Amendment right, perhaps checking his or her identification and doing a background check to see if he or she is a convicted felon or is otherwise restricted from carrying a firearm. If all checks are clear, the individual would be sent on his or her way without any citation, as he or she is exercising his or her Second Amendment rights.

In some states, one needs a permit to carry a concealed firearm. The states typically require the individual to demonstrate to the court or other legal authority that he or she completed a firearm safety course and passed a background check administered by the state. If all is clear, the individual is granted a "concealed carry" permit, which can be good for 5 or more years, depending on the state. This means he or she can then carry a concealed firearm at any time as long as his or her permit is accessible. These permits are valid in the state of issuance and any other "reciprocity" state.

On a daily basis, police officers encounter armed individuals with and without permits and open carry licenses. They are trained to identify such persons and verify their permission to carry firearms, as well as to determine a course of action if they are, in fact, violating the law.

Fourth Amendment

> *The right of the people to be secure in their persons, houses, papers, and effects, against unreasonable searches and seizures, shall not be violated, and no Warrants shall issue, but*

> *upon probable cause, supported by Oath or affirmation, and particularly describing the place to be searched, and the persons or things to be seized.*

The Fourth Amendment is perhaps one of the most applicable amendments to policing. It entails the key words and phrases "**search**, **seizure-arrest**, **reasonable suspicion**, **probable cause**, **search warrant**, **arrest warrant**, **investigative detention**, and **warrantless searches**."

A search as described by the Fourth Amendment involves exploring, looking for, or inquiring about something. Searches comprise a majority of police and investigative work, as the act of inquiring is fundamental to investigating anything. There are several steps that an officer has to take in order to conduct a proper search; those steps will be discussed later in this section. However, it is important to note that searching is one of a police officer's core duties.

A seizure, on the other hand, is similar to an arrest. It is basically the taking of someone into custody or physically preventing an individual from freely leaving. For example, placing someone in handcuffs and restricting his or her movement is a custodial arrest. Stopping someone for a speeding ticket and telling the individual to wait while the citation is being issued is a temporary seizure. While the officer is in the process of issuing the citation, the violator is not free to leave and therefore is temporarily seized.

For an officer to legally seize someone, he or she must have either reasonable suspicion or probable cause to believe that a crime was committed, is being committed, or is about to be committed. Reasonable suspicion is the belief, thought, or feeling that an officer has that an individual is about to commit a crime, is committing a crime, or has just committed a crime. (Cornell Legal Information Institute, n.d.a.)

For instance, reasonable suspicion could be an officer following a driver and seeing that the driver is swerving across lanes and into oncoming traffic. The officer has reasonable suspicion that the driver is under the influence of drugs or alcohol. He or she initiates a stop and approaches the vehicle, when he or she smells the odor of an alcoholic beverage(s) coming from the driver. The officer conducts field sobriety tests, and the driver fails all of them. He or she is then arrested for driving under the influence.

On the other hand, probable cause is defined as follows:

> Probable cause is a requirement found in the Fourth Amendment that must usually be met before police make an arrest, conduct a search, or receive a warrant. Courts usually find probable cause when there is a reasonable basis for believing that a crime may have been committed (for an arrest) or when evidence of the crime is present in the place to be searched (for a search). (Cornell Legal Information Institute (n.d.b.)

Another simple definition of probable cause from Worrall and Schmallegar (2010) is the following: "[P]robable cause is the facts and circumstances that would convince another reasonably intelligent person to believe another has committed a specific crime" (p. 254). These authors also defined reasonable suspicion as a belief based on the consideration of the facts at hand that a reasonable person can draw from in order to conclude that a crime is being committed or has just been committed.

Reasonable suspicion is more of a feeling and therefore requires less evidence than "probable cause," which is more direct and physical at times. Probable cause is based on solid facts and evidence to support that a crime has been, is being, or will be committed.

For instance, in the prior example, probable cause to arrest the driver is developed through the field sobriety tests that the officer administers to determine if the driver is intoxicated. The fact that the driver failed all the tests, along with proper documentation of the tests and the driver's responses, is evidence to support that the driver was indeed intoxicated and arrestable (Cornell Legal Information Institute, n.d.b.).

Research this case and discuss its application to current times.

A "search warrant" is a document issued by a judge or magistrate authorizing a police officer or other governmental authority to search a location without the owner's consent. A majority of the time, the requesting party must indicate justifiable and proper reasons for the warrant (e.g., evidence will be recovered, a crime will be prevented, an arrest will be made, etc.). An applicable case is *Katz v. United States.*

An arrest warrant is similar to a search warrant in that it can be issued by a judge or magistrate. It authorizes an officer or other governmental official to take someone into custody because he or she has committed a crime. Usually, the requesting party would indicate on the warrant what his or her probable cause is for making the arrest (Cornell Legal Information Institute, 2019).

Research the case *Terry v. Ohio* and discuss its applications to law enforcement today, giving examples.

An investigative detention is the brief seizure of an individual by an officer or investigative official, for the purposes of investigation. This type of detention can also be compared to a term called the Terry stop or stop and frisk. The concept of a Terry stop originated from the case *Terry v. Ohio,* which determined that an officer may stop someone based on reasonable suspicion that he or she is armed, engaged, or about to be engaged in a criminal activity (Cornell Legal Information Institute, 2019).

Warrantless searches are searches that can be conducted without first obtaining a judicial warrant. There are several types, including but not limited to stop and frisk, search incident to arrest, vehicular searches, consent searches, border searches, open fields, plain view, public schools, government offices, and prisons. Search incident to arrest means that an officer can search someone who has been legally arrested prior to transporting or placing him or her in a holding facility.

Vehicular searches are searches of automobiles that are abandoned on public highways/roads, are towed, or are stored. The officer should have probable cause that a crime was committed, is being committed, or is about to be committed before searching the vehicle.

Consent searches can be done without a warrant only if the person being searched gives the consent to be searched. However, the individual can withdraw his or her consent at any time during the search, and the officer must cease if that happens.

The remaining types of warrantless searches mentioned are permitted because they involve searches of open or public areas. A law enforcement or a governmental officer can search government locations and premises without a search warrant as long as there a reason to believe that a crime has been committed, will be committed, or is about to be committed within said premise or location.

Fifth Amendment

> *No person shall be held to answer for a capital, or otherwise infamous crime, unless on a presentment or indictment of a Grand Jury, except in cases arising in the land or naval forces, or in the Militia, when in actual service in time of War or public danger; nor shall any person be subject for the same offence to be twice put in jeopardy of life or limb; nor shall be compelled in any criminal case to be a witness against himself, nor be deprived of life, liberty, or property, without due process of law; nor shall private property be taken for public use, without just compensation.*

The Fifth Amendment also plays an important role in policing. According to the Cornell Legal Information Institute (2019), this amendment is broken into five specific sections: (a) right to indictment by grand jury before any criminal charges for felonious crimes; (b) a prohibition on double jeopardy; (c) a right against forced self-incrimination; (d) a guarantee that all criminal defendants have a fair trial; and (e) a guarantee that the government cannot seize private property without making due compensation at the market value of the property.

The two most applicable parts of this amendment are the concepts of double jeopardy and self-incrimination. Double jeopardy means that if an individual is acquitted of a specific charge, he or she cannot be tried again for that same crime. It exists to protect individuals from repeated emotional and financial strains involved in multiple trials for the same offense. The right to avoid self-incrimination is also a hugely important concept to understand. This allows an individual to refuse to testify against him- or herself in a criminal trial, if speaking truthfully would force him or her to admit to committing a crime. The defendant may "plead the Fifth," which means he or she is declining to answer any more questions.

A famous case that provides an understanding of this concept is *Miranda v. Arizona*, which lead to the concepts of Miranda rights and Miranda warnings. Miranda warnings educate the person being arrested that he or she has the right to remain silent, the right to have an attorney present during an interview with law enforcement, and the right to an attorney paid for by the government if he or she cannot afford one. Police are trained extensively about the proper use of Miranda warnings, which help protect the individual's right against self-incrimination.

Research this case and discuss its applicability to policing.

Sixth Amendment

> *In all criminal prosecutions, the accused shall enjoy the right to a speedy and public trial, by an impartial jury of the State and district wherein the crime shall have been committed, which district shall have been previously ascertained by law, and to be informed of the nature and cause of the accusation; to be confronted with the witnesses against him; to have compulsory process for obtaining witnesses in his favor, and to have the Assistance of Counsel for his defense.*

The Sixth Amendment has implications for police procedure, as the police are the gateway to the criminal justice system. After the advisement of Miranda rights, the individual is given the opportunity to have an attorney present who can further explain his or her rights. The Sixth Amendment has four major parts: the right to a public trial without delay; the right to an attorney; the right to an impartial jury; and the right to know who is accusing him or her of having committed a crime (Cornell Legal Information Institute, 2019). The Sixth Amendment also enshrines the right of the individual to know the charges being brought against him or her, as well as the evidence that will be used at trial.

Fourteenth Amendment

> *All persons born or naturalized in the United States and subject to the jurisdiction thereof, are citizens of the United States and of the State wherein they reside. No State shall make or enforce any law which shall abridge the privileges or immunities of citizens of the United States; nor shall any State deprive any*

person of life, liberty, or property, without due process of law; nor deny to any person within its jurisdiction the equal protection of the laws.

Recently, there has been much political debate about the first section of this amendment, known as the citizenship clause. It indicates that anyone born on U.S. soil is an American citizen. Enacted to enshrine the citizenship of African Americans, some are now expressing opposition to automatic citizenship for children born to non-citizens. Still, changing the amendment and its interpretation would be a monumental task. It would spark its own massive political blowback, as the very origins and justification of this amendment are based on principles of non-discrimination.

The phrase "equal protection of laws," however, is perhaps the most relevant aspect of this amendment for policing. A close reading of the amendment text shows that "equal protection" is guaranteed to "any person within [a State's] jurisdiction," not to citizens alone. State and local police agencies assist everyone in their communities, regardless of citizenship status.

An area where this comes into tension for state and local police is when federal agencies request assistance in enforcing federal immigration laws. Chapter 5 talks about this in greater detail. Still, public safety remains the number one priority for local law enforcement. Most agencies operate under the notion that crime witnesses, victims, and other reporting parties are exempt from any immigration inquiries, except for "criminal aliens" or individuals who have been physically arrested for an arrestable offense.

Research *Brown v. Board* of Education (racial discrimination) and *Roe v. Wade* (reproductive rights) and discuss their applications to policing in current times.

Some of the landmark cases associated with this amendment are *Brown v. Board of Education* (racial discrimination) and *Roe v. Wade* (reproductive rights). See also *Almeida-Sanchez v. United States*, *Wong Wind v. United States*, *Plyler v. Doe*, and *Boumediene v. Bush*.

Exclusionary Rule and Fruit of the Poisonous Tree Doctrine

The exclusionary rule and fruit of the poisonous tree doctrine are two concepts that are often confused, as they are very close in their literal meanings. They flow from the Fourth and Fifth Amendments and help shape the professionalism and ethical constraints of policing on a daily basis.

Research and discuss this case and its applications to current policing.

A U.S. Supreme Court case, *Elkins v. United States,* provided the basis for the exclusionary rule, which holds that any evidence obtained in violation of the law cannot be used in court (is "inadmissible"). By respecting this principle, the U.S. government is basically setting an example about how the rule of law works, even if it could mean that a crime goes unpunished. The government does not have the right to violate a criminal's rights, and if it does, the evidence it obtained cannot be used against the criminal.

The fruit of the poisonous tree doctrine is an extension of the exclusionary rule. If a piece of evidence, obtained illegally and subject to the exclusionary rule, leads to the discovery of another piece of evidence, this second piece of evidence is also inadmissible in court. If the original evidence (the "tree") was bad, then the "fruit" or secondary evidence stemming from it is also bad. For example, if an officer arrests someone without probable cause and the individual provides some information regarding the case—whether it be a verbal statement or physical evidence—this information could be considered a fruit of the poisonous tree and excluded from use at a future trial.

Another court case that demonstrates these principles is *Mapp v. Ohio*.

Exceptions

There are, however, exceptions to these concepts. Cornell Legal Information Institute (2019) recognizes some of the most common ones as the **good faith exception**, **independent source doctrine**, **inevitable discovery doctrine**, **attenuation doctrine**, and **evidence admissible for impeachment**. **Qualified immunity**, a privilege of government officials, makes these exceptions to the rules all the more important.

The good faith exception provides that if an officer believed "in good faith" that he or she was legally obtaining evidence and did not deliberately try to break a law, the evidence may be used in court. The proof that the officer acted in good faith is to show that he or she had no knowledge of an infirmity with the evidence-gathering process utilized.

The other exceptions apply to specific situations and cases. Evidence obtained through an illegal search may not be used in court. However, if a warrant or legal justification is sought independently—one that has no affiliation with the previous, tainted search—that resulting evidence may be used in court. This particular exception is known as the independent source doctrine.

The inevitable discovery doctrine allows evidence seized through illegal means to be admitted in court if the prosecution or representing party asserts that the evidence would have been discovered anyway ("inevitably"). The party must prove that there was an active investigation underway and that the evidence would have been clearly discovered following proper procedures.

The attenuation doctrine asserts that evidence gathered illegally may still be used in court if the connection between the illegal action in obtaining the evidence and the evidence itself has become diminished. (USLEGAL.com, 2016). This can happen, for example, if someone is illegally stopped but, upon further investigation, the officer discovers that there is an outstanding warrant for the subject's arrest. The outstanding warrant "attenuates" or reduces the concern over the original constitutional violation, because it turns out that probable cause does exist to arrest this person. Evidence admissible for impeachment is a doctrine that also allows evidence that is illegally obtained to be presented in court if it is used to discredit the credibility of the defendant during trial. For example, if the evidence can prove that the defendant is lying on the stand, it can be admitted. Still, this is a limited exception, as the evidence may only be used to attack the "character" of the defendant, not to prove he or she is guilty of the specific charges brought against him or her.

Qualified immunity prevents government officials from being held liable for acts, committed during the course of their duties, that unintentionally violate the letter of the law. In principle, it assumes that officials are not attempting to break the law as they attempt to enforce the law. According to Cornell Legal Information Institute (2019), qualified immunity exists to hold officers accountable for their actions if they violate an individual's rights, while also protecting officers from being sued and harassed when they are performing their duties and responsibilities reasonably.

Qualified immunity is the subject of major public debate, in light of concerns about officer-involved shootings and other incidents. Some believe it goes too far in inoculating government officials from consequences for unlawful actions. Law enforcement officials, however, express a feeling of being unable to do their jobs if their every interaction with the public could lead to personal and individual liability.

As explained, the exclusionary rule and the fruit of the poisonous tree Doctrine have various exceptions, but the accepted use of these exceptions is constantly being argued, decided, and re-decided in our nation's courts. The field of policing is constantly evolving because of this.

Box 10.1 Perception Versus Reality

While it is true that policing is an ever-evolving field, we still have a lot to learn from a 1995 article from the University of California, Santa Barbara, "Perceptions of the Criminal Justice System: Television Imagery and Public Knowledge in the United States" by McNeely. Much of the public's understanding about and perceptions of the criminal justice system is derived from television and other entertainment sources (McNeely, 1995). Due to rapid changes in technology in the 1990s, such as the explosion of the Internet and cable TV, this connection was further concretized for many across the nation and world. This statement brings recognition that even over 2 decades ago, when social media was not as prevalent as it is today, it still plays a role in how the criminal justice system is perceived. Through the media, the excessive use of force against Rodney King by the LAPD on March 3, 1991, was broadcasted on several television stations and viewed by many. This event heightened the public's many doubts and questions, even then. Moving to current times, in 2016, Samantha Rhinerson and Ronald Mellen published a study titled "Perceptions of the Criminal Justice System" that came to similar conclusions. They posited that an individual's perception of the criminal justice system is shaped by two concepts: his or her ethnic background and his or her exposure to social media outlets. This was evidenced based on reactions to the killing of Michael Brown in Ferguson, Missouri and several other high-profile police-involved deaths of unarmed African American males.

The researchers stated that African Americans are three times more likely to believe that the criminal justice system is prejudiced than White Americans (Rhineserson & Mellen, 2016). Furthermore, they found that incidents involving police use of excessive force seem to receive more attention, and for longer periods of time, when the victims are African American or Latino.

More than 20 years has passed between publication of these two distinct studies, but their conclusions were the same: Americans' perceptions of the criminal justice system are heavily affected by the information they receive through popular culture, social media, TV and movies, and other sources of entertainment. The reality is that the criminal justice system has its flaws, and ethnic groups have their expectations, whether based on interactions or just by social influences. Social media is there to present information to a mass audience, regardless of its confirmed accuracy of the situation. All of these influence the perceptions people have about the criminal justice system and specifically the police.

Police Professionalism

Police professionalism is an important topic that includes both police accountability and agency accreditation. This section will discuss both in detail and provide examples of each.

Police Accountability: Internal and External

Why do we need police accountability? Several incidents have transpired between the police and communities they serve, resulting in pressure from civil rights groups such as the NAACP, Black

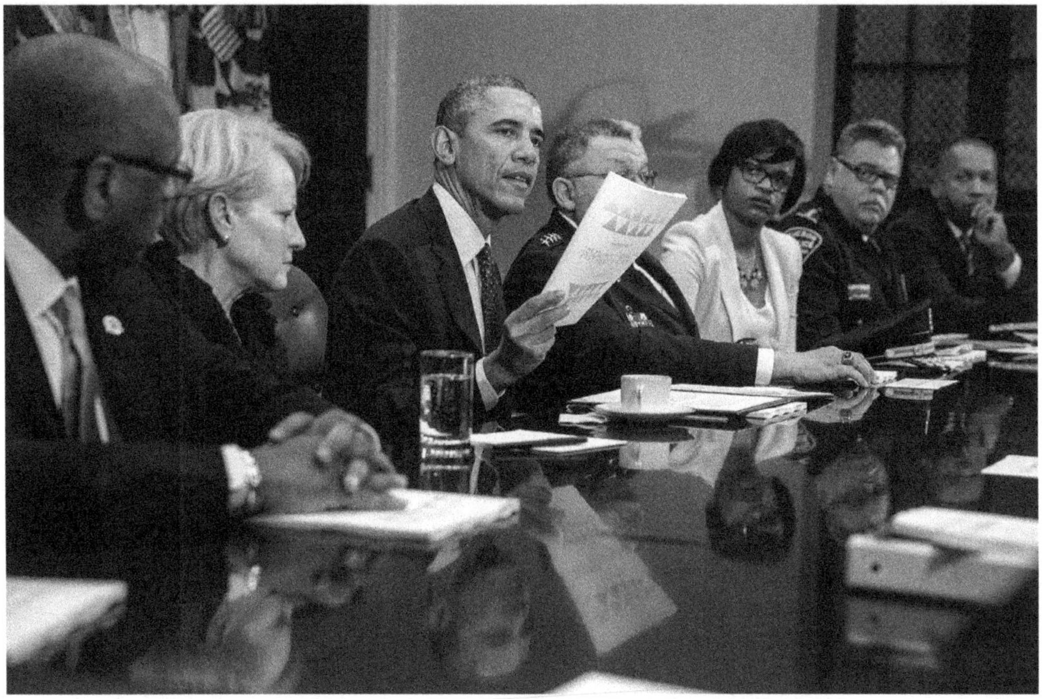

Figure 10.1 President Barack Obama speaks to the press after a meeting

Lives Matter, and others, asking for more police oversight and consistency. In addition, police accountability is much needed, as noted in the final report of former President Obama's Task Force on 21st Century Policing in May 2015, which listed six major pillars: building trust and legitimacy, policy and oversight, technology and social media, community policing and crime reduction, training and education, and officer wellness and safety (see figure 10.1).

Building trust and legitimacy is the most applicable pillar in answering the question of why we need police accountability. The communities that are served by the police need to hold the police accountable for their actions, and the agencies need to demonstrate that there is a checks-and-balance system in place wherein police officers can be held accountable for their actions. Several steps are being addressed by various police agencies in order to demonstrate they are meeting the requirements of pillar 1.

Nicholas Chagnon, Meda Chesney-Lind, and David Johnson (2018) noted in the article "Cops, Lies, and Videotape: Police Reform and the Media in Hawaii" that police accountability is one of the most important topics within the criminal justice system in the United States. Recent actions of police misconduct, combined with technological advancements like body-worn cameras and cell phone cameras, have combined to elevate this issue.

A simple definition of police accountability is holding both individual officers and the agencies they represent to high standards for delivering fair, just, and effective police services to their communities. If problematic actions are taken by the police, they are expected to be able to explain what they did, how they did it, and why.

In a publication by the National Institute of Justice titled "Police Accountability and Community Policing," George Kelling, Robert Wasserman, and Hubert Williams note that police accountability is a fundamental issue for police executives, as they are the public-facing representatives of their agencies and officers. As mentioned in chapter 7, police management involves three core components:

leadership through values, accountability to the community, and administrative mechanisms of control (Kelling et al., 1988).

Leadership through values is when police administrators work in a positive and effective manner, setting an example for their peers and subordinates, thus fostering a greater accountability within the force. Accountability to the community is what police agencies are striving for by including their community members in decision-making processes regarding hiring, recruiting, retaining, and disciplinary measures.

The administrative mechanisms of control relate to supervisory structures, training, audit mechanisms, discipline, rewards, and peer control (Kelling et al., 1988). These are all strategies that the agency can utilize to strengthen its internal accountability endeavors. Crucial to success is the agency employing strategic means in addressing officers' actions, promptly responding to them, and being as transparent as possible.

Police Accreditation

What is police accreditation and why do agencies need to be accredited? The most notable accreditation for law enforcement in the United States is handled by the Commission on Accreditation for Law Enforcement Agencies (CALEA). CALEA calls itself the "gold standard in public safety." It was founded in 1979 and reviews law enforcement agencies, communications centers such as 911, training academies, and campus security agencies.

CALEA is comprised of the following professional organizations: International Association of Chiefs of Police (IACP), National Organization of Black Law Enforcement Executives (NOBLE), National Sheriffs Association (NSA), and Police Executive Research Forum (PERF).

According to the agency's website (CALEA, 2019), "CALEA Accreditation programs provide public safety agencies with an opportunity to voluntarily meet an established set of professional standards, which require:

- Comprehensive and uniform written directives that clearly define authority, performance, and responsibilities;
- Reports and analyses to make fact-based and informed management decisions;
- Preparedness to address natural or man-made critical incidents;
- Community relationship-building and maintenance;
- Independent review by subject matter experts; and
- Continuous pursuit of excellence through annual reviews and other assessment measures."

Once an agency decides to apply for accreditation, it fills out an enrollment package on the agency's website. After it is determined that the agency is eligible to be accredited, a CALEA site-based assessment team member will be sent out to visit the agency and examine policies, procedures, reports, buildings, vehicles, holding units, and several other aspects of the agency's operations.

After the assessment, there is a commission review and decision regarding the agency's accreditation. Once an agency is accredited, there is a compliance maintenance period that lasts for 3 to 4 years, at which time the agency will have to apply for re-accreditation.

The CALEA accreditation process or evaluation has three main audiences: the agency's leadership, the agency's personnel, and the community. It helps the agency leadership by letting the public know that this is a strong, well-run agency. It helps agency personnel by ensuring that they receive high-quality training and have strong internal policies to be supported in doing their work. For the community, it offers mechanisms for transparency, information sharing, and accountability (CALEA, 2019).

For some agencies, accreditation may be cost prohibitive. It is also noted on the CALEA website that the cost associated with various agencies varies. For instance, there are cost variances from law enforcement agencies, public safety communications, public safety training academies, campus security accreditation programs, and the CASP-community agency support program. These costs vary based on the standards, requirements, staffing, jurisdiction and agency size, manpower and personnel, and so on. According to the pros and cons of accreditation, some may say it is too expensive and their agencies cannot afford becoming accredited. Others may say the standards are not applicable to their unique agencies.

CALEA believes that accreditation improves the agency's relationship with the public and government officials and reduces its other benefits: increased community advocacy, support from government officials, stronger defense against civil suits, and reduced risk and liability exposure (CALEA, 2019).

A 2001 study from McCabe and Fajardo, published in the *Journal of Criminal Justice*, provides some arguments in favor of accreditation. It compared accredited and non-accredited agencies across five categories: field training hours, minimum educational requirements for starting officers, drug testing, operation of a specialized drug unit, and operation of a specialized child-abuse unit. Accredited agencies were found to require more training, education, and drug testing of their officers, and to operate more specialized units to combat specific types of crimes.

However, a 2017 study by Steven Hougland and Woss Wolf, "Accreditation in Police Agencies: Does External Quality Assurance Reduce Citizen Complaints?" found that, in at least some areas, accreditation may not be a determinative factor for success. The study examined 628 agencies: 314 accredited and 314 non-accredited. The two variables studied were the total number of complaints received and the number of sustained citizen complaints at each agency. "Sustained citizen complaints" refers to complaints where there was enough evidence to confirm the allegations against an officer accused of an action that warrants mediation, remedy, or discipline.

According to the 2017 study, there were no significant differences between CALEA accredited and non-accredited agencies regarding the volume of citizen complaints and the investigatory outcomes. The researchers referenced several other studies that also found no significant differences between accredited and non-accredited agencies, such as Alpert and MacDonald (2001) and Doerner and Doerner (2012).

For some agencies, accreditation may be cost-prohibitive. Accreditation fees vary by size and type of agency, but as of this writing, range from around $8,500 for small law enforcement agencies to nearly $20,000 for the largest agencies. These fees do not include the cost of the on-site assessment, which agencies must also cover, as well as annual continuation fees and officer and management time. A list of costs by agency type is available at the CALEA (2019) website.

Others say the standards are not applicable to their unique agencies, "unique" meaning that they are small-town agencies with less than 10 officers. These agencies definitely have standards and operatives to follow and adhere to. However, because these agencies are so small, they do not have the resources and manpower to perform some of the more major policing tasks, such as investigating felony crime scenes, fingerprinting and transporting suspects, and maintaining holding facilities for securing prisoners temporarily. These are all major standards that CALEA measures in various larger agencies in order to determine compliance. These agencies primarily call on the larger surrounding agencies for major events, investigations, prisoner processing, and many other functions and duties through a mutual aid system between the agencies.

The issue of accreditation is certainly up for debate. Some studies suggest a benefit to accreditation, while others indicate the process may not be determinative of an agency's quality and success. At the end of the day, each law enforcement agency's leadership must determine whether accreditation is the right fit and a worthy pursuit for their organizations.

A Lesson on Policing From the UK

The United States is not the only country engaged in a public debate about the role of police in local communities. In the United Kingdom, Karen Bullock (2010) from the Department of Sociology at the University of Surrey wrote in article, "Improving Accessibility and Accountability: Neighbourhood Policing and the Policing Pledge," that is highly recommended. The article explains that two concepts have increased police accessibility and accountability within their communities: neighborhood policing (what we call "community policing") and the policing pledge.

A policing pledge is a commitment that police agencies make to their communities about how they will operate. It lays out the expectations that police are required to meet and be accountable for. The paper indicates that success is evaluated against two criteria: (a) whether the agencies provide community updates about progress and what they are doing to address certain issues, and (b) whether the agencies are transparently providing information to the public, such as crime statistics and maps. According to this analysis, agencies in the UK, mostly in Wales and England, have seen positive interactions and responses between their agencies and the communities they serve.

Another police accountability tool that warrants mentioning is the **COMPSTAT** program, which was developed by the New York Police Department in the 1990s. COMPSTAT is a strategy of collecting and analyzing data on crimes and calls for service to inform law enforcement's response. It is a form of police accountability because it provides information behind the reasons for certain decisions made by law enforcement. Some say that the COMPSTAT program is used to target specific groups of people or neighborhoods, while others say that it is being used appropriately for resource allocation and policing strategy development.

Chapter Summary

This chapter discussed the most relevant constitutional amendments that police officers need to understand: the Second, Fourth, Fifth, Sixth, and Fourteenth Amendments. It also covered the relationship between police and the citizens they serve. Strengthening this relationship will always be an ongoing endeavor.

This chapter also discussed the exclusionary rule of evidence and the fruit of the poisonous tree doctrine. These concepts are related, and their distinctions are best understood through different examples. The exclusionary rule encompasses the fruit of the poisonous tree doctrine—it opens the way for the fruit of the poisonous tree to take effect. As mentioned, though, there are several exceptions. The concept of qualified immunity also gives state and local officials the benefit of the doubt when it comes to holding them liable for acts that unintentionally violate the law.

Last, this chapter tackled two of the many pressing topics in policing today: police accountability and police agency accreditation. Police accountability is necessary in order to build trust between police and the communities they serve. Transparency shows accountability and brings respect.

Police accreditation has its champions and its opponents. Some say it is a positive step that improves the reputation of the accredited department, while others say it is too expensive and there are not any significant differences between accredited and non-accredited agencies when it comes to citizens' complaints. The accrediting organization, CALEA, and various police agencies dispute this notion. They say that being accredited provides stability, transparency, and professionalism.

Discussion Questions

1. List four amendments to the United States Constitution that are applicable to policing. Provide detailed examples or scenarios.

2. What is the difference between the exclusionary rule and the fruit of the poisonous tree doctrine?

3. What is police accountability? List two internal and two external examples of police accountability.

4. What is police accreditation? What are the pros and cons of police accreditation?

5. Research and discuss the *Tennessee v. Garner* and *Katz v. United States* court cases. What are their applications to policing today?

6. Research the *Terry v. Ohio* and *Miranda v. Arizona* court cases. What are their applications to policing today?

References

Alpert, G., & MacDonald, J. (2001). Police use of force: An analysis of organizational characteristics. *Justice Quarterly* 18(2), 393–409.

Bullock, K. (2010). Improving accessibility and accountability—neighbourhood policing and the policing pledge. *Safer Communities, 9*(1), 10–19. doi:10.5042/sc.2010.0009

CALEA. (2019). *About us.* Retrieved from https://www.calea.org/about-commission

Chagnon, N., Chesney-Lind, M., & Johnson, D. T. (2018). Cops, lies, and videotape: Police reform and the media in Hawaii. *Crime, Media, Culture, 14*(2), 171–190. doi:10.1177/1741659016677328

Cornell Legal Information Institute. (2019.). Reasonable search. Retrieved from https://www.law.cornell.edu/wex/reasonable_suspicion

Cornell Legal Information Institute. (2019). Probable cause. Retrieved from https://www.law.cornell.edu/wex/probable_cause

Doerner, W., & Doerner, W. (2012). Police accreditation and clearance rates. *Policing: An International Journal of Police Strategies and Management* 35(1), 6–24.

Flanders, C. & Welling, J. (2016). Police use of deadly force: State statutes 30 years after Garner. *Saint Louis University Law Journal.* Retrieved from www.slu.edu/colleges/law/journal/police-use-of-deadly-force-state-statues-30-years-after-garner/

Hougland, S., & Wolf, R. (2017). Accreditation in police agencies. *Police Journal, 90*(1), 40–54. doi.:10.1177/0032258X16671030

Kelling, G., Wasserman, R., & Williams, H. (1988). *Police accountability and community policing.* Retrieved from https://www.ncjrs.gov/pdffiles1/nij/114211.pdf

Legal Dictionary. (2019). *Tennessee v. Garner, 471 U.S. 1 (1985).* Retrieved from https://legaldictionary.net/tennessee-v-garner/

McCabe, K. A., & Fajardo, R. G. (2001) Law enforcement accreditation a national comparison of accredited vs. non accredited agencies. Journal of Criminal Justice, 29(2), 127. doi:10.1016/S0047-2352(00)00088-X

McNeely, C. (1995). Perceptions of the criminal justice system: Television imagery and public knowledge in the United States. *Journal of Criminal Justice Culture and Popular Culture, 3*(1), 1–20.

President's Task Force on 21st Century Policing. (2015). *Final report of the President's Task Force on 21st Century Policing.* Retrieved from https://cops.usdoj.gov/pdf/taskforce/taskforce_finalreport.pdf

Rhinerson, S., & Mellen, R. (2016). Perceptions of the criminal justice system. *American Jails, 30*(1), 33–36.

USLEGAL.com. (2016). *Attentuation doctrine law and legal definition.* Retrieved from https://definitions.uslegal.com/a/attenuation-doctrine/

Worrall, J., & Schmallegar, F. (2010). *Policing today.* Saddle River, NJ: Prentice Hall.

Figure Credits

Fig. 10.1: Source: https://obamawhitehouse.archives.gov/blog/2015/03/02/what-21st-century-policing-means.

CHAPTER ELEVEN

Future Initiatives in Policing

Learning Objectives

- Understand transcontinental crimes and INTERPOL
- Explore the concept of a globalized police force
- Examine the trends of policing to include crime-fighting strategies, privatization, technology, and partnerships
- Illustrate the characteristics of predictive policing strategies
- Understand crime analysis and its types
- Examine police interaction with individuals with mental disorders

Chapter Outline

1. A Real-Life Police Scenario for Discussion
2. Transnational/Transcontinental Crimes
3. Future Trends in Policing
4. An Overview of Crime Analysis
5. Encountering Individuals With Mental Disorders
6. Perception Versus Reality in the Future of Policing
7. Chapter Summary
8. Discussion Questions

This chapter will cover the ever-changing police practices in combating emerging crimes such as terrorism, cybercrimes/computer crimes, and other technological crimes. The controversial concept of a globalized police force, or a universal police force, as well as predictions of the future crime landscape made by police scholars and researchers will also be examined in this chapter. This chapter will also address the purpose of this book, perception versus reality in the future of policing. Based on recent events involving police and the community nationwide, perceptions about policing have been shifting significantly. Several agencies have started various initiatives to rebuild the trust that once existed between the community and these agencies.

A REAL-LIFE POLICE SCENARIO FOR DISCUSSION

On July 7, 2016, days after the fatal shootings of Alton Sterling and Philando Castile in Louisiana and Minnesota, several people gathered in Dallas for what was supposed to be a peaceful protest. That evening turned into one of the deadliest police officer ambushes in United States history.

A gunman, armed with what appeared to be a high-powered rifle, took cover in an elevated position in a parking garage and opened fire, killing several Dallas police officers and injuring many others, including civilians. The gunman was a 25-year-old Army veteran Micah X. Johnson. Investigation into his social media accounts revealed his frustration over recent shootings of unarmed Black men by police around the country.

Police Chief David Brown, who is himself African American, oversaw the law enforcement response and negotiations with the suspect. For the first time in U.S. law enforcement history, he ordered police to use a bomb disposal remote control vehicle. These types of robots are typically used by the military but had never been used in law enforcement before. During the incident in Dallas, the device was used to locate the suspect and plant an explosive, which killed him.

Using this type of device in domestic law enforcement immediately caused controversy. Although the device accomplished its objective, critics feared that American policing was becoming too militarized. Incidents like this raise questions: What is the future of policing? As controversial as police use of force is today, what will happen when robots and other mechanical devices are utilized regularly to mitigate threats, including through use of lethal force against humans?

Are machines replacing conventional policing? Are human crimes becoming too dangerous for conventional police officers to handle? These are all relevant questions for discussing the future of policing. Police departments are exploring the newer technologies (discussed in chapter 9) to stay ahead of the evolving criminal world. This chapter addresses some of the futuristic strategic goals and initiatives that police agencies are using within the United States and internationally.

Transnational/Transcontinental Crimes

As society evolves, so do crime trends; the trends shift globally and need global attention by law enforcement organizations. One concept that is being addressed by both national and international police agencies today is transnational or transcontinental crimes. According to the renowned criminologist Jay Albanese (2017), transnational crimes are various types of crimes that involve more than one country in their planning, execution, or impact.

Albanese noted that this type of crime can be divided into three major categories: (a) provision of illicit goods, (b) provision of illicit services, and (c) infiltration of business or government. The provision of illicit goods involves drug trafficking, trafficking in stolen property, weapons trafficking, and counterfeiting. Provision of illicit services includes commercial sex and human trafficking. Infiltration of business or government covers fraudulent activities, racketeering, money laundering, and various types of corruption-related offenses (Albanese, 2017).

Other scholars have divided transnational crimes into two categories for discussion: **transnational organized crime** and **transnational environmental crime.**

Transnational Organized Crime

The FBI (2019) offers this definition to describe groups that engage in transnational organized crime (TOC):

Figure 11.1 Human trafficking is a global problem. In this photo, border patrol agents remove seven illegal aliens including three children from hot car trunks.

> Transnational organized crime (TOC) groups are self-perpetuating associations of individuals who operate, wholly or in part, by illegal means and irrespective of geography. They constantly seek to obtain power, influence, and monetary gains.

These groups go to great lengths to protect their illegal activities through violence, exploiting jurisdictional boundaries, and multifaceted communication strategies. As the FBI further notes, these groups can affect and target victims all over the world; therefore their exact location is difficult to pinpoint. They are organized in both the Eastern and Western Hemispheres, including Europe, Asia, Africa, and the Middle East (FBI, 2019). Their vast and growing numbers is a result of advancements in technology, which makes it easier for them to reach and target victims from across the globe. This has implications not only for public safety but for public health, border security, human trafficking, and other fraudulent activities taking place nationally and internationally.

Consider a specific example from the work of Christian Leuprecht, Oliver Walther, David Skillicorn, and Hillary Ryde-Collins: "Hezbollah's Global Tentacles: A Relational Approach to Convergence With Transnational Organized Crime," published in 2017. They consider Hezbollah a prime example of this type of organized crime syndicate. The organization was originally formed in Lebanon in 1982 during the Lebanese Civil War (BBC News, 2018). The researchers suggest that Hezbollah, also known as the "Party of God," may be one of the most secure organized crime groups globally. The members of this elite group believe that "the ends justify the means," so they participate in fraudulent and illegal activities in order to raise money to fund humanitarian causes (Leuprecht et al., 2017).

Although this group is based in one small country, it has global networks and continues to evade sanction by law enforcement due to its fluid means of dismantling and restructuring as needed. Some of the most common activities engaged in by Hezbollah include sham marriages, passport fraud, credit card and other financial fraud; money laundering; intellectual property crimes; diamond trading; human, arms, and cigarette trafficking; and so on (see figure 11.1). Their actions are not always viewed as criminal by those on the outside, since profits gained from such activities are remitted to funding religious, social, educational, and military activities within southern Lebanon's Shiite community (Leuprechet et al., 2017).

Transnational Environmental Crime

In addressing transnational environmental crimes—also known as TEC—in a 2011 paper, "Conceptualising and Combating Transnational Environmental Crime," Glen Wright (2011) points out that this topic is often not given a lot of attention, but it should be thought of and treated as a form of organized crime. The author notes that this type of crime can be summed up in two categories: the illegal trade in natural resources and the illegal trade in hazardous materials.

The illegal trade and trafficking of natural resources involves endangered species, as well as other natural resources such as logging and mineral resources from the earth. The illegal trade in hazardous substances includes harmful chemicals that are not being properly regulated as they are transported outside of existing structures and regulations. This has the potential for stripping away the ozone layers. The effects of environmental crimes are detrimental to the entire world, as they affect every aspect of life. For instance, illegal logging and fishing leads to depletion of natural resources, and the illegal dumping of chemical wastes strips away natural resources by killing wildlife (Wright, 2011).

These types of activities are heinous, as they are done for greed and financial gain by criminal organizations. In his paper, Wright (2011) theorizes that TECs are being neglected by international enforcement bodies, since protection of natural resources is often left to individual states and countries. Also, because they are not as obviously and directly seen as crimes against humans, they may not be taken as seriously. However, the effects of these types of crimes are devastating and do affect humans, ultimately. So, how are these types of crimes being addressed on a global scale? Not all nations are on the same page when it comes to these types of crimes. Some view them as important whereas others do not see them as such and therefore do not enforce or address them.

Whether we are talking about transnational organized crime or transnational environmental crime, both can be considered forms of terrorism. There are significant similarities between these types of organizations and "known terrorist organizations." Transnational crime organizations thrive due to their mass connections, with tentacles all around the globe, their ability to reach many, and their ability to make many believe in their ultimate causes. They also frequently operate under "religious" justifications and promise to improve the lives and properties of their communities. This makes combating transnational organized and environmental crimes even more difficult for international agencies.

What agencies are addressing these issues globally? Who is involved? The next section talks about one of the major policing agencies that operates globally to enforce a common set of rules and regulations, under agreement from various countries.

INTERPOL and the Concept of a Globalized Police Force

Addressing international crimes is a global initiative that requires all nations' efforts. There are various global agencies charged with fighting international crimes, but for the purposes of this text we will discuss the two leading organizations: International Criminal Police Organization (ICPO-INTERPOL or just INTERPOL) and the United Nations (UN).

INTERPOL has 194 member countries and the United Nations is comprised of 193 member countries and two observer states. The major responsibilities of INTERPOL are to make the world a safer place and provide police worldwide with technological support to combat crime trends in the 21st century (INTERPOL, 2019). INTERPOL works to support police worldwide in their efforts to prevent and fight crime through cooperation and innovation, regardless of the political situation in a given country (INTERPOL, 2019). INTERPOL offers a wide range of services to law enforcement including data exchange/sharing, training and education, maintaining global database systems, criminal intelligence analysis, I-Checkit/document verification, forensics, response teams, border management, fugitive investigations, and many other criminal detection and enforcement strategies.

The United Nations operates more on the political and humanitarian side of things. According to the UN website, the organization focuses on five major responsibilities: maintaining international peace and security; protecting human rights; delivering humanitarian aid; promoting sustainable development; and upholding international law. Maintaining international peace and security is one of the foundations of this organization, which emerged after the second World War with the need to foster peace amongst nations (UN, 2019). Protecting human rights is also a fundamental goal of this organization, as some nations do not place the same value on human rights as others do.

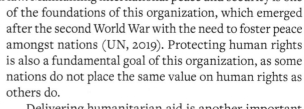

Figure 11.2 INTERPOL flag

Delivering humanitarian aid is another important service of the UN, since some nations, whether due to wars, natural disaster, or some other source of strife, have significant needs that can only be met through outside support. The UN promotes sustainable development because it is important for all nations to develop in a way that fosters prosperity, greater social well-being, economic opportunity, and protection of the environment (UN, 2019). As mentioned under the "Transnational

Environmental Crimes" section, some nations do not understand the importance of protecting the environment, so the UN makes it a priority to spread this as a global value.

The mission responsible for upholding international law is mostly carried out by the United Nations Security Council, a body that administers peacekeeping missions, imposes sanctions, and authorizes use of force where there is justification to do so in various instances (UN, 2019). There are various courts, tribunals, and multilateral treaties as well that exist to hold individuals accountable for their actions and for international crimes.

Several other agencies have ties with these agencies and work collectively, such as the Federal Bureau of Investigations (FBI), Central Intelligence Agency (CIA), and Europol. While new types of crimes and criminal organizations are emerging both domestically and internationally, myriad agencies are also working to stay ahead of the game in combating these types of crimes.

Future Trends in Policing

What challenges are police facing in the near future, as crimes and society evolve? Various agencies have developed strategies to address emerging crimes. Walker and Katz (2018) explain that the main areas of evolution in the future of policing, encompass police technology, crime analysis, police employment, police research, and the impact of the war on terrorism.

Police technology and crime analysis can be viewed collectively. Police agencies are investing in new technologies to fight crimes such as advanced cybercrimes and cyber-enabled crimes. Crime analysis helps agencies determine the specific types of crimes and what specific resources to use to address these crimes, along with the benefits that can be gained from an investment in new technologies.

Trends in police employment is a vital area of study for the future of policing. Although this is an illustrious career, policing has been met with low recruitment; many agencies have reported that their application numbers have decreased in recent years. Chapter 2 documented this phenomenon in detail. Agencies are continuously striving to beef up their recruiting initiatives, with an emphasis on hiring diversity and strategies for retaining their officers.

The future of policing research and the impact of the war on terrorism are also two areas in a state of change. As the various types of crimes are ever changing, police agencies are relying more and more on educational and private research institutes to collaborate with and conduct meaningful research projects that address crimes of the future, such as organized crimes and property crimes. Almost every police agency is also dealing with the impact of the war on terrorism, as they are at the forefront of responding to such attacks; again, this is an area of constant evolution. Most police agencies are currently training their members in tactics and strategies to identify, prevent, and respond to terrorist acts. In addition to these major areas of evolution in modern-day policing, a study from the Police Executive Research Forum (PERF), published in 2014, identifies a number of other areas going through significant change. With support from the Office of Community Oriented Policing Services (COPS) at the U.S. Justice Department and Target Cooperation, PERF (2014) distributed a "future of policing" survey to over 500 agencies nationwide and issued a report summarizing the study's findings. We will discuss the results.

Information-Based Strategies

When exploring crime trends and crime-fighting strategies domestically, two major information-based strategies were examined: predictive policing and intelligence-led policing. Predictive policing is a concept used by various departments that involves collecting data from various systems and using the collected data to prevent, respond, and strategically allocate resources to respond to specific types of crimes or incidents (PERF, 2014). Intelligence-led policing is about equipping police administrators with strategic information from multiple sources so that they can analyze it and make specific decisions to disrupt, reduce, and prevent serious criminal offenses (PERF, 2014).

Predictive and intelligence-led policing strategies are being used nationwide to address emerging crimes and reduce crime rates. In implementing these strategies, civil liberties have to be taken into account, as there is often a fine line in these systems between making accurate and actionable predictions and intruding into the private lives and liberties of ordinary people. PERF (2014) recommends that police administrators be vigilant in ensuring that all policies and regulations are adhered to before implementing such strategies. Data should be examined thoroughly before making any negative implications that may affect the public innocently.

Furthermore, predictive policing and intelligence-led policing is truly data driven; so, it is advisable for administrators to understand the limitations of this data. For example, crimes may go unreported due to various reasons, including the information source's fear of potential retaliation, deportation, or community ostracization. If a crime is not reported it will not show up in the data, therefore skewing the overall picture.

The LAPD is at the forefront in using predictive policing by partnering with UCLA Institute for Pure and Applied Mathematics (PERF, 2014). Using a program called PredPol, UCLA researchers examined several sets of crime data from the LAPD and identified mathematical patterns within the data. With the help of the National Science Foundation, the researchers were able to build algorithms with the patterns that helped them predict various types of crimes. The LAPD, Santa Cruz Police Department, and several other agencies around the country are now using this software.

Tailoring Partnerships to Maximize Public Safety

Partnerships are key to building effective crime-fighting methodologies for the future. These go hand in hand with community policing, requiring relationship and trust building among all parties involved. It is recommended that police agencies continue to forge partnerships with police research organizations such as PERF, National Police Foundation Project, and others. Second, police agencies should continue to partner with federal, state, and local law enforcement agencies as well as colleges and universities. Finally, partnering with various business such as local pawn shops will also reap law enforcement benefits.

Partnering with police research organizations will expose agencies to resources to help them target specific crimes that require strategic understanding and analysis. These organizations have high-level, skilled researchers who can properly analyze and understand a crime trend. Partnering with federal law enforcement agencies is something that most agencies are already doing, although relationships can always be strengthened. Partnering with federal agencies helps state and local police maximize their investigative capabilities and allows them to extend their capacity when budgetary constraints would otherwise come into play.

Figure 11.3 Speech at Scheller College

Partnering with local and state higher educational institutions is also paramount, and the reasons are twofold. It provides law enforcement with access to the educational population and young and eager criminal justice scholars or researchers. In addition, partnering with these colleges and universities, as shown in Figure 11.3, gives agencies a wide range of understanding into certain crime trends that affect young adults in particular (PERF, 2014). Finally, partnering with local businesses such as pawn shops is a strategic way to reduce thefts and other crimes.

There are some potential challenges with these strategies since, for example, not all pawn shops would be mandated to participate in this program and less-than-complete participation could lead to gaps in detecting thefts. Still, there is a lot to be learned from agencies that have worked for years to improve relationships with their cities, counties, local officials, and businesses.

Private, public, and nonprofit sectors working collectively to address evolving crimes is a very promising development for the future of crime fighting. Several of these collaborations are directed by the crime-prevention units of police agencies, which form coalitions to facilitate information sharing such as updates on crime reports, calls for service, crime-prevention strategies, and tips from community members.

Implementing Strategies to Increase Efficiency

With the rise of technology and the invention of new types of crimes using technology, police agencies are working in overdrive to implement appropriate and effective responses. This requires them to also search for ways to maximize agency efficiency. Agencies actually reduce police response to minor crimes as one step toward increased efficiency. In addition, agencies develop relationships with private security officers in their jurisdiction and have policies regarding off-duty employment by officers to ensure that their workforce is not overextended (PERF, 2014).

Before PERF's recommendations, agencies would typically respond to all calls for service. However, after surveying various departments and determining their needs, changes to call response priorities began to emerge. They learned that calls about crimes such as burglaries, larcenies, vandalisms, and so on are often made several hours after the incident, when there is little to no chance that the suspect is still on the scene. Some agencies have implemented new strategies so that victims of such similar crimes can simply report these crimes online.

Crimes such as minor thefts or vandalism, where the victim does not necessarily need to meet in person with the police, could be reported online. Officers will review these online reports on a daily basis and determine whether a follow up is needed to collect pictures or other evidence or conduct further investigation. By implementing online reporting capabilities for minor crimes, agencies have reduced their overall response times and strategically directed their resources to improve efficiency.

There are some concerns with this type of system. First, there is greater potential for someone to file a false report for insurance purposes. Second, some agencies want to make sure that they are not completely cutting out officer interaction with crime victims. Some victims may feel traumatized by the crime they have experienced and personally want to speak to an officer while making their complaint. These are all valid concerns, and agencies are making several strides in addressing them.

In regards to private security, as mentioned in chapter 4, these establishments can be used as eyes and ears for police if there is a well-established partnership. Some private establishments such as apartment complexes hire security personnel. These individuals are thought of as, essentially, community officers who have gained the trust of their tenants and can also act as an information-sharing liaison to local and state police agencies, regarding crimes committed within or around their establishments.

Since private security personnel are hired to cover a designated place, their presence can also enhance coverage over such establishments and allow police officers to focus on other areas or calls.

In regard to off-duty assignments, in some states, police agencies can enter into legal, paying opportunities with private firms, and their officers can earn additional income. These opportunities also benefit the law enforcement mission. The officers are legally covered by their agencies if they have to take law enforcement action such as making an arrest or citing someone, or if they exhibit use of force while working an off-duty assignment. However, they still have to report to the private establishment regarding any actions taken on the property.

There are positives and negatives to this activity. On the one hand, working jobs like these allow officers to form relationships with residents or individuals in the area, which can be useful during a law enforcement incident. However, if an officer becomes very familiar with a particular establishment or group of people, there is also the possibility that someone may accuse him or her of biased or unethical conduct. Some agencies prohibit their officers from working certain off-duty assignments that are more prone to these scenarios, such as being bouncers at nightclubs and escorting celebrities.

In some agencies, officers are permitted to solicit outside employment and individually enter into agreements with private entities, as long as they notify their police agency of their off-duty work. Outside employment can be established with faith-based organizations, entertainment organizations and establishments, and other private entities. The responsibility is placed on the officer to accurately report the hours worked while off duty so that they do not conflict with their current work schedules or responsibilities.

Future Trends in Technology

The PERF study covered several issues related to emerging technology, as this is the one of main drivers of change in criminal activity and, therefore, policing. The study reviewed use of social media; implementing a nationwide public safety broadband network system for first responders; next-generation 911; partnering with real-time crime centers; fighting cybercrimes; and using technology to fill in personnel gaps (PERF, 2014).

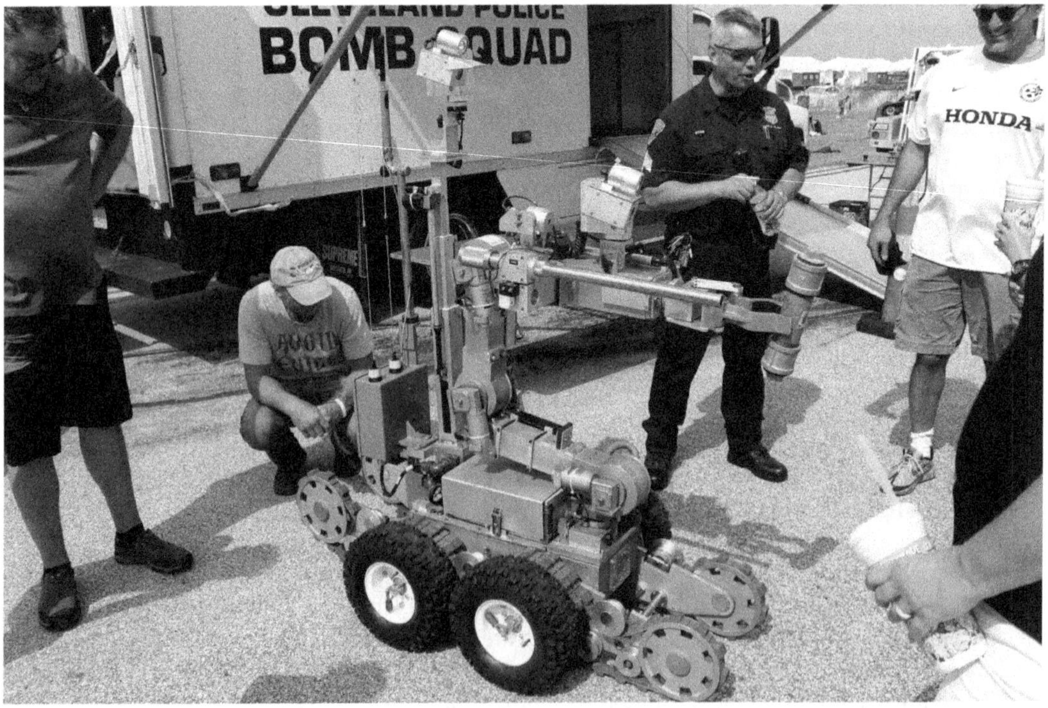

Figure 11.4 Cleveland Police Bomb Squad robot

The use of social media by police was discussed in chapter 9. Social media is used by many in the public and it is an excellent way for police to share information regarding suspects being sought, emergent public safety threats such as fires or other incidents, and routine notices about department services and programs.

As a result of the major communications failures during September 11, 2001 terrorist attacks, it was apparent that first responders needed a nationwide communications system that is clear and accessible to all agencies. The Nationwide Public Safety Broadband Network (NPSBN) was signed into law by President Obama in 2012. It is a nationwide public safety broadband network that enables first responders—including police, fire, and other emergency responders—to communicate clearly and effectively in times of emergency, across agency lines.

Next-generation 911 is another step forward in technology. It improves communications between individuals calling 911 and dispatchers responding with help and services. With next-generation 911, users can contact 911 from any device connected to the Internet; operators can receive enhanced information including texts, images, and video in an accurate and rapid way; and dispatchers can easily save and transfer emergency calls from one station to another (PERF, 2014).

Several agencies are currently using this technology to great effect, and some have partnered with Motorola Solutions to further maximize their reach. In this day and age, most individuals have a cellular phone or an Internet-capable device wherein messages and images can be transmitted quickly and easily to other communication devices. Police agencies are seeing this as an advantage to not only reach more people but to obtain more information from the citizens they protect.

Real-time crime centers, also referred to as RTCCs, provide police agencies with a variety of technologies that help them respond to calls effectively and efficiently. RTCCs equip officers with various technologies so that they can respond effectively to calls that are currently happening or have recently occurred. Agencies spend significant time collecting data on multiple aspects of crime and criminals; secure sharing of information with other law enforcement officers as needed helps avoid duplication and enhance efficiency.

As technology evolves, so do cybercrimes. Cybercrimes are types of crimes that involve electronic means, such as sharing, transferring, exploiting, stealing, destroying, or any other illegal exchange conducted, facilitated, or assisted by technology. These types of crimes were explained thoroughly in chapter 5. Law enforcement agencies must rev up their forensic units and partner with federal and state agencies with state-of-the-art laboratories to assist in preventing and investigating computer crimes. This is one way that agencies expand their capacities and ensure efficiency.

Law enforcement agencies are also using technology to help fill in personnel gaps (see figure 11.4). For example, several agencies have flooded their streets, buildings' exteriors, and entry and exit points with security cameras. These cameras are controlled at one location or several stationary locations by the department so that operators can conduct virtual patrolling of streets, locations, and structures. This reduces the number of patrol officers needed in a given location. It has also helped solve crimes, where a still picture or video of a suspect is captured and can then be broadcast to the public for identification.

Of course, deployment of these cameras must be done carefully, and consideration must be made to ensure privacy rights of citizens. If the cameras are placed in truly public places, though, there is no expectation of privacy there, and some jurisdictions do not need permission to record or photograph people, places, or structures.

An Overview of Crime Analysis

The concept of crime analysis has a long and illustrious history. Some of the influential police reformers who were mentioned earlier in this text, such as August Vollmer and O.W. Wilson, strived to understand the various types of crimes, why they occur in certain locations, and why some offenders repeat offenses, with the goal of trying to predict crime patterns so that agencies can better allocate patrol and investigative resources and actually prevent future crimes.

Crime analysis is an area of constant change as technology and policing evolve. It is also central to crime prevention. The Law Enforcement Assistance Administrator's Integrated Criminal Apprehension Program (ICAP) defines crime analysis as

> [a] set of systematic, analytical processes directed at providing timely and pertinent information relative to crime patterns and trend correlations to assist operational and administrative personnel in planning the deployment of resources for the prevention and suppression of criminal activities, aiding the investigative process, and increasing apprehensions and the clearance of cases. Within this context, crime analysis supports a number of department functions, including patrol deployment, special operations and tactical units, investigations, planning and research, crime prevention and administrative services (budgeting and program planning). (Gottlieb & Arenberg, 1992, p. 12)

In its simplest form, crime analysis is the collection of information from multiple sources that is then analyzed by crime specialists in order to speculate regarding future crimes so that police administrators can strategically plan their approaches.

As crimes evolve, so too do the techniques that law enforcement agencies use to analyze crimes and determine the patterns and methods used by today's criminal offenders. Patrol budgets and other criminal investigation resources are always limited, and so strategic prioritization is needed to ensure that resources are allocated properly and the goal of public safety is met.

A majority of the nation's police agencies in the United States, and even internationally, have crime analysis units because they assist with the prediction (Figure 11.5), prevention, and detection of crime. The International Association of Crime Analysts (IACA, 2019) has more than 3,000 members across the globe in 61 countries, including the United States, Canada, Mexico, Ireland, Trinidad and Tobago, and Chile. This professional association delivers state-of-the-art training to its members, which include both law enforcement and civilian crime analysts. Some jurisdictions choose to have civilian employees serve this role, as they can bring different types of experience and education to the agency, such as advanced degrees and other specialized skills such as critical thinking and analytical strategies.

The major functions of a crime analysis unit are identification of evolving or existing crime patterns and series; forecasting future crime occurrences; initiation of target profile analysis; provision of investigative leads; provision of support data to crime prevention programs; assisting in case clearance processes, and provision of trends and other data to support resource allocation, departmental planning, and budgeting (Gottlieb & Arenberg, 1992; see figure 11.5).

TYPE	RELATIONSHIP TO VICTIM	PROBLEMATIC	LIKELIHOOD OF VIOLENCE
I	None	High	"Limited"
II	None	High	"Limited"
III	None/slight	Moderate	Moderate
IV	Slight	Moderate	Moderate
V	Moderate	Moderate	Moderate
VI	Intimate	Slight	High
VII	Extended/intimate	Slight	Very high

Figure 11.5 "Threat Assessment of Stalkers as a Series of Continuums" from "Stalkers and Other Obsessional Types: A Review and Forensic Psychological Typology of Those Who Stalk"

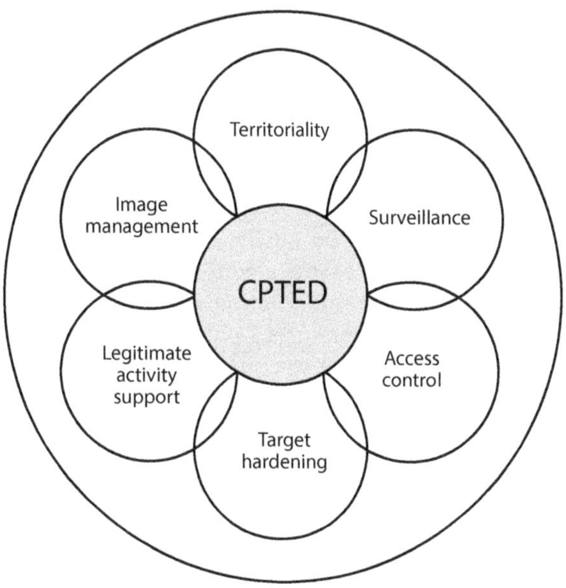

Figure 11.6 Geographical juxtaposition

The function of crime analysis operates through several layers. For instance, when a crime analyst receives information or a question about a suspect, he or she can then use demographic information from available databases to see if there is a match. Then, he or she can explore known associations of that individual and establish various patterns in order to share this information with requesting parties. The most common trajectory of the crime analysis process looks like this: information collection, collation, analysis, dissemination, and feedback.

The first step, information collection, involves pulling data from various sources, including crime reports, calls for service, calls to dispatchers, case dispositions, and other sources such as community reporting initiatives such as crime tips and other neighborhood watch information.

In the collation phase, a crime analyst organizes and makes sense of what has been collected mainly by thoroughly examining the data, rearranging it, and creating codes and themes mostly from calls for service and crime statistics. The third step is analyzing the data in light of what information is being sought by the requestor. Analyzing the data is basically making sense of it, placing specific data sets into specific categories in order to be easily read and explained.

After the data has been collected and analyzed, analysts present the information to other officers or police administrators whose job involves the interpretation of such data and putting its findings into action—to reduce crime and/or address social problems within their designated districts. Administrators may also give feedback to the analysts regarding the information shared and requests for further information or clarification.

Crime Prevention Through Environmental Design (CPTED) is an example of a major, internationally utilized strategy involving crime analysis (see figure 11.6). In this process, crime prevention specialists evaluate data regarding businesses, residences, and other locations and provide concrete recommendations about how to prevent criminal acts from occurring in these locations, places, or residences. In some jurisdictions, the CPTED process is something that local business owners and other related establishments are actively taking part in, in order to prevent future crimes from taking place, again showing the importance of different types of community partnerships.

Intelligence Analysis and Criminal Investigative Analysis

It is also important to know the various types of crime analysis. Before examining the three major types, let's discuss two "relatives" of crime analysis: **intelligence analysis** and **criminal investigative analysis**. Intelligence analysis is more focused on certain types of crimes or criminal entities, gathering and analyzing information dealing with gang-related crimes, drug trafficking, prostitution rings, financial crimes, and other organized criminal syndicates—and the individuals involved in them. Criminal investigative analysis involves profiling individuals who have committed serious offenses. This type of analysis seeks to gather information about the individual's lifestyle, patterns, frequent locations, social habits, and method of operation in criminal activities in order to prevent him or her from committing future crimes or to prevent similar future offenders.

Tactical, Strategic, and Administrative Crime Analysis

Gottlieb and Arenberg (1992) posited that there are three main types of crime analysis: tactical, strategic, and administrative. **Tactical crime analysis** focuses on the recency of the crime and direct information about the type of crimes in order to isolate a pattern or patterns. It specifically focuses on the how, when, and where the incident happened in order to develop a specific pattern useful in deterring or apprehending potential suspects. Tactical also refers to the quick response in addressing a specific issue with swift action steps. **Strategic crime analysis** focuses on long-term crime patterns to be addressed through effective police responses. Long-term strategies could include planning, financial obligations, manpower, and resource allocations to address specific set of crimes or findings.

Administrative crime analysis targets a specific audience such as police administrators, public officials, and other private groups to receive information vital for decision-making and resource allocation strategies relevant to these groups/audiences (Gottlieb & Arenberg, 1992).

Encountering Individuals with Mental Disorders

Another topic of discussion regarding the evolution of policing is the issue of police interactions with individuals suffering from mental health problems. According to the National Alliance of Mental Illness (NAMI), the mental health crisis in the United States has led to a situation where police officers are now acting as crisis intervention specialists (see figure 11.7). To support law enforcement in carrying out this role, NAMI teaches agencies how to implement crisis intervention teams (CITs; see figure 11.8).

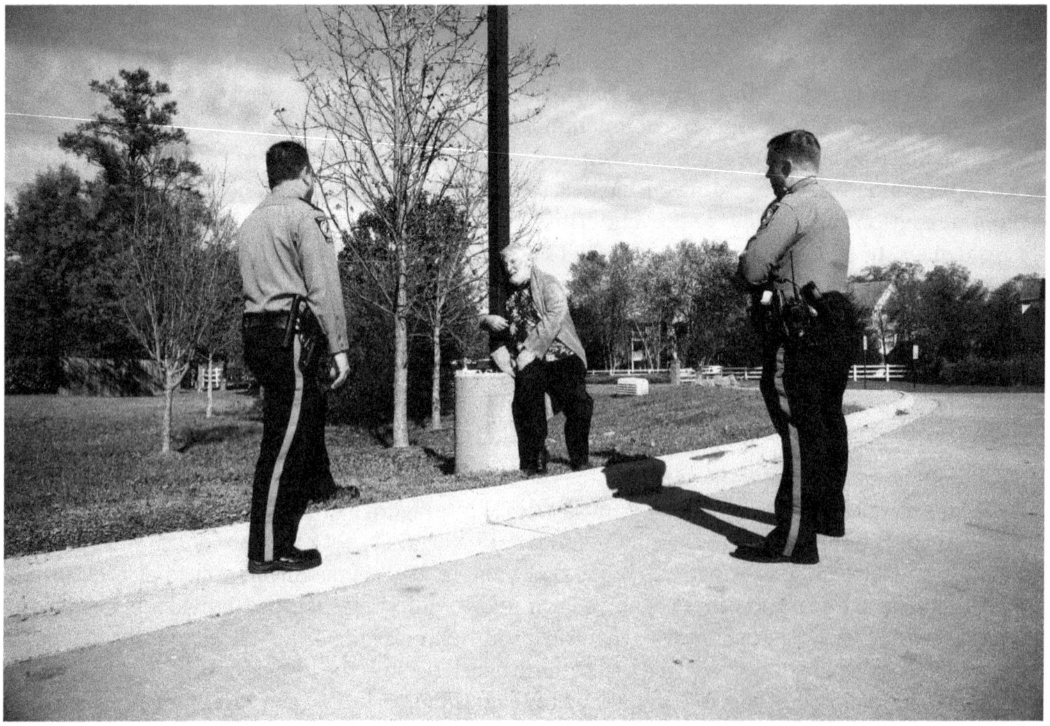

Figure 11.7 Example of Crisis Intervention in progress

Over 2,700 communities in the United States have CITs in place, where law enforcement officers partner with local and state mental health specialists to receive training in how to deal with persons with mental illness (NAMI, 2019).

Amy Watson, Michael Compton, and Jeffrey Draine wrote "The Crisis Intervention (CIT) Model: An Evidence-Based Policing Practice?" in 2017, which provides a brief introduction to the history behind this concept. In the late 1980s, police in Memphis encountered an individual wielding a knife and threatening to harm himself. The man was fatally shot by police, and it was later discovered that he had extensive mental issues. Responding to community outcry, the mayor initiated a task force comprised of police administrators and officers, mental health specialists, advocacy organizations, and educational institutions to review the situation. Thus, the first CIT program was formed—also known as the Memphis Model.

Figure 11.8 CIT training with NAMI-AL

CIT consists of 40 hours of training for law enforcement officers to complete, which includes visits to mental health facilities, practical learning, and rigorous mental health scenarios to engage in and learn from (Watson et al., 2017). Upon completion of the training, officers are certified CIT officers and can be called on to handle service calls regarding anyone displaying possible signs of mental illness.

It is recommended that 20–35% of all police agencies in a given locality have CIT-trained officers, as this reduces the chances of officers using force on individuals with mental health issues. Six to 10 percent of all police encounters with civilians in the United States involve people with mental health issues (Watson et al., 2017). What's more, the researchers also noted that when police use excessive force to arrest, detain, or apprehend an individual, quite often that individual has some sort of mental illness crisis. With the high volume of interactions officers have with individuals on a daily basis, having a program that educates them about how to properly handle situations involving mental illness is clearly necessary.

NAMI says that CITs benefit law enforcement by giving police officers more tools to do their jobs safely and effectively. With the implementation of CIT, physical injuries sustained by officers encountering individuals with mental illness have fallen by over 80% (NAMI, 2019).

When officers are equipped with knowledge through programs like CIT, they also become more efficient. Further benefits are improved community relationships, a more effective crisis response system, better training response to behavioral health crisis calls, reduced unnecessary arrests and use of force, reduced officer/citizen injuries, increased officer confidence in skills, reduced liability, and more efficient use of criminal justice resources, including increased jail diversion (CIT International, 2019).

These benefits are thoroughly supported by the growing demands for this program nationwide and internationally. NAMI says these programs are also cost effective, because it is more expensive to house and provide mental health services to inmates in prison than to enroll individuals in community mental health programs. For example, in Detroit, caring for an inmate with mental health issues costs over $31,000 annually, whereas a community mental health program costs closer to $10,000 (NAMI, 2019). Further research shows that CIT programs reduce procedural costs, such as hospital and jail costs.

As agencies see the benefits of CITs, their use is expanding. As always, though, there are some possible drawbacks to take into consideration. Some officers feel that CITs' mission is in tension with officers' duty to "enforce" the law and is taking away their discretion to use force when necessary.

One way to deal with this concern is to have officers take this training on a volunteer basis, rather than making it mandatory. Clearly, responding effectively using CIT training takes compassion and commitment to the program's goals. Agencies should ask officers who wish to explore their talents in using oral communications in these types of situations to volunteer for the specialized program.

Still, some officers who were not initially interested in the training but required to complete it found that they learned a lot and actually feel more comfortable approaching all individuals they come into contact with, regardless of their mental health status, because of the training. Some administrators have prioritized the training for officers simply because it teaches them to use more verbal communication measures. There are significant considerations for police administrators to make while selecting individuals to attend these trainings, but what is important is that they are being provided.

Box 11.1 Perception Versus Reality in the Future of Policing

We will close this chapter with a brief note on the varying perceptions in the future of policing. The reality to point out here is that positive and negative perceptions of policing will always exist. The negative perceptions can be shaped by recurring incidents or one-time experiences.

There are two parties involved here: the police and the communities they serve. For both groups, the perceptions of the past cannot be changed, and the perceptions of the present can be addressed too quickly. But the perceptions of the future can be prevented by having both parties work collaboratively and transparently. Chapter 2 presented several strategies that police agencies and community members can use to enhance trust and collaboration and to effect positive future perceptions.

One concept to introduce that has negatively affected the perceptions of policing is the Ferguson effect. Justin Nix and Justin Pickett noted that following the fatal shooting of Michael Brown in Ferguson, Missouri, police began to be heavily scrutinized. This resulted in police reducing enforcement in order to avoid criticism, which then resulted in increased crime rates, especially murders. Even though the so-called Ferguson effect has not been theoretically proven, some agencies have toned down their strategies to the point where they are essentially taking a hands-off mentality because they are unable to operate under such constant public scrutiny. There are two ways to look at this scenario: One is that it is perceived that the police are taking a more hands-off approach and that this is leading to an increase in crime. On the other hand, it may be that the negative publicity about police interactions with civilians, shared on social and news media, have increased individuals' hostility toward the police, resulting in more serious injuries and fatalities (Nix & Pickett, 2017).

It could be that individuals are becoming more resistant toward law enforcement because of what they see on social media and in the news. The police may perceive the individual who is resisting or not obeying their commands as a threat and use other forms of force to effect the arrest. But individuals who they encounter may believe they are "asserting their rights" and law enforcement agents are the ones violating the law. The Ferguson effect can also be referred to as the "YouTube effect," or the "viral video effect." Constant portrayals of negative interactions between police and civilians may contribute to community members placing lower trust in the police and therefore being less likely to report crimes or assist in investigations, which of course keeps criminals in business and increases local crime.

Social media is engulfing the spectrum of information sharing. Whether the information put out on social media is accurate or inaccurate, it will be disseminated. The question now becomes, "What is law enforcement's greatest challenge today: the threat of serious crimes such as organize crimes, terrorism, and gangs, or trying to build a strong relationship between agencies and their communities despite the negative portrayals on social media?"

As a researcher, professor, and former police officer, I can offer my personal insight. The reality is that crime will always be evolving, and if agencies are equipped with the right amount of information, technology, and funding, they will be able to keep up with and address new types of crimes.

But building relationships between policing and the communities they serve takes work, time, effort, and dedication on both sides. A short video clip shared hundreds of times on social media has the potential to rupture the entire reputation of an agency. Rebuilding from this will take much more time than the few seconds contained in the video clip.

Some agencies have become proactive and are using social media to their advantage, portraying positive stories about their officers in action within their communities. Even though these are not viewed by as many constituents as the negative portrayals, they are being shared and more agencies are getting on board with creating this type of content that shows community partnership building. As Rachel Stein and Candace Griffith (2017) point out in their paper, "Differences Between Resident and Police Perceptions Can Affect the Success of Crime Prevention Strategies," law enforcement actively needs a strong relationship with our local communities in order to be successful at our public safety mission.

Police response to serious crimes such as organized crimes, terrorism, and gangs are all important topics to address, but if the foundational basis of community policing is not reinforced between police and the communities they serve, then police agencies will be more alienated in fighting these and other crimes.

Chapter Summary

This chapter covers several ways that crime is evolving with technology and communications, and the myriad ways agencies across the globe are responding. We explained what transcontinental, organized, and environmental crimes are, and the role of globalized police forces such as INTERPOL.

We explored the ways that the future of policing depends on diverse partnerships, cutting-edge strategies, and adaption of new technologies. We drilled deep into the concept of crime analysis and learned how crime analysis units are helping law enforcement detect, predict, and event prevent future crimes. Finally, this chapter reviewed ways that agencies are adapting to concerns voiced temporally by members of their communities, such as use of force toward individuals with mental illnesses and the perception of police bias flourishing due to social media.

Fostering a positive relationship between police and the communities they serve is key in all future policing protocols, which have the potential to ignite debates over privacy issues and perceived or real biases. If not handled well, social media can only fan these flames.

Some agencies have dedicated significant resources to their community policing sections, and the importance of this relationship-building work continues to grow. Positive interactions and relationships with law enforcement, along with strengthened communication, transparency, and accountability will help mitigate against unfounded and negative attacks on law enforcement via social media or other sources. Once again, community policing is the key to preventing crimes—including the crimes of the future.

Discussion Questions

1. What are transnational organized crimes? List and describe the types and provide detailed examples of these types of crimes.

2. Describe in detail the concept of CEPTED, list the benefits of this concept, and provide two examples wherein it has been used successfully.

3. What is the concept known as "crime analysis"? What are its major functions?

4. What is CIT? What are its benefits and drawbacks?

5. In reading this chapter, what is the key ingredient to successfully addressing crimes of the future and why?

References

Albanese, J. (2017). *Transnational crime. Oxford Bibliographies.* Retrieved from http://www.oxfordbibliographies.com/view/document/obo-9780195396607/obo-9780195396607-0024.xml

BBC News. (2018). *Who are Hezbollah?* Retrieved from http://news.bbc.co.uk/2/hi/middle_east/4314423.stm

CIT International. (2019). *Improving responses to people in crisis.* Retrieved from http://www.citinternational.org/resources/Documents/CIT%20Program%20Overview.2017.pdf

Federal Bureau of Investigation (FBI). (2019). *What we investigate: Transnational organized crime.* Retrieved from https://www.fbi.gov/investigate/organized-crime

Gottlied, A. & Arenberg, S. (1992). *Crime analysis: From concept to reality.* Retrieved from https://www.ncjrs.gov/pdffiles1/Digitization/137374NCJRS.pdf

International Association of Crime Analysts (IACA). (2019). *About IACA.* Retrieved from https://iaca.net/

INTERPOL. (2019). *Connecting police for a safer world: Overview.* Retrieved from https://www.interpol.int/About-INTERPOL/Overview

Leuprecht, C., Walther, O., Skillicorn, D. & RydeCollins, H. (2017). Hezbollah's global tentacles: A relational approach to convergence with transnational organized crime. *Terrorism and Political Violence, 29*(5), 902–921. doi:10.1080/09546553.2015.1089863

National Alliance on Mental Illness (NAMI). (2019). *Crisis intervention team (CIT) programs.* Retrieved from https://www.nami.org/get-involved/law-enforcement-and-mental-health

Nix, J., & Pickett, J. T. (2017). Third-person perceptions, hostile media effects, and policing: Developing a theoretical framework for assessing the Ferguson effect. *Journal of Criminal Justice, 51,* 24–33.

Police Executive Research Forum (PERF). (2014). *Future trends in policing.* Retrieved from https://www.policeforum.org/assets/docs/Free_Online_Documents/Leadership/future%20trends%20in%20policing%202014.pdf

Stein, R. E., & Griffith, C. (2017). Resident and police perceptions of the neighborhood: Implications for community policing. *Criminal Justice Policy Review, 28*(2), 139–154. doi:10.1177/0887403415570630

United Nations. (2019). *What we do.* Retrieved from http://www.un.org/en/sections/what-we-do/index.html

U.S. Department of Justice. (n.d.). *Special litigation section cases and matters: Law enforcement agencies.* Retrieved from https://www.justice.gov/crt/special-litigation-section-cases-and-matters0#police

Walker, S. & Katz, C. (2018). The police in America: An introduction. New York, NY; McGraw- Hill Education

Watson, A. C., Compton, M. T., & Draine, J. N. (2017). The crisis intervention team (CIT) model: An evidence-based policing practice? *Behavioral Sciences & the Law, 35*(5/6), 431–441. Okdoi:10.1002/bsl.2304

Wright, G. (2011). Conceptualising and combating transnational environmental crime. *Trends in Organized Crime, 14*(4), 332–346. doi:10.1007/s12117-011-9130-4

Figure Credits

Fig. 11.1: Source: https://www.flickr.com/photos/cbpphotos/26832862983.
Fig. 11.2: Copyright © 2016 Depositphotos/frizio.
Fig. 11.3: Source: https://www.usar.army.mil/News/Images/igphoto/2001733688/.
Fig. 11.4: Copyright © 2014 by Raymond Wambsgans (CC BY-SA 2.0) at https://www.flickr.com/photos/cak757/15091090331.
Fig. 11.5: Source: Stalking Crimes and Victim Protection: Prevention, Intervention, Threat Assessment, and Case Management.
Fig. 11.6: Source: https://www.researchgate.net/figure/The-seven-crime-prevention-through-environmental-design-CPTED-principles-Source_fig1_281604957.
Fig. 11.7: Copyright © by Henrico County Police Division. Reprinted with permission.
Fig. 11.8: Source: https://www.youtube.com/watch?v=V6Vz9mTk-vA.

CHAPTER TWELVE

Policing in the 21st Century

A REAL-LIFE POLICE SCENARIO FOR DISCUSSION

"Please, please, please, I can't breathe, Please, man, I can't breathe." These were George Floyd's last words before his death in custody of then-police officer Derek Chauvin on May 25, 2020. This was no mistake; the officer smirked heartlessly as he amplified the pressure on Mr. Floyd's neck. As a result of that action, George Floyd's life was cut short. This was just one of many incidents involving police excessive use of force that triggered the worldwide police reform movement. Similar cases occurred in the hands of police officers, such as the death of Breonna Taylor following a no-knock warrant; the killing of Rayshard Brooks after having fallen asleep in a fast-food drive-through; the fatal shooting of Ahmaud Aubery who, while jogging, was perceived as suspicious in the eyes of a former detective; and the paralysis of Jacob Blake as he was breaking up a domestic argument. As mentioned in previous chapters, policing has gone through several eras: the political era, the reform era, and the community policing era. Each of these periods significantly contributed to policing. The political era implemented policing; however, it was very corrupt due to its dynamic. The reform era strived to transform policing through the aggressive reforms and proposals by August Vollmer and O.W. Wilson. Lastly, the community policing era continues today without much change, even despite the social climate. This leaves us with the unwavering question: Will policing ever be perfect? The community era was originally described as emphasizing the understanding and active cooperation between communities and the police. In actuality, this era continues to ensnare strife between the police and the communities they serve. Due to historical events dealing with policing and the communities they serve, several jurisdictions have proposed a number of reforms such as: **creating citizen review boards**; **banning choke holds**; **banning no-knock warrants**; **encouraging officers to hold their coworkers accountable through intervention**; **reclassifying the charge for assault and battery on a police officer**; **ending qualified immunity**; **developing police officer misconduct database systems**; **passing laws such as the Community Policing Act**; **responding to calls to defund, disband and or replace the police**; **examining current use of force policies to include lethal, nonlethal, chemical and electric agents**; and **enacting the George Floyd Law Enforcement Trust and Integrity Act**.

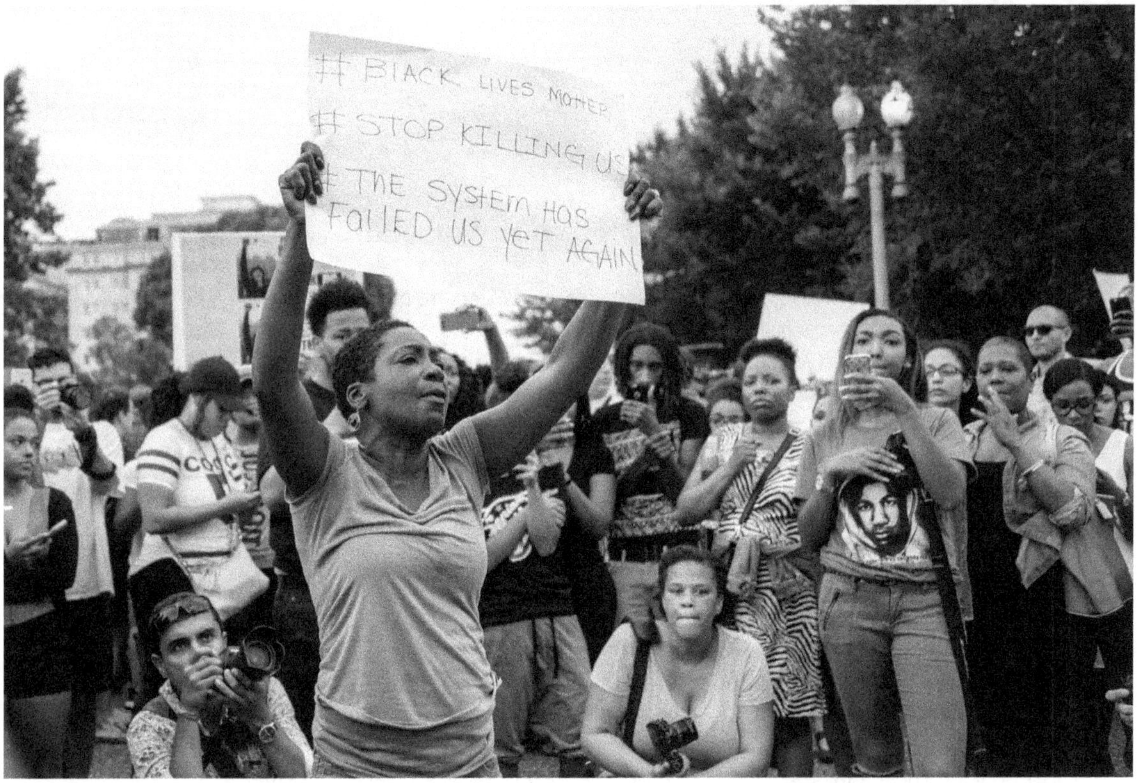

Figure 12.1 March Against Police Brutality and Racism

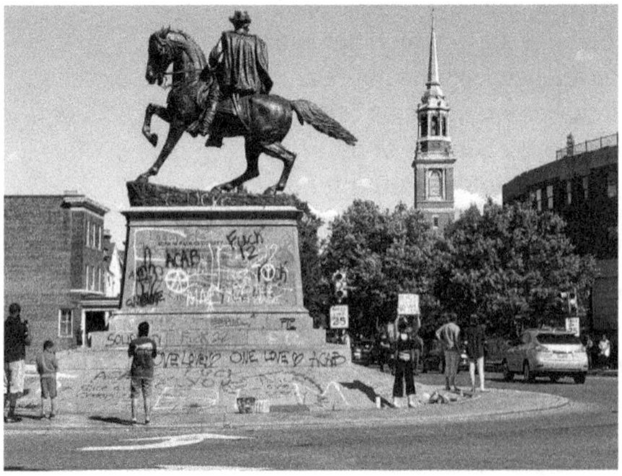

Figure 12.2 J.E.B. Stuart Monument

Figure 12.3 Black Lives Matter 2020

Citizens Review Board

The use of citizen review boards (CRB), also known as civilian oversight boards, is not a new concept in policing. They were initially implemented in the early 1950–60s. However, they recently gained renewed popularity in 2020. Following the high-profile killings of Michael Brown in Ferguson, MO in 2014 and several others, a public cry for CRBs was inevitable. These efforts started in Los Angeles, Chicago, Kansas City, Missouri, and Detroit. Over 140–150 CRBs are in existence (see table 12.1), according to the National Association for Civilian Oversight for Law Enforcement (NACOLE, 2020).

Figure 12.4 Gonzalez Police Reform 9

Most common models:

- **Investigation-focused model**
  - conducts routine, independent investigations of complaints made against police officers
  - may replace or duplicate internal affairs processes
- **Review-focused model**
  - focuses on completing or reviewing completed investigations or complaints by internal affairs
  - recommendations are made to the chief, but they can also hold community meetings
- **Auditor/Monitor model**
  - focuses on broad, holistic patterns of complaint, quality of complaint, discipline and punishment rendered
  - conducts systematic reviews on policies, practices, training, and recommendations for improvement

Types of authorities:

- Varying levels of authorities ranging from:
  - independent complaints
  - subpoena records

  - impose discipline
  - recommend discipline
  - review discipline
  - hear citizen appeals
  - hear officer appeals

Internal and external complaints:

- External complaints:
  - excessive force
  - use of force
  - courtesy
  - profiling
  - improper arrest
  - driving
- Internal complaints
  - use of force
  - unbecoming conduct
  - driving
  - harassment

Features of CRBs:

- Size: ranges from 2–50 individuals
- Term length: limited (1–3 years) or unlimited
- Qualification of members
  - Knowledge or experience
  - Training
  - College education
  - Must be former law enforcement officer
  - Must not have family law enforcement officer
  - Must not be elected official
  - Residency
  - Registered voter
  - No criminal history
  - Recommendation or appointment by city official

TABLE 12.1 Examples of Civilian Review Board Models in North America

INVESTIGATION	REVIEW	AUDITOR/ MONITOR	OTHER	NONE
Atlanta, GA	Baltimore, MD	Calgary, AB	Los Angeles, CA	Arlington, TX
Chicago, IL	Boston, MA	Fresno, CA	Louisville, KY	Baltimore County, MD
Honolulu, HI	Charlotte-Meck, NC	Los Angeles, CA	Memphis, TN	Columbus, OH
Long Beach, CA	Detroit, MI	Wichita, KS	Minneapolis, MN	Fairfax, VA (both)
Montreal, QC	Houston, TX		Ottawa, ON	Miami-Dade County, FL

INVESTIGATION	REVIEW	AUDITOR/ MONITOR	OTHER	NONE
New York, NY	Las Vegas, NV		Peel Region, ON	Montgomery County, MD
Philli, PA	Milwaukee, WI		St. Louis, MO	Nashville, TN
Salt Lake City, UT	Oklahoma City		Toronto, ON	Pittsburg, PA
Seattle, WA	Omaha, NE		Vancouver, BC	Raleigh, NC
	Orlando, FL			Tulsa, OK
	Phoenix, AZ			Virginia Beach, VA
	Prince George's County, MD			
	San Antonio, TX			
	San Diego, CA			
	Tampa, FL			
	Tucson, AZ			

Investigative model:

- Atlanta PD, *Atlanta Citizen Review Board* (ACRB)
- Seattle PD, *Office of Police Accountability* (OPA)

Review model:

- Philadelphia PD, *Police Advisory Commission* (PAC)
- Las Vegas PD, *Partnered with Office of Community Oriented Policing Services* (COPS Office)
- Tampa PD, *Citizens Review Board*

Auditor model:

- Fresno PD, *Office of Independent Review* (OIR)
- Los Angeles County Sheriff, *Sheriff Civilian Oversight Commission* (SCOC)

Other type models:

- Fairfax PD has a blend of review panel and auditor models. The auditor will review all investigations related to death and serious injury cases, use of force, and issues a report to the board of county supervisors on a yearly basis. The auditor also acts as an ongoing administrative support to the Fairfax County Civilian Review Panel.
- The citizens review panel will serve a 3-year term with a 2-term limit and will review abuse of authority complaints and serious misconducts. Both auditor and CRP will issue reports to the public, county board, and police chief yearly reports of complaints, policies, training, and practices, etc.

Objectives of CRBs:

- transparency
- independent investigations
- improving accountability
- improving public trust and legitimacy

- engaging the community
- demystifying police internal affairs investigations
- deterring police misconduct

Advantages and disadvantages:
Varies per jurisdiction and per model type.

- Advantages:
  - independence, transparency, public confidence, community perspective, officer acceptance, broad range of oversight, policy focus
- Disadvantages:
  - investigative experience, expense, complaint reception, timeliness, report challenges, diversity representation

Resolution and types or dispositions:

- unfounded—nothing occurred
- exonerated—actions were justified, lawful, and proper
- not sustained—investigation failed to find evidence to clearly prove or disprove allegation
- sustained—investigation shows enough evidence to clearly prove allegation

Overall summation/cautions:

- community has a role in complaint review
- oversight works best when it is triggered automatically
- oversight should be transparent
- standalone from police and political affairs
- there is no one best model that fits all—local needs, structure, history
- each agency is different in its culture, political makeup, and social climate
- best fit rather than best practice

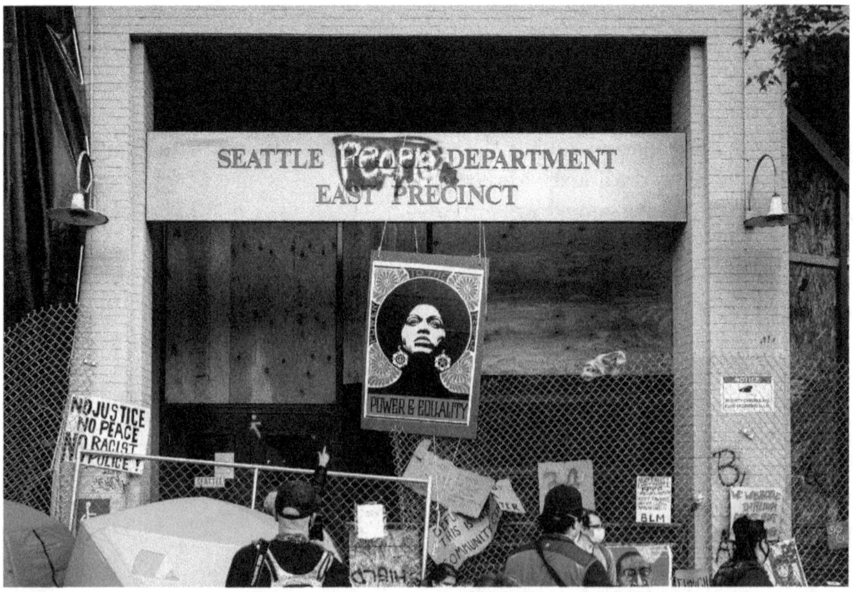

Figure 12.5 Seattle People Department

CRBs are being explored nationwide. However, the reality of their recent popularity is ironic when, in fact, most of the high-profile incidents across the country occurred in jurisdictions that already had CRBs in place. One common error is the assumption that one jurisdiction's successful implementation of a CRB will be successful in their community as well. An important fact to note is that there is no one specific CRB strategy that will fit all agencies and jurisdictions, each agency and jurisdiction should examine what exactly their community members, along with their public safety agencies, want when determining the specific brand that will fit their locality. The mentality of having one strategy fit for all localities is presumably flawed.

Box 12.1 Police Chief Larry D. Boone: What Does the Future of Policing Look Like?

Figure 12.6 Police Chief Larry Boone

Considering an ideal future of policing, I recall the 1987 film *RoboCop*, which presented a futuristic cyborg hardwired to serve, protect, and uphold the law without bias—but that future has still not arrived.

However, technology will continue to be the most noticeable evidence of the transformation in police and criminal conduct. This high-tech "catch me if you can" game will place demands on law enforcement to strategically hire those that are technologically savvy in policing software and cybercrime investigations. Nearly every police department across the nation is facing manpower challenges due to personnel vacancies. Recruiting the next generation of law enforcement officers reflective of the community will be a challenging task, as the profession is no longer viewed as a career, but merely a job. Considering current events surrounding high-profile, conflicting law enforcement encounters with minorities, diversifying police organizations will be daunting. Hence, some police departments, regardless of their efforts, will never realize a diverse police force. Nonetheless, they will need to focus their recruiting efforts on candidates who are culturally competent, emotionally intelligent, and possess a solid foundation in critical decision-making regardless of diversity. Currently, some police departments are actively seeking those skill sets to improve performance and reduce the number of incidents involving officer misconduct.

Police departments will continue to be measured in two areas: crime reduction and public trust developed through community engagement. Research suggests that evidence-based policing strategies such as focused deterrence do have a measurable, positive effect on crime. Conversely, research also suggests community relations strategies have no positive impact on crime. Yet, during recent protests in response to the George Floyd incident, some cities experienced no rioting or looting because of 'authentic and legitimate' police and citizen relationships. This did not go unnoticed by city government and community stakeholders. Moreover, in the future, police departments will need to invest in 'authentic' social capital with the communities they serve, particularly those in urban settings where historically civil unrest has occurred. In my opinion, the future of policing will continue to be influenced by the same two variables that exist today—technology (record management systems, body worn cameras, social media, and smart phones) and human capital.

Far too often, there is a tendency to place too much confidence in technological tools. As I reflect on the Minneapolis incident and how it forever changed the law enforcement profession, the following held true in 1829 and still holds true today, but we have given it a fancy name—procedural justice:

Police, at all times, should maintain a relationship with the public that gives reality to the historic tradition that the police are the public, and the public are the police; the police being only members of the public who are paid to give full-time attention to duties which are incumbent on every citizen in the interests of community welfare and existence.

—Sir Robert Peel

In the future, would it not be wonderful if we could hardwire future officers to a high degree of confidence through the selection process and training, to serve, protect, and uphold the law without bias? Perhaps this is not such a stretch. As a profession, we are better today than we were yesterday, and we will be better tomorrow than we are today.

Choke Holds

Question to Students

What are your thoughts on this specific proposed reform? Give pros and cons along with examples to support your position.

What are choke holds? When are officers permitted to use choke holds? The basic definition of this technique is a hold that consists of applying strong pressure to the neck that prevents blood and oxygen circulation to the brain. Choke holds or neck restraints have been permitted in law enforcement training for decades. Most are applied and justified in a life-or-death situations. However, recent events involving this technique being unjustly used on individuals has caused it to be revisited or banned in several localities. Prior to the incident with Eric Garner in New York, there had actually been several other chokehold deaths, to include but not limited to: James Thomson in Chicago, IL; Allen Simpson in Dallas, TX; Rodney Lynch in Gallup, NM; Dustin Boone in Las Vegas, NV; Roger Owensby, Jr. in Cincinnati, OH; Carl Glen Wheat in Amarillo, TX; Gerald Arthur in New Orleans, LA; Torris Harris in Chattanooga, TN; and many more (Daugert, 2020).

When Can Officers Use the Choke Hold Technique?

As mentioned above, it is justified only in a life-or-death situation wherein the officer's life is in grave danger and they have no other means of being freed from the physical restraint of a suspect. The move to ban this technique may have both positive and negative perceptions. In the positive aspect, it lessens overzealous and macho officers from abusing their physical authority and restraint over innocent subjects they encounter. On the other hand, if an officer is involved in a physical altercation where a choke hold is necessary to break free or to subdue a hostile subject, the officer may not be able to pursue this technique if their locality has banned it, potentially leading to death or grave injury of the officer involved. Ultimately, this technique can be a deadly force if applied without due regard, and each locality should have to examine their use of force policy and determine its compliance or not.

No-Knock Warrants

According to Cornell Law School, a no-knock warrant is a search warrant that authorizes officers to enter a premise or structure without announcing or making their presence known. The basis for this type of warrant is to prevent suspects in an investigation from destroying or concealing pertinent evidence from the police. This type of warrant has its positive and negative perceptions and is mainly issued by a magistrate or a judge. Due to the number of high-profile deaths that have resulted from the no-knock warrant, such that of Breonna Taylor, several agencies are starting to reevaluate this search initiative, and even ban this type of practice. Even though it is advantageous not to knock and alert the presence of law enforcement officers, no-knock warrants can be risky when there is no regard for liability nor quality of life. Some localities are seeking to abolish this practice, whereas others are increasing the criteria needed to issue them, only allowing sitting judges to evaluate, administer, and sign them rather than magistrates. There are significant differences between a magistrate and a sitting judge. While they can both hear facts to determine probable cause; a judge has more authority, experience, and leverage in deciding whether the warrant is justified or not. Ultimately, as mentioned with the other proposed reforms, each locality can thoroughly examine this practice and advise on a case-by-case basis whether it is advantageous or not for execution in an active investigation.

On December 7, 2020, Virginia's governor signed Breonna's Law, banning the no-knock warrant in the commonwealth of Virginia. Virginia is one of a few states that have implemented this law into action since the death of Breonna Taylor. Others may follow this initiative depending on their constituents.

Question to Students

What are your thoughts on this specific proposed reform? Give pros and cons along with examples to support your position.

Peer Intervention Programs

Mr. George Floyd did not die instantaneously. He suffocated, suffering a slow death while three other officers watched. This was noted by Paul Noel, the deputy superintendent of the New Orleans Police Department. Noel further explained that his department has started peer intervention training several years prior to this incident. This training consists of officers acting swiftly to intervene when others are engaged in misconduct such as excessive use of force, planting evidence, falsifying police reports, and other various types of misconduct. Peer intervention may lead to a reduction

Question to Students

What are your thoughts on this specific proposed reform? Give pros and cons along with examples to support your position.

in criminal charges, firings, or deaths of those persons that are recipients of officer misconduct. Matt Vasilogambros, a staff writer for Pew Research Center, noted this clearly in his 2020 article "Training Police to Step in and Prevent Another George Floyd." This training is being implemented nationwide, wherein officers are obligated to act if another is engaged in misconduct. Some jurisdictions are only requiring officers to say something if they *see* something, whereas others are charging their officers to *do* something. In some localities, criminal charges can be brought against officers who stood by and watched misconduct actions without intervening. This reform is necessary. While the New Orleans Police Department has faced significant challenges in the past with their handling of various situations, they are in the forefront of administering and enforcing peer intervention training. This reform is meant to bring down the long-standing blue wall of silence—the concept that officers have stood by and watched other officers perform acts of misconduct and not said or done anything. Some say this concept is a myth. However, others contradict this notion by pointing to the variety of instances wherein it occurred. The Northern Virginia Criminal Justice Academy has noted that they will be implementing this training for incoming recruits very soon, and several other agencies have started implementing it. Another local agency noted their use of the Ethical Policing is Courageous program. This training seeks to teach officers to intervene if they see a situation arising between another officer and a subject—they can de-escalate the situation and separate both parties. It also teaches officers to withstand harsh verbal insults and non-serious physical contact, such as pushing, shoving, and spitting, rather than reverting to the old ways where they justified the use physical force for such minor occurrences. Regardless of the implementation, this type of police reform is being explored in multiple agencies nationwide. The implementation of peer intervention programs has the potential to cultivate a new culture among police that encourages growth by reinforcing positive conduct.

Assault and Battery on a Police Officer: Felony or Misdemeanor?

While this particular reform is not being examined in most states, Virginia is leading the reexamination of this code section. According to the current Virginia code, 18.2-57 Section A, anyone who commits a simple assault on another person is guilty of Class 1 misdemeanor and can be convicted to a sentence of at least six months. Section B states if the assault is done because of the victim's race, sexual orientation, color, national origin, disability, or gender identity, then the person shall be guilty of a Class 6 felony and convicted to a term of confinement of at least six months. Section C covers assault against several professions to include law enforcement officers, judges, corrections officers, emergency medical service workers, and also behavioral health and human services workers. Such a person will be guilty of a Class 6 felony and be sentenced to a mandatory minimum of six months confinement (Commonwealth of Virginia, 2020). Certain lawmakers in Virginia are exploring the possibility of reclassifying the charge for assault on the aforementioned workers from a felony to a misdemeanor in instances where the assault does not result in serious bodily injury. This proposal is gaining traction in Virginia legislature. However, partisan politics places a substantial obstacle in the way of such reform passing the general assembly. Proponents of this reform argue that it will

Box 12.2 Brian Hackett: Thoughts on the Future of Policing

Figure 12.7 Agent Brian Hackett

The future of policing will be more complex in an everchanging environment due to the attention from politicians, academics, and United States citizens who are demanding the change in policing. A review of policing in the past gives us a good indication on how far policing has evolved and what it is likely to become. Policing half a century ago is much different than in today's climate. Policing even a decade ago was much different due to the more modern technology used by police officers today.

The future of policing will feature more police accountability, transparency in investigations, better training, de-escalation techniques, laws that protect citizens, and possibly the changing of when qualified immunity can be asserted by police officers. Citizens demand that officers be held accountable for use of force and that transparency in investigations become public investigations. Citizen review boards are becoming more normal. Citizens also ask for better trained officers to be able to deal with individuals with crisis, substance abuse, and mental health problems. Crisis intervention training, de-escalation technique training, and body-worn cameras are the focus of strong requests citizens make to heads of police organizations. There have been calls to protect the citizens from police misconduct. Much of those calls are for ending qualified immunity. Supreme Court rulings in previous police Use of Force cases makes this very hard to do. *Graham v. Connor* (1989) and *Tennessee v. Garner* (1985) rulings have made it harder to prosecute police officers when there is not a clearly established law and also gives reasonable officers the ability to make split-second decisions without 20/20 hindsight from persons who were not there with the officer. There is potential for future legal cases brought to the Supreme Court to change this through case law or politicians drafting legislation that gives more leeway for prosecutors to charge officers in the future.

Lastly, policing in the future should evolve into a different approach to achieve better outcomes with the citizens. There is no arresting away all of society's ills. Agencies can no longer wait for a use of force incident in their communities before trying to enact change in their departments. After the 1999 Columbine High School shooting, departments changed the way they responded to active violence incidents. The mindsight changed from "if it can happen here" to "when it happens this is how we will respond." The same approach has to be taken toward use of force that often-become national incidents, sparking large scale protests. Solving a community's problems should not be left to only law enforcement when there is a breakdown or failure of the system. Agencies need to establish an approach that involves public and private organizations. The future of policing is identifying the needs of the community and using these established relationships before, during, and after someone is involved in the criminal justice system to solve problems. There can be no cookie cutter approach as each community is different and has their own distinct people and needs.

Question to Students

What are your thoughts on this specific proposed reform? Give pros and cons along with examples to support your position.

reduce jail time as well as decrease the overwhelming population of those incarcerated within our criminal justice system. Others opposing this proposal advise that the statute will send the wrong message to those who wish to do harm to law enforcement officers, one that conveys that assaulting an officer is okay. Additionally, such opponents argue that it will lead to more negative physical interactions between the police and the citizens they protect.

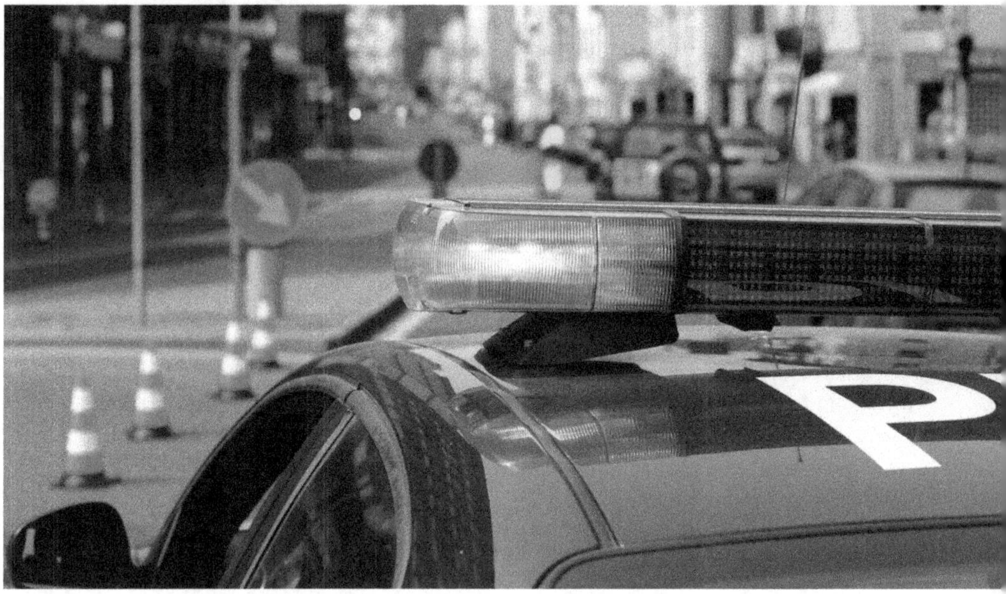

Figure 12.8 Blue Sirens of Police Car

Qualified Immunity

Question to Students

What are your thoughts on this specific proposed reform? Give pros and cons along with examples to support your position.

What is qualified immunity? Discussed briefly in previous chapters, qualified immunity, according to Cornell Law, addresses two distinct interests. First, it attempts to hold public officials accountable for their actions if irresponsibly and inappropriate while in performance of their duties and responsibility. The second interest is that qualified immunity protects these officials from harassment, liability, and distraction when they perform their duties and responsibilities reasonably. This concept can present some confusion, and I will try my best to explain it as clearly as possible. Qualified immunity protects or prevents public officials, including law enforcement officers, from frivolous civil lawsuits alleging that they violated an individual's rights (Cornell Law School, 2020). It still allows citizens to sue police officers, but only in cases where there are clearly established statutory or constitutional violations. While officials are perceived to be fully protected from legal consequences, this is not the case when misconduct violates the Constitution, specifically the 8th and 14th amendment.

The discussion of ending qualified immunity has caused a divide among several legislators in specific parts of the country. According to some current social contributions, proponents argue that ending qualified immunity will keep officers from abusing their power. Opponents to ending qualified immunity argue that this reform is being garnered by the private attorneys who will benefit financially if qualified immunity is taken away from public officials.

It is also important to know the history of qualified immunity and its historical applications. This concept has ties that goes back to the civil rights movement, specifically the Civil Action for Deprivation of Rights (Miller, 2020). In response to the widespread harassment of freed slaves following the Civil War, the US government put words into action, putting legal protections in place. In a nutshell, every government official who clearly violates someone's constitutional rights is liable to pay damages to the person who suffers the incursion—so freed slaves had an avenue for legal recourse if their rights were violated. A prominent example is the *Connick v. Thompson* (2011) case.

It is noted clearly that the origin of this concept has strong historical applications, and therefore several states are examining whether it is needed in this current day.

Research the *Connick v. Thompson* (2011) case and discuss its application to the topic of qualified immunity.

Police Officer Misconduct Database System

This particular initiative is being explored nationwide, and while Chapter 8 provided a clear and effective definition of police misconduct, it is important to expand on this concept in light of the police reform movement. There are various nonprofit, private, and for-profit institutions readily available that strive for such a database. In essence, the community is seeking a nationwide system that tracks officer misconduct for various acts. The major reason for this push is to deter the officer from obtaining police employment in a different locality after committing misconduct. Before we fully discuss this section, it is important to know the meaning of lateral transfer. Lateral transfer means that an already certified police officer can transfer to another agency that accepts lateral transfers with the proper training and experience. The accepting agency will also conduct a shorter and condensed academy for the lateral transferee to become acclimated to their policies and practices. There have been several incidents in which police officers were involved in misconduct, such as lying and other minor issues, and were given the chance to resign in lieu of termination. When they resign, their personnel file will not indicate they were terminated. It will only indicate that they resigned with no further detail. As a result, in rare occasions, they can obtain full police employment within other localities without communication with the officer's host agency where they engaged in misconduct. To resolve this issue, the public demanded a database that would note officer misconduct and thereby provide transparency among departments as well as to outside agencies prior to hiring an officer laterally into their agency. How far can this system extend? Would it be made public for all to see and know these officers that have committed such acts? Or would the database only be accessible by other governmental agencies that are actively conducting a background check on an officer? These are all intriguing questions that need to be further addressed in the ongoing debates on this subject. Lastly, President Donald Trump recently signed an executive order that gives authority to the US attorney general to create a nationwide database to track police officer's history of misconduct. The database will primarily track officers' terminations, criminal convictions, and any civil judgements against officers for excessive use of force (Executive Orders, 2020). Such an action signals that a nationwide database is inevitable. Some jurisdictions may choose to implement theirs locally or await the federal mandate when the time comes.

Question to Students

What are your thoughts on this specific proposed reform? Give pros and cons along with examples to support your position.

Figure 12.9 Denouncement

Community Policing Act

This bill was recently passed in Virginia and has the potential of being explored in other states. Its intention is to reduce biased policing. The statute requires local and state officers to record the following information for every motor vehicle or investigative stop made: race; ethnicity; age; gender; reason(s) for the stop; the location of the stop; whether there was a citation, warning, or arrest; if any arrest or citation was issued and what it was issued for; and lastly, whether the person or the vehicle was searched (Torian, 2020). Furthermore, the bill requires each local agency to collect and report all complaints on excessive use of force to the state police. The bill also requires the director of the Department of Criminal Justice Services (DCJS) to furnish a report to the governor, the general assembly, and attorney general by July of the following year. Such reports serve to track various trends within agencies in order to reduce biased policing. Will this reporting process be accurate? Will all incidents be captured? These are some of the limitations most state, federal, and state agencies face in reporting crime data to the public. It captures somewhat accurate information only if the important is reported correctly or reported at all. These are some of the issues some agencies would have to work diligently on. Limitations such as these will require further research to determine the efficacy of these reports in mitigating biased policing.

Defund, Disband, and Replace the Police

This concept has been voiced by various groups that seek to reform policing (see figures 12.11 and 12.12). These terms seem to be used interchangeably, but it is important to understand the distinct meaning of each of them. "Defund" the police does not mean abolishing or disbanding policing entirely. It instead refers to reallocating the resources, particularly financial, from local, state, and federal agencies to other governmental and nonprofit sectors that assist in societal and humanitarian services such as social services, human services, violence prevention programs, drug and alcohol prevention programs, etc. The premise behind this is to limit police involvement wherein civilian social workers and other trained therapists could be better suited to address such issues. Resources will be channeled to train more of these services rather than toward active police intervention. The terms "disband" and "replace" the police go hand-in-hand, through which proponents are calling

Box 12.3 Deputy Chief of Police Dan Kelly: Thoughts on the Future of Policing

I am a son of an officer (retired), the father of an officer, and I am currently an officer. As I begin my 34th year in the field of policing, I am highly encouraged about its future. While it may appear daunting, it is also exciting because the future of policing is influenced daily through the collective choices we make.

Figure 12.10 Deputy Chief of Police Dan Kelly

The future of policing depends on shared leadership and the ability to function simultaneously with change and tradition in a dissonant and transforming environment of crime, politics, civil unrest, and reforms. Policing must demonstrate vulnerability to effectively collaborate on a holistic policing model to safeguard against infinite threats within finite boundaries. Policing must thrive in change while remaining structured and accountable.

The future will foster change through policing reforms and implementing national standards. Expanding procedural justice, social justice, diversity, and bias-free training will elevate in importance. Changes in technology will challenge the limitations of current laws and new court decisions will alter the boundaries of police training, tactics, and community relations. New laws will be written, societal expectations will evolve, and what is acceptable today may not be acceptable tomorrow. While national reforms and standards are needed to further accountability and professionalism, it is vital to remember police agencies earn trust and legitimacy locally with the community they serve.

In unison with external change, there is tremendous value for the future of policing to focus on what it controls: upholding the constitution, protecting rights, ethics, transparency, hiring, training, community engagement, leadership, and assisting elected and community leaders to understand issues as they weigh changes to law and policy. Remaining principled in these areas is critical to navigate change and constructs that may not change, including that a primary purpose of government is to provide for public safety, that government will enact laws which require enforcement, and that enforcement involves human interaction. Therefore, investing in recruitment, retention, training, and wellness of officers is a priority.

I am enthusiastically optimistic for the future of policing because we can deliberately and continuously choose to improve our collective tomorrow with choices we make today. When I envision the future of policing, it seems reasonable to imagine the efficacy of being safe anytime and anyplace in your community. The only way to accomplish this aspiration is through engagement and collaboration, not division. We will become stronger as a nation, a community, and a profession by embracing transformational growth, building resilience through vulnerability, and strengthening our commitment through leadership.

to abolish the police all-in-all and make recommendations for people to police themselves. Others have noted that they are in favor of having regular citizens police themselves. Several influential factors have fueled these outcries of defunding and disbanding the police. One notable factor is frustration from the recent highly publicized police encounters, particularly with minorities (as mentioned at the beginning of the chapter). Some of these outcries are influenced by professional affiliations, and the remainder have been going on since the Civil Rights Movement. From a criminal justice point of view, policing is much needed to provide law and order. From a personal standpoint, what would society look like without the presence of the police? These are tough questions that each locality will have to discuss moving forward. There is always the balance of power wherein the police are held accountable for their actions by the federal government. However, who holds the federal government accountable for their actions? There should always be one level of higher accountability in order to have a peaceful society.

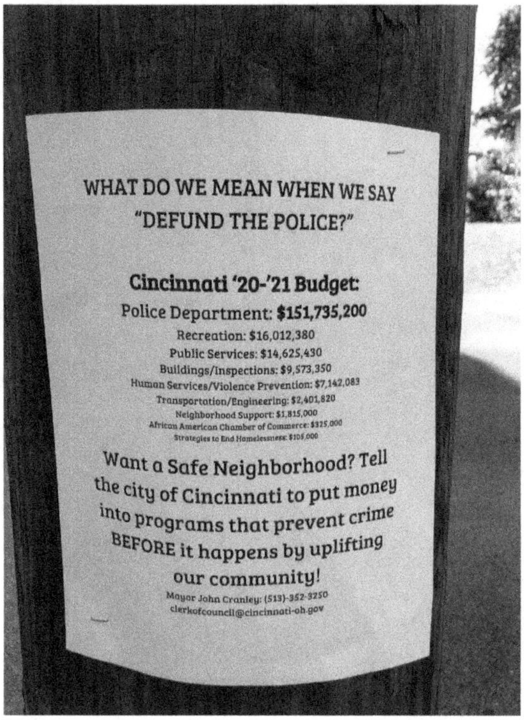

Figure 12.11 Defund the Police: June 9, 2020

Figure 12.12 Defund the Police

Use of Force Polices: Lethal, Nonlethal, Chemical, and Electric Agents

In Chapter 9, under the less-lethal force section, use of force is discussed briefly. However, based on the recent high-profile incidents involving police and minorities, several locality officials are urging their police agencies to re-examine their use of force policies. Some have pushed for their agencies to make use of force policies public for all to see. Some additional reforms surrounding police use of force policies include: enabling officers to use more verbal judo in de-escalating physical situations, banning choke or strangle holds on civilians, developing a stronger use of force continuum plan, banning officers from shooting at moving vehicles, requiring officers to intervene and stop excessive force, ensuring that officers report each time they use force or threaten to use force on those they interact with, and reexamining "shooting at fleeing felons" policies. These are all recommendations that are being actively discussed at various localities. Several other agencies are exploring the more frequent use of less-lethal force options, such as chemical and other electric agents, to disable an active and resisting subject. Such options reduce the mentality that the officer always resort to their firearm to address a violent individual. Most of these types of equipment are already being developed, or are on the market for use. Some are very expensive, whereas others have already been circulating the policing and protecting arena, such as the pepper ball and taser projectiles. These technologies can be effective at preventing loss of life with proper usage.

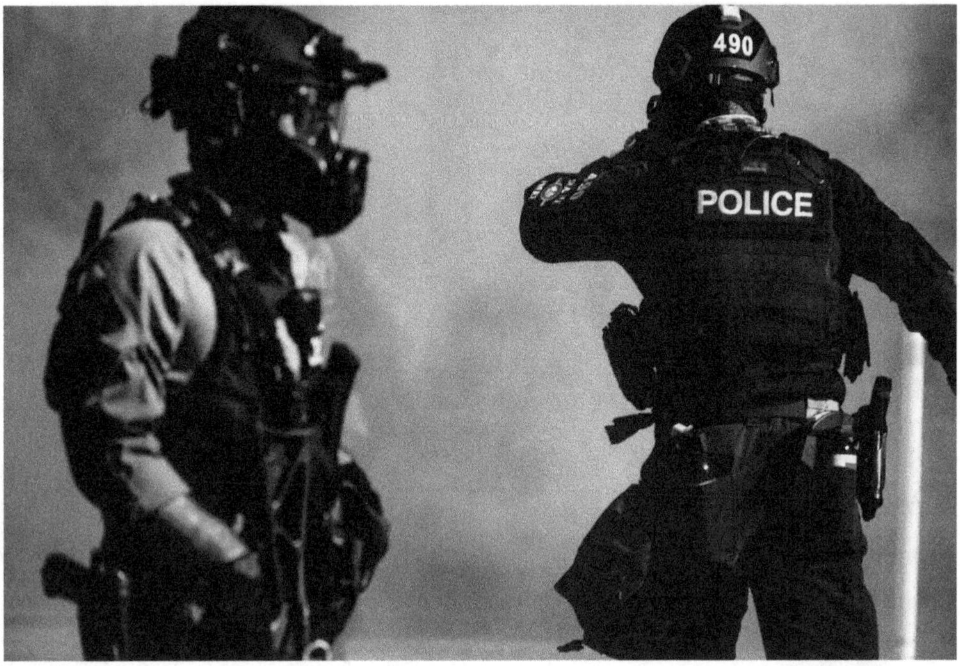

Figure 12.13 Fog of War

According to the International Association of Chiefs of Police the two most applicable supreme court cases in police use of lethal force are the *Tennessee v Garner* and the *Graham v Connor* cases, the comparison is collectively noted as the **Garner-Graham Standard** (Callahan 2020). In comparing the Tennessee v Garner case and the Graham v Connor case, it is evident that their outcomes are similar. Mike Callahan, a supervisory special agent for the FBI, noted in his article "Jettisoning the lethal force gold standard" that "law enforcement officers may use deadly force when they have probable cause similar to an objectively reasonable belief, that a suspect poses a significant threat of death or serious bodily harm to the officer or others." (Callahan 2020). Major local and state agencies are amending their use of force policy statements away from *just* "a fleeing felon". The felon must be an *imminent* threat, or a *violent* fleeing felon, at which point an officer can justify the use of lethal force. These groundbreaking cases lay the foundational basis for agencies and local and state governments to amend their policies as the community policing era progresses.

Research both cases and discuss their applications to current policing style regarding use of force policies.

In addition, in order to reduce further use of lethal force incidents between officers and individuals with mental illness or emotional disorders, several large municipal agencies are also exploring establishing unarmed crisis intervention teams to respond to non-violent calls for service-on a completely opposite scale such as the fire department, San Francisco Fire Department. The LAPD fully supports this endeavor as well as noted by (CBSLA Staff, 2020) in This endeavor can be discussed in two parts. Firstly, it may be advantageous in reducing the negative encounters between officers and individuals with mental illness or emotional disorders. Second, it places the crisis intervention member in the presence of most unpredictable situations. These situations are mostly very calm, but can turn violent within minutes. Some agencies are responding to this concern by sending social service workers with the officers on these special crisis intervention details.

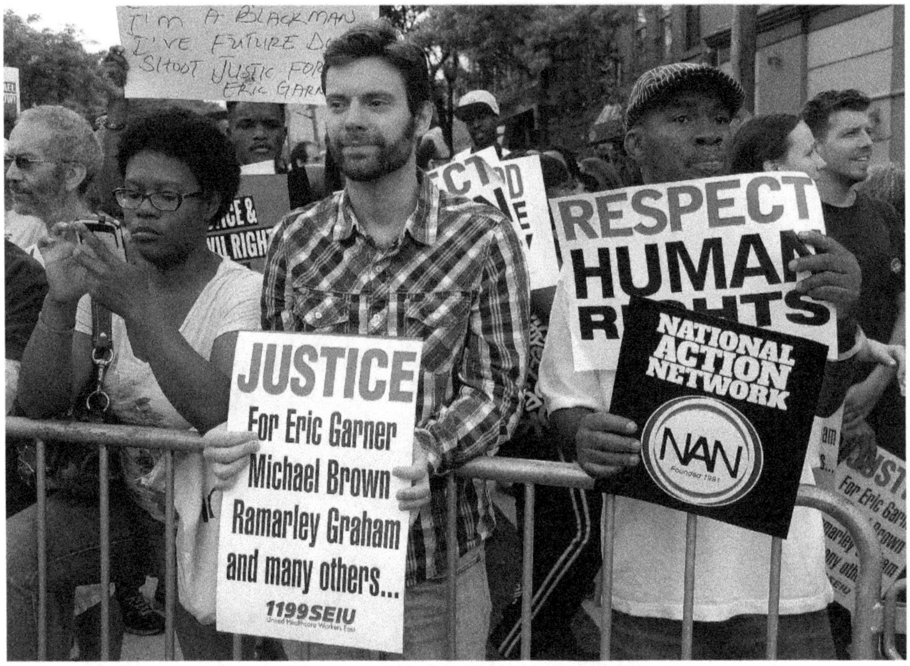

Figure 12.14 TAG Garner Protest

George Floyd Law Enforcement Trust and Integrity Act

This bill was named in memory of George Floyd (see figures 12.15 and 12.19). It is currently being discussed by the nation's top lawmakers and covers the following reforms (Jackson Lee 2020):

- mandating all local, state, and federal law enforcement bodies report data to the Justice Department on uses of deadly force involving police officers
- giving federal grants to law enforcement agencies which devise new programs for oversight or hiring, such as bringing on more diverse officers and agents
- creating a federal task force to coordinate the investigation and prosecution of law enforcement agencies
- creating a set of federal minimum standards for police departments, standards which do not currently exist

It is important to note that these bills are introduced and have yet to go through the procedural process of being voted on and passed by Congress. Some bills can be politically charged, wherein they must overcome partisan obstacles before finally being voted on. If this one is passed, police agencies will have to adhere to the four mandates noted above.

These proposals have either been implemented or are currently being reviewed by various localities. This chapter will highlight each of these proposals and will also discuss its applicable advantages and disadvantages to both sets of groups. It is also important to note that these reforms are everchanging, and by the time of the publication of this textbook several more will have been proposed. However, these are the foundational points for current 21st century police reforms.

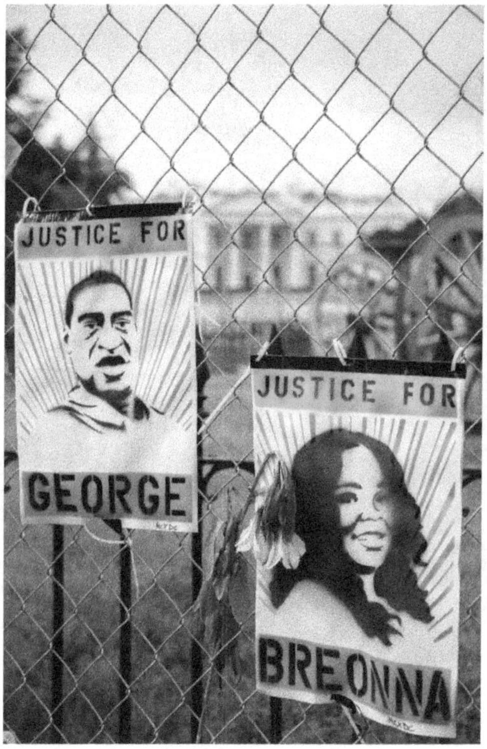

Figure 12.15 Signs in Front of the White House Show Support for the Black Lives Matter

Figure 12.16 Street Art, Chicago Avenue Minneapolis

Moving Forward

Much can be said on the topic of moving forward from a personal, professional, and academic standpoint. From a personal standpoint, I spent a decade of my life as a police officer. I wore my badge proudly and performed my duties and responsibilities with respect to my department, my family, and my integrity. A lot has changed since my departure; however, my passion toward this illustrious career has fueled me to stay active with local police agencies in assisting with policy implementation, delivering efficient and diversified trainings for both in-service and recruits, assisting with selection and promotional processes, examining crime statistics, and being actively involved in the chief's advisory boards. In maintaining connections with local police departments, I have come to understand the necessity of police reform. With this knowledge, it is now my own responsibility to influence positive change in the field. Professionally, I am working with various neighboring police agencies and community organizations to assist in fostering and enriching this relationship. The rise of active community initiatives such as faith-based organizations working, business, neighborhoods, and localities wherein community members have stepped forward to address the tension that has risen between both groups is noteworthy. From an academic standpoint, Christopher Donner and David Olson (2020) presented a very informative study in their article titled "Fair Treatment in Policing: Testing the Relationship Between Internal and External Procedural Justice." In this article, 113 officers were surveyed from a local Illinois police department, focusing on the recommendation of "legitimacy" by President Obama's 21st century policing report. Legitimacy can be measured both internally and externally regarding procedural justice by how officers

Box 12.4 Retired officer Steven J. Thompson's Thoughts on The Future of Policing

In the history of policing, whenever there was a social issue that was too big for other agencies, it was assigned to the police to handle. The unfortunate result was criminalizing things which would be better handled and solved long-term by other agencies equipped to address the problem. With the events of 2020, police were forced to limit the kinds of calls for service they responded to, and citizenry nationwide have made it clear that they want less police involvement in calls. The future of policing will have police removing some of the hats they have been forced to wear for far too long so they can focus on preventing and solving violent crime, and spend more time building the relationships they need to accomplish those tasks effectively. To continue as we have for so long would be a disservice to policing and the communities we serve.

Figure 12.17 Steven Thompson Deputy Chief (Ret.)

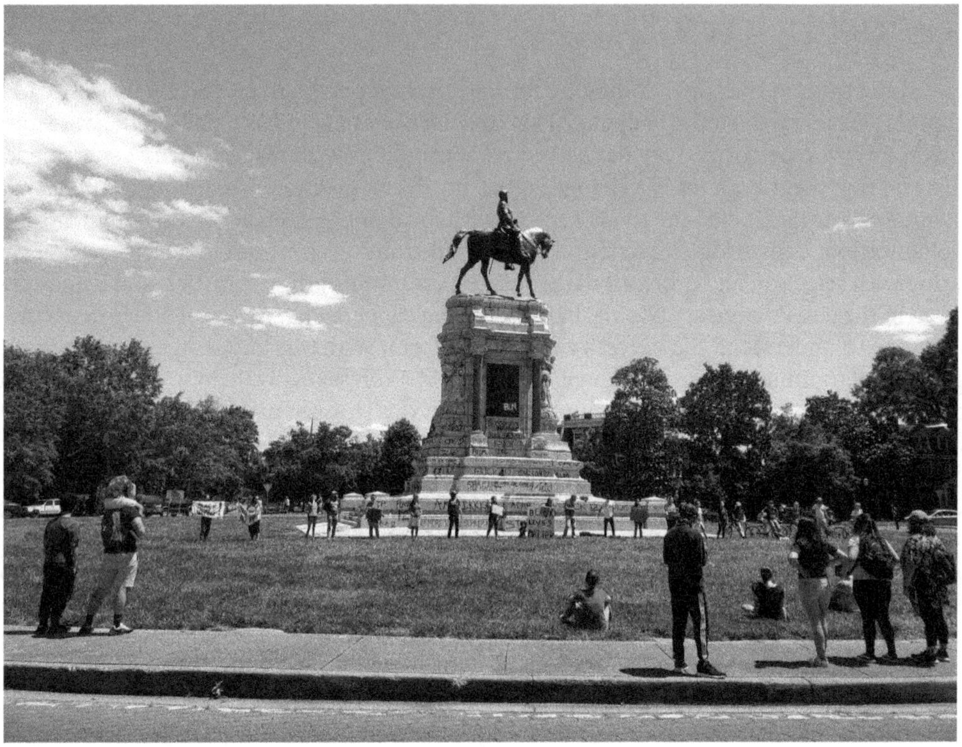

Figure 12.18 Robert E. Lee Monument

treat each other and citizens. The study evaluated if officers who were treated fairly within their own organizations would treat citizens fairly. According to their results, officers who were treated fairly within their own agencies are more likely to treat citizens with respect (Donner & Olson, 2020). Obviously, there are limitations with this study as it only captures the perceptions of one local agency. Other jurisdictions may vary in their policies, perceptions, and other factors, which may generate a different result. However, it is important to note that being treated fairly influences officers in their constant dealings with community members.

One last applicable component that has yet to be discussed and requires attention of current policing reform is the **suicide by cop** (SbC) ideation. There have been limited talks and trainings on this particular topic. According to the Police Executive Research Forum (PERF), this encounter involves an individual who attempts to commit suicide by enticing or forcing a law enforcement agent to use lethal force (2020). There are current studies that denote the prevalence of these incidents and what steps can be put in place to prevent them. Some individuals may attempt such acts due to mental illness—especially depression—or personal motivations. The following will be covered in this section: types of SbC and how to recognize SbC incidents.

PERF (2020) noted that there are two major types: planned and spontaneous. Planned SbC involves an individual who has been thinking about how to end their life but cannot bring themself to act on the ideation. Instead, they rationalize a plan in which they would attempt to threaten the police into using lethal force to end that individual's life. Spontaneous SbC is characterized by the absence of a plan or thought leading up to the event. Typically, the individual involved would make the decision to end their life during the commission of a crime in which the police were on the scene.

Training is now being circulated on this topic due to its prevalence, so that law enforcement can attempt to understand the mindset of the suicidal person. By understanding the individual and their body language, mannerisms, and demeanor, the officer can make an informed decision

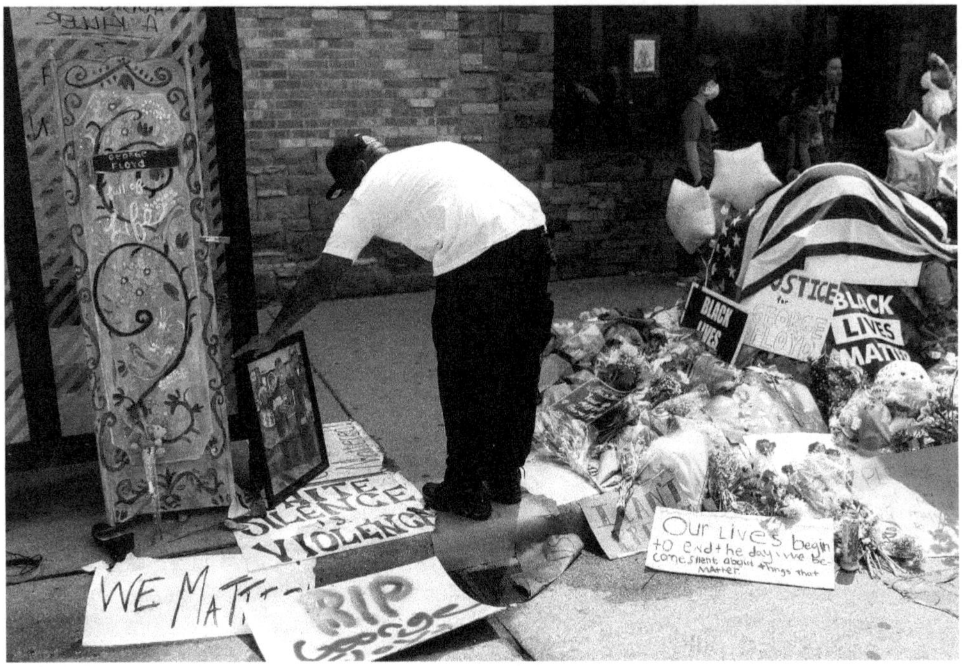

Figure 12.19 George Floyd Memorial

on how to react whether it be relating, distracting, or de-escalating the situation. Various agencies are partnering with renowned psychologists, such as Dr. John Nicoletti, in delivering high-end training for their officers when responding to these scenarios. Such trainings are being offered to police dispatchers as well, because they are oftentimes the first responders to such incidents. Some recommended steps in responding to these types of incidents include: staying calm, using less than lethal force options, engaging in continuous conversations with the individual, trying to understand the individual's position, relying on crisis intervention team training, keeping a safe distance, slowing the situation down, speaking slowly, asking 'what' questions instead of 'why' questions, and making limited requests to keep it simple. All suggestions by various policing experts to include police psychologist Dr. John Nicoletti.

Chapter Summary

Policing will continue to change as it strives to address outcries from the public while maintaining professional standards. Building the community's trust is paramount for any police chief, commissioner, and superintendent moving forward. To rebuild trust between both parties, two things need to be taken into consideration: investing in the community, and having the community invest in the police. This broad statement accounts for various initiatives such as having a chief's advisory boards consist of both community members and police; allowing the community and police to air out concerns within community organizations, events, town halls or open forums; and examining the need to shift some policing positions to be more akin to community liaison officers.

As regards a chief's advisory board, it should consist of highly engaged community members as well as former or retired police officers. Both groups can act as a sounding board to the chief regarding policing, training, recommendations, and assisting in any way possible at the discretion of the chief. This variation will bring in a diverse set of community members and police into the same working space to achieve goals for a designated agency.

Community events, townhalls, and forums wherein both groups can air out differences and concerns can be troubling for some police executives, because they often do not like or want to be in such positions. However, it is vital to have these uncomfortable conversations in order to foster a great relationship between community and police moving forward. Faith-based and business leaders can also help in providing the space and forum for such conversations or events. These leaders have access to several community outlets as well.

Several agencies are reexamining their community policing officers, altering their positions to be more of a community liaison officer. These positions can vary from a civilian with some law enforcement experience, to specialized trained officers on community policing wherein they can represent their assigned communities. These officers are ideally very knowledgeable in their assigned areas and build long lasting relationships with the key players in each community. They are tasked

Box 12.5 Perception Versus Reality

During the majority of 2020, and thus far in 2021, our nation has faced several adversities, including the pandemic, racial injustices, staggering crime rates, mental and emotional health impacts on individuals, the presidential elections, the insurrection on the nation's capital, and so on. During all these trials, one major facet that remains stagnant is law enforcement. Regardless of the untold history of law enforcement from the slave patrols to current law enforcement standards, these agencies are there to protect and serve as they have been for centuries during various eras. It is important to note that negative interactions between law enforcement agencies and the community members they serve have shaped current policing reform standards. The age of policing is undergoing an unprecedented and rapid reformation, and it will continue to evolve. This reformation will affect these agencies in a positive and a negative way: Positively, it will open the way for more opportunities for others to serve in a civilian capacity and for passionate individuals to pursue this career. Negatively, such reformations can be too drastic and can lead to a mass exodus from this career.

In the end, protecting and serving is the pivotal goal as mentioned in the community policing chapter. The serving of our community and citizens is as important as protecting them. Law enforcement advocates have echoed for years that 21st century policing has redirected from a serving mentality to more of a protecting mentality. It is imperative to note that serving the citizens will eventually lead to more citizen satisfaction for law enforcement. The reality I would like to propose to all law enforcement advocates, students, recruits, and current and former officers is that refocusing on serving our constituents fairly, effectively, and in a non-biased way will eventually lead to a more collaborative initiative between law enforcement agencies and the communities they serve. When citizens feel as they are been served without bias, without stereotype, and fairly, they will act in accordance with the laws and policies that govern their localities. Lastly, a motto I coined states, "Generalization = negativity, separation, and biases; collaboration = positivity, unity, and amicable social change."

I firmly believe once a collaborative mindset exists between both facets (community members and law enforcement), then positivity, unity, and an amicable social change will occur in this movement.

in building trust and confidence, which can take time, resources, and dedication on the officer's part. It may be a lot to ask of an officer, so these positions should be filled by willing and wanting officers who are passionate about building and reestablishing the broken trust between police and the communities they serve.

Lastly, training initiatives for both academy and in-service members ought to incorporate the topic of slave patrols into the history and current state of policing. The topic of slave patrols is critical because the phrase "rebuilding police relationships with their communities" involves acknowledging that these tumultuous relationships originated from slave patrols in the southern and colonial states and counties. These relationships between police and communities had been further eroded by the enforcement of Jim Crow laws, other segregation laws, and instances in which marginalized populations have been negatively affected by such interactions. Acknowledging these actions while working to create safer and more equitable relationships between the agencies and their communities, is a ceaseless endeavor. Future initiatives must continue building and evaluating these relationships, and agencies and communities must work in tandem to achieve shared goals.

Discussion Questions

1. What are some of the pros and cons of Citizen Review Boards? List and describe the three most common types.
2. Explain the No-Knock Warrant concept, what are some pros and cons?
3. Evaluate the assault and battery on a police officer proposed reform, note your personal and professional stance on this concept.
4. Qualified immunity has been much debated in various legislature chambers whether to keep or end it, explain its origination and provide a brief note on your position on this debate.
5. What would an ideal police officer misconduct database system look like? What are some advantages and disadvantages for this proposed national database system?
6. There have been many talks on defunding the police, give a short justification if you are for or against these proposed police reform

Resources

Atlanta Citizens Review Board (Explore online website for an example of a well-developed CRB example- https://acrbgov.org/)

National Association for Civilian Oversight for Law Enforcement (Explore online website for updates on CRBs and other applicable documentation- https://www.nacole.org/).

Bureau of Justice Statistics (This online resource/website provides countless resources on policing and its future endeavors relating to crimes, employment, and other applicable artifacts- https://www.bjs.gov/)

President's Task Force on 21st Century Policing (This guide provides the basis for several police reforms we are seeing currently, president Obama put together a brilliant team of researchers, police officers, community members, and other applicable social and healthcare workers to come up with applicable suggestions and recommendations for improving the community and policing relations- https://cops.usdoj.gov/pdf/taskforce/taskforce_finalreport.pdf)

References

Callahan, M. (2020, October). Jettisoning the lethal force gold standard. *Police Chief Magazine.*

Commonwealth of Virginia (2020). § 18.2-57. Assault and battery; penalty. *Virginia Law Library.* Retrieved from https://law.lis.virginia.gov/vacode/title18.2/chapter4/section18.2-57/

Cornell Law School (2020). Qualified immunity. *Legal Information Institute.* Retrieved October 9, 2020 from https://www.law.cornell.edu/wex/qualified_immunity.

Daugert, K. (2020). How decades of bans on police chokeholds have fallen short. *NPR.* Retrieved September 21, 2020 from https://www.npr.org/2020/06/16/877527974/how-decades-of-bans-on-police-chokeholds-have-fallen-short

Donner, C. M., & Olson, D. E. (2020). Fair treatment in policing: testing the relationship between internal and external procedural justice. *Journal of Crime & Justice, 43*(3), 393–408. https://doi-org.proxy.library.vcu.edu/10.1080/0735648X.2019.1677262

Executive Orders (2020, June 16). Executive order on safe policing for safe communities. *Whitehouse.gov.* Retrieved on October 9, 2020 from https://web.archive.org/web/20210102002202/https://www.whitehouse.gov/presidential-actions/executive-order-safe-policing-safe-communities/

Jackson Lee, S. (2020). H. R. 7100: George Floyd Law Enforcement Trust and Integrity Act of 2020. *Govtrack.* Retrieved on October 9, 2020 from https://www.govtrack.us/congress/bills/116/hr7100

Miller, M. (2020, June 9). Qualified immunity is a blank check for government overreach. *Pacific Legal Foundation.* Retrieved on October 9, 2020 from https://pacificlegal.org/qualified-immunity-government-overreach/

Torian, L. (2020). Community Policing Act: data collection and reporting requirement. *Virginia's Legislative Information System.* Retrieved on October 9, 2020 from https://lis.virginia.gov/cgi-bin/legp604.exe?201+sum+HB1250

PERF (2020). Suicide by Cop: Protocol and Training Guide. *Policeforum.org.* Retrieved October 9, 2020 from https://www.policeforum.org/suicidebycop

Vasilogambros, M. (2020, June 5). Training police to step in and prevent another George Floyd. *Pew Research.* Retrieved on October 9, 2020 from https://www.pewtrusts.org/en/research-and-analysis/blogs/stateline/2020/06/05/training-police-to-step-in-and-prevent-another-george-floyd

Figure Credits

Fig. 12.12: Andrew Ratto, "Defund the Police," https://commons.wikimedia.org/wiki/File:Defund_the_Police_(50163804498).jpg, 2020.
Fig. 12.13: Copyright © by Derek Simeone (CC by 2.0) at https://www.flickr.com/photos/dereksimeone/50161828816/in/photolist-2jqCu6w-2j716YX-2j8fe9W-2jdKk8K-2jdv9hQ-2j6E8eH-2jdsmLA-2j7YgCQ-2jaG9dN-2jhCJWZ-2jdv9mY-2jdnThf-2jb92bX-2j86u0g-2j715h5-2j715K4-2j6YzEG--2jhz2qn-2juHUwi-2jb92a9-2jrtCBU-2j64j2j-2jgiwfj-2j6.
Fig. 12.14: Copyright © by Thomas Altfather Good (CC BY-SA 4.0) at https://commons.wikimedia.org/wiki/File:TAG_Garner_Protest_02.jpg.
Fig. 12.15: Copyright © 2020 Depositphotos/renaschild.
Fig. 12.16: Copyright © by Chad Davis (CC by 2.0) at https://www.flickr.com/photos/146321178@N05/50252291881/in/photolist-2jyC8Bx-2jbJai9-2jhQZYN-2jqvhMR-2jgpX1p-2jhGUkE-2jdRVyH-2jhNNEL-2j9HcT9-2jsV6kb-2j8JBhW-2j9FVGc-2j7174w-2jeHN3V-2jqCu6w-2j716YX-2j8fe9W-2jdKk8K-2jdv9hQ-2j6E8eH-2jdsmLA-2j7YgCQ-2jaG9dN-2j.
Fig. 12.18: Copyright © by Quidster4040 (CC by 4.0) at https://commons.wikimedia.org/wiki/File:-George_Floyd_protest_Robert_E_Lee_statue_2020-05-31.jpg.
Fig. 12.19: Copyright © by Lorie Shaull (CC BY-SA 2.0) at https://commons.wikimedia.org/wiki/File:George_Floyd_Memorial_2020-05-27.jpg.

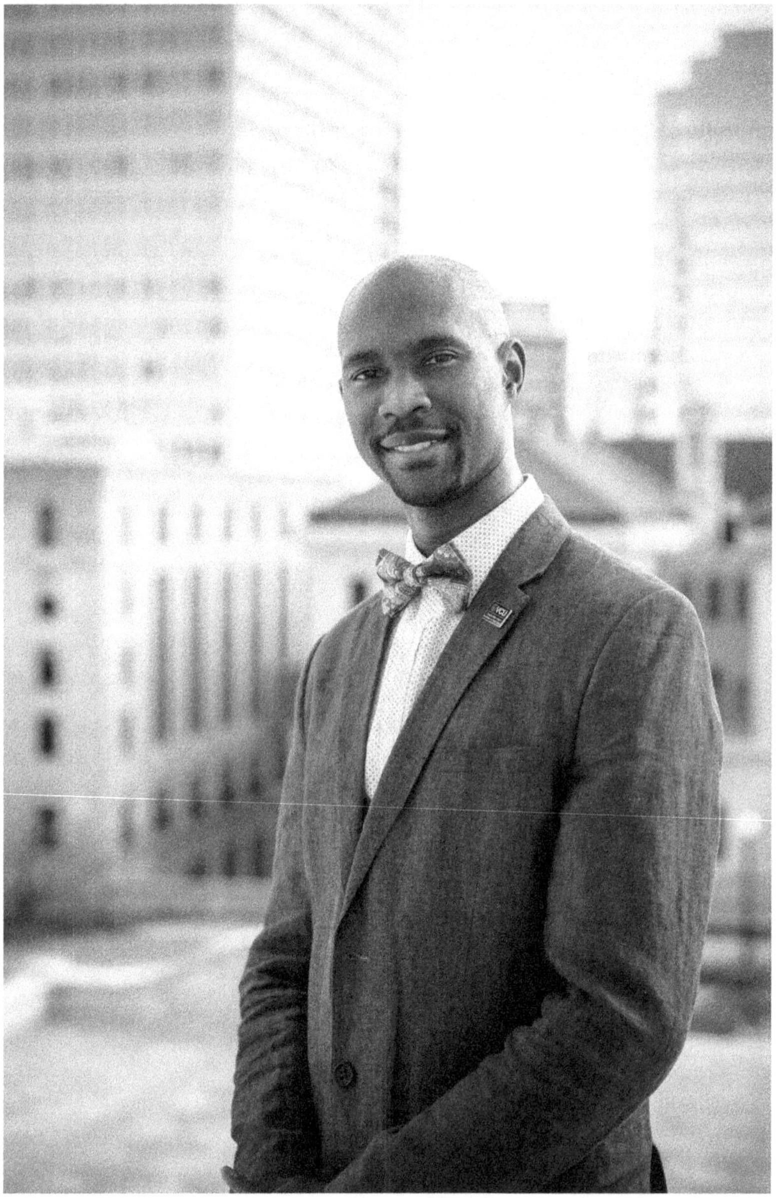

ABOUT THE AUTHOR

Chernoh M. Wurie was born in a small town called Kenema, in Sierra Leone. Navigating childhood in the midst of this nation's savage civil war, Chernoh dreamed about living in the United States. When he was 16 years old, rebels—known for amputating their victims' limbs—robbed Chernoh and his family at gunpoint, in their own home. As he stood there and watched the intruders rip his mother's wedding ring off her finger, Chernoh vowed to become a police officer and protect people in the face of violence.

Now Dr. Chernoh M. Wurie is a highly respected law enforcement expert, and a veteran of the Prince William County (VA) Police Department, where he was the first non-citizen to become a commissioned officer. Dr. Wurie has since gotten married and started a family with his wife, Jennifer. After ten years on the police force, Dr. Wurie transitioned into teaching future generations of law enforcement, although he is still active in the law enforcement community.

Dr. Wurie is currently a criminal justice professor at Virginia Commonwealth University (VCU). He completed his bachelor's degree in criminal justice at Radford University, and his Masters and PhD in public administration with a concentration in public safety at Walden University. Dr. Wurie is the faculty advisor for the National Association of Blacks in Criminal Justice (NABCJ) chapter at VCU, and was awarded the Excellence in Faculty Mentorship Award from the University Academic Advising Board (UAAB) in 2018. He was also the chair of the Wilder School's Diversity, Equity, & Inclusion Committee at VCU from 2017 to 2019.

Dr. Wurie is a noted expert on law enforcement and police–community relations. His unique background as a refugee, a Black man, and a law enforcement professional—as well as his strong bonds to family and faith—give him the ability to bridge divisions and find common ground in the national conversation about the role of police in our communities. Dr. Wurie's academic and scholarly work, as well as his mentorship of future law enforcement leaders, breaks down stereotypes and promotes better understanding on all sides.

Dr. Wurie's publication credits include *Impact: A Compilation of Positive Police Encounters* (2013: AuthorHouse); and Chapter Six in *Black Men Changing the Narrative Through Education* and Chapter Three in *Breakthrough Mentoring in the 21st Century: A Compilation of Life Altering Experiences*, edited by Walter R. McCollum (2018: McCollum Enterprises).

Dr. Wurie also serves as Safety and Security Response Team (SSRT) Director of his church, Hill City, and vice president of the Barrels of Hope international charity, which he co-founded with his wife and best friend, Jennifer M. Wurie. Barrels of Hope provides the women of St. Peter's Women's Community Vocational Center in Sierra Leone with donations that support vocational skills training. St. Peter's Vocational Center was started by Dr. Wurie's mother, Annie Maude Wurie, who is a pivotal figure in his life. Chernoh and Jennifer Wurie have two children, Eliza and Jamessin.

INDEX

S

T

U

V

W

Printed in the USA
CPSIA information can be obtained
at www.ICGtesting.com
LVHW080912290824
789545LV00008BA/64

9 781793 536143